The Praeger Encyclopedia of Old Masters

JOACHIM FERNAU

FREDERICK A. PRAEGER, *Publishers*

NEW YORK

TRANSLATED FROM THE GERMAN
BY JAMES CLEUGH AND MONICA BROOKSBANK
UNDER THE SUPERVISION OF OLIVE COOK

BOOKS THAT MATTER
Published in the United States of America in 1959
by Frederick A. Praeger, Inc., Publishers
15 West 47th Street, New York 36, N. Y.

Library of Congress catalog card number: 59-7456

© 1958 BY DROEMERSCHE VERLAGSANSTALT TH. KNAUR NACHF.
MUNICH AND ZURICH
ILLUSTRATIONS PRINTED BY MANDRUCK MUNICH THEODOR DIETZ
TEXT SET IN GREAT BRITAIN BY THE CAMELOT PRESS, SOUTHAMPTON
PRINTED IN GERMANY

The following kindly supplied illustration material:

Hugo Böhm, Stuttgart 2; Eva Bollert, Karlsruhe 1;
Verlag F. Bruckmann KG., Munich 2; Conzett & Huber, Zürich 50;
Editions Aimery Somogy, Paris 38; S. Francesco, Arezzo 1;
Heinz Gleixner, Munich 12;
Franz Hanfstaengl, Munich 8; Hirmer Verlag, Munich 8;
Instituto Geografico de Agostini, Novara 3; Foto Kempter, Munich 29;
Verlag Mensch und Arbeit, Munich 3; Karl Meyer, Vienna 1;
Hildegard Müller, Hanover 1; Musée Condé au château de Chantilly 1;
Galleria Nazionale della Sicilia, Palermo 1; Olivetti & Co., Milan 2;
Galerie Pardo, Paris 1;
St Pierre, Louvain 1; Die Piperdrucke, Munich 3;
Preiss & Co., Munich 1;
Private Collection 2; Schleinitz-Foto, St Heinrich 1;
Verlag E. A. Seemann, Cologne 1;
Walter Steinkopf, Berlin 13;
Uitgeverij W. Gaade, The Hague 4.

The author wishes gratefully to acknowledge
the co-operation of the following

Professor Leo van Puyvelde, Brussels
Honorary Director of the Musées Royaux des Beaux-Arts

Professor Roberto Salvini, Florence
Professor of the History of Art at the University of Trieste
Former Director of the Uffizi Gallery, Florence

Dr. Heinrich Zimmermann, Berlin
Former Director of the Staatl. Gemäldegalerie, Berlin

INTRODUCTION

A GREAT many dictionaries of painters have appeared in the past two hundred years, varying in scope and degree of scholarship from amateur works, such as the Rev. M. Pilkington's *Dictionary of Painters*, edited by Fuseli and published in 1810, and the monumental, exhaustive work of our own century the *Allgemeines Lexikon der bildenden Künstler*, edited by Ulrich Thieme and Felix Becker. It would seem almost impossible to make a new contribution in this field. Yet there exists no popular reference work on the old masters arranged alphabetically, of handy size and moderate price, which incorporates the results of modern research without entering into the more minute problems of style and attribution which are the concern only of the connoisseur and expert. The present volume aspires to fill this gap. To increase its usefulness the compilers have availed themselves of the opportunity, unimaginable before the present age, of including a wealth of illustrations in colour, which give a better idea of differences in style than any verbal description. The sizes of the originals are given in every case and occasionally when it is impossible to judge the main characteristics of a painter from a reproduction of the whole work on so miniature a scale, a detail of the picture is shown.

A dictionary of such relatively small compass could not embrace more than some 750 names. So there are unavoidable omissions: many of the more modest but by no means negligible masters have no place in these pages. About the inclusion of the truly great there could be no doubt; and of the hundreds of less talented painters the compilers have selected those whose work the general reader might most frequently encounter, not only in the principal European galleries, but in provincial museums, private collections and the sale-room, and those whose work has some point of interest, like that of Denis van Alsloot, the painter of the remarkable historical Procession Pictures in the Victoria and Albert Museum, or like that of Arcimboldi, the painter of those curiously surrealist portraits composed of fruits, vegetables, birds and fish-heads. No painter is included whose style was not already formed by the time the eighteenth century came to its close. The book owes much to such standard reference works as the dictionaries of Thieme-Becker, Wurzbach and Bénézit, but in the majority of cases both the original source-books and recent opinions have been consulted.

The object of this book is not only to give the reader the basic facts about each painter and to indicate whenever possible where at least some of his works may be found, but also to attempt some appreciation of the painter's achievement. It is not within the scope of a dictionary to describe in detail the development of each branch of painting, but the importance of individual painters in the evolution of a particular *genre* is pointed out with reference to other entries by means of which the reader can form an outline picture of the growth of such categories of painting as landscape, portraiture, or history painting. Thus if the reader has recourse to the entry on the marine painter Willem van der Velde, he will find references to Vroom, Porcellis, Vlieger and Cappelle and by looking up these artists he will gain some general idea of the progress made by the Dutch painters of seascapes.

In addition to entries on the masters themselves such technical terms have been explained as are necessary to the understanding of old master paintings and the conditions under which they were produced. The various mediums in which the old masters worked are briefly defined and one or two entries are included on general subjects, such as fakes for instance, which are closely connected with the study of the old masters. The contents of the more important public picture galleries are also very shortly listed.

The names of many of the old masters have often come down to us in a confusing variety of forms. The names Brueghel occurs also as Bruegel and Breughel; Saftleven is sometimes written as Sachtleeven, Quinten Massys appears in some catalogues as Quentin Matsys or Metsys; Patenier is spelt in some documents Patinir and in others Patinier. As a general principle the simplest forms of the painters' names have been adopted here with a mention of variations in spelling where they are considerable.

At the end of the dictionary a list is given of some of the chief source books which are essential to any detailed study of the old masters, together with a few of the best-known encyclopaedias of painters compiled by modern art historians.

J. F.

AACHEN

The golden age of German painting was already over when Hans von Aachen (1552-1615), who was born in Cologne, began his work. At that time neither he nor any other painters in Germany had developed an independent style comparable with that of Italian Mannerism (q.v.). But he, too, visited the 'promised land' of Italy, where he studied Tintoretto and Michelangelo. On his return, owing to the lack of really important native masters, he was appointed Court Painter to the far from exacting Emperor Rudolf II. Von Aachen was, however, a brilliant technician, undertaking all sorts of subjects, from Biblical and mythological illustration to portraiture. He died in Prague, where at that time the Emperor resided. A man of the world, von Aachen moved in 'high society'. It is significant that his wife was a daughter of the great composer Orlando di Lasso.

ABBATE

Born at Modena, Niccolo dell' Abbate (c. 1509-1571) was undoubtedly an Italian, though he almost ranks as a Frenchman. For at least twenty years, until his death, he worked at the Court of the French King in Fontainebleau (q.v.). He was an interesting, though not a great artist, whose rare authenticated works are highly prized. Stylistically derived from those of Correggio and Parmigianino, they are often much more surprising in their invention. The more his work is studied, the more important it seems. Some art historians now consider him responsible for the charming picture in which a well-dressed couple, surrounded by fields of wheat, are watching a number of horses on long leads held by a farm servant, the animals galloping round him in a wide circle as they thresh the corn with their hoofs. This fine canvas is preserved in the palace at Fontainebleau. *The Death of Eurydice*, one of Abbate's most important pictures, is in the National Gallery, London.

ABILGAARD

Nicolai Abraham Abilgaard (1743-1809), born in Copenhagen, adopted the current classical style. He studied antique works, and those of Raphael, in Italy. The first of his more notable compositions was accordingly not a still-life, a *genre* picture or a landscape, but depicted a heroic subject,

H. VON AACHEN · THE TRIUMPH OF TRUTH
24¼″ × 19″. Munich, Alte Pinakothek

The Wounded Philoctetes. This canvas is preserved, like most of his other works, in the Royal Gallery at Copenhagen. Abilgaard considered throughout his life that his stately but unfortunately somewhat frigid illustrations of such themes were the only sort of painting worth while. In this belief he decorated a room in the royal palace with four allegorical frescoes representing respectively primitive times, the Roman Empire, the Papacy and modern Europe. The palace was destroyed by fire in 1794. Classically minded as ever, Abilgaard exclaimed: 'My glory is going up in flames!' But he was mistaken. His reputation lives on in that of his pupil Thorwaldsen and in certain of his own works, which acquire more and more historical interest as his period recedes and the few Scandinavian names recorded in the history of art are left still further behind.

ACADEMIES OF ART

The prototype of all academies was to use the word 'academy' in connection with art, and such was the academy of the Carracci in Bologna. But another form of academy sprang into existence with the founding by Vasari in 1563 of the *Accademia del Disegno.* Its intention was frankly pedagogic, and it also aimed at freeing the young painter from the jurisdiction of the guilds. Painters still learnt the rudiments of their art in the workshops of the masters (see *Bottega*), but the Accademia del Disegno was the first of those institutions which gradually began to oust the bottega, until by the nineteenth century they had gained the monopoly in all matters of artistic education. The immediate offspring of Vasari's academy was the *Accademia di San Luca* in Rome (1593), the organisation of which became the pattern of Lebrun's and Colbert's *Académie Royale de Peinture et de Sculpture,* founded in 1648. The latter in turn, with its elaborate order of precedence, method of training, doctrines and its parent institution in Rome, was the model for similar enterprises throughout the seventeenth and

P. AERTSEN
THE PANCAKE MAKER
*34½″ × 68″. Rotterdam,
Boymans Museum*

Plato's Academy in the groves beside the Cephissus outside Athens. The name was revived in humanist circles during the early Renaissance to designate the informal meetings of learned men to discuss problems of science and philosophy. The earliest academies of art were gatherings of mature artists in a private workshop for the purpose of discussion and drawing from life. Such was the academy of B. Bandinelli (1531), the first establishment eighteenth centuries (Dresden 1647, Berlin 1694, Vienna 1704, Madrid 1752, Venice 1755, Munich 1760). The Royal Academy of Arts in London was founded in 1768, with Reynolds as its first President. All these official academies were dependent on court patronage and society; and they were instrumental in fostering the 'grand style' which degenerated into 'academicism'.

See N. Pevsner: *Academies of Art,* 1940.

ACCADEMIA, VENICE

This important picture gallery occupies the old Scuola di Santa Maria della Carita, the oldest brotherhood in Venice. It was made a public gallery in 1798 by Napoleon after the fall of the Venetian Republic. The pictures exhibited are chiefly by Venetian masters and were assembled from churches and private palaces in Venice, when the gallery was first opened, though much has since been added to the collection. Among the more important works in the gallery are a *Madonna* by Jacopo Bellini; Gentile Bellini's *Miracle of the True Cross* and *Corpus Christi Procession in the Piazza of St Mark's*; the S. Giobbe Altarpiece, the *Madonna with SS. Catherine and Magdalen*, the *Madonna and Child* and five allegorical pictures by Giovanni Bellini; Carpaccio's famous series illustrating the legend of St Ursula, the *Martyrdom of the Ten Thousand Virgins, Healing of Madman in View of the Rialto* and ten pictures illustrating the legend of St George, formerly in S. Giorgio degli Schiavone; representative works by Cima and Basaiti, *The Tempest* by Giorgione; the *Rich Man's Feast* by Bonifazio; Titian's *Presentation of the Virgin* and *Pietà*; a number of large, important canvases by Tintoretto; Veronese's celebrated *Feast in the House of Levi* and *Battle of Lepanto*, interesting allegories, a *Circumcision* and *Christ before Pilate* by Schiavone; typical works by Tiepolo and unparalleled examples of genre by Longhi.

AELST

Born at Delft, Willem van Aelst (1625-1683?) belonged to the generation of Vermeer, Pieter de Hooch and Carel Fabritius, founders of the city's artistic reputation. He did not, however, reside there, but spent much time (1645-1656) in France and Italy, dying at Amsterdam. He was a pupil and nephew of Evert van Aelst, who specialised, like Willem, in still-life. Willem's pictures are remarkable for the charm and brilliance of their colour and their outstanding draughtsmanship. They are however somewhat overcrowded with a quite unnecessary display of subsidiary objects of Italian antiquarian interest, such as Renaissance beakers, the shafts of columns, marble slabs and reliefs. His simpler paintings of flowers, hunting gear, snipe and partridges are more attractive.

AERTSEN

His contemporary, Vasari, enthusiastically sings the praises of Pieter Aertsen (1508-1575), though the distance between Amsterdam, where Aertsen was born, and Florence, where Vasari wrote his biographies, is well over a thousand miles, and Raphael, Michelangelo, Leonardo da Vinci and Titian were active in Italy at the same time. What caused the Italian Vasari to be as fascinated by Aertsen as were the Dutch and the Germans?

Aertsen was an older contemporary of Pieter Brueghel the Elder. In view of this early date, the homely scenes painted by Aertsen show a wonderful mastery of colour. There is much turbulence in his illustrations of popular gatherings, even the Biblical scenes having a riotous character. But they are never coarse. The pictures are not psychologically moving. They convey no deep emotion. But it is impossible to pass them without a twinkle in the eye and a feeling of amusement.

Unlike those of his contemporaries who were influenced by Italy, Aertsen is as typically Dutch as Brueghel. This characteristic was clearly recognised in Holland at the time and accounted for his popularity there. Aertsen spent twenty years (possibly from 1535 to 1555) in Antwerp and then returned to Amsterdam, where he died.

ALBANI

Born at Bologna, Francesco Albani (1578-1660) enjoyed like his fellow-student, Guido Reni, much favour among the rising middle classes and artistic circles of the nineteenth century. Today little remains of his high reputation at that time. He is regarded at best as a painter of some consequence, historically not without interest. But in his own lifetime he was much

ALBERTINELLI · THE ANNUNCIATION
66" × 79" (*Detail*). *Munich, Alte Pinakothek*

admired and employed. He worked at first in Bologna, then for fifteen years in Rome, where he attended the studio of his former teacher, Annibale Carracci, who had settled in Rome in 1600. Eventually Albani, after the death of his first wife, a wealthy Roman lady, returned to Bologna. The last decades of his life were embittered by litigation and the loss of his fortune through embezzlement by his brother.

He handled both Biblical and mythological themes in much the same way, whether depicting cupids, or cherubs, sentimental nymphs or sentimental Magdalens. He is often reminiscent of Domenichino. Most museums, including the Dulwich Gallery, possess specimens of his work.

ALBERTINELLI

A lifelong friend of Fra Bartolommeo, whose stages of development he faithfully shared, Mariotto Albertinelli (1474-1515) was born and died at Florence. The two painters even employed the same form of

signature. In Albertinelli's pictures the influences of Credi, Leonardo and Raphael are often very evident. Traces of Mannerism (q.v.) are also already discernible. His most attractive paintings are small Raphaelesque Madonnas. The large religious works are as a rule figuratively stiff, architecturally hard and compositionally loose and incoherent.

ALLEGRETTO NUZI

The name of the painter Allegretto is mentioned for the first time in the Florentine guild-lists in 1346 and for the last time in a testamentary document dated 1374. Pictures bearing his signature in full—a rare piece of good fortune in the case of Gothic paintings—are to be found in the Vatican, at Apiro near Cingoli, in Macerata Cathedral, at Fabriano, where he was long active, and in the Kaiser Friedrich Museum, Berlin. His subjects are Madonnas and saints modelled on those of the Sienese School and Giotto. But his colours are bright and pleasing. He favours yellow and pink against a gold background, as well as rich brocades, which are represented, exceptionally, without the folds regularly introduced by him in other materials. The question may well be asked, though it has not been answered up to now, whether he found folds in brocade too difficult to paint or whether he preferred the splendid effect of an unbroken surface in this material.

ALLORI

Two painters of the Late Renaissance in Florence bore this name, Alessandro (1535-1607) and his son Cristofano (1577-1621). Alessandro grew up as an orphan in the house of his uncle, Agnolo Bronzino, Court Painter to Cosimo I. After studying under Bronzino and later under Michelangelo in Rome, Alessandro soon became famous in consequence of his two frescoes in the Chapel of the Annunziata Order of Knighthood, *Christ among the Scribes* and *The Expulsion of the Money-changers*. His success appears to have been mainly due to his shrewdly calculated introduction of portraits of Duke Cosimo, Bronzino, Pontormo and other prominent men of the day among the spectators in these pictures. He was in great demand as a painter for the decoration of churches but is of slight importance as an artist.

Cristofano was more accomplished. His altar pictures still show the influence of his father. But his small half-length figures, his Virgins, Magdalens and portraits, give him a place among notable painters. His most famous work, *Judith and Holofernes*, is in the Pitti Palace at Florence.

ALSLOOT

Denis van Alsloot was a Flemish painter, mentioned in the Register of the Painters' Guild of Brussels in 1599, by which time he was already established. Later he was made Court Painter to the Archduchess Isabella and the Archduke Albert. He died in 1626. With Pierre Snayers and Antoine Salaert, he belongs to a group of realists between the school of religious painting which was coming to an end and the Antwerp masters of whom Rubens was the foremost. Alsloot specialised in processions which he painted with meticulous accuracy and minute detail. Paintings of fêtes are in the Brussels and Antwerp museums and his most ambitious work, a painting of the Ommeganck of 1615, a Pageant-Procession in Brussels, is in the Victoria and Albert Museum, London.

ALTDORFER

Nothing is known for certain about Albrecht Altdorfer's family. In 1478 one Ulrich Altdorfer, a painter, was enrolled as a burgher at Regensburg, but left the city ten years later. In 1505 a second Altdorfer, named Albrecht, returned to Regensburg from abroad and acquired

ALTDORFER · THE NATIVITY
14½" × 10". Berlin, Staatl. Museen

citizenship, a privilege at that time not available to those under twenty-five. It is therefore a fair inference that Albrecht was born in 1480 and that Ulrich was his father. Accordingly, it was most probably the latter and not, as was formerly assumed, Dürer, who trained Albrecht. The elucidation of such trifling points illustrates in a small way the meticulous research which has built up the history of art during the last hundred years.

Altdorfer is not one of the greatest masters. But he is certainly one of the most attractive. His awkward early style, as in the Berlin picture representing St Jerome or St Francis (1507) had by 1510 acquired all the charm of his characteristic romantic manner. His first masterpieces include *St*

ALTDORFER · LANDSCAPE WITH BRIDGE
17″ × 14″. Berne, J. Koefer Collection

The *Battle of Arbela* (1529) in the Alte Pinakothek at Munich is usually considered his chief work. But the most detailed and 'difficult' of a painter's productions is by no means always necessarily his most important and best. Anyone is at liberty to give the preference, as pure painting, to the *Landscape* just mentioned, the *St George in the Woods* at Munich or the magical nocturne *Florian's Leave-taking* in the Uffizi Gallery. Nevertheless, no one can fail to be deeply impressed by the *Battle of Arbela*, which has the double aspect of a large-scale work painted by a miniaturist. It is built up of hundreds of exquisite details. But when observed from a considerable distance, it becomes what the artist must always have felt it to be, essentially timeless landscape, the earth on the first day of creation, as seas and chasms broke out and the sun's globe rose above the horizon. The armies of Alexander and Darius then merge into a single many-coloured field of flowers.

At the time of Altdorfer's death in Regensburg he enjoyed great respect and prosperity. A foreign drawing portrays his

George and the Dragon at Munich and the *Holy Family at the Fountain* in Berlin. About 1511 he seems to have undertaken a fairly long journey down the Danube, which taught him a great deal and also perhaps brought him into contact with northern Italian painting. But his style underwent no change.

He painted tirelessly whatever appealed to him, depicting the birth of Christ as though it had occurred in 1512 a hundred yards outside the gates of Regensburg, St George as though he had fought with the dragon in the woods near the town's bridge over the Danube, and Susanna bathing in the gardens of such a Renaissance palace as only an architect like himself could imagine. For Altdorfer was in fact the city architect. He also repeatedly painted the valley of the Danube, in a series of uncommonly beautiful small canvases now at Munich, pioneer works of the subsequent Danube School. His *Landscape with Footbridge* in the collection of J. Koerfer at Berne may be regarded as the first landscape painted purely for its own sake.

AMBERGER · CHRISTOPH FUGGER
38¾″ × 31½″. Munich, Alte Pinakothek

noble and elegant figure at a meeting of the Town Council. Both the Emperor and the Duke of Bavaria employed him. He could well afford to decline the post of mayor of this ancient free city of the empire.

ALTE PINAKOTHEK, MUNICH

The origins of this celebrated Munich Collection date back to the early sixteenth century when Duke Wilhelm IV of Bavaria (reigned 1508-1550) commissioned heroic and biblical subjects for his pavilion in the Hofgarten at Munich. Among the pictures executed for this purpose were Altdorfer's *Battle of Alexander* and works by Burgkmair and Barthel Beham. The collection as we know it today began to take shape, however, under Archduke Maximilian I (1598-1651), who built a gallery to house his pictures and made an inventory of them which has been preserved. Among the works acquired by Maximilian were Dürer's *Paumgartner Altar*, the *Heller Altar* (destroyed by fire in 1729) and the *Four Apostles*, and Rubens' *Lion Hunt*. Max Emmanuel (1679-1726) added to the collections more works by Rubens, including *Helene Fourment and Her Eldest Son Franzs*, Van Dyck's *Portrait of the Sculptor Colyn de Nole, The Wife of Colyn de Nole and Her Daughter*, and *Portrait of a Man*, fine examples of the work of Brouwer, Titian's *Vanitas* and Poussin's *Pietà* and *Midas and Bacchus*. When the Bavarian line of the House of Wittelsbach died out in 1777 and the inheritance passed to the Palatine line the contents of the Mannheim Gallery, consisting chiefly of works of the seventeenth-century Dutch and Flemish painters, became amalgamated with the Munich collections. In 1803 when the religious houses and ecclesiastical estates were secularised, several great altarpieces, including works by Holbein, Burgkmair and Grünewald, became the property of the Bavarian state. In 1806 the Munich Collection was further enriched, again by inheritance, by the contents of the

Düsseldorf Gallery, a collection formed by Johann Wilhelm of Pfalz-Neuburg, Elector Palatine, 1690-1716. It included outstanding examples of the work of Rubens, such as *The Battle of the Amazons*, *Rubens and Isabella Brant* and the *Rape of the Daughters of Leucippus*, Rembrandt's series of *Scenes from the Passion* and Raphael's *Canigiani Holy Family*. Ludwig I (1825-1848) built the Alte Pinakothek in the style of an Italian palace to house the vast Munich Collection and acquired the Boisseries Collection of early Flemish and German paintings, including works by the Master of St Bartholomew, the Master of the Life of the Virgin, Bouts, Bernard van Orley and Altdorfer; Italian fifteenth-century pictures, including Ghirlandaio's high altar from S. Maria Novella, Raphael's *Madonna Tempi* and *Madonna della Tenda*, Perugino's *Vision of St Bernard* and Botticelli's *Pietà*. In 1827 Ludwig I acquired the collection of the Dukes of Wallerstein-Rechberg with works by Altdorfer, Cranach and other German masters. Additions to the collection during the present century include works by Tintoretto, Signorelli, Antonello and Goya, but it still retains the character of a family collection. The Alte Pinakothek building was severely damaged in the 1939-1945 War, but the pictures themselves were all preserved.

ALTICHIERO

The reputation of the Gothic painter Altichiero da Zevio (c. 1320-1385) is increasing. He came from Verona and is acknowledged to be the head, founder and master of an entire school of painting. His work survives mainly in the neighbourhood of Verona and Padua. One example is the fresco in the church of Sant' Anastasia at Verona representing saints recommending members of the Cavalli family to the Madonna. In Padua he has a fresco in the San Giorgio Chapel, while the church of Sant' Antonio contains his masterpiece, a large Crucifixion. The latter was discovered by Ernst Foerster in 1837 under thick layers of whitewash.

FRA ANGELICO
THE ANNUNCIATION
76¾" × 76¾". *Madrid, Prado*

Altichiero's pictures, for all their Gothic charm, reveal a new spirit in art. The figures are still Giottesque. But their attitudes no longer suggest a miracle play. The faces express ordinary human emotions. The bodies are given the logical movement which Masaccio was the first to repeat later. The personages look interested in what is going on, intently observant of the other figures. Such treatment was revolutionary at the time. Altichiero's horses might have been painted by Uccello, though Italy was to wait a whole generation for the latter's work.

AMBERGER

Christoph Amberger who was probably born in Amberg c. 1500 and died in Augsburg c. 1561-1562 was appointed a Master of his guild at the age of thirty-two, on the death of the aged Bernhard Striegel, his respected predecessor. Am-

berger became an important portraitist, trained in the Venetian style. At Augsburg, where the famous and powerful were wont to meet at that time for Congresses and Imperial Diets, he painted Fugger, Peutinger, Frundsberg and the young Emperor Charles V. The latter, when he saw the portrait, paid three times the price asked and presented the artist with a gold chain. This picture, entitled *Portrait of a Man*, is now in the National Gallery, London.

AMIGONI

The life of Jacopo Amigoni (1675-1752) was an unbroken series of triumphs. It is remarkable in view of the extent of his travels, the honours bestowed upon him, the invitations he received and the number of his works, how soon posterity revised the verdict of his own generation. He was born in Venice and died in Madrid. For some years he was in the service of the Elector of Bavaria. He supplied the latter with allegorical paintings for palaces and portraits of handsome saints for churches. He also spent a few years in London, where he stayed at the residences of peers and painted portraits of the gentlemen of the day. For years, too, he lived in Paris, Venice and eventually Spain. Everywhere he remained a perfect specimen of the Rococo age, as elegant, charming and gay as his showy paintings, which were too facile to be taken very seriously. It was Tiepolo, twenty years his junior, who first showed the world how far this style could be taken.

ANGELICO

One of the most important painters of the early fifteenth century, Fra Angelico (1387-1455) was only rivalled by his equally great contemporary, Masaccio. Both devoted their artistic gifts entirely to the service of the Church and were deeply religious, but Masaccio in the liberal style of a layman, Angelico as a monk. The former concentrated on dramatic events, the latter on pictorial sermons.

Angelico's real name was Guido di Pietro. Born in Vicchio di Mugello, Tuscany, he died in Rome. At the age of twenty he entered the Dominican convent at Fiesole, near Florence, taking the name of Fra Giovanni. St Antoninus was an influential teacher at this establishment, where Angelico also met the subsequently canonised Dominici. The youthful Fra Giovanni became an enthusiastic adherent of the doctrines of St Thomas Aquinas. The young man's eloquence and learning soon gained him the name, both among the laity and his brother monks, of Angelico, just as Aquinas had once been called the 'angelic' doctor, implying that he was heaven's messenger.

At this period Angelico had never used a brush. He was over thirty when he suddenly began to paint. He probably started by decorating the convent manuscripts in about 1418. He then turned to fresco, on the walls of the cells at the convent of San Marco at Florence. Some of his panels are also to be referred to this

early date. His intention at that time was to teach the monks Christian history by means of pictures. His mild and tranquil figures of angels, saints and layman stand together in perfect harmony. Their gestures are passionless. Their features express unearthly calm. The world which Fra Angelico painted throughout his life, not in a state of rapture but with extreme deliberation, was meant to represent not the real world but that planned by God, full of solemnity, brightness and exaltation. Bernard Berenson has expressed its character in noble language: '"God's in His heaven, all's well with the world." Fra Angelico felt that intensely. It prevented him from finding evil anywhere. Whenever he was obliged to represent it, his imaginative gift deserted him and he became no more than a child.'

In the pictures of his first years the struggle to draw correctly and achieve perspective remains evident. His outlines

ANTONELLO · PORTRAIT OF A MAN
13¾″ × 10″. London, National Gallery

often still seem Gothically stiff. The surfaces of his robes resemble coloured illuminations. These early paintings convey a special effect of purity and innocence.

Between 1440 and 1446 he created a number of masterpieces which, like the *Lamentation for Christ* at San Marco in Florence, display surprising new colours. The background landscape has become dark. The figures press forward to the centre of the picture. The colours of the garments range from the deepest brown to sea-green and rich red. In 1447 Pope Eugenius IV summoned Fra Angelico to Rome. Hitherto he had always lived in seclusion and avoided the rising tide of humanism. But in Rome he inevitably encountered the new spirit that foreshadowed the Renaissance. His Vatican frescoes of this period have less inner but more external richness. They are less absorbed in God and more concerned with a stately glorification of the Church. In their details, however, for instance in the head of a groping blind beggar or the standing figure of a woman and child at the picture's edge, the humility and simple charity preached by Fra Angelico are given vivid expression.

His most important works include the altarpiece of the Madonna at Perugia, the *Coronation of the Virgin* in the Louvre, the frescoes of the convent of San Marco in Florence, and the Cortona *Christ* and *Christ Surrounded by Angels, Patriarchs, Saints and Martyrs* in the National Gallery, London. The National Gallery of Rome contains a *Last Judgment*, which is probably one of his very latest works.

He acquired fame and honour in his own lifetime. For three years he acted as Prior of San Marco. According to Vasari, the Pope wished to appoint him an archbishop. He is the only painter recorded to have been canonised after his death.

ANONYMOUS

The painters of a large number of important pictures have not so far been identified by art historians. The fact is not surprising, as the older artists generally, especially in the Gothic period, have remained modestly obscure in comparison with their works. If the same hand is occasionally recognisable in several paintings, the artist is provisionally named from the most characteristic of them, e.g. 'the Master of the Life of the Virgin'. But painters by whom only a single picture seems to have survived cannot even be designated by the consoling title of the 'Master of' this or that work. They have to be referred to merely, with resignation, as 'Anonymous'.

ANTONELLO

Antonello di Giovanni degli Antoni da Messina (c. 1430-1479) the son of a sculptor and stonemason, was born at Messina, and probably died there in February 1479. In order to appreciate the significance of this painter it is necessary to have some idea of the Italy of 1430.

ANTONELLO · THE VIRGIN ANNUNCIATE
14″ × 13½″. Palermo, Mus. Nationale

At that time the 'good king', René of Anjou, ruled the united kingdom of Naples and Sicily. Artistically, it was much under Flemish and Dutch influence. Van Eyck, Campin and Rogier van der Weyden were known in the so-called School of Naples. Their pictures could be found in the houses of rich merchants, for there was close intercourse between Italy and the Netherlands. The great Italian banks and commercial firms had branches in Ghent, Bruges, Antwerp and Brussels. Flemish paintings reached the south in the form of valuable gifts or purchases. This situation was hardly affected when the 'good king' died in 1442 and Alfonso of Aragon succeeded him. Alfonso was, to be sure, a Spaniard. But Spain itself was also influenced artistically by the Netherlands. Alfonso enjoyed pictures by Van Eyck and Rogier, which he collected. Accordingly, too, Antonello undoubtedly studied Flemish painting.

His next steps are chiefly recorded in contemporary sources, which were long believed. But they were suddenly proved to have been, in the main, entirely unfounded. Documentary research in Naples and Sicily finally corrected the current fancies, legends and errors of these statements and threw some light on Antonello's actual career. The supposed years of his birth and death (1444 and 1493), his twenty years' residence in Venice, his journeys to Spain and Flanders and his invention of oil-painting, or introduction of it into Italy, were all shown to be legendary.

A few facts only were retained. He was probably trained at Naples under Colantonio, by whom no authenticated work survives. But the latter's style is known to have been based on that of Van Eyck. Certain dates are also unquestioned. But they refer with one exception to time spent in Sicily, Naples and Calabria. The exception, 1475, is by far the most interesting of these years.

In 1475 Antonello, a painter from the extremely remote province of Messina, visited the brilliant cosmopolitan centre of Venice. That was the first time the 'great world' had ever heard of him. When he left the city a year later, half its inhabitants lamented his departure. A genius had abandoned them. A star had passed away. Their only consolation was that Giovanni Bellini still remained among them. Such was the intense interest of Venetians in art at that time. When, at a later date, Titian's *Assumption of the Virgin* was exhibited, a civic holiday was declared.

Bellini, one of the most outstanding figures in Venetian painting, was the same age as Antonello. The Sicilian's pictures were a revelation to him as to everyone else. We can understand this feeling even today after a single glance at a typical work by Antonello. It contains no depth of devotion, no reverent narrative, no graceful tribute to authority. It gives an impression, on the other hand, in some inexplicable way, of disdainful daring, imposing arrogance and fierce pride. The artist had managed, in his provincial seclusion, to achieve a hitherto unknown synthesis of the styles of Van Eyck and the Renaissance. He had not passed from one to the other, but combined the two. This feature of Antonello's art, evident to all, captivated Venice. Painting took a great stride forward. The new spirit culminated twenty-five years later in Giorgione.

Bernard Berenson argues in interesting fashion against the customary opinion that Giovanni Bellini himself was also fascinated by Antonello's work. But we need not hesitate to diminish the stature of the great Bellini by believing that he borrowed from Antonello. The latter's influence leaps to the eye. For example, the composition, colouring and spirit of Bellini's madonna from the San Giobbe altarpiece in Venice strikingly resemble those of Antonello's incomplete Madonna at Vienna, painted five years before Bellini's picture. Moreover, Bellini's later portrait of the Doge Leonardo Loredano immediately brings to mind Antonello's *Portrait of a Man* in London.

A further remarkable feature of the surviving works by Antonello is the fact that they reveal no sign whatever of hesitation or internal stress. Yet we know that at some period during his provincial life at Messina he must have undergone the exciting experience of turning from his Flemish style to revolutionary innovation. But in none of his pictures is the process evident. Not for a moment does their quality vary. His works compose an unbroken series of masterpieces, of which the most important are to be found in the galleries of London (a head of Christ, a Crucifixion, a St Jerome and portraits), Paris, Antwerp (a Crucifixion), Berlin, Vienna (an altarpiece), Dresden, Rome, Palermo, Syracuse and Philadelphia, where an ironically smiling portrait dated 1475 is preserved in the Johnson Collection.

APT

Ulrich Apt the elder has set art historians a number of problems owing to a single, supposedly false signature. There is evidence that he was living in Augsburg after 1486. Ten years later he painted frescoes in the St Afra Chapel on the Lechfeld, where Otto the Great had once defeated the Hungarians and saved

ARCIMBOLDI · SUMMER
32¾" × 20¾". Munich, Alte Pinakothek

Europe. Documents refer to his execution of paintings for the Town Hall and also to his responsibility for the so-called Rehlinger altarpiece of 1517, which includes an Annunciation and a Crucifixion.

In the nineteenth century a *Portrait of a Young Knight*, now in Berlin, was discovered in England. This portrait bore a striking stylistic resemblance to a group of pictures hitherto considered to be by Apt. But unfortunately the letters L.S. appeared on the battle-axe carried by the knight in the painting. This fact seemed to prove that it could not be Apt's work. Comparisons were made and Apt was deprived of the attribution of a whole series of pictures of high merit. The Mathaus altarpiece and the *Lamentation for Christ* at Munich were also ascribed to the unknown painter L.S. It was not until our own day that credible evidence was provided by K. Feuchtmayr that these letters in the Berlin portrait had simply been copied by Apt from the initials engraved by the armourer on the weapon. Apt's apparent rival was thus disposed of and all the painter's works were restored to him.

His most interesting painting is the small wooden panel of the *Lamentation* at Munich. The colour is surprisingly vivid for an Augsburg artist. The subject is handled in the dramatic style at which the young Cranach aimed, combining features characteristic of the Dutch painter Scorel with those of Dürer's early work. In this case the shadowy figure of Apt suddenly acquires the aspect of a strenuously experimental artist.

He maintained a studio in which his sons Jacob and Ulrich the Younger also worked. But their share in its productions has not yet been determined. They may have been responsible for the vehement style of the final period of this painter.

ARCIMBOLDI

Guiseppe Arcimboldi, sometimes known as Arcimboldo, was born in Milan in 1530 and died there in 1593. Many Renaissance artists were eccentric and went in for peculiar hobbies. Arcimboldi was the most capricious of them. He has a place in the history of art not because he was of eminent patrician birth and consequently had easy access to the Imperial Court, nor because he became Court Painter to three Emperors, nor even on account of his portraits of princes. He is remembered because he was permanently obsessed by the idea of concocting portraits and entire pictorial allegories out of apples, pears, cucumbers, onions, birds and fish-heads. He thus anticipates modern surrealism by about four hundred years. Oddly enough, his experiments sometimes amounted to more than a joke, producing on occasion amazing still-life compositions. Paintings by him are preserved in the galleries of Milan, Brescia, Cremona, Innsbruck, Vienna, Copenhagen, Paris and Hartford in the United States. American private collectors made a point of acquiring Arcimboldis. They were so delighted to find such curiosities among so much that was ancient and venerable.

ASSELYN

Jan Asselyn's appearance is known to us from an etching by Rembrandt. He was born at Dieppe in 1610 and died in 1652 in Amsterdam. His early paintings generally depict cavalry combats and still owe much to his first model, Palamedes Palamedesz. After a visit to Rome he produced chiefly landscapes with vivid yellow lighting effects, pictures of ruins with brightly coloured figures and a few wildly romantic winter scenes, which are highly prized. Asselyn's Italianate pictures were among the first of this kind to be produced in Holland. This fact gives importance to an otherwise minor painter.

ATTIRET

Jean Denis Attiret, a French painter, was born at Dole in 1702 and studied in Rome. He worked at first in France as a portrait painter, but after becoming a Jesuit in about 1732 he was sent to China as a missionary. There he became Court Painter to the Emperor and his works were hung in the Royal Palace at Peking. His earlier works in China were in the Western manner, but later he painted a series of landscapes and still-life pictures in the Chinese style. He died in China in 1768.

AVERCAMP · WINTER SCENE 31″ × 52¼″. *Amsterdam, Rijksmuseum*

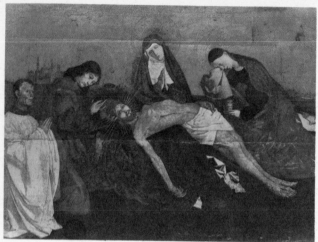

SCHOOL OF AVIGNON
(c. 1474). THE PIETÀ OF
VILLENEUVE-LES-AVIGNON
64¾" × 47¼". Paris, Louvre

AVERCAMP

The beautiful filigree style of the spacious landscapes and wintry scenes of Hendrick van Avercamp, who was born in 1585 in Amsterdam, only indicate by a certain severity of handling that they are of much earlier date than those of Van Goyen, Esaias van der Velde and Van der Neer. In other respects they have all the attractive features developed in later Dutch landscape painting, such as fidelity to natural atmosphere, much arresting detail, beguiling perspective, variety in the figures and discreet touches of comedy. The accessories remind one that Avercamp had already seen the landscapes of the peasant-painter Brueghel, by that time deceased.

Hendrick van Avercamp was called the 'Dumb Man of Kampen'—where he died in 1663—owing to an impediment in his speech. His pupil and nephew Barent van Avercamp is sometimes mistaken for him. But Barent was a much inferior painter.

AVIGNON

For almost a century after 1309 the Popes and anti-Popes lived in exile from Rome at the small town of Avignon in southern France. The artists, poets and scientists who attended them lent a sudden brilliance to the local society. It attracted many students from elsewhere, the great Simone Martini himself coming in 1339 to spend the rest of his life at Avignon. The French painters in the city forthwith abandoned their rigid, icon-like style and produced some remarkably novel pictures. Provence was at this time far in advance of the north in many respects. It remained so until the rise of the Netherlanders of genius, Van Eyck and Campin, whose influence immediately enlightened the adjacent regions of northern France. At this period, distance and national frontiers began to lose their former significance. Avignon's artistic revival in the fifteenth century was quite cosmopolitan in character.

The 'School of Avignon', however, usually means the previous age and refers to a great many works in the Gothic style by painters whose names are unfortunately not known.

BACCHIACCA

Francesco Ubertino Bacchiacca was born in Florence in 1494. He was a pupil of Perugino and Franciabigio, but the strongest influence on his work was that of Andrea del Sarto. Bacchiacca worked in Florence all his life, except for a short interval in Rome some time after 1524. He died in 1557. He painted religious subjects, such as *The Magdalen* in the Pitti, the *Descent from the Cross* (Uffizi) and the *Noli me tangere* (Christ Church, Oxford), and also decorative panels, often of subjects taken from literary sources. These panels, of which the *Legend of the Dead King*, formerly in the Dresden Galleries, and the two episodes from the life of Joseph in the National Gallery, London, are examples, were intended to be let into walls or furniture. Bacchiacca also designed a series of tapestries representing the months of the year. In style he stands between Florentine Mannerism and the High Renaissance, deriving many of his characteristics from the Quattrocento.

BACKER

Jacop Adriansz Backer, a pupil of Rembrandt, was born at Harlingen in 1608 and died in Amsterdam in 1651. Backer copied the style of his master closely in portraits of individuals and groups, with some admixture from the works of Frans Hals. He produced many admirable paintings of this kind. His biblical and mythological pictures, on the other hand, are insignificant. His portrait of an old woman is preserved in the Wallace Collection, London.

BACKHUYSEN

Ludolf Backhuysen was born in Emden in 1631 and died in Amsterdam in 1708. He is regarded as essentially a marine painter, though there are also pictures of biblical subjects by him. He studied under Allart van Everdingen and the marine painter Hendrik Dubbels. His early seascapes show ships and boats, labouring in rough weather near the coast, with extraordinarily effective and bold lighting of the waves. Some of these paintings almost attain the standard of Willem van der Velde. The later pictures have a greater range of subject and are more dramatic and pretentious. He crowds surfaces three or four yards square with piers, cities, towers, warships, flags and human figures. But the more he fills up his canvases the emptier they seem.

Backhuysen gave lessons to Peter the Great, who often visited him in his studio. The artist is represented at the National Gallery, London, and in the Wallace Collection.

BAEGERT

Derick Baegert (active 1470-1515) was entirely neglected until a short time ago. But it now appears that he was responsible, among other works, for the Nikolai altarpiece from Kalkar (now in Antwerp) and the splendid altarpiece of the Crucifixion in the church of St Lorenz at Cologne. Sections of this painting are now preserved at Munich, Nuremberg and Brussels. The *Judgment* in the Town Hall of Wesel-am-Rhein, where Baegert lived, and the charming, idyllic panel of *St Luke Painting the Madonna*, which is at Münster, are also attributed to him. Baegert's figures gesticulate vigorously and are sometimes also provided with inscribed streamers to indicate speech. The style is thoroughly Dutch.

BALDOVINETTI

Alessio Baldovinetti (1425-1499) was born and died in Florence. A painter with intellectual interests, Baldovinetti occupies a position midway between the still devout generation of his teacher Domenico Veneziano and that of the Renaissance masters, with their wider outlook. He was famous in his day for his scientific study

BALDOVINETTI · MADONNA AND CHILD
41¼″ × 30¼″. Paris, Louvre

Hans also reached a high position in the service of the Bishop, dying as a town councillor. After 1509 he resided permanently in the city.

It is now considered certain that he had previously studied under Albrecht Dürer in Nuremberg. There is a tradition that Dürer, when he left for Holland, took with him woodcuts and plates by his friend 'Green Hans'. On Dürer's death a lock of his hair was sent to Baldung as a keepsake. The connection is also supported by the style of Baldung's early paintings. Two triptychs of 1507 are so completely in Dürer's manner that they can only be the work of a studio pupil. It is even possible that the copies of Dürer's *Adam and Eve* at the Uffizi Gallery, Florence, are by Baldung.

He was one of the first in Germany after Cranach to paint a regular series of nudes, in which both Renaissance sensuousness and Gothic naïvety are in evidence. Even his pictures of young witches, now at Frankfurt, can be studied today with as

of painting. But his experiments seem to have resulted in the rapid decay of all his important works. He treated biblical themes naturalistically in a somewhat hard, brittle and frigid manner. But his landscape backgrounds are often surprisingly successful. He set a new example in this direction. Some idea of his linear style can be obtained from the ruins of his fresco of the Nativity in the cloister of the Annunziata at Florence. His sense of humour is delightfully revealed in the well-preserved profile entitled *Portrait of a Lady* in the National Gallery, London.

BALDUNG

Hans Baldung, who was born at Weyersheim in Alsace c. 1476-1484, and died at Strasbourg in 1545, was called Grien by his friends, either because he preferred this colour in his pictures or because he liked to dress in green. His father was legal adviser to the Bishop of Strasbourg, and

H. BALDUNG · THE MARGRAVE VON BADEN
18¾″ × 14¼″. Munich, Alte Pinakothek

much pleasure as he took in painting them.

But these allegorical works, in which the flesh-colour is often strangely wan and the modelling weak, did not make Baldung famous in his lifetime. His reputation rested rather upon the great, rich altar pieces preserved at Freiburg, Basle and Berlin and upon the beautiful and touching compositions entitled *Holy Night* and *Rest on the Flight* to be found at Nuremberg, Vienna, Frankfurt, Karlsruhe and Munich. His portraits are of equal importance. They are refined in colour and brilliant in drawing. The delineation of character is sometimes extremely subtle, as in the case of the young Count Palatine Philip at Munich. Sometimes the artist shows a playful superiority in the treatment of his sitter which could never have occurred to the sober Holbein, the serious Dürer and the paternally-minded Cranach. No one but Baldung would have dared to represent so plainly the ancient nutcracker visage of the Margrave Christoph von Baden in the portrait now at Munich. The artist's amusement is quite unconcealed. But at the same time he gives the sitter's features so amiable an expression and renders them so pictorially effective that the Margrave himself was probably just as much amused as the painter. A robust delight in comedy—for people who lived about the year 1500 were passionately addicted to laughter—can be found even in Baldung's seriously conceived painting of the *Flood*, now at Bamberg.

H. BALDUNG · THE HOLY FAMILY
18¾″ × 14¾″. Vienna, Academy

Balen often introduced mythological figures into the landscapes of the artists Momper, Vrancx and Uden, while other friends helped him with his flowers and fruit. In spite of the skill displayed on these occasions and the stylistic resemblances between the friends, this procedure did not exactly improve the coherence of such routine productions. Balen had two important pupils, Antony van Dyck and Frans Snyders.

BALEN

Resident at Antwerp throughout his life, Hendrik van Balen (1575-1632) produced charming little landscapes somewhat reminiscent of those of Jan Brueghel the Elder. His allegorical pictures are of less account. Owing to the close friendships between the painters of the Antwerp Guild,

BARBARI

Jacopo de' Barbari (c. 1450-1515), was born at Venice and died in Holland. A pupil of Vivarini and perhaps also of Bellini, he stayed in Venice, of which city he was very fond, until about 1500. The singularly beautiful woodcut affording an aerial view over the five thousand houses of Venice to the foothills of the Alps is ascribed to this artist. The work attracted much attention at the time. Even today this panorama, three yards long, arouses admiration of the painter's skill. But stylistically Barbari remained entirely dependent upon his models, in particular Bellini.

Dürer admired the sculptural ideal of beauty cultivated by the Renaissance masters and wished to find out how they represented mass. He once asked Barbari to enlighten him. 'But the aforesaid Jacobus,' he writes, 'was quite obviously unwilling to reveal his procedure to me.' Dürer was mistaken, for Barbari himself had no idea of the secret. All he had done was to learn his trade well. He was a very able painter. But he remained something of an apprentice all his life.

He proved it in 1500, when he felt the urge to travel. He went to work in Wittenberg, where he must have met the then rising young painter Cranach, later in Nuremberg, where he renewed acquaintance with Dürer, then in Frankfurt on the Oder and finally at the Netherlandish Court. In the north he was called Jakob Walch, i.e. 'Jacob the Foreigner'.

BARBATELLI

Bernardino Barbatelli (c. 1550-1612) was a Florentine painter, a pupil of Michael Tosini and Bernardo Buontalenti. He visited Rome c. 1570-73 and was much influenced by the works of Raphael. He early acquired a reputation as a painter of grotesques, of which examples were those executed for the decorations of the villa of Pratolino for the Grand Duke Francesco, which have since perished. His excellence as a painter of decorative effect can, however, be seen in examples in the Pitti Palace and the Uffizi. Barbatelli also painted five frescoes in the lunettes of the cloister of S. Maria Novella representing scenes from the life of St Dominic; frescoes of the life of St Bruno in the Certosa, near Florence; five frescoes in S. Maria Maddalena de' Pazzi; and fourteen lunettes in fresco representing scenes from the lives of founders of the Order of Servites in the Convent of Sa. Annunziata. Specimens of Barbatelli's oil painting include the *Annunciatio* and *S. Catherine* (Seminario Patriarcale, Venice).

BARLOW

Francis Barlow (c. 1626-c. 1702) was born in Lincolnshire and is known as the father of British sporting painting. At a period when English painting was largely dominated by foreign influence, Barlow concerned himself with the birds and animals of his native county, depicting them with remarkable exactitude and often including landscape settings, as in the *Plover Shooting* at Shardeloes, which were far in advance of his time. Barlow was also a talented etcher.

BAROCCIO

Federigo Baroccio (1526-1612), who was born in Urbino and died there, modelled himself on Correggio. His pictures are mostly altarpieces. But they are already

F. BAROCCIO · THE NATIVITY
53¼" × 42". Madrid, Prado

characterised by the dilution of Correggio's style and its transition to the insipidity and sentimental colouration of the school of Guido Reni. Baroccio is represented in the National Gallery, London, by his *Holy Family* (*La Madonna del Gatto*).

BARTOLOMMEO

Fra Bartolommeo (1472-1517) was the son of a mule-driver, so obscure and poor a man that little more is known of the childhood of his son, who was one day to be so famous, than that he was called Baccio (short for Bartolommeo) della Porta (because he lived near the Porta Romana in Florence) and the date of his birth in that city, where he also died.

At seventeen he entered the studio of Cosimo Rosselli, where one of his fellow-pupils was the painter Mariotto Albertinelli, destined to be his lifelong friend. With Albertinelli he subsequently began painting in his own home. He became deeply affected by the sermons of Savonarola. He burnt his secular pictures and resolved in 1500 to enter a monastery. Four years later he resumed painting. Two journeys, to Venice in 1508 and to Rome in 1514, proved decisive for his technical development. On returning from the former city he produced his most successful works, related to those of Bellini in composition and brilliant in colour. After the Roman visit his drawing was excessively influenced by that of Michelangelo, while his designs grew monumental and his colour more subdued. But the works of Raphael, Credi and Leonardo had also made a deep impression on the studious monk. Bartolommeo was no pioneer. He translated, exploited and furthered the ideas of others. Typical examples of his work are in the cathedral at Lucca (*Madonna with the Baptist and St Stephen*) and in the National Gallery, London (*Madonna with the Child and St John*).

BARTOLOMMEO DI GIOVANNI

Two panels by this Florentine artist, representing the miracles of St Benedict, hang in the Uffizi Gallery. Others are in the United States. These works prove him to have been no more than a subordinate, though he served an important master—namely, Domenico Ghirlandaio. He acted as an apprentice, entrusted with the decoration of predelle (q.v.). Ghirlandaio employed him, for instance, on those of the altar of the Foundling Hospital at Florence. The papers relating to this work were recently discovered, the find being a notable proof of the acumen in matters of style of two specialists, Ullmann and Berenson.

They both maintained that two pictures supposed to be by Ghirlandaio were from another hand. Berenson, in the course of his researches, assembled a whole *œuvre* by this unknown Ghirlandesque painter, refusing to regard these works simply as inferior productions by Ghirlandaio and asserting in the face of all objections that a different person was concerned, whom he called the 'Alumnus' (pupil) of Domenico. Years later Berenson's theory was confirmed by the discovery of the document referred to, giving the name of the 'Alumnus', Bartolommeo di Giovanni. But an interesting mystery had been disposed of.

BARTOLOMMEO VENETO

(*See* VENETO)

BASAITI

Though of Greek parentage Marco Basaiti (c. 1470-c. 1527) was probably born in Venice, where he can be traced as living between 1490 and 1527. Little as his life is known, his works are highly prized. They are mainly altarpieces, with often remarkably fine delineations of landscape. But he cannot be absolved from charges of imitating Vivarini and Giovanni Bellini, who were his teachers. Fine examples of his original treatment of landscape occur in his *San Sebastian* in Berlin and his *Christ on the Mount of Olives* and *The Calling of the Sons of Zebedee* in the Accademia at Venice.

BASSA

Like almost all the early Spaniards, Ferrer Bassa (c. 1290-1348) is still much under-estimated. His unusual, adventurous personality and the fantastic beauty of his works are only now being recognised. He was the first important painter of Spain, being born surprisingly early, a younger contemporary of Giotto, and dying in Barcelona eleven years after the Italian master.

Bassa was first known to art historians, before any of his pictures were discovered, from unmistakable information in the criminal records of the Kingdom of Aragon. He was again and again pardoned in the Courts. On one occasion he was accused of violating three virgins in succession, on another his deportation was demanded and on another the forfeiture of his property. He contracted a late marriage, after which he seems to have lived more quietly. Many documents attest his work as a painter for the King and for wealthy monasteries. These commissions must have been of considerable import-

ance. Despite our detailed knowledge of him, however, none of his paintings was unearthed until quite recently. Then eight duly authenticated frescoes were found in the chapel of a nunnery at Pedralbes, representing the lives of the Virgin and Christ. The pictures were strong in colour, large in scale and composed in a severe, archaic style. The faces of the personages recalled those by Duccio and the early Florentines. But an unprecedented assurance in their gestures more indicative of character than in the case of Duccio and less formal than Giotto's, showed an advance on former masters.

Further investigation proved that oil had been the medium a century before it was used by Van Eyck.

BASSANO

Several members of the Bassano family are known to art historians. Their real name was da Ponte. But the Venetian country town in which they all grew up became permanently associated with their work and was regarded in time as their surname.

The first of the family to acquire a reputation as a painter was **Francesco** (c. 1470/5-1541). Four signed pictures by him have been preserved. They are today, with one exception, to be found in small churches near Bassano. Francesco was an accomplished but conventional painter in the style of Bartolommeo Montagna.

But the name Bassano, when used without a Christian name, commonly refers to Francesco's famous son, **Jacopo** (Giacomo). The latter lived in the town of Bassano all his life (c. 1510-1592), occupying a house surrounded by extensive gardens. Not much is known of the first decades of his long life. His reputation did not begin to grow till he was thirty-one or thirty-two. In all likelihood, his father's death obliged him to think of earning his own living as well as of artistic immortality. His pictures of country life, with

J. BASSANO · THE ADORATION OF THE SHEPHERDS
(Reduced in height) 96" × 60¼". *Bassano, City Museum*

its popular entertainments and pastoral scenes with herdsmen and animals, give the impression that he had long known and loved it. These paintings are his best work.

But he soon became best known for his altarpieces. These were modern versions of biblical stories, introducing episodes of life in the streets of Bassano and in the neighbourhood. Such depictions of simple rusticity became more and more popular in Venice as life in that city grew ever more fashionable and ceremonious. Before long orders were pouring in at such a rate that Jacopo was obliged, in order to retain some sort of personal freedom, to establish a big studio. He could do so the more easily since four of his many sons were already of an age to assist him. Francesco junior, Giambattista, Leandro and Gerolamo all took up painting with enthusiasm. Procedure seems to have been thoroughly domesticated. While one of the brothers primed, another drew, a third laid on the colours and a fourth added glazing. Then Jacopo would return from the Town Hall, where he was acting as Consul at the time, and join in the work. Unfortunately, in these circumstances, pictures from his own hand alone are not always readily distinguishable from those carried out by others in the studio. They can best be recognised from the high standard of colour organisation which is his chief merit. He troubled himself little, especially in religious subjects, about drawing and composition. He was in the habit of repeating himself in the most ingenuous manner and on occasion adopting the devices of others as a mere matter of convenience.

Yet at times he would produce a work as daring as the *Execution of John the Baptist* at Copenhagen, such a picture as Pontormo himself could barely have imagined, or the astonishing splendour of the *Banquet of the Rich Man* at Cleveland, Ohio.

His native city has been able to retain most of his pictures, which are to be found in the local gallery. Nine, however, are at Hampton Court, and there are three good examples of his work in the National Gallery, London.

BAZZANI

Giuseppe Bazzani was born in 1690 at Reggio and worked in Mantua, where he died in 1769, having become Director of the recently established Academy of Art. He was influenced by the work of Veronese and in particular of Van Dyck and Rubens. *Annunciation* (Venice); *St Anthony of Padua and the Infant Christ* (National Gallery, London).

BECCAFUMI

Though living in the High Renaissance period, Domenico Beccafumi (1486-1551) still retains traces of the earlier Sienese style. They are immediately obvious in his predelle (q.v.). His manner was first formed on that of Perugino. But after studying in Rome between 1510 and 1512 he drew more and more inspiration in his large mythological and biblical paintings from Raphael and Michelangelo. His colour was always personal and highly original. Born at Cortina, he died at Siena, where his most important frescoes are also to be found. His *Esther and Ahasuerus* is in the National Gallery, London.

BEECHEY

Sir William Beechey, R.A., was born at Burford in Oxfordshire in 1753 and studied law before becoming a student at the Royal Academy. He became portrait painter to Queen Charlotte and teacher of the Princesses. Unlike many of his contemporaries, Beechey never attempted the 'grand manner'. His portraits, though not of the first rank, provide an interesting record of personalities of the period. Beechey died at Hampstead in 1839, long after Lawrence had succeeded to the monopoly of fashion and reputation as a portrait painter. He is well represented in the National Portrait Gallery, in the National Gallery, London, and at Windsor.

BEERSTRAATEN

A series of large winter landscapes, all somewhat hard and dry in style, have survived from the hand of **Anthonie** Beerstraaten, an Amsterdam painter who was working from 1639 to 1665. They represent snow-covered castles and walled-in churches by the side of frozen canals and rivers. The bare branches of trees form filigree patterns against invariably overcast and clouded skies. Crowds of elegant figures in formal dress disport themselves on the ice. The pictures are easy to identify.

The painter **Jan Abrahamsz** Beerstraaten (active 1622-1666 at Amsterdam) was perhaps related to Anthonie. The former travelled much, producing large-scale views of towns and the sea, more rhythmically but also more conventionally composed than those of Anthonie. The question whether these two were or were not one and the same person was long debated among art historians.

A. VAN BIEJEREN · STILL-LIFE
44″ × 39¼″. Amsterdam, Rijksmuseum

BEGA

A resident of Haarlem and pupil of Adriaen Ostade, Cornelis Bega (active 1620-1660) painted, like his master, poor folk seated in their dark, untidy workshops amid cases, boxes and chests of drawers, or else tippling at the village inn. The reason why Bega's paintings do not bear comparison for a moment with Ostade's is that the former's figures do not convince us in the least. His singers have their mouths wide open and his hammers descend. But the spectator cannot imagine himself to be hearing anything. In spite of the resemblance in subject-matter, Bega's works can hardly be mistaken for those of Ostade, supreme in this field. Both as draughtsman and painter the pupil is more timid than his master and his settings are more gloomy. *The Philosopher*, in the National Gallery, London, is an example of his style.

BEIJEREN

The name is also spelt Beyeren. Abraham Hendricksz was born at The Hague c. 1620, and worked there and at Delft, Amsterdam and Gouda, dying at Overschie c. 1680/90. He was in the main a painter of still-life, influenced by his teacher and uncle, de Putter, and by the eminent Jan Davidsz de Heem. His debt to de Putter is evident from the fish, lobsters and crabs, which appear in nearly all his pictures. His long residence at The Hague, where this kind of still-life was then very fashionable, probably confirmed his taste for it. But his eternal preoccupation with such subject-matter, painted though it was in a glistening style anticipating impressionism, often gives his work a whiff of the market-barrow which does not appeal to everyone. In his later paintings the exposed entrails of his scaly carp and cod are replaced by the less offensive oyster, associated with highly colourful velvet materials and gorgeous table-ware, in the sparkling depths of which Beijeren's own features can sometimes be obscurely discerned.

BEHAM

Hans Sebald Beham (1500-1550) and **Barthel** Beham (1502-1540) were brothers who were born in Nuremberg. They were both painters and etchers on copper and were both influenced by Dürer. The paintings of Hans have for the most part unfortunately disappeared. He died at Frankfurt. Barthel also left Nuremberg and was appointed Court Painter to the Duke of Bavaria in Munich. He executed a number of portraits. His chief work, *The Miracle of the Cross*, is preserved in the Alte Pinakothek, Munich.

BEERVELT

Pieter Poele van Beervelt (active 1375-1414) worked in Ghent and had an extraordinarily eventful life. Scarcely any other painter of this early date is so often mentioned in contemporary documents, dealing with actions for slander, pilgrimages enforced by legal sentences, charitable donations and appointment to the Embassy in London. He must have been an extremely busy man. One of his pictures, dated 1411, is expressly referred to by Würzbach as having been painted in oils. Yet, strangely enough, not a single example of his output survives.

BELLEGAMBE

The works of Jean Bellegambe (c. 1480-c. 1535), who seems never to have left his native town of Douai, are almost exclusively altarpieces, remarkably and disappointingly conservative in style for his period, already that of humanism. Such pictures were being produced fifty years previously at Antwerp. They were overcrowded with figures and dealt with mystical events, amid swarms of cherubs —a favourite motive with Bellegambe— or with panoramic Last Judgments. Only an occasional architectural background of Renaissance type recalls the fact that times had changed.

Bellegambe was discovered in the nineteenth century, which conferred a belated glory upon him, perhaps too easily acquired. Examples of his work are to be found at Douai, Lille, Arras, Brussels, Berlin and New York.

BELLINI

'He is the best of painters,' Albrecht Dürer exclaimed when he met Giovanni Bellini in Venice. At that time Bellini stood alone at the height of his powers. The revolutionary impact of Antonello da Messina lay thirty years behind him and Titian's triumphant career was still to come. Giorgione was a youth, few of whose works were yet known. Palma Vecchio had just finished his apprenticeship. Dürer could think of no one anywhere of the same stature as Giovanni Bellini. Bellini himself appears to have agreed with him. For he behaved like a patriarch, with an air of detachment and aristocratic grandeur. When he visited the young Dürer at his lodgings in Peter Pander's inn near the Rialto, the Nuremberg painter naturally felt highly honoured. He wrote home: 'He came to see me in person, telling me he would like to have

GIOVANNI BELLINI · DOGE LOREDANO
24" × 17½". London, National Gallery

31

GIOVANNI BELLINI · MADONNA AND CHILD
32¾" × 24¾". Milan, Brera

something of mine. He asked me to do something for him and he is sure to pay for it.'

Giovanni was born in Venice, c. 1430, and died there at an advanced age in 1516. He came from a highly respected family of artists. His father, **Jacopo** (c. 1400-1470), was well known in the brilliant circle of Venetian society. The city already had at that time over a hundred thousand inhabitants. It was a sovereign state, with a Doge at its head of almost royal prestige. Jacopo had studied under no less an authority than Gentile da Fabriano. Examples of his work are to be found in the Uffizi Gallery at Florence, in Venice and in Madrid, while two of his sketch-books are preserved in the Louvre and in London respectively. They were mentioned by artists in his own lifetime with such respect as is only accorded to standard manuals. These albums dealt with perspective, anatomy,

types of subject-matter, biblical themes, ancient architecture, sculpture, coins, ornamentation and physiognomy. To possess them was to acquire remunerative capital. The Venetians thronged to Jacopo's studio.

His sons, Gentile and Giovanni, were both, of course, his pupils. Giovanni, the most alert and receptive of the two, also eagerly studied, in the neighbouring city of Padua, works by the Tuscan artists Uccello, Donatello, Castagno and Filippo Lippi. In a few years he had outstripped his father, his brother and everyone he knew, with one exception, Andrea Mantegna of Padua, who was the same age as himself. When eventually the two men met, Giovanni recognised that Mantegna towered above him like a rock.

Fascinated by the Paduan, Bellini could not resist his influence. It is conspicuous in all the Venetian's Madonnas and Pietàs of this period, marked by the unprecedented severity, reserved strength, gravity and linear power of Mantegna's spirit. One of the most characteristic of these paintings is the *Transfiguration of Christ* in the Correr Museum at Venice, where there is much foreshortening, in Mantegna's manner, of the figures of the Apostles. The rock on which they lie is also treated in his style. Other typical pictures of this kind are *The Agony in the Garden* in London and the Milan *Lamentation over Christ* and *Madonna and Child*. Many connoisseurs consider that Giovanni Bellini never achieved again, in any of his famous late works, the stern beauty of repressed emotion in the features of this Madonna.

Mantegna married Giovanni's sister. The two painters thus became still more closely associated. But in 1475 a new artistic comet rose above the horizon. Antonello da Messina visited Venice. 'The work of this Sicilian of genius during the year he spent in the city of the Lagoon can hardly be over-estimated in its effect on Venetian painting. The fact that the leading painter of Venice, Giovanni Bellini, assimilated the other's revelations and incorporated them in his work made Antonello's influence paramount in the city' (L. Dussler).

The change of direction involved release from the pressure of Mantegna, which had forged Bellini's steel, but now ceased just at the right moment. Bellini proceeded to develop his true nature. His pictures acquired a harmonious and soothing beauty not hitherto associated with his work. He did not repudiate either Mantegna or Antonello. Their influences remained effective in his portraits. But after 1490 his style became wholly his own. In that year he painted the so-called *Christian Allegory*, now in the Uffizi Gallery. It is easy to understand the deep admiration felt even by Giorgione, fifteen years later, for this picture.

By the turn of the century Giovanni Bellini's European reputation was well established. His long life enabled him to produce an abundance of good work. He is represented in every important gallery and large private collection.

His elder brother, Gentile, died nine years before him.

Gentile Bellini, like his brother, was at first strongly influenced by the Paduan School, but his individuality is apparent in the early study of St Lorenzo Giustianini in the Venice Academy, which must be one of the first full-length portraits in existence. The portrait of a mathematician in the National Gallery, London, painted a little later, after Gentile had become acquainted with Antonello, exhibits an aspect of portraiture in the unusual accent on the hands which was to become a feature of later Venetian painting. In 1429 the Sultan Mehemet requested the Signoria to recommend to him a good portrait painter and Gentile Bellini was chosen. He spent some months in Constantinople, where he was given the title of Bey. He returned to Venice laden with gifts and with many sketches of Eastern personages, and the picture now in the Louvre representing the reception of a Venetian embassy by the Grand Vizier. He immediately received further commissions from the Schools of St Mark and St John, for whom he painted *The Procession of the Relic of the True Cross* and *The Miraculous Preservation of the Relic*. These remarkable compositions anticipate the great Venetian pageant pictures of later date and also the records of Venetian architecture made more than two hundred years later by Canaletto and Guardi.

BELLOTTO

It was out of respect and affection for his uncle and teacher, Antonio Canaletto, that Bernardo Bellotto (1720-1780) assumed the latter's name. Many collectors, even today, prefer to call him by it. But Bellotto's pictures are much inferior to Antonio's. The uncle's works stand head and shoulders, so to speak, above the best of the nephew's. Bellotto is most successful when he relies on his own talent, as in the Varese landscape at the Brera Gallery, Milan, in his small pastoral studies and in the panoramas in glassily cold colours and sharp outlines painted during prolonged visits to Munich, Dresden—where he spent twenty years—Vienna and Warsaw. He died in the latter city.

BENSON

Ambrosius Benson (active 1518-1550), came from Lombardy and settled in Bruges. He was a highly talented but eclectic painter who borrowed from Rogier van der Weyden, Gerard David and also from Italian sources. His Madonnas are particularly reminiscent of Gerard David, while his portraits recall Memling. His principal works are in Antwerp (*Madonna with Prophets*) and the Prado (*Pietà*). Benson would appear to have received many commissions from abroad, for there are more pictures by him in Spain than in the Netherlands. A *Magdalen Reading* by Benson is in the National Gallery, London.

BERCHEM

Born in Haarlem in 1620 and dying in Amsterdam in 1683, Nicolas Berchem must have been a perpetual student if he in fact passed through the hands of so many teachers, including Van Goyen, as are attributed to him by his great admirer,

G. BERCKHEYDE · THE GROOTE KERK
16″ × 13¼″. Cambridge, Fitzwilliam Museum

Amsterdam. He was equally successful there and remained so until his death, exercising great influence on his contemporaries. If we are to believe Houbraken in this instance, his pupils included Karel du Jardin, Pieter de Hooch, Ochtervelt, Huchtenberg, Dirk Maas, Vermeer van Harlem the Younger and Huysum the Elder.

BERCKHEYDE

Opinions have always differed, according to the taste of the day, as to which of the two brothers, **Job** (1630-1693) or **Gerrit** Berckheyde (1638-1698), was the better painter. Both produced mainly views of streets and towns. Job was a fearless and powerful colourist. Gerrit often failed in this respect. He was a facile imitator of Heyden and Saeuredam. From a purely artistic standpoint, Job was the better and more important painter.

Both were born and died in Haarlem. Gerrit is said to have been drowned there. The brothers and their unmarried sister lived together in a rare state of concord, only once leaving Haarlem for any considerable time, when they visited Cologne, Bonn, Mannheim and Heidelberg.

BERMEJO

Little is known of the life of this supposedly most important Spanish painter of the fifteenth century. Bartolomé Bermejo came from Cordoba, his real name being Bartolomé de Cardenas. 'Bermejo' or 'Vermejo' simply means 'the red-haired'. The years of his birth and death are unknown. He only dated one of his signed works, a Pietà in the Chapter House of Barcelona Cathedral. The date is 1490. He may have been between fifty and sixty at the time. The pictures ascribed to him with more or less certainty at the present day are puzzling if regarded as all by the same artist. His impressive

Houbraken. We may be content today to assume that he studied under his father, Pieter Claesz, who was an excellent painter. Berchem may also have worked for a short time with Moyart and Jan Wils. The character of his painting was, however, decided by a journey to Italy, proved by two contemporary references. Returning in 1642, he joined the Haarlem guild.

His earliest pictures closely resembled stage backcloths. But he soon began to limit his scale and subject-matter, tentatively including a few rustic landscapes among his battle pieces, hunting scenes and Court ceremonies. The landscapes sold surprisingly well. As he grew more and more interested in them, and in the placid beauty of pastoral life, his painting improved. Certain pictures of his best, middle period are unquestionably important.

In 1677 he moved from Haarlem to

Christ Crowned with Thorns in the Vich Museum is surprisingly reminiscent of Mantegna. It bears hardly any resemblance to the dramatic and feverishly coloured triptych of the Virgin at Agui, an altarpiece signed 'Bartolomeus Rubeus', the adjective meaning 'the Red' in Latin. Both pictures, moreover, differ completely from the devotionally stiff and formal *Engracia* of Boston. If Bermejo in fact covered so wide a stylistic field, he must certainly be regarded as the most interesting Spanish artist of his time.

BERRUGUETE

There were four Castilian painters named Berruguete, members of the same family. Two of them became important artists. **Pedro,** born at Paredes and dying in 1503, probably in Toledo, may have visited Italy. A note in the Court records of Urbino seems to refer to him. His frescoes and altar-panels at times show traces of the influence of Perugino on their Spanish formality and traditional iconographic style.

But it was his son **Alonso** (c. 1486-1561) who was first to introduce Italian Renaissance painting and sculpture into Spain. He, too, was born at Paredes and died at Toledo. Vasari (q.v.) mentions him several times in his biographies of Michelangelo, Sansovino and Filippino Lippi. Michelangelo himself, in a letter, makes a single passing reference to his name. But the Spanish gentleman evidently did not make any great impression on Michelangelo. Berruguete, however, was deeply influenced by his Italian visit. On his return in 1520 he had become a typical man of the Renaissance. In reality he was a modest enough disciple of Italy. But his Spanish contemporaries considered him a regular Michelangelo. The Archbishop of Toledo paid him 50,000 reals (£20,000) for the sculptures of the choir-stalls and throne of the Cathedral.

Alonso's works have unfortunately only survived in part, while some pictures attributed to him are not authenticated. It is a great pity that they do not bear his signature, for it is one of the finest specimens of calligraphy extant, in a most elegant Moorish script, set down by a Western hand.

BERTRAM

Master Bertram of Minden is one of the first names in the history of German art. The few records in which his name occurs mention commissions for altarpieces and also for sculpture, so that Bertram was more than a painter. He was probably born in 1345 at Minden in Westphalia. He must have gone at an early age to Hamburg, for he was little more than twenty years of age when he painted his first important work there. In his long life he must have painted more pictures than the few which have come down to us. Fire accounted for the loss of many priceless works, and others were destroyed during the Reformation. Master Bertram died in Hamburg in 1415. The date has been ascertained from a document referring to the claims of relatives who benefited from his will.

Bertram was a generation in advance of Konrad Witz and Stefan Lochner, and his work represents the beginning of German painting. Painters did indeed exist prior to Master Bertram, but they were without distinctive personality. So when he came to Hamburg he found no tradition, no one upon whom he could model himself. He was the first German painter to impose a definite, individual character upon his work. His pictures are particularly distinguished for their colour and texture. His principal works are divided between the galleries of Hamburg and Hanover.

BEUCKELAER

Joachim Beuckelaer (c. 1533-1573) belonged to the group of early Dutch painters of common life and manners led by Pieter Aertsen, under whom he probably studied. At any rate the two men, knew each other well. Aertsen being Beuckelaer's uncle by marriage. Modern judgment sets Beuckelaer considerably below Aertsen. The case is arguable, but is unfair to the former, who died at forty

MASTER BERTRAM · THE CREATION OF THE ANIMALS
(*From the Grabow Altarpiece*) *Overall size* (*six panels*)
68⅜″ × 68″. Hamburg, Kunsthalle

and market-women, relegating the specifically Christian elements to the background.

The merits of this artist have been under-estimated.

BLAKE

William Blake, poet, painter and engraver, was born in London in 1757, the son of a hosier and dissenter who read Swedenborg. From the age of four Blake believed himself to be in touch with spirits, angels and prophets. He was a nervous child and was not sent to school but when he was fourteen he was apprenticed to the engraver James Basire and spent part of his working time making drawings of Gothic monuments and sculpture in Westminster Abbey. He also learnt something of Renaissance and Baroque art, for Basire was at the time engraving the Raphael cartoons at Hampton Court and a number of pictures by Guercino. Among his acquaintances a little later were Flaxman and Fuseli. These were the influences that formed his style. Blake married Catherine Bouchier, a peasant, in 1782. He received help at various times from admirers of his work; one of them, Thomas Butts, bought many of Blake's remark-

and endured much humiliation. It was quite usual for the countless painters of the second rank in Holland to earn their livings as bakers or schnapps-sellers. But Beuckelaer must have suffered greatly from having to paint for a daily wage of 1 gulden. There can be little doubt, therefore, that he also acted as an anonymous assistant to Aertsen and that many fine passages in the latter's works are by Beuckelaer.

Pictures painted exclusively by himself are rare. There are several in Stockholm, mostly large market or kitchen scenes. Even his few religious works give a conspicuous place in the foreground to stalls

able tempera paintings and numerous watercolours over a long period. Blake died in 1827, believing himself to be surrounded by the visionary presences that had always been part of his inner existence.

He painted chiefly in watercolour. His tempera paintings, in which he used glue instead of albumen to bind the pigments, have partly perished, and we can only guess at their original appearance from the one fine example to survive, *Satan smiting Job with Sore Boils* in the Tate Gallery. Blake was not interested in the naturalistic imitation of what he called 'vegetable' phenomena, but only in exteriorising his spiritual experiences. Instead of using his eyes as the means of providing himself with the material for his pictures, he took his subjects from the Bible, Milton, Dante and his own writings. The unique quality in his work is a sweeping rhythm of movement which not only governs his figure drawing, but is caught up and harmonised by the complementary features so often introduced in the border designs. He employed a skilfully controlled system of distortion, and in his last period, in the *Illustrations to Comus* and the *Illustrations to the Divine Comedy* he found a perfect pictorial equivalent to the art of words and arrived at the complete exteriorisation of his visions. Blake cannot be 'placed' in the history of painting. The power of his imagination, his genius in objectifying it, and the sense of the supernatural which animated it set him aside from all currents and tendencies. His influence is perhaps stronger today than it was in his own lifetime, when he was unknown and unregarded except for a short time among his disciples, Samuel Palmer, Edward Calvert and John Linnell.

Blake was among the most original and fertile of engravers and illustrators, inventing new processes of reproduction, by means of which he was able to produce editions of his own writings and print editions of his coloured drawings.

His watercolours and paintings are divided between the British Museum, the Tate Gallery, and the Victoria and Albert Museum, London.

BLES

Herri Met de Bles (c. 1480-c. 1550) was probably responsible for better work than has yet been proved

to be his. It is certain, in the first place, that he was identical with Herri (Heinrich) Blesius, Henrico Civetta (Heinrich Käuzchen), Henrico da Dinant (Heinrich von Dinant), perhaps with 'The Monogramist' and probably also with Herri de Patenier, appointed guild-master at Antwerp in 1535. The Patenier family, including the important painter, Joachim Patenier, came from Dinant. The anonymous 'Master of 1518' represented in the Kaiser Friedrich Museum in Berlin may also perhaps be identified with Herri Met de Bles.

He was in his day equally well known in the Netherlands, Germany, France, Italy and Spain, where one of his pictures was found by Bredius in Barcelona. Mander (q.v.), who lived not long after him, declares that 'Bles' is simply the common Flemish word for a white patch in the hair. Mander ascribes to him a picture of 'monkeys and a sleeping merchant' which is preserved at Dresden and is inscribed with the emblem of an owl, the crest of Bouvignes-Dinant.

More and more works are now being ascribed to this painter. They are attractive in a peculiarly harsh and vigorous style,

A. BLOEMAERT · PASTORAL SCENE
24″ × 29¾″. Hanover, Landesgalerie

recalling in some respects Joachim Patenier and in others Hieronymus Bosch. The *Sermon of John* in Dresden, a portrait in Berlin, the *Copper Mine* at the Uffizi Gallery, the *Holy Family* in Basle and the *Disciples of Emmaus* in Vienna have all been ascribed to Herri Met de Bles. He is a painter who should not be overlooked in any gallery. His landscapes, incidentally, are noticeable even at a distance for the bewildering intricacy of their rock formations. The artist was born in Bouvignes and died at Lüttich.

BLOEMART

Born at Dordrecht in 1564 and dying at Utrecht in 1651, Abraham Bloemart was the first of his name to acquire a reputation as a painter. Nor did any of his sons or grandsons exceed him in importance.

He initiated a new style at Utrecht, founding a whole school of what might perhaps be called 'homely Mannerism'. He himself never visited Italy, but was deeply attached to what he felt it represented. He succeeds best where he is most Dutch in his interpretations of the country, as in his rural landscapes, akin to Bassano's in feeling, where he expresses his love of nature in a rustic type of Mannerism. After 1620 he toned down the dramatic element in his earlier pictures, such as his *Judith* at Vienna, but fortunately retained the brilliance of his unbroken greens, reds and yellows. One of his best late works is the *Pastoral* at Hanover, painted when he was sixty-three.

His works are crowded with detail and lacking in symmetry. His academic mythological scenes are weak, his portraits unimpressive. But his Biblical subjects are well handled and his landscapes beautiful. He was greatly respected at Utrecht. The Emperor owned pictures by him. He was visited by Queen Elizabeth of Bohemia and entertained Rubens. He obtained permission to erect a studio in the church of the Nuns of St Clare, where his pupils included at various times Terbrugghen, Jacob Cuyp, Honthorst and Weenix.

BOCCACCINO

Born at Ferrara in 1466, Boccaccino died in 1524 at Cremona, where his masterpiece, frescoes in the Cathedral depicting scenes from the life of the Virgin, is preserved. In addition to frescoes, Boccaccino painted certain pictures characterised by peculiarly subtle, singing colour, as in his small *Gipsy* at the Uffizi Gallery. In his religious themes, as in his *Madonna* at Hamburg, the gentle, sensuous harmony of Bellini predominates.

Other works include a *Procession to Calvary* in the National Gallery, London, and a *Santa Conversazione* in the Accademia at Venice.

An unknown painter who imitated Boccaccino, though his style is distinct, is credited with pictures entitled *The Washing of Feet*, *Christ among the Doctors* and *Madonna with Saints* in the Accademia at Venice, *Adoration of the Magi* in the Brera Gallery at Milan and *Madonna and Two Donors* at Naples. This artist, called Pseudo-Boccaccino, was probably a pupil of Bramantino.

BOILLY

Louis Leopold Boilly, a portraitist and painter of scenes from ordinary life was born at La Bassée in 1761 and died in Paris in 1845. His agreeable facile little pictures were popular during the First Republic. No less than five thousand of them survive.

BOL

The surname Bol was borne by fourteen painters during the sixteenth and seventeenth centuries in Holland. But mention of the name commonly refers to only one of them, Rembrandt's most distinguished pupil, Ferdinand Bol (1616-1680).

He was born in Dordrecht, the son of a respected surgeon, and died in Amsterdam, where he was one of the first pupils received by Rembrandt, as well as the one, apparently, who stayed longest with him. There is documentary evidence that Rembrandt's studio was already selling numbers of Bol's pictures by the end of the 1630s. These paintings are so much in his master's manner that many were long attributed to Rembrandt himself.

Bol's works are of exceptional quality so long as he follows in the footsteps of his teacher. But, strangely enough, when his desire to please the public and his innate tendency to decorative elegance led him, in the 1660s, to go his own way, the strength of his former style declines into unpleasant theatricality. During the last ten years of his life he seems to have given up painting and to have lived only for his own pleasures and social obligations. But he had already done enough to establish a high reputation. Such pictures as the *Governors of the Leper Hospital* and the *Governors of the Poorhouse* in Amsterdam, his self-portrait at Munich and some of his other portraits are numbered among the show-pieces of the great national galleries. He is represented in the National Gallery, London and in the Wallace Collection.

A certain **Hans Bol** (1534-1593) is recognised as a painter of graceful portraits and miniature landscapes.

FERDINAND BOL · SELF-PORTRAIT
30¼" × 28¾". Munich, Alte Pinakothek

BOLTRAFFIO

Less is known of Giovanni Antonio Boltraffio (1467-1516), who was born and died at Milan, than might be expected from the distinction of his family, a conspicuous one in the city, as he was himself no doubt a conspicuous personality. He was in Bologna about 1500 and in Rome about 1513.

As a pupil of Leonardo da Vinci he, like the rest, such as Luini, Predis, Melzi, Giampietrino and d'Oggione, remained so completely dominated by that tremendous figure, from the time of Leonardo's arrival in Milan, that it is now impossible to say what that generation of painters would have achieved if Leonardo had not crossed their path and made them utterly dependent upon himself. It is certain that Boltraffio had great talent, revealed in his *St Barbara* in Berlin and in his portraits. The best of his paintings of the Madonna are preserved in the Louvre, London and Bergamo.

BONIFAZIO

Bonifazio di Pitati or Bonifazio Veronese was born at Verona in 1487 and died in Venice in 1553. He was a pupil and assistant of Palma Vecchio and established a large workshop in Venice. Bonifazio was influenced by Giorgione and his favourite theme was figures in a landscape. He gradually abandoned the traditional group of Madonna and saints and painted scenes of fashionable country life, music parties in the open air, the pleasures of the chase and picnics in forest glades, giving them such titles as *The Rich Man's Feast* (Venice) or *The Finding of Moses* (Florence). Bonifazio is well represented in Florence, Rome and Venice.

BONSIGNORI

Francesco Bonsignori was born at Verona, probably in 1453, and studied at Venice under the Vivarini. In 1489 he moved to Mantua, where he came under the influence of Mantegna. He died in 1519 at Caldiero, near Verona. Bonsignori was a monumental portraitist, excelling with older sitters (examples at Bergamo, Milan and in the National Gallery, London), and it is for these rather than for his firmly composed altarpieces that he demands attention. His work in portraiture is a bold development of the style of Alvise Vivarini and of Antonello.

BORDONE

Paris Bordone, a pupil of Titian, was born at Treviso in 1500 and died in Venice in 1571. As one of the successors of Giorgione, Palma and Titian, he benefited from the study of the great Venetians who had preceded him. He noted their depth of colour, their grandiose composition, the psychological refinement of their portraits and their splendid handling of landscape and nocturnal illumination. He reproduced all these elements well and his pictures are often very fine. But they never reveal any original features. Bordone's very lack of inventive powers may have rendered his life an easy one. He was admired everywhere, in Venice, Treviso, Vicenza, Turin and Genoa. He travelled a great deal, painting at the Court of Francis I, King of France, between 1538 and 1540 and also working for Fugger at Augsburg. He produced altarpieces, mythological works, portraits of both men and women and historical pictures. Nearly all the big galleries possess paintings by Bordone. The best known of them is in the Accademia of Venice. It depicts the delivery to the Doge, in gorgeous surroundings, of the ring retrieved by the fisherman.

BORGOGNONE

Ambrogio Borgognone (1455?-1523) was a Milanese painter who, together with his venerable older contemporary, Foppa, whom he imitated, stood at the head of the Lombard School before Leonardo arrived at the Court of the Sforza dynasty. Borgognone's character was simple, honest and devout. His pictures are notable for their subdued, graceful rhythm, their harmonious disposition of space and their

unusual tact in the juxtaposition of low-toned greyish blues. Berenson has labelled him the 'Whistler of the Renaissance', an extraordinary description which, for all its daring, may perhaps help to define the peculiar nature of Borgognone's style.

After the turn of the century his colour grew more animated and his figures somewhat less relaxed and unrelated to one another. His masterpieces are the Certosa altarpiece and the frescoes at Lodi and in San Simpliciano at Milan. He is well represented in the National Gallery, London.

A certain Ambrogio di Giorgio Borgognone, active in Pavia between 1481 and 1518, is sometimes confused with him.

BOSCH

Hieronymus Bosch, as he signed himself on some of his pictures, was active at Hertogenbosch, where he died, after 1480/1. This enigmatic artist did not become the subject of documentary research until a late period—in fact, only after the publication of Carl Justi's study of him in 1889. The results, however, were meagre. Contemporary records refer to him repeatedly as Hieronymus van Aken. It appears therefore that his family was originally settled in Aachen. He is mentioned as a guild-master for the first time in 1480. This information is followed by references to contracts for pictures placed with him by the municipality and the 'Brotherhood of Our Lady', a body to which he belonged. The catalogue of the Escorial, Madrid, lists the names of works by Bosch which were collected by King Philip II. But that is the sum total of our knowledge.

His period is believed to be pretty well understood today. Yet this great painter remains a lonely and most puzzling figure to modern scholars. His works prove that we can really grasp very little of the religious symbolism and basic psychology of those who lived five hundred years ago. For it is certain that the weird and ghostly surrealistic visions painted by Bosch were then intelligible, not merely enjoyed, as they are today, for their painterly skill and their fantasy. He was representing definite ideas, not simply endless variations on the Witches' Sabbath theme. The *Hay-wain* triptych at Madrid and the *Temptation of St Anthony* at Lisbon may well be mistaken for purely personal fancies. But *The Garden of Delights* of Madrid and especially the uncanny *Last Judgment* of Vienna surely suggest pictorial versions of a symbolic language familiar from sermons. To put the matter another way, while a modern observer only sees a 'damned soul' trapped in a forged ball, the painter's contemporaries would know why he was there—what sins, in fact, he had committed. Either the technical proceedings represented in the *Last Judgment* alone must have been above the heads of the men of 1500 or else they conveyed something to the spectators of that age which we cannot now conjecture. Nor is there any point in our trying to understand their meaning. It is better to admit ignorance and take these refined miracles of colouring as purely painterly phenomena. Only so can we enter in any way into the thoughts and feelings of the artist.

BOSCH · THE GARDEN OF DELIGHTS
(*Detail from "Hell"*) *88″ × 39″. Madrid, Escorial*

In addition to these masterpieces, Hieronymus Bosch produced a further series of equally splendid paintings. They include *Stations of the Cross*, such as the famous one in Ghent, the *Ecce Homo* pictures of Frankfurt and Philadelphia, the *Christ Crowned with Thorns* in London, *Adorations of the Magi* in Madrid and Philadelphia, the *Seven Deadly Sins* of Madrid, *Paradise and Hell* in the Doges' Palace at Venice, the *Ship of Fools* in the Louvre and the *Tramp* at Rotterdam.

A chalk drawing of unknown authorship in the Library at Arras purports to be a portrait of Bosch. The face is that of a man about sixty, square-headed and full-fleshed. The corners of the narrow lips and the skin of the thick neck are furrowed by the wrinkles of age. But the eyes are large, piercing and ironical in expression. If this portrait corresponded with the reality, Bosch was by no means an austere mystic.

BOSSCHAERT

The older artist of this name, Ambrosius, born at Middleburg in 1565 and dying at The Hague in 1621, painted flowers. His sons, **Ambrosius** and **Abraham,** were also flower painters. The works of all three look very much alike to the ordinary observer. Some slight indication of the hand of the elder Bosschaert may be deduced—in addition to qualitative considerations—from the niches containing his luxuriant bouquets and the faint, watercolour treatment of his background landscapes. His pictures resemble those of his friend Jan Brueghel, but lack the latter's attractive warmth.

BOTH

Of two brothers, **Jan,** who was born in 1618 and died in Utrecht in 1652, achieved a much higher level. His landscapes, influenced by Claude, have a curiously modern air, as of the romantic school of the nineteenth century. His herdsmen, riders and travellers are shown moving through misty woods or over a broad expanse of open, sunlit country, towards a low-lying horizon. The long shadows of evening lie across the scene. His mythological works are rarer. Jan Both's pictures were much admired—and often forged—in the Rococo Age.

Andries was born in 1608 and died in Venice in 1641. It is difficult to imagine brothers so utterly different. The elder painted crude scenes of peasant life and alehouse tippling.

BOTTEGA

Italian shop, working place. Every successful artist of the Renaissance kept a workshop or *bottega* in which his commissions were executed. In many cases the *bottega* was a family enterprise inherited by successive generations. Here the master trained his apprentices, who commonly began to learn a craft on the completion of their thirteenth year. The master's assistants also worked in the *bottega*. These were either apprentices who had served their time, but had not yet set up for themselves, or they were artists from outside who were co-operating with a famous master to improve their own practice or to earn a living. The master provided drawings and designs for the commissions that came to him. The preparation of the materials, the cartoons and, in the case of painting, of the panels and colours needed was the business of the assistants, who also painted the accessories of large works and often entirely executed less important orders from the designs which the master finished. When the apprentices and assistants left the *bottega* to work elsewhere they naturally took with them all that they had acquired of their master's style and technical mannerisms, so that even when they were no longer actively connected with the *bottega* their work would be stamped as belonging to his school. This was, of course, only the case with men of mediocre talent; the more gifted apprentices would develop independently and probably set up their own *botteghe*.

BOTTICELLI

The real name of this world-famous painter was Alessandro Filipepi. He was born in 1445 and spent all his life in Florence, where he died in 1510. He was a slightly older contemporary of the greatest of the Medici, Lorenzo the Magnificent (1449-1492). At that time Florence had become a paradise for painters, poets and scholars. The power of the Medici was not exercised in an oppressive but in a liberating sense. It encouraged self-reliance to an extraordinary degree. The unprecedented wealth of Lorenzo flowed in abundance through the city, conjuring up palaces and gardens among the streets. Within the walls of Florence in those days lived not only Botticelli, but also Leonardo da Vinci, Verrochio, Pollaiuolo, Filippino Lippi, Jacopo Sellaio, Piero di Cosimo, Ghirlandaio, Perugino and Lorenzo di Credi.

But this brilliant setting ought not to mislead one into regarding Botticelli as a typically radiant being of the Renaissance period. He was nothing of the kind. The radiant, joyous painters of the High Renaissance came a generation later. It is easy to understand Botticelli on the evidence of his two most famous paintings, *The Birth of Venus* and the *Primavera*, both in the Uffizi. They seem wholly given up to Greek mythology, Arcadian dreams and paganism. But this view is an illusion due to the subject-matter and the sweeping, apparently carefree linear rhythms. The ultimate impression is not one of gaiety and freedom from care, but of melancholy and Orphic lament. Botticelli's female heads, in particular, convey this feeling of painful experience. Their eyes seem to look through and beyond the spectator. When, as is often the case, the features have great sensuous beauty, the appeal suggests at the same time helplessness, timidity and submission. None of his female figures, no picture of his, in fact, looks exuberant. Every movement, every gesture represented, appears tentative. Roberto Salvini once most effectively observed that in Botticelli 'movement changes to rest, action to memory'.

His inimitable charm resides in this hint of melancholy, morbidity, low-toned lament and dreamy abstraction. It is reinforced by his wonderful colour sense and inexhaustibly imaginative draughtsmanship. He had, of course, also studied under a teacher of outstanding ability, Fra Filippo Lippi.

Botticelli's life, for which the principal source is Vasari (q.v.), was not very rich in outward events. But it was repeatedly troubled by psychological problems. His youth may well have been undisturbed and carefree, for his father earned good wages as a tanner. But how the legend of his cheerful nature arose is incomprehensible. It was probably due to Vasari, who relates at great length the story of a trick he played on one of his companions. The trick, however, was a somewhat sinister one.

He was at first apprenticed to a goldsmith, from whom he may have adopted the name he used professionally. But the boy's extraordinary talent for drawing eventually induced his father to allow him to become a painter. After studying under Filippo Lippi, he began to work independently about 1470, when he was engaged, with the brothers Pollaiuolo, in painting for the Commercial Tribunal of Florence. The influence upon him of

BOTTICELLI · THE BIRTH OF VENUS
(Detail) 70" × 111¼". Florence, Uffizi

Antonio Pollaiuolo must have been exceptionally strong. For in the righthand group of his *Primavera*, painted ten years later, the design of Pollaiuolo's *Rape of Deianira* can be recognised. The third of Botticelli's great teachers was Verrocchio,

BOTTICELLI · PIETÀ
(Detail) 55¼″ × 81¼″. *Munich, Alte Pinakothek*

an extraordinary personality, who made a deep impression on everyone he met.

In 1481 Pope Sixtus IV invited Botticelli to Rome, commissioning him to execute three frescoes in the Sistine Chapel. His fame increased to such an extent, as a result, that on his return to Florence he was overwhelmed with offers of contracts. 'But instead of painting,' laments Vasari primly, 'he turned, for he was a man of subtle intelligence, to the elucidation of Dante's poems. This work greatly impeded his career.'

When Savonarola, in 1490, started his fanatical penitential activities, Botticelli was among those who fell under his influence. An idea of the artist's violent change of heart can be obtained from a study of his later works. There is no further trace in them of Hellenism and Arcadian poetry. The *Calumny of Apelles* in the Uffizi and the *Lamentation for Christ* in Munich were designed in the throes of an intense dread of punishment. The style of both paintings is austere and menacing, though splendid. They were executed at the very time when such sentiments had already ceased to be congenial to the age. The 'radiant' next generation had arrived. Botticelli had in a sense died before he physically expired. Vasari ends his account with the words: 'But at last he grew old and incapable of work, as well as so lame that he was obliged to use two crutches. He died in his seventy-eighth year.'

Botticelli's chief works are to be found in Florence, Munich, Berlin, London and Washington.

BOTTICINI

It is clear, though it has not been proved, that Francesco Botticini (active 1446-1497), originally a pupil of Neri di Bicci, worked subsequently in Verrocchio's studio. His pictures are typical examples of the work of an imitator. In some the copying—the result one feels, of sincere admiration—appears quite undisguised. He started by following Cosimo Rosselli in a somewhat forced and gaudy style. Then it seems that he encountered Verrocchio, forgot Rosselli, studied 'from Botticelli' and painted the *Ascension*, now in London, and the *Madonna with Angels scattering Flowers* in the Pitti Palace at Florence. Later scholars found his works difficult to identify. Vasari confidently ascribed the *Ascension* to Botticelli. The Pitti Madonna was also attributed to another artist. Both paintings, incidentally, are of high quality.

Today Francesco Botticini has been recognised for what he was. His works can be named without much trouble. The pictures in London and Florence have long since been given their correct ascriptions. A fine *Young Tobias* in the Uffizi Gallery is also now stated to be by Botticini.

BOUCHER

It could almost be said that François Boucher (1703-1770), who was born and died in Paris, remained at his easel to the

BOUCHER
NUDE ON A SOFA
$23\frac{1}{4}'' \times 28\frac{3}{4}''$. Munich,
Alte Pinakothek

st, working, as might have been ex-
ected, at a Venus.

Boucher, Watteau and Fragonard be-
ween them compose a brilliant trinity of
ainters at the Rococo Court of Louis
V. The rise of the first-named was
apid. He began by studying under Le
Moine, who had produced the ceiling
escoes at Versailles. He then concen-
ated on Watteau. He proceeded to pay
is first visit to Italy at the age of twenty-
ur to see the works of Tiepolo. He
eturned a master, with nothing more to
arn in the way of technique. He was
nade a member of the Academy, succeeded
udry as Inspector of the State Gobelins
actory and became a professor, a Gentle-
an of the Bedchamber and official
ainter to the King. He was patronised by
Madame de Pompadour, for whom he
ainted portraits, and decorated her
oudoir.

During the fifty years after his death
oucher was gradually forgotten, though
uite undeservedly. It is true that he is
ot to be compared for a moment with
Watteau and that his reputation was
xaggerated in his lifetime. But there is
o doubt that he was an important
alant. His pictures are not merely
alant. They have genuine artistic merit,
eing often delightfully coloured and
ways brilliantly drawn. His beautiful

designs for tapestry are unquestionably
outstanding, of much greater value than
his pictures.

The best of the latter are in the Louvre.
They include *Venus in the Forge* and
Diana After Bathing. One of his most
erotic compositions, the *Reclining Girl*, is
at Munich. The Wallace Collection contains a selection of his paintings of the
highest quality. Diderot's verdict was:
'What marvellous colour, what wealth of
invention! He had everything in him
except the truth. A charming profligate!'

BOURDON

Born at Montpellier, Sebastien Bourdon
(1616-1671) moved, while he was still very
young, to Paris, Bordeaux, Toulouse and
eventually Rome, where he spent the
years 1634-1637, studying Poussin and
Claude. He visited Venice and returned
to Paris in 1643. His dashing portraits,
very modern in style, and a picture he
painted for Notre Dame, soon made him
famous. In 1648 he founded, under the
patronage of Cardinal Mazarin, the Paris
Academy of Art. In 1652 he went for two
years to Stockholm, where he was
appointed Court Painter to Queen Christina. His work in Sweden was mainly
portraiture. In this field and in landscape
his style now seems most original.

Returning to Paris in 1654, he received a number of commissions for decorative schemes. Apart from four years spent at Montpellier, he remained in the capital for the rest of his life, working in a manner increasingly based on that of Poussin, blended with a lyrical sweetness and a coolness of colour that are his own.

BOUTS

Born at Haarlem, c. 1415, Dirk Bouts settled at Louvain about 1448, where he was appointed painter to the municipality, a great and rare honour, which had formerly been conferred by Brussels on Rogier van der Weyden. Bouts seems to have remained in Louvain until his death in 1475.

Little more is known of the life of this great late Gothic master. He must have been already famous when he arrived in Louvain. None of his youthful works is known. The first of his extant pictures are perfectly mature. His influence on all Flemish painting and that of the Lower Rhineland was very great, only being exceeded by that of Rogier van der Weyden. Bouts may lack the brilliance, the imaginative energy and resource of Rogier. But his form and line are as admirable as the latter's. His unique greatness, however, resides in his delineation of human facial expression. Such effects cannot be 'contrived'. They must be pictorial renderings of personal feeling. The features of his personages express modesty and reserve, often, expecially in representations of Christ, e.g. the *Rex Regum*, an embittered resignation. The eyes gaze intently, with a positively hypnotic solemnity. Bouts was far in advance of his age in his feeling for

D. BOUTS · THE LAST SUPPER
(Centre Panel) 72″ × 58″. *Louvain, St Peter's*

atmosphere and as a painter of landscap

Two of his works are attested b documentary evidence. These are th altarpiece for the church of St Peter : Louvain, and the two panels for the La Courts, now in Brussels. One of th latter, *God's Judgment*, is of absolutel unique beauty. Recent documentary re search has relieved scholars of the nee to regard the other, weaker panel, repre senting a knight being led to execution as entirely by Bouts. It was only finishe after Bouts's death.

In addition to these pictures, a numbe of others are unquestionably his. Th most important of these is the *Entomb ment* in the National Gallery, Londo Others include some paintings of th *Madonna and Child* in Berlin, London an the Metropolitan Museum of New York, a portrait in London, the *Paradise* at Lille, *Hell* in the Louvre, the *Martyrdom of St Hippolytus* at Bruges, the Munich *Resurrection* and the Berlin *Passover* and *Christ with Simon*.

One of the most striking works of his old age is the *Martyrdom of St Erasmus* at Louvain. It reveals his personal magnanimity. At this period (1458) Gothic mentality regarded the sufferings of others with childish curiosity. But Bouts was incapable of cruelty even in a picture. He adhered faithfully to his instructions in clearly representing the extremely repulsive details of the martyrdom, in which the intestines of the living victim were extracted on a turning spit. Yet in some inexplicable manner the operation appears to be occurring in a dream, without the infliction of real pain. 'No stress whatever is laid upon the inhumanity of the act. Realism is strictly subordinated to pathos. The face of the martyr remains calm, for all his sufferings and imminent death. All the personages present appear wholly unconcerned, with the exception of one of the executioners, whose lips are involuntarily compressed' (Jacques Lassaigne).

Bouts had two sons, **Dirck the Younger** (c. 1448-1491) and **Aelbrecht** (c. 1460-1549), who worked in their father's renowned studio. Both their production and their reputations are still the subject of controversy. An *Assumption of the Virgin* at Brussels, around which some works of a 'Master of the Assumption' have been grouped, has been ascribed to Aelbrecht Bouts. No documented work by Dirck Bouts the Younger exists, though it is thought that he may be the author of a group of pictures labelled as by the 'Master of the Pearl of Brabant', after a picture at Munich.

BRAMANTE

Born in Fermignano near Urbino in 1444 and dying in Rome in 1514, Donato d'Angelo Bramante, one of the foremost architects of the Early Renaissance in Italy, was also a painter. His few extant pictures show in the first place the influences of two great masters, Piero della Francesca and Mantegna, secondly, Bramante's own uncommon skill, and thirdly that he was not a natural painter. The apparent inconsistency here is explained when his sculptural *St Sebastian* in the Brera Gallery at Milan is examined. It is an impressive, very clever and entirely unobjectionable picture by an architect. One must regret, however, that Bramante did not paint many more pictures. He was resident in Milan from 1472 to 1499 and might have been the one artist capable, in his level-headed sobriety, of checking the all-conquering influence of Leonardo.

BRAMANTINO

The Milan painter Bartolommeo Suardi (c. 1475-1536) adopted the name of his teacher, the great architect, Bramante, and is generally known as Bramantino. His pictures vary considerably in quality. But they always convey a certain charm owing to a surprising magnificence of conception, much fertility in colour organisation and agreeably faultless composition, Bramantino, too, being an architect. His chief works are in Milan. They

BREKELENKAM · INTERIOR
20" × 18½". Zurich, Kunsthaus

47

include a fine fresco of a *Madonna with Angels*. He is represented in the National Gallery, London.

BRAY

Born and dying in Haarlem, Jan de Bray (1627-1697) was taught by his father, Salomon de Bray. Jan's portraits of groups and young women are so well painted that they may be compared with early works by Frans Hals. It scarcely seems possible that his name should be so little known to the public at large. The fact is probably due to the positively immense number of good painters active in the Netherlands during the century of Rembrandt and Hals. One of Jan de Bray's pictures, *The Painter, His Wife and Children in the Guise of Antony banqueting with Cleopatra*, is at Hampton Court Palace.

BREKELENKAM

Born at Zwammerdam, in 1620, Quiryn Gerritsz van Brekelenkam spent most of his short and probably much-troubled life at Leyden, where he died in 1668. In 1648 he joined the Leyden Guild. He was twice married, had nine children and earned his living in his latest period, like so many minor painters in the Netherlands, by selling schnapps. He accordingly ceased to depict the conventional subjects favoured by his teacher, Gerard Dou, and began to paint scenes of common life in the streets and at the homes of craftsmen and labourers. His pictures vary a great deal in quality. The *Tailor's Workshop*, for instance, now at Amsterdam, is a fine, imposing work. His female types, with their high foreheads, recalling those of Pieter de Hooch, have great charm. But many of his other paintings are crude and ugly, as are also some of the hermits he often represented. Three of his pictures are in the National Gallery, London.

BRERA

The Palazzo di Brera in Milan originally belonged to the Jesuits; the present building was begun in 1591, but its final appearance owes most to the architect F. M. Richini, who worked on it from 1651 to 1686. During the eighteenth century, under Austrian rule, the Brera was handed over to the State and became an academy of art. It was made a public museum in 1882. The famous picture gallery on the first floor is one of the finest existing collections of North Italian painting. Among the most celebrated works in the gallery are Francesca's *Federigo, Duke of Montefeltro* and *Madonna with Angels and Saints*, Carpaccio's *Presentation of the Virgin*, Mantegna's *Dead Christ*, Foppa's *Madonna and Saints*, a collection of pictures by Luini and works by Titian, Veronese, Bonifazio, Cima, Moroni, Moretto, Palma Vecchio, Tintoretto, Bassano, Bellini and the Vivarini.

BREU

Jörg Breu (1480-1534), born and dying in Augsburg, belonged to a family of weavers, a class from which his father's employers, the Fuggers, also originally came.

Jörg Breu, at twenty-two, was already independent after prolonged travels through Austria, such as the great Altdorfer undertook ten years later. Much could be learnt in that way. The monastery at Herzogenburg in Austria contains the earliest of Breu's works to be signed in full, an altarpiece. In 1514 he set out on another journey, this time to Italy. The experience led to drastic changes in his style, as it had in the case of his compatriot Burgkmair, whose influence over him now became generally paramount. Breu, too, could thenceforward be regarded as a 'modern' painter.

His works were surprisingly varied in character. They included altarpieces, portraits, battle pieces, frescoes—now destroyed—drawings, woodcuts, topical sketches—for example an illustration of Frundsberg's victory at Pavia, the latest news in February 1525—designs for fortifications and military operations and a manuscript chronicle of public events.

His son, Jörg the Younger, is only

PIETER BRUEGHEL THE ELDER   THE MASSACRE OF THE INNOCENTS
44½" × 64". Vienna, Kunsthistorisches Museum

known today, as a painter, through a single picture. He appears to have been primarily a draughtsman.

BRILL

Paul Brill, or Bril, was born in Antwerp in 1554 and died in Rome in 1626. Religious and allegorical subjects were really only a pretext for his main preoccupation, which was landscape. His small, early pictures are particularly admired. The dazzling, whitish-yellow highlights in the interstices of meticulously drawn foliage and the separation of the foreground from the middle distance, as in theatrical design, are characteristic of his style. At a later date, under the influence of Elsheimer and the Italians, his landscapes became more decorative, were larger in scale and contained fewer figures. They grew more empty, often in both senses of the word. His signature consisted either of his written name or a pair of spectacles, this

being the meaning of the Dutch word *bril*. He is represented in the Louvre.

BRONZINO

Born of poor parents at Monticelli in 1503 and dying in Florence in 1572, Angelo Bronzino repaid in full, throughout his life, the generosity of his patrons and older friends. He was at first trained by a house-painter, then attended the studio of Raffaelino del Garbo and eventually met Pontormo, who treated him like a son, doing all he could for him. The interest of this Schopenhauerian misanthrope was decisive for Bronzino's professional career, though he was also influenced by Michelangelo. Pontormo took steps to ensure that Bronzino should succeed him in the favour of the ruler of Florence, Duke Cosimo I de' Medici.

Innumerable paintings by Bronzino, in particular extremely interesting and decorative portraits, have survived. They

PIETER BRUEGHEL THE ELDER · THE PEASANT WEDDING
45⅞" × 65¼". Vienna, Kunsthistorisches Museum

BROUWER

The general public knows the name of Adriaen Brouwer, born in Oudenarde in c. 1603 and dying in Antwerp in 1638, so well as to be in no doubt of its association with groups of boors, tippling peasants, unkempt smokers, card-players and village barbers, dentists and fiddlers. These lively subjects had already rendered him famous in his lifetime. But Brouwer's pictures are also of exceptional merit from a purely artistic standpoint. Rubens recognised their quality, for he repeatedly visited the extravagant and dissolute painter, supported him financially, and bailed him out of prison for debt. He owned seventeen paintings by Brouwer.

The latter was a pupil of Frans Hals in Haarlem about the year 1623. In 1631 he was enrolled in the Guild of St Luke at Antwerp. His early style is linked with that of Pieter Brueghel the Elder. But after 1631 he painted *genre*, particularly tavern and peasant pictures, with a breadth of brushwork and subtlety of tone which was in defiance of his time. He holds an important position in the development of *genre* painting. David Teniers the Younger and Adriaen van Ostade were influenced by him.

Brouwer, throughout his life, had nothing good to say about Hals. But this evidence cannot be taken seriously. Hals was certainly difficult to get on with. But Brouwer, for his part, had a lurid reputation for telling fairy tales.

When not drunk or in gaol he painted fanatically. Nearly all the big galleries contain pictures by him. Munich, with sixteen, has the most. Two of his rare landscapes are in Berlin. In London he is represented, at the National Gallery and the Wallace Collection, by lesser works.

are unmistakable in their firmly outlined features, of a courtly impenetrability and impassivity, resembling masks. The eyes are often rather prominent, the ceremonial dress rendered with great care, greys and browns composing a colour scheme of much refinement. His portraits of children are also of high quality. He was the first Tuscan to paint such subjects for their own sake.

Bronzino's portraits were not only fine works of art. They determined the character of Court painting all over Europe. The Uffizi portraits of Eleonora di Toledo, Prince Ferdinand and Princess Maria are outstanding.

BROOKING

Charles Brooking (1723-1759), a London painter, produced almost exclusively sea-scapes. They are of astonishing merit for a man who had spent many years on paintwork of the crudest description in a shipyard. When he began to compose pictures, the dealers treated him, since he had no influential friends, with such shameless rapacity that he must have lived in the direst poverty. His *Dead Calm* is preserved in the National Gallery, London.

BRUEGHEL

Pieter Brueghel the Elder, known as 'Peasant Brueghel', also spelt Bruegel and Breughel, was born near Breda in 1525, probably at the village of Brueghel. He died in Brussels in 1569 while still under fifty. The popular idea of him as an old man is therefore as false as that which represents him as a simple peasant squinting at village life through the thick, convex windows of his cottage and proceeding to paint it.

He was in fact a widely travelled man. After his training at Antwerp under the versatile and well-informed Coecke van Aelst (1502-1550) he was appointed guild master in 1551. But for some reason still unknown he did not go on to work independently. He was employed by the copper etcher Hieronymus Cock, the first Fleming who both dealt in and issued works of art. In 1553 Brueghel went to Italy. It is very improbable that he did so for personal or financial reasons. Most likely Cock sent him there to etch copies of Italian pictures on copper, as he had already done at Antwerp in the case of Bosch's works. Brueghel's journey took him through France and Italy as far as Sicily. It lasted about a year.

Shortly after his return he left Cock's service, settling at the cosmopolitan centre of Brussels. At that date he had some thirteen years more to live. In that brief period he achieved immortality with no more than three dozen pictures.

It is to be noted in the first place that the contemporary art of Italy had practically no visible influence on his work. It is true that he treated subjects such as the harbour at Naples—this work is now in Rome—and that the deeply fissured southern landscape and that of the Alps are repeatedly recalled in his paintings. But his early *Landscape with the Fall of Icarus*, now in Brussels, with its ploughman and clumsy, massive horse, has more relation to old Italian frescoes than to the works of Titian, Raphael and Leonardo which Brueghel had seen.

Actually, his style owes nothing to anyone, not even to Bosch, whom he admired and whose technique, rather than spirit, he followed in his famous portrait of the termagant, *Dulle Griet*, now at Antwerp. It was not, however, either this picture or those representing hell and the temptation of St Anthony, with their nightmare figures, fine as these works are, that made him one of the greatest of painters. It was his depictions of peasants and landscape. Here he broke quite new ground, doing so, moreover, by methods which are often overlooked in the study of art, a minimum of subtlety in drawing, the simplest possible handling of surfaces and a most unobtrusive organisation of colour. But he was capable of combining individual passages into a superb harmony.

When in 1565 he conceived the idea of

BRONZINO · ELEONORA DA TOLEDO AND DON GARZIA · *46" × 38⅜". Florence, Uffizi*

painting the so-called pictures of the months, the notion was not an original one at that date. But no one now remembers the many previous series of this kind. On the other hand, Brueghel's *Homecoming Hunters*, now in Vienna, has remained an eternal symbol of winter. The picture perfectly represents the typical scenes of frost and snow which any homesick northern exile in the south longs to see. The *Gloomy Day*, standing for February and March, which is also now in Vienna, reaches the same high standard. Each member of the series typifies two months. One of the six is missing. The *Homecoming Herd*, for October and November, is another at Vienna, while *Haymaking*, for June and July, is at Raudnitz, and *The Corn Harvest*, for August and September, in New York.

One of the finest of his winter landscapes is *The Bird-trap*, in a private collection at Brussels. His skill in the depiction of pure white was positively miraculous. He often employed it to the most delicate effect. Even his *Adoration of the Kings* in the Winterthur Museum, a most remarkable painting of an ordinary crowd in a village street, consists for the most part simply of a winter landscape of magic beauty. Such also is the character of the *Slaughter of the Innocents in Bethlehem* at Vienna, and the *Census in Bethlehem* at Brussels. It is a stirring experience to note an entirely new vision in these pictures, corresponding, no doubt, with the personal feelings of the artist. Even the most impressive events, including the appearance of Christ Himself, occur as inconspicuously and casually as any ordinary proceeding. Brueghel's attention is not concentrated, in the *Census*, upon the Virgin and Child, scarcely visible in the foreground among peasants, carts and miscellaneous lumber. He is absorbed in awestruck contemplation of a snow-covered world, of the earth itself, the red globe of the sun and the inexplicable, ant-like swarming of human life.

By far the biggest collection of Brueghel's works is preserved in the Kunsthistorisches Museum at Vienna. It includes his two well-known pictures

A. BROUWER · THE BITTER DRAUGHT
19" × 16¼". Frankfort, Staedelsches Kunstinstitut

of village life, the *Wedding Feast* and the *Fair*. An important *Adoration of the Kings* is in the National Gallery, London.

Pieter Brueghel the Younger (1564-1638), known as 'Hell' Brueghel, was his father's eldest son. Innumerable copies by him of the elder Brueghel's pictures are extant, but few of his own.

Jan ('Velvet') Brueghel (1568-1625) was the youngest son, twelve months old when his father died. He shows hardly any traces of the latter's style. Both technique and representation are refined to a miniaturist's scale. Jan was wealthy and respected, a Court painter and friend of Rubens, in association with whom he painted several pictures. The gorgeous wreath of flowers in Rubens's *Madonna with Wreath* at Munich is by Jan Brueghel. The figures of Adam and Eve, in the latter's *Paradise* at The Hague, on the other hand, are by Rubens.

Both the younger Brueghels also worked

in association with Joos de Momper. Jan's works are still highly prized today.

BRUSSEL

Paul Theodor van Brussel (1754-1795) was a popular Dutch painter who specialised in still-life pictures painted in the style of the previous century. *Flower Piece* in the National Gallery, London.

BRUYN

Born at Wesel am Rhein in 1493 and dying at Cologne in 1555/6, Bartholomaus Bruyn painted mainly portraits. He was the 'fashionable photographer', so to speak, of the Cologne aristocracy. Remarkably unimaginative in his work, he saw no objection to placing his model regularly, in conventional style, against a neutral background and behind a parapet or imparting some artificial gesture to the hand. Yet not one of his portraits resembles another. All are psychologically interesting, from the Town Councillors and Counts to the stout, smug merchants and dandified scholars, from the comfortable matrons to their meek daughters.

Bruyn's early work was influenced by that of Jan Soest. His portrait style resembles that of Joos van Cleve. Later, through contact with Scorel, his manner became increasingly Italianate. His *Dr Fuchsin* and *St John and the Holy Women* are in the National Gallery, London. He grew rich and was elected to the Town Council, living in the house near St Alban's church formerly occupied by the painter Stephan Lochner.

BUITEWEG

Willem Buiteweg or Buitenwegh (1590-1630) was a Dutch painter born in Rotterdam. He was influenced by Dirk Hals and Esias

Van der Velde. Buiteweg's pictures are rare. His etchings and drawings are well known and of great interest. His son **Willem Buiteweg the Younger** (1625-1670) was a well-known animal painter.

BURGKMAIR

The few paintings ascribed to **Thomas** Burgkmair are in a stiff, provincial style, but not without a certain charm of their own. His son **Hans,** however, achieved a great reputation.

He was born 1473 and died in 1531 in Augsburg, where he was trained by his

H. BURGKMAIR · ST JOHN ON THE ISLAND OF PATMOS · (*Centre panel of the St John Altarpiece*) *61¼″ × 50″. Munich, Alte Pinakothek*

father and subsequently by Martin Schongauer, by then already famous. Burgkmair also formed an association with Dürer, who was about his own age. By 1498 Hans had begun work on his own account. His earliest surviving picture, dated 1490, is a portrait of the preacher, Gailer von Kaisersberg, who was also painted by Cranach. It is a far cry from this work by Burgkmair as a student to his last production, dated 1529, melancholy in mood but superbly handled, a portrait of himself with his wife, which is now at Vienna. Some brief visits he paid to Venice had a decisive influence on his style. The portraits of his middle period clearly show his debt to the school of Bellini and to Carpaccio. At times, as in the Nuremberg

Madonna of 1509, they recall Crivelli. But by 1518 he had worked the Italian influences out of his system and developed his own manner, e.g. in *St John on the Island of Patmos*, now at Munich. Here the passionate vehemence of the saint's gesture, the self-contained dignity of the landscape, the luxuriance of which marks it out as the main contrapuntal theme, could have been achieved by no other painter in Germany at this early date except Grünewald.

In Burgkmair's last years his creative energy declined. It was only in *Esther and Ahasuerus*, now at Munich, and the self-portrait, that the old mastery was again in evidence. His son, Hans the Younger, was not an important painter.

CALCAR

Jan Joest van Calcar, who died in Haarlem in 1519, seems to have travelled a great deal. His chief work is the great triptych, in sixteen sections, which he painted at Kalkar in the Rhine Valley near the Dutch frontier for the church of St Nicholas. Joest had become a citizen of the town in 1490. His pictures are not very numerous. They reveal a somewhat complacent, middle-class temperament, closely observant of nature, especially in the faces of his personages. Even his nocturnal lighting effects, natural or from torches, are anything but subtle. They are thoroughly prosaic. He seems to have been in association with Geertgen, perhaps as the latter's pupil. His excellent small-scale portraits can be seen in Munich and the National Gallery, London. They prove his unpretentious but discerning insight into psychology. He was a painter without personal ambition.

CALVART

Born at Antwerp in 1540, Denis Calvart went to Italy at the age of twenty-two. At first, like all northern painters coming with empty hands to a land where artists had achieved such distinction, he joined their followers, attending the studio of Fontana at Bologna and that of Sabatini in Rome, whom he assisted with his frescoes in the Vatican. Calvart then returned to Bologna, where he surprised the city by his youthful talents for organisation. He started his own school in competition with that of the famous Carracci brothers. The enterprise was successful and was maintained by Calvart for forty-five years, until his death in 1619. At various times Albani, Domenichino and Guido Reni were his pupils. Puyvelde states that 'he was popular with the Italians, who considered his palette more brilliant and his brushwork more delicate than those of the Carracci school. But his productions, like theirs, remained highly eclectic and academic.'

Calvart's best painting, inspired by Piombo, is a *Scourging of Christ*, now in the Villa Borghese at Rome.

CAMBIASO

Luca Cambiaso (1527-1585), the son and pupil of the painter Giovanni Cambiaso, was born at Moneglia near Genoa. He died in Madrid after leaving Genoa in 1583 to comply with an invitation from Philip II. Innumerable frescoes by Cambiaso have survived in the palaces and chapels of Genoa and at the Escorial. Their subjects are usually biblical or mythological. He also painted a very large number of serious, somewhat conventional pictures in the older Genoese style. But the inadequacy of all generalisations is evident from a study of the mysteriously dark *Madonna in Candlelight* in the Palazzo Bianco at Genoa, which Cambiaso must have painted in a reckless mood. It anticipates Georges de la Tour by a century.

CAMPAGNOLA

Giulio Campagnola was really only discovered in modern times. The notices of him in even fairly recent comprehensive works of reference strike one today as relating to a different person altogether. He is stated there to have been a Venetian lawyer who spent his spare time engraving on copper in the manner of Giorgione. But in fact Giulio Campagnola was a professional painter belonging to the famous school of Bellini. One after another of the paintings of this school is now being attributed to him. He has even already been credited with works a few years ago supposed to be entirely by Giorgione, though inexplicably weak specimens of his style.

Campagnola was the son of a notary. He was born in Padua in 1482 and died young, like his model, Giorgione, in

Venice in 1516. Two attempts by his influential father to establish him as a lawyer, at the Courts of Mantua and Ferrara, came to nothing. Shortly after 1500 he was already active in Venice as a painter. He seems to have formed a friendship with Giorgione, for he imitated the latter's manner with extreme fidelity.

In point of fact, he is no more than Giorgione's shadow. Giuseppe Fiocco, responsible for the latest research in this direction, attributes to Campagnola the frescoes in the Scuola del Carmine at Padua, as well as parts of the *Ordeal of Moses by Fire* and its companion picture, the *Judgment of Solomon*, both in the Uffizi Gallery, where they still bear the name of Giorgione. Fiocco adds the *Romulus and Remus* at Frankfurt and the *Golden Age* in London. The small Munich picture of the *Shepherd Boy*, still officially ascribed to Giorgione, may also be Campagnola's.

CAMPHUYSEN

Rafael Camphuysen (1598-1657) and Govert Dircksen Camphuysen (1624-1672) were brothers, both born in Gorcum, Holland, and dying in Amsterdam. **Rafael** painted romantic riverside views in rather monotonous studio browns which, by the simple process of darkening, have come to look like moonlight scenes. Aert van der Neer, who was his pupil, beat Rafael at his own game.

Govert Dircksen probably held the post of Court Painter at Stockholm from about 1652 to 1663. He specialised in the depiction of animals. His renderings of cattle and sheep under clumps of trees, with a river or the roofs and spires of a small town behind them, are rather like the paintings of Paul Potter, to whom much of Govert's work may have been attributed. He also produced pictures of an entirely different character, two yards square, in which lifesize oxen seem about to emerge from the canvas, giving the

JOEST VAN CALCAR · THE ADORATION OF
THE CHILD
(Right Wing) 18¾″ × 5¼″. *Munich, Alte Pinakothek*

CAMPIN · VIRGIN AND CHILD WITH A
FIRESCREEN
25" × 19¼". London, National Gallery

The name of this predecessor and probable teacher was not known. He was therefore called, after the place where one of his productions was found, the Master of Flémalle. One memorable day, however, documents were found stating that Robert Campin had trained two pupils who were subsequently appointed masters. They were Rogelet de la Pasture—the French for Rogier van der Weyden—and Jacquelet Daret, both the names of painters already known. The logical conclusion was drawn that Robert Campin and the Master of Flémalle must be one and the same person. Hitherto no evidence has been discovered to contradict this assumption.

A great Old Master had been rescued from obscurity. He must have played the same sort of pioneering part in southern Flanders as Hubert van Eyck played in northern Holland. His chief works are the *Birth of Christ* at Dijon, the *Annunciation* at Waterloo-Tongerloo, the *Virgin and Child* in London, the *Standing Madonna* and *Two Thieves* at Frankfurt and the *St Barbara* at Madrid. Far superior to these still somewhat archaic productions are three portraits as good as any by Rogier van der Weyden and possibly in fact by him. These are the two fine, intensely vivid paintings of a married couple in London, and the massive, luminously treated head of the Ducal Counsellor Robert de Masmines in Berlin.

spectator quite a fright. Examples of his work are to be seen in the Wallace Collection, London, and in the Dulwich Gallery.

CAMPIN

It was known in the nineteenth century that a painter of this name was appointed guild-master at Tournai in 1406, carried out a number of commissions, maintained a large studio and died in 1444. But his pictures were thought to have disappeared, and no importance was therefore attributed to him.

Then discoveries were made which suddenly elevated Robert Campin to the status of a great master. It had long been realised that one of the greatest painters in the world, Rogier van der Weyden, had a predecessor whose works, though more old-fashioned and less talented than his, nevertheless bore the same relation to them as would a teacher's to a pupil's.

CANALETTO

The name is the affectionate diminutive applied by his Venetian fellow-citizens to Antonio Canale, who was born in 1697 and died in the city in 1768. He was probably a member of the aristocratic Canal family. At any rate, he signed his name in that form. But his father had come down in the world and earned his living as a scene-painter for the theatre. The point is of some interest, as possibly explaining the tradition that Canaletto had a *camera obscura* made for him, taking his pictures from the images thus obtained. The apparatus in question was at that time used for projecting images with the effect of a theatrical or cinematographic

CANALETTO · THE RIVA DEGLI SCHIAVONE, VENICE
29¾" × 49¼". Berlin, Staatl. Museen

performance. It was simply a form of the modern lens camera without its photographic action. The images seen through the lens could be reflected on to a canvas and painted over.

This remarkable and little-known circumstance does not, of course, in the least detract from Canaletto's fame as a painter of classical rank. He represents, with Guardi and Tiepolo, the most important of the later Venetians.

He learned his art by eye. Pannini, with whom he worked during a visit to Rome in 1719, merely taught him how to handle his materials, though he may have owed something more to Luca Carlevaris, whose pictures he proceeded to study on his return to Venice.

He soon achieved a high reputation, especially among the English colony at Venice. His admirers in that quarter sent cases of his pictures to London and encouraged him to follow them himself. In 1746 he undertook the journey. It is not certain when he returned but by 1755 he was again in his beloved Venice, which he was never tired of painting.

His views of London, fine as they are, seem a little hard and cold in comparison with those—apart from a few weaker specimens—produced in Venice, which are full of warmth, dazzling in their perspective and saturated in luminous colour. Canaletto has not the loose, delicate touch of Guardi or the latter's impressionist vision. His Venice is not the city of flashing blades and amorous passions, but the royal mistress of her miraculous lagoons. He is a classical painter, allowing no turbidity in his colour or humour in his scenes. His extremely broad yet precise drawing forms a perfect harmony with the light in which it bathes.

Almost all the big galleries possess works by Canaletto. One of his finest pictures, the *Stone-breakers' Yard*, is in the National Gallery, London.

CANO

Alonso Cano (1601-1667) of Granada belonged to the generation of Spaniards fated to be completely overshadowed by the towering figure of Velasquez. Fortunately, the Court of Madrid was able to employ many of them, attracting and furthering their talents, bestowing glory upon them and relieving them of anxiety. Cano himself was Court Painter to the King from 1637 to 1651. His exceptional versatility as painter, sculptor and architect permitted him eventually to give his restlessness free rein, resign his post and return to Granada. His pictures are symbolic and religious, with the bright colouring of Veronese, his typical golden-yellow, gleaming violet and brownish-green. The contours, however, are often cold and conventional in the Spanish style. Nevertheless, he was somewhat influenced at a later date by Murillo's softness. Cano, both personally and as an artist, lacked integration.

His outward appearance is known from a splendid portrait by Velasquez. The lean, haughty features are those of a grandee, devoted to intellectual rather than aesthetic pursuits and resembling, in fact, Cano's own works.

CAPPELLE

Born 1624/5 and dying in Amsterdam in 1679, Jan van de Cappelle had the luck to inherit a dye-works and some houses from his father. He could live on the income from his property and afford to be painted by Rembrandt and Frans Hals, as well as keeping a yacht and collecting five hundred drawings by Rembrandt. He left 90,000 florins in hard cash to his heirs. He only painted for his own pleasure. He evidently had no teacher and there is therefore no record that he ever belonged to the guild. He was, however, regarded in his lifetime as an important painter. His seascapes recall those of Simon de Vlieger, of whose drawings, also, he possessed no less than 1,300. Cappelle's are fine works in which sunlight is reflected from waves under a sky with clouds at a great height and the misty outlines of vessels can be seen. The Carstanjen Collection at Berlin formerly possessed a picture by Cappelle in which the sun was shown unclouded, an unprecedented exploit at the time. Cappelle also painted a few winter landscapes, village scenes on a small scale. But they are much inferior to his seascapes. The best of his works are to be found at the National Gallery, London, and in the Dulwich Gallery.

CARAVAGGIO

The son of an architect, Michelangelo Merisi Caravaggio was born c. 1560/5 at the village of Caravaggio, near Bergamo, from which he took his name. After an adventurous life, full of duels, prosecutions and escapes from pursuit, he died in 1609 at Porto Ercole on the coast of southern Tuscany. Caravaggio was a good painter, but an extremely difficult man to get on with.

Very little is known of his youth. He had some training in Milan, then wandered off to Venice, whence he tramped southwards. In Rome he was sometimes taken for a vagabond. The turning-point in his life came when Cardinal Francesco noticed him at work as a studio apprentice. In the Cardinal's palace he painted his first great pictures, the *Card-players*, today in the Rothschild Collection, Paris, and the *Woman with a Lute*, now in the Liechtenstein Gallery at Vienna. These two astonishing works brought him commission after commission. But soon trouble arose. He was involved in a duel and bolted to Genoa to escape prosecution. Eventually he was permitted to return to Rome. But he had no sooner arrived than he ran another man through. Again he fled, this time to the small village of Pogliano, where he painted for a while. Then he continued his flight to Naples, painting more pictures there. Whenever he was not fighting, he was painting. At last he seemed to have found a haven under the protection of the Grand Master of the Knights of Malta. He painted in the island for a time, then fought another duel, with a Master of the Order. The same pattern of events was repeated. One foggy night he escaped from prison, making his way to Sicily, where he painted all over the island. No sooner had he fulfilled some commission for an altarpiece than his pursuers from Malta would catch up with him and he would rush on to the next village, the next church and the next commission. His last flight, to the Italian mainland by boat, proved fatal. He fell ill on the journey and died.

It seems a wonder that Caravaggio painted so many pictures in so short and adventurous a life. His temperament was exceptionally violent. To twentieth-century eyes his works do not seem to reveal the fact. They appear perfectly normal to ourselves. But they disturbed his contemporaries. At that date Mannerism (q.v.) was the prevailing style in art. Caravaggio, on the other hand, was the first to practise 'naturalism'. He wanted to represent ordinary people, and succeeded in doing so. Even his biblical scenes are often of this popular character depicting the mercenary soldiers and ordinary Roman citizens of his day. He meant to have done with 'affectation and mental refinement' and substitute the psychology of the plain man. His famous *Bacchus* in the Uffizi Gallery is a handsome rascal of the Campagna, startling in his frank lasciviousness. Caravaggio's figures are large in scale, with lifelike colouring and markedly indolent gestures. On the slightest pretext he would introduce

CARAVAGGIO · BACCHUS
39¼" × 34". Florence, Uffizi

dazzling illumination and contrasting shadows to throw his modelling into high relief, a method which later exercised an irresistible fascination on the Dutch painters Terbrugghen and Honthorst. His influence on posterity was immense, though he himself cannot be considered a really great artist, his work being too often confined to mere outward representation. His *Christ at Emmaus* is in the National Gallery, London.

CARIANI

Giovanni Busi, called Cariani (c. 1485/90-c. 1547), came of a Bergamo family. From 1509 to 1547 he was in Venice. Though a pupil of Giovanni Bellini, he inclines in style rather to Palma Vecchio and Giorgione, under whom he also studied. He painted a great many versions of the Madonna with Child theme for private citizens. In most of his religious pictures, secular subjects and portraits the influence of Giorgione is predominant. The greater number of his works are at Bergamo. There are three fine portraits and a *Holy Family* in the Accademia, Venice. He is well represented in the National Gallery, London.

CARLEVARIS

Born at Udine in 1665 and dying in Venice in 1731, Luca Carlevaris inaugurated a further great age of painting in the latter city, which had produced no significant works for many years. He preceded Canaletto, whom he trained. Carlevaris's pictures are not true *vedute* (q.v.) in the sense of the term as applied to the works of Canaletto and Guardi, because in his case the interest is still invariably concentrated on throngs of people. But his works do at least depict the city. He is really a Carpaccio two hundred years nearer to our own time.

CARON

Antoine Caron, born in Beauvais c. 1515, probably died in Paris in 1593. He was Court painter to the King and worked for ten years at Fontainebleau (q.v.), being generally considered as belonging to that school. Its members treated mainly mythological subjects, and were concerned for the most part with wall decoration, productions for festivals and designs for Gobelins tapestries. It was no wonder that their works, after a promising start, sank to the level of mechanical ornamentation. But if Caron really painted, as has been assumed since the researches of Gustav Glück, the portrait of a princess, signed with the initials A.C. and dated 1577, which is now in the Alte Pinakothek at Munich, he certainly achieved in this case, surprisingly enough, work comparable with that of François Clouet. The features of the sitter are pale and degenerate, surrounded by a glittering display of flashing silks and gleaming jewels.

CARPACCIO

Although the archives of Venice record hundreds of dates relating to Vittore Carpaccio's life, they do not give those of his birth and death (c. 1450/65-c. 1526). There are similar doubts about his name, though several of his signatures exist. They are written in the ten different forms, Carpatio, Carpathio, Carpazio, Carpacio, Capatius, Carpathius, Scarpaza, Scharpaza, Scarpazo and Scarpatio. Only his Christian name, Vittore, never varies.

He came of an old Venetian family of craftsmen. A document dated in the summer of 1526 refers to him as already dead. The name of his first teacher is not known and does not matter, for Carpaccio owed nothing to anyone but Gentile Bellini. He probably not only knew the famous brothers, but also assisted Gentile in his work. It was from the latter that he learnt how to tell a story and render the vast panorama of the houses and canals of Venice. He soon surpassed his master in such subjects. The style of a younger generation is recognisable in Carpaccio's lighter draughtsmanship, the more graceful motion of his figures, his finer colouring and the soft realism of his daylight. In particular, the delightful

CARPACCIO · THE ARRIVAL OF THE AMBASSADORS
(Detail) 110″ × 235½″. Venice, Accademia

details which appear from time to time in a corner of his pictures are of astonishing beauty. They may represent figures leaning from a balcony, a clerk at his desk or a gondola being rowed to a distant isle in the lagoon by an oarsman in red breeches, while some historic event proceeds in the foreground, attended by councillors, ambassadors, bishops, merchants and ladies. Typical of his work is the series of nine large pictures of episodes from the life of St Ursula, painted for the School of that saint and now in the Accademia at Venice.

Carpaccio was an important painter. Unfortunately, his work is very uneven. The altarpieces are definitely inferior to the narrative works from which one learns to love the Venice of his period. Among his best productions are the *Presentation of the Virgin* in the Brera Gallery at Milan, the *Story of St Ursula*, the *Healing of a Madman with a View of the Rialto* and the *Meeting of Joachim and Anna* in the Accademia at Venice, ten pictures

ANNIBALE CARRACCI
BACCHANTE
44¾" × 56¾". Florence, Uffizi

illustrating the *Legend of St George* in the church of San Giorgio degli Schiavoni at Venice and *St Ursula Taking Leave of Her Father* in the National Gallery, London.

CARRACCI

In the second half of the sixteenth century the three Carraccis were revered as infallible at Bologna. The question how they came to enjoy such respect and influence is of some interest, for not one of them was a genius.

Lodovico (1556-1619) spent many years in Florence, Parma, Mantua and Venice. On his return to Bologna he surprisingly announced that he had found the ruling fashion of Mannerism (q.v.) to be a blind alley and was determined to revive classicism. His recipe comprised a collection of the ingredients of this style, which he had studied in venerable examples seen on his travels. The term 'eclectic', which first came into use in relation to the Carraccis, may serve to describe his method, though the word is too strong to be quite fair to him.

Later research has tended to allow the Carraccis more independence and genuine merits of their own. True poetic features are now discerned in Lodovico's emotional productions and in those of his cousin Annibale an impressive classical note and a joyous appreciation of pagan sensuality.

Lodovico persuaded his cousin **Agostino** (1557-1602) and shortly afterwards the latter's younger brother **Annibale** (1560-1609) to join him in founding an 'academy'. Their school was so perfectly organised and conducted on such comprehensive lines—teaching anatomy, perspective and mathematics—that it soon acquired a monopoly. Lodovico was its guiding spirit, the shrewd Agostino its theorist and Annibale its energetic practical exponent.

The latter was the most talented of the three. His chief works are *Christ and the Woman of Samaria at the Well*, now in Vienna, and the Villa Farnese frescoes in Rome, on which he worked with his brother Agostino. The mythological and biblical personages of the Carraccis are all characterised by a certain indolence of gesture, suggesting emotion held 'in suspense', which imparts a rhythmic nobility to every movement, in strong contrast to the vigour and pseudo-realism of the Mannerists. Poussin later fell under the influence of the Carraccis. But they show no trace of his attractive handling of broad passages and landscape. Lodovico died in Bologna, Agostino in Parma and Annibale in Rome.

CARREÑO

Born at Avilez in Asturias in 1614 and dying in Madrid in 1685, Juan de Miranda Carreño, was taught by Cuevas and Roman, but shows little trace of their influence. His historical and religious works are based on Van Dyck, his portraits on Velasquez. It is interesting to compare his portrait of the Infante Charles II, now in Berlin, with one by the latter artist. The unnecessary abundance of marble tables, bronze lions and golden eagles framing two mirrors in their wings proves Carreño's ambition to achieve the 'grandeur' so highly prized in Spain at the time, which Velasquez nevertheless succeeded in representing with simple black and grey. Carreño was appointed chief Court painter after the death of Velasquez.

CARRIERA

Rosalba Carriera was born in Venice in 1675 and died there in 1757. She was fortunate for a while in finding herself without a serious rival. The last great Mannerists were no longer active to compete with her and the next generation—Guardi, Canaletto and Tiepolo—had not yet begun work, while Carlevaris was only just becoming known.

She had little success until she turned to the medium of pastel (q.v.), holding an exhibition in Paris which at once brought her fame. Subsequently she produced hundreds of portraits of princes and princesses. The Dresden Court alone possessed 157 of her pictures. In her last years she suffered a terrible affliction. At seventy-five she went blind. The rest of her life was passed in darkness and despondency.

CASTAGNO

Andrea del Castagno was born near Dicomano in 1423, spent his childhood at Castagno and died in Florence in 1457. A sensational start with his biography might be made by repeating the report of Vasari (q.v.) that he murdered his friend, Domenico Veneziano. Unfortun-

ately, Vasari seems to have forgotten that the allegedly murdered man blissfully survived his alleged murderer by some four years. It is obvious that such legends arose in consequence of Castagno's peasant-like obstinacy and tempestuous character.

The great Masaccio was still alive during Castagno's childhood. As an adult the latter studied his frescoes with the deepest interest, traces of which continue to appear in the younger man's religious paintings even after the influence of Donatello had begun to prevail in his work. The point may be illustrated by reference to Castagno's *Crucifixion* fresco, which is preserved, like most of his other pictures, in the Santa Apollonia Museum at Florence. His personal style, however, is more readily recognisable in the *St Julian* at Florence and the *Young David* at Washington. The latter painting is highly statuesque in the supple grace

A. DEL CASTAGNO · PORTRAIT OF A
YOUNG MAN
20¾″ × 14¾″. *Munich, Alte Pinakothek*

and refined energy of the figure, the impetuous and lifelike attitude of which, in its Renaissance naturalism, owes nothing to any of Castagno's predecessors. His important pictures also include the over-life-size portraits of Florentine scholars and warriors, preserved at Florence, the first of their kind. The artist's personality is immediately evident from the deliberately unaffected pose and aggressive realism of these portraits. He was perfectly conscious of his own revolutionary spirit, which he had expressed at the age of only seventeen, when Cosimo de' Medici had ordered from him a picture celebrating one of that ruler's victories. The young painter had submitted a work representing the hanging of Cosimo's defeated opponents. The picture has not survived. L. Venturi writes: 'His preference for vigorous movement ran counter to the taste of the day. In that respect he was a pioneer. It can be confidently affirmed that he introduced the dramatic phase of Florentine painting.'

CASTIGLIONE

Born in Genoa in 1616 and dying in Mantua in 1670, Giovanni Benedelto Castiglione was inexplicably called by his contemporaries 'Il Grechetto', though his work bears absolutely no relation to that of the Spaniard known as El Greco.

Castiglione was one of the most talented and agreeable of the artists who flourished in the somewhat barren period of the seventeenth century in Italy. He was devoted to animals and ransacked the entire Old Testament for mentions of them. His pictures have such titles as *Noah entering the Ark with the Animals* and *Noah leaving the Ark with the Animals*, to be found at Florence and Vienna, *Jacob with His Herds* at Madrid and Dresden, *The Israelites with Their Herds*, at Milan and *Abraham with His Herds* at Genoa. But Castiglione also often painted such purely rural scenes as Bassano had introduced. They are strongly coloured, effectively Mannerist in their lighting

and somewhat exotic. He obviously knew Rembrandt's pictures and had studied his chiaroscuro. As an etcher Castiglione is unquestionably important.

CATENA

Though the date of his birth is not precisely known, calculation based on stylistic considerations is now so accurate that Catena's first pictures can be confidently assigned to a period limited to five years. When their maturity is taken into account, it is clear that Vincenzo di Biagio Catena must have been at least twenty-five about the year 1500. He was born in Venice c. 1470/75 and died there in 1531. As pupil and apprentice he spent some years in the best studio available in Venice at the time, that of Giovanni Bellini, where he met the young Titian, Palma, Sebastiano del Piombo and Giorgione, men who afterwards made very great names for themselves.

Many of Catena's paintings survive. His altarpieces resemble Bellini's in their composition and are very close to Giorgione's in spirit and intention. One of the finest, representing a knight approaching the Virgin and Child on bended knees, is in London.

It is now believed that Catena painted many more pictures than were signed by him or otherwise authenticated. A number of works seem to have been produced in common by the young men from Bellini's studio. Thus Catena is supposed today to have been mainly responsible for the *Ordeal of Moses by Fire* in the Uffizi Gallery, formerly regarded as wholly by Giorgione. Its companion picture, *The Judgment of Solomon*, in that gallery, is also considered partly Catena's, though he was probably assisted by Campagnola. Apparently Catena painted excellent portraits. That of Fugger in Berlin is certainly his. That of a senator, now in Vienna, is actually signed by him. Both are outstanding works.

His reputation was much exaggerated in his lifetime. He became extremely wealthy. But posterity soon revised this estimate. Catena must be regarded in the last analysis as a 'follower'.

CAVALLINI

Pietro Cavallini is referred to in documents between 1291 and 1308. He seems to have been a Roman. Vasari (q.v.) wrongly calls him a disciple of Giotto. In fact, Cavallini's art is derived from the classical influence of Byzantium. He was only slightly younger than Cimabue and probably developed his own style. The latest research actually concludes that he may have been to some extent a forerunner of Giotto. Cavallini's contemporaries undoubtedly regarded his frescoes—panels did not yet exist—as revolutionary in the same way as Giotto's. Traces of his work have survived in Rome and Naples, in the former city at the churches of Santa Maria in Trastevere and Santa Cecilia. The latter contains his most important surviving painting.

CAVAZZOLA

Paolo Morando, known as Cavazzola, was born in 1486 and died in Verona in 1522. He seems to have paid little attention to contemporary Venetian painting, turning more and more, as he grew older, to Raphael. His best-known work is the *Descent from the Cross*, part of the Passion Series at Verona. His portraits, preserved at Dresden, Milan and Florence, are realistic, both eyes of the sitter being always intently fixed upon the spectator. Psychologically he seems to have been less akin to Raphael than to Domenico Morone, who trained him. He was also influenced by Domenico's son, Francesco Morone.

CHAMPAIGNE

Philippe de Champaigne was born in Brussels in 1602 and came to Paris at the age of nineteen, spending the whole of the rest of his life, until his death in 1674, apart from a few journeys, in that city. His early friendship with Poussin is evident in his first works. In 1628 he became painter to the Queen Mother and subsequently gained the favour of Louis XIII and Richelieu. His work at this time was a modification of the Baroque of Rubens, which had strongly influenced his early years. The colour is cold, draperies are stiff and sculptural.

In the 1640s Champaigne joined the religious sect of the Jansenists and for the rest of his life worked in close association with the convent of Port-Royal. Here his gift for portraiture, in which art he was to be one of the most important painters of his century, was discovered. His portraits owe nothing whatever to any of his forerunners. Painted in sober tones of grey and brown, with flat, delicate washes, the faces of his sitters all

CHARDIN · LA MÈRE LABORIEUSE
19¼″ × 15¼″. Paris, Louvre

express his own embittered and melancholy temperament. There is not the least reason to credit him with the 'profound psychological insight' so often attributed to him. No one who observes the truly Jansenist features, suggesting, in other words, a certain irresolution, of his portrait of the Vicomte de Turenne, could see in such a face that of the man who sacked Heidelberg. Three portraits of Cardinal Richelieu and one of Cardinal de Retz are in the National Gallery, London.

CHARDIN

Jean Baptisto Simeon Chardin seems, as a personality, to have been as attractive, modest, unassuming and highly esteemed as are his pictures. He was born in Paris in 1699, the son of a master carpenter who made billiard tables for the Court. The artist himself never left the city. He became extremely popular with the Parisians in his lifetime, though the fact did not prevent them paying very low prices for his works. He received, for example, a mere 25 livres for his *Boy Spinning a Top*. The picture was later acquired by the Louvre for 175,000 gold francs.

Chardin studied under Cazes and Coypel and assisted Vanloo in restoration work at Fontainebleau. He was elected a member of the French Academy in 1728 and its Treasurer in 1755. He was finally granted an apartment in the Louvre. But his old age was troubled by illness, bereavement, by the mysterious suicide of his son and by straitened circumstances which were largely due to his refusal to bargain for higher prices than he was offered for his pictures. He died in 1779.

It is surprising enough that he achieved any success at all. The taste of the period was for Watteau and Boucher rather than for a painter who produced, like the Dutchmen of Delft in earlier times, softly tinted, greyish, misty canvases depicting kitchenmaids, toiling housewives, very simple still-life studies or a playing child, a girl writing a letter, a governess. But it is recognised today that these works put

an end to the Rococo style and that his last pictures look forward 150 years to the paintings of Manet.

The largest collection of Chardin's works, comprising some thirty items, is in the Louvre.

CHARONTON

Euguerrand Charonton, also called de Quarton, was born at or near Laon in c. 1410. In 1447 he moved to Avignon, where he died in 1466. He was one of the most important members of the Avignon School (q.v.) in its second phase of prosperity. Being entirely French, he is of great interest to art historians as a conspicuous example of the success with which the arts of France at that time continued to maintain independence of the great influence of Flemish painting.

Charonton's works must formerly have been very numerous. Few are extant today. His chief surviving picture is the *Coronation of the Virgin* in the hospital at

PETRUS CHRISTUS · PORTRAIT OF A YOUNG GIRL · *10¼" × 8¼". Berlin, Staatl. Museen*

Villeneuve-les-Avignon. This painting, over six feet in height, attracts attention by a broad passage in the red tint characteristic of the contemporary French artist Fouquet. It dominates the top section, resembling a burning bush, with the figures of the Virgin, God the Father and Christ. Immediately below this glowing cloud, composed of ornamental features and tongue-like angels' wings, stand a crowd of persons whose upturned faces indicate an extraordinarily intense devotion, unprecedented in Avignon painting. The lower half of the picture is also unmistakably by Charonton. It shows a remarkably level Provençal landscape with the sea in the distance. The effect is that of a *predella* (q.v.) integrated with the work as a whole. The style is harsh but technically subtle, to the absolute exclusion, however, as already mentioned, of the highly picturesque and atmospheric handling of contemporary Flemish artists. In a word, it may be considered that Charonton continued to be deeply influenced by the Sienese painters who had come to Avignon a century before.

CHIAROSCURO

A technique in painting whereby objects are brought out in the round by means of bold contrasts of light and shade. The entire picture is usually dark relieved by light accents (see *Highlights*). The possibilities of chiaroscuro were first explored in the dramatic compositions of Caravaggio, but it is the art of Rembrandt which provides the most striking instances of the use of chiaroscuro. Although chiaroscuro lends itself to illusionist effects, it is not a property of representational painting: as used by Rembrandt, it is an essentially non-naturalistic convention.

CHRISTUS

This unusual name was borne by a painter who also sometimes called himself Petrus Christophorus. He was a contemporary and probably a pupil of Jan van Eyck, though apparently no more than ten or

CIMA · MADONNA AND CHILD
24″ × 19″. Bologna, Royal Gallery

fifteen years younger. The name of the village where he was born c. 1400/10 was Baeerle, in Brabant. But the identity of the place is uncertain. From 1444 until his death in 1473 he lived in Bruges, where Jan van Eyck also resided.

The reputation of Petrus Christus will always be overshadowed by that of his great fellow-citizen, though he was undoubtedly a fine artist in his own right the more to be admired on account of his very early date. His inspiration remains purely Late Gothic, so that he retains for us the fascinating charm exercised upon the modern world by medieval piety. He kept this tradition alive in the Netherlands long after Jan van Eyck died, till it merged with that founded by Bouts and Ouwater. Petrus resembles van Eyck very closely in style, though a comparison soon shows the difference. The younger man's work is then at once seen to be more conventional, stiffer, more prosaic and technically less smooth. There is a world of difference, for example, between the betrothed couple in the 'Eligius' picture by Petrus in New York and the Arnolfini husband and wife depicted by Jan van Eyck. The former picture is a fine one, the latter a sublime work of art. The former is perfectly intelligible, the latter enigmatic. Petrus, great painter as he was, seems to have been almost deaf, in comparison with Van Eyck, to the voices of the spirit. On only one occasion did a really noble and mysteriously suggestive work, the *Portrait of a Young Woman*, now in Berlin, slip, so to speak, through his fingers.

Another work, the *St Jerome in His Study*, also in New York, was recently freed from a superimposed picture, and is very likely a genuine Van Eyck. It was hoped at first that it might be one. But in all probability it is simply an exceptionally fine painting by Petrus. Berlin possesses a *Madonna with Carthusians*, Brussels a large *Lamentation* which reveals for the first time some traces of the influence of Rogier van der Weyden, and New York another treatment of the same subject in the artist's typical style. The only picture known with any certainty to have been painted by Petrus and Van Eyck together is the *Madonna with a Prior* recently acquired by the National Gallery of Washington. (See also *Eyck*.)

CIGNANI

Born in Bologna, in 1628 and dying in Forli in 1719, Carlo Cignani belonged to a respected family of lawyers, members of the minor nobility. In honour of the painter, the family were given the rank of counts by the ruling prince. Carlo Cignani studied under Albani and was the last considerable representative of the famous Bolognese School. With him Late Italian Baroque painting comes to an end. In other words, this style had already become obscure, pedantic and over-decorative. But since Cignani not only continued the line of development leading from the Carracci through Albani to Reni, but also admired the limpidity of Poussin, he stands, too, for an improvement in neatness in draughtsmanship, and simplicity and elegance in composition. He painted mainly biblical and mythological subjects. Nearly all the galleries of the world possess pictures by him.

CIMA

Born at Conegliano 1459/60 and probably dying there 1517/18, Giovanni Battista da Conegliano Cima seems to have lived in Venice for more than twenty years, until 1516. It was here, after studying under Alvise Vivarini, that he underwent his deepest influence, that of Giovanni Bellini. Cima's Madonnas are usually accompanied as in the case of the older Mannerists, by two or four saints ranged to right and left, while the lifelike features of a patron often emerge, as though beheaded, from the lower edge of the picture. The artist belonged to a numerous band of the followers of Montagna and Bellini, difficult to distinguish from one another and characterise individually. Cima himself lacks the outstanding gift of Bellini for harmony. His style is more angular and severe, in the manner of Montagna. He had little sense of humour. There is never the faintest trace of a smile in any of his works. Even his fine landscape backgrounds are solemn 'concessions' made to the progressive ideas of his

P. CLAESZ · STILL-LIFE · *14¾″ × 20¼″. Switzerland, Private Collection*

time. At present his paintings are in high favour. They are represented in nearly all large galleries. But the finest collection of Cima's work is to be found in Venice, in the Accademia and in the churches of SS. Giovanni e Paolo, San Giovanni in Bragora and Santa Maria dell' Oroto.

CIMABUE

Born in Florence, Giovanni Cimabue (1240?-1302?) was the last great artist of the Byzantine tradition, though his work already shows signs of a break with earlier conventions. His art was the basis of that of Duccio, who combined it with Gothic elements. In modern times, despite Cimabue's great fame in his own day, his work is known from tradition rather than fact, as no extant picture can be ascribed to him with absolute certainty. He was formerly considered to be the painter of the Rucellai Madonna in the church of Santa Maria Novella, Florence. According to Vasari, this picture was carried in a triumphal procession through the streets of the city. But the work is now attributed to Duccio. The *Virgin Enthroned* in the Uffizi Gallery, the *Madonna with Angels* in the Lower Church at Assisi and some frescoes in the Upper Church, including the *Crucifixion*, are today ascribed by some critics to Cimabue. A comparison of these works with the art of Duccio and that of Giotto shows Cimabue to have been at once one of the last painters of the Middle Ages and a precursor of the early Renaissance. This view is also suggested by Dante's familiar lines:

Credette Cimabue nella pittura
tener lo campo, ed ora ha Giotto il grido,
si che la fama di colui è oscura.

Cimabue thought he held the field in painting and now the cry is for Giotto, so that the fame of the former is obscured.)

JOOS VAN CLEVE · MADONNA OF THE CHERRIES
$29\frac{3}{4}'' \times 21\frac{1}{4}''$. *Aix-la-Chapelle, Private Collection*

CLAESE

Peter Claese, the father of Nikolaus Berchem, was born at Steinfurt in Westphalia in 1597 and died in Haarlem in 1661. His pictures represent magnified sections of objects which may be found 'accidentally' on the corner of a table, such as a knife, a plate of fruit, a piece of cut cake, a cup, a roll of bread and sometimes even a gutted fish. The colour scheme is mainly brownish-grey, with here and there a deeper, more glowing accent. The style resembles that of Willem Heda, though it is less tastefully refined.

CLAUDE
See LORRAINE.

69

F. CLOUET · ELIZABETH OF AUSTRIA
14½″ × 10¾″. Paris, Louvre

CLEVE

Joos van Cleve the Elder was born in Cleve c. 1480/90. There is documentary evidence of his activity as guild-master at Antwerp between 1507 and the year of his death, 1540. It was for long impossible to distinguish him, the Joos who studied under Calcar, from a certain Joos active in London, known as 'mad Cleve', from a Cornelis van Cleve and finally, from the anonymous 'Master of the Death of the Virgin'. The confusion was mainly due to Mander (q.v.), whose account of the Cleves in his memoirs is completely unintelligible. The conclusions of the latest research are as follows: Joos van Cleve the Elder undoubtedly painted the pictures which are referred to as by 'Cleve'. These comprise the attractive studies, turned out by the dozen, of the Virgin and Child, which are described by Max Friedländer as 'easy to live with, understand and appreciate for their obvious prettiness', together with the many portraits in light colours, the features shown in relief against the dark hair and equally dark background and illustrating, in their expression of tranquil unconcern, humanity at large rather than any particular person. But Joos has also now been identified for certain as the author of another group of works, including the very fine small altarpiece for a praying-desk in Berlin and the altar panels depicting the death of the Virgin which are preserved in the Cathedrals of Cologne and Munich. Joos is therefore no other than the hitherto anonymous 'Master of the Death of the Virgin'. These discoveries constitute important additions to his production. The documents and dates, moreover, relating to the two large altarpieces are consistent with the supposed circumstances of Joos's career. How far certain portraits painted at the Court of the French King should be ascribed to him, not to Clouet, is still a matter of dispute. Joos certainly visited France. No doubt he heard talk there of Leonardo da Vinci, who had only just died in the south of the country, and possibly saw some of his pictures. Joos's own works show traces of the Italian master's influence.

It is clear that the family name was van der Beke. The son, **Joos van Cleve the Younger,** born at Antwerp in 1520, seems to have been the person known as 'London Cleve', as he soon left for London, where he painted most of his surviving portraits and died insane in 1554. He excelled in portraiture. The small work in Berlin, representing a young man, has the quality of a Holbein.

CLOUET

Jean Clouet (1485-1540) came to France from the Netherlands. Apparently he was the same person as Janney Clauet of Valenciennes. In 1516 he arrived at the Court of Francis I at Tours, where he married a Frenchwoman and was appointed Court Painter—producing only portraits. He moved to Paris in 1529 and died there.

His son **François** (1522-1572) born at Tours, grew up in Paris and followed in his father's footsteps at the Court, holding office also under Francis's successors.

Ienry II, Francis II and Charles IX. He, oo, died in Paris.

The lives of these two men were as uneventful as the above summaries indiate. No doubt they experienced a certain mount of disappointment and common orrow, more or less keenly felt enjoyment, rosperity and affection. François, in parcular, left two natural daughters. But ate dealt them no staggering blows. No race of their temperaments, characters or assions, not even a hint of personal pride, an be detected in their pictures.

It is important to stress the point. For iese two painters were surrounded by iose of the Fontainebleau School (q.v.). warms of them were active at Court, ancing at its balls, executing decorations, itriguing, declaiming and generally playig the courtier. They arranged festivals, ainted halls and produced landscapes and llegories to please the Renaissance taste f the King. In the midst of all this giddy irmoil, with the King visiting one castle fter another and most of the artists accomanying him, the two Clouets sat at work i their small house in the rue Sainte voye, next door, not to a peer, but to the pothecary Cutte, whom François painted. They continued to behave like typical Dutch craftsmen. It was from this basic ttitude that their pictures developed.

Their work is of brilliant quality. That f Jean or Jehannet, the father, derived as whole from Barent van Orley and Joos an Cleve, only gradually succeeded in nparting greater vividness to the repreentation of draperies and jewellery. His ountenances are far less 'speaking' than iose by François, much less animated, iore drawn than painted. Yet it would ertainly be a superficial judgment to call im an inferior psychologist. Neither rtist probed very deeply into the mind. ean's pictures, at any rate, wear very ell.

François, out of respect for his father id to the confusion of historians, somemes used to sign his work 'Jannet'. But ie silken sheen and sparkle of his colour, ie amazing precision and elaboration of is drawings, surpass his parent's. More emarkable still, the gemlike lustre of his

paintings does not seem at all forced or obtrusive.

The equestrian portrait of Francis I in the Uffizi Gallery, that of the same king at the Louvre, that of Claude in the Pitti Palace at Florence and of the Dauphin at Antwerp are all by Jean Clouet.

The most important portraits by his son are those of the apothecary Cutte and of Elizabeth of Austria in the Louvre, of *Diane de Poitiers Bathing* at Washington, those of Henri II in the Uffizi, Pitti and Versailles Galleries and that of Charles IX at Vienna.

CODDE

Pieter Codde of Amsterdam (1599-1678) was admired and well known in his day, being given the task of finishing Frans Hals's great canvas of the *Marksmen* after Hals had abandoned the work. But the dashing style of a genius did not really suit Codde. He was far more drawn to Frans Hals's brother, Dirck, who produced small, cheerful pictures of officers carousing in guard-rooms or dissolute ladies and gentlemen enjoying themselves. Dirck Hals and Codde were the leaders of a whole group of painters of such scenes. It was the period of the terrible Thirty Years' War in Germany, which had given the young people of Holland, safely out of danger themselves, a taste for romantic swashbuckling.

Two of Codde's pictures are in the National Gallery, London.

COECKE VAN AELST

The Flemish painter, Pieter Coecke, Cock, Koecke van Aelst was, according to an inscription on his funeral monument quoted in Sweertius' *Monumenta Sepulchria* (1613), born in 1502 and died in 1550. Van Mander says that he was a pupil of Bernard van Orley and that he visited Rome. He worked principally in Antwerp. In 1533 he visited Constantinople. He was painter to Mary of Hungary and the Emperor Charles V; he also designed buildings, stained glass and tapestries, tried his hand at sculpture and translated Vitruvius and Serlio. Some of his Turkish drawings were published in engravings by his widow in 1553. Our knowledge of Coecke's work is based on a series of repetitions of the *Last Supper*, all influenced by Leonardo's design, and Friedländer attributed to him a triptych of the *Virgin and Child Enthroned* in the National Gallery, London.

COELLO

Claudio Coello, the son of a Portuguese immigrant, was born in 1630/40 and died in 1693 in Madrid, where he was the last important representative of the Madrid School. He was little influenced by his teacher, Rizi, an artist of no consequence. It was not until Coello met Carreño, who patronised him and arranged for him to copy paintings by Titian and Rubens in the Escorial, that he developed a style of his own. His designs are on a large, often monumental scale, as in his figures of saints. The drawing is sometimes pedantic. Compared with Carreño he lacks imagination and zest. But his colours glow. Their 'saturation' is admired by A. L. Meyer, who is the chief authority on his work.

Success came early to Coello. Like his older contemporary, Carreño, whom he reverenced, he was appointed Court Painter to the King, and produced innumerable easel-pictures, frescoes and portraits—for example, that of Charles II of Spain, now at Frankfurt. His masterpiece is the 'Sagrada Forma' altarpiece in the Escorial.

Claudio Coello was not related to **Alonso Sanchez** Coello, who was born at Valencia in 1515 and died in 1590 at Madrid, where he was the pupil of Antonis Mor during that important Dutch painter's residence in the city. But unfortunately he derived little profit from these lessons. He could never get rid of his typical Spanish melancholy and continued to produce 'ancestor portraits', few of which are to be seen outside Spain. His portrait of Philip II is preserved in Berlin.

CONINXLOO

It would be a labour of Sisyphus to gi an account of Gillis van Coninxloo origin and family. Seventeen artists of t name are known to have lived short before or after Gillis and he himself h to be called Gillis III if there is to be a hope of distinguishing him from the res

The task is easier when all the pictur of this clan are examined. Only one of t painters concerned, Gillis III, is of a importance. Born in Antwerp in 1544 an dying in Amsterdam in 1607, he gaine his decisive inspiration from a journey France in his youth, where he hit upon new theory of landscape painting. For t next thirty-seven years he laboured to p it into practice. The usual procedure those days was to paint landscapes in thr distinct stages of perspective, employin 'studio brown' for the foreground, lig green for the middle distance and ve pale ochre near the horizon. The meth is most strikingly illustrated by Joos Momper and Paul Bril in their early work Gillis van Coninxloo was the first to away with this conventional treatment perspective. His prolonged struggle achieve this aim seems, of course, almo incredible today. His pictures gradua acquired the correct gradations of atm sphere, together with an unromantic ar unpretentious view of nature, a coherer colour scheme and lower and lower ho zons to indicate distance.

These results were a revelation and liberation to his colleagues. Momper, Br Jan Brueghel, Schoubroeck, Savery an Vinckeboons all learnt from him. Eve etchers on copper felt bound to attempt t reproductions of these innovations hundreds of plates. The most interestin pictures by Coninxloo—many have be lost—are to be found in Vienna, Stra bourg and Brussels.

COPLEY

John Singleton Copley (1737-1815) w born in Boston, Massachusetts, of a English father and an Irish mother. 1774, having already made a name f

CORREGGIO · LA NOTTE
102⅞" × 75¼". Dresden, Gemäldegalerie

himself as a portrait painter, he set out for Italy. A year later, on his return journey, he came to London and settled there for good. He soon embarked on a series of scenes from contemporary English history, among which were *The Death of Chatham* and, the finest of the series, *The Death of Major Pierson* (Tate Gallery). This picture is one of the best 'historical' paintings produced by the English school. The Duke of Wellington pronounced it the finest battle picture he had seen. Copley was the father of Lord Lyndhurst, three times Lord Chancellor.

COQUES

Born in 1614 and dying in Antwerp in 1684, Gonzalez Coques, who sometimes spelt his name Cocx, owed little to his teachers, Pieter Brueghel III, grandson of the great 'peasant' Brueghel, and David Rychaert. The greatest benefit Rychaert conferred on him was his daughter in marriage.

The style of Coques was based on those of Terborch and Van Dyck, improbable as this combination may appear. His figures, even when seen on a small scale in Terborch-like interiors, have the courtly and self-conscious air of Van Dyck's. Coques was employed by several Continental rulers and by Charles I of England. For the Stadtholder Frederick Henry of the Netherlands he painted a series of life-size compositions of the story of Cupid and Psyche. He is best known for his portraits, Van Dyckian in character, but on a small scale. He is represented in the National Gallery and the Wallace Collection, London.

CORNEILLE DE LYON

Corneille de Lyon was not a Frenchman by birth. In some records he is called Corneille de la Haye, Cornelius of The Hague. The circumstances which brought him to Lyon, where he was working by 1536, are unknown. A portrait painter of his talent and standing would have been more at home in Paris. In Lyon he was quite cut off, and indeed painted a number of his portraits from drawings made by other artists. He nevertheless soon made a name for himself. French courtiers who had occasion to travel through Lyon sought him out for the pleasure of having a quick portrait painted. The Queen herself once visited Corneille de Lyon. He was a Protestant, and his last years were darkened by the religious persecutions. He became a Catholic in 1569 and so escaped the Massacre of St Bartholomew. He died in 1575 and for centuries was forgotten.

Corneille de Lyon was not an important painter. His portraits, with their unvaried green or blue backgrounds are highly conventionalised. He was not much interested in the psychology of his sitters, and even if his portraits seem sometimes to show penetration this is probably due to his pleasing technique and to the fact that we are so far removed from that age of lace collars and black velvet doublets. Three attractive portraits by Corneille de Lyon are in the National Gallery, London.

CORNELISZ VAN AMSTERDAM

Called also Jakob van Oostsanen, from his birthplace, this artist (b. 1468/70) died in Amsterdam in 1533. While his namesake, Cornelisz van Haarlem (b. 1562), ranks as a Late Mannerist, Cornelisz van Amsterdam must be regarded as a relatively early representative of the Dutch School. His religious pictures belong essentially to the old style of Dutch composition. Their only innovation is their Renaissance setting, also to be found in the works of the contemporary painter Engelbrechtsen. This feature, which Cornelisz really did not know how to employ, introduces elements of superfluous ornament and unconvincing elegance into the productions of an artist fundamentally of Late Gothic type. His paintings, moreover, are not all equally good. Even the best, such as the *Altarpiece of the Virgin* in Berlin, the St Jerome altarpiece in Vienna and the

Nativity in Naples, do not make Cornelisz van Amsterdam one of the outstanding but only one of the respectable painters of a brilliant period.

CORNELISZ VAN HAARLEM

Born in 1562 and dying in Haarlem in 1638, this highly esteemed and wealthy artist belonged to a group of learned Humanists, such as Mander, Spranger and Goltzius, in association with whom, following the example of the Carracci, he founded a Haarlem Academy.

His portraits were much admired. The large *Banquet of Marksmen*, still at Haarlem, later made a considerable impression on Frans Hals. Cornelisz used mythological and biblical subjects merely as an excuse for the portrayal of nudes in vigorous movement, thus proving himself to be, in theme as well as in style, a true Mannerist (q.v.). The Rijksmuseum at Amsterdam recently acquired his *Bathsheba Bathing*, the most perfect realisation in existence of the ideal of the Haarlem Late Mannerists. Of the two robust, waxen-hued female figures depicted that to the left emerges from the bath with the haste of one of the soldiers represented in Michelangelo's cartoon of the Battle of Cascina. By way of contrast, an attendant Negress is painted in ashen grey against the dull gold of a park in the background. It is, of course, an insincere work, unquestionably without the least trace of genuine feeling. But it is extremely interesting and even attractive.

PIERO DI COSIMO · THE DEATH OF PROCRIS · 25½″ × 72″. *London, National Gallery*

CORREGGIO

Antonio Allegri took his name from the village of Correggio, near Modena, where he was born. The year of his birth is not known with absolute certainty. If the statement of Vasari (q.v.) that Correggio died at forty is correct, it must have been 1494, for he died in 1534, either at his birthplace or the neighbouring city of Parma. Outwardly, he led a quiet life, in modest, provincial circumstances, far from the great centres of civilisation. It is all the more astonishing, therefore, that his work should be characterised by such vehemence, sensuality, technical innovation and boldness. Soon after his death he was regarded as one of the greatest painters who ever lived.

He was first influenced by Costa, whom he probably met in Mantua. Mantegna, too, impressed him at this time. It was long before the pictures he then painted were recognised as his, since they were altogether different from those which afterwards made him famous. The *Madonna with St Francis* at Dresden is to be referred, on documentary evidence, to this early period. It has enabled other pictures painted at that time, which were discovered later, to be identified as Correggio's.

He changed his style completely about 1518. This development can only be explained by supposing that he visited Rome, where he must have seen paintings by Leonardo and Raphael, or at any rate Milan, where he would undoubtedly have found the former's work. Vasari, however, denies that he made any such journey, declaring that Correggio must have dreamt it. If so, it is remarkable that he recreated such features of Leonardo's productions as the tender smiles of his women, their submissive poses and the beauty of the boldly sketched, girlish faces of his angels. Unfortunately, Correggio was not content with this achievement, but went a step further in his delineation of 'charm', 'sweet surprise' and general effusiveness. The slight exaggeration involved has prevented Correggio from being regarded as a really great painter.

F. COSSA · ALLEGORY OF AUTUMN
46″ × 28⅜″. Berlin, Staatl. Museen

He also reproduced to a certain extent Leonardo's effects of haziness. He could hardly have done so without studying the latter's works. In the course of time, he developed the new technique of chiaroscuro from this element. In certain of his pictures this effect, extraordinarily beautiful in itself, actually becomes a source of light, without justification in nature, and thus constituting an exciting problem for the observer. In the famous painting, for example, at Dresden entitled *Holy Night*, all the figures bending over the crib are brightly lit from below, not from any natural source, but from the Child Himself.

The passionate attitudes of Correggio's figures, his sensuousness, softness and supernatural lighting effects all exerted a decisive influence on the Post-Mannerists.

He decorated the Cathedral of San Giovanni Evangelista at Parma with ceiling-paintings of amazing virtuosity. But he left a fresco in the same building unfinished. His oil-paintings are more important. They include the *Holy Night* and *Madonna with St George* in Dresden, the *Madonna with St Jerome*, which has an enchanting angel's head, and the *Return from Egypt* at Parma, the *Repose on the Flight* at Florence, the *Danae* in Rome, the *Io*, with its astonishing back view of a nude in a cramped pose, and the *Ganymede* in Vienna, the *Mercury Instructing Cupid before Venus* and the *Madonna of the Basket* in London and the *Antiope* in Paris.

Berenson said of Correggio that 'he was only too receptive to sensual impressions and therein lies his limitation'.

CORTONA

Born at Cortona in 1596, Pietro Berrettini went to Rome at the age of only sixteen. He studied Raphael and Michelangelo in that city, and was soon overwhelmed with commissions.

In 1640 he moved to Florence for seven years to fulfil a long-standing engagement to undertake frescoes in the Pitti Palace and certain architectural work.

On his return to Rome, where he had been impatiently awaited, the Pope raised him to the rank of 'Cavaliere'. He died in Rome in 1669. He painted both frescoes and easel-pictures, on religious, mythological and allegorical themes. But he was himself already aware that his frescoes were his most important and permanent contributions to art. They had, in fact, the strongest possible influence on Roman Baroque. A direct line of development leads from Cortona, through his pupils Luca Giordano and Gaulli, to the frescoes of Tiepolo.

COSIMO

Piero di Cosimo (1462-1521) was born in Florence and became a pupil of Cosimo Roselli. In about 1480 he accompanied his master to Rome and helped him with the decorations for the new chapel of the Vatican for Sixtus IV. Except for this one visit to Rome Piero di Cosimo remained all his life in Florence. Vasari describes him as living in misanthropic solitude and taking little part in the life of the town, though he designed some of the most fantastic masquerades for the celebrated carnivals of the time of Lorenzo the Magnificent. Piero's fanciful and wayward genius found its chief source of inspiration

J. COSSIERS · THE ADORATION OF THE SHEPHERDS
66″ × 75¼″. Cassel, Gemäldegalerie

in classical antiquity, especially in those legends told by Ovid of the early history of man, such as the story of Prometheus bringing fire to mankind. There is often an element of terror and violence in the frenzied figures and primeval landscapes in his pictures, as, for example, in his painting of the battle stirred up by the Centaur Eurytus at the marriage feast of the King of the Lapiths with Hippodamia (National Gallery). Pictures of a similar character in the Ashmolean Museum, Oxford, and the Metropolitan Museum, New York, are admirably discussed by E. Panofsky in the *Journal of the Warburg Institute*, I (1937). Other pictures by Piero include *La bella Simonetta* (Chantilly), *The Death of Procris* (National Gallery), *The Story of Perseus and Andromeda* and *Portrait of Caterina Sforza* (Uffizi), *The Coronation of the Virgin* (Louvre) and *The Destruction of Pharaoh* (Sistine Chapel).

COSSA

Son of a master-mason, Francesco Cossa was born at Ferrara in 1435 and died at Bologna in 1477. To art historians he is an important personality of special significance. It was he, with Cosimo Tura, who strikingly resembles him, who founded a new school of painting at Padua in the province of Emilia, between the two focal points of Florence and Venice. He owed nothing at all to the contemporary art of either city. But at Padua he was stimulated by Mantegna. Piero della Francesca had the greatest influence of all upon him. Cossa, who began to paint very early, had become aware of this artist at the age of fifteen. Piero had come to Padua from Urbino to carry out two contracts for frescoes. He stayed a year. Cossa was enraptured by the archaic, monumental style of the Tuscan and based his own upon it. In 1470, owing to disagreements with his patron, the Duke of Ferrara, Cossa moved to the Court of Bologna, where he died of the plague while still at the height of his powers.

His paintings, of a religious and allegorical character, show crowded scenes occurring amidst the tremendous desola-

tion of biblical regions, the people in composed but graceful movement. Sometimes, as in the famous *Autumn* at Berlin, he sets against such a background a single tall figure, in this case a peasant girl, proud as any by Piero della Francesca, who has paused on her way back from the vineyard, her foot resting upon the edge of the picture-frame as if it were the head of the vanquished Goliath. This is a most remarkable work.

Most of Cossa's frescoes and many of his panels have disappeared. But his fanciful frescoes in the Schifanoia Palace at Ferrara, with their numerous figures, have survived. A work of his maturity, the Mercanzea altarpiece, is in the Pinacoteca at Bologna. Another of his chief works, an altarpiece representing St Vincent Ferrer, is shared by London, which has the centre panel, Milan which possesses the two wings, and Rome where the *predella* (q.v.) are preserved.

COSSIERS

The works of Jan Cossiers of Antwerp (1600-1671) are unfortunately seldom found in museums and galleries. A pupil of Cornelis de Vos, he was an accomplished and daring artist, producing large biblical and mythological scenes, crowded with figures in vigorous movement, brilliantly lit and glowing with colour.

COSTA

Born in Ferrara in 1460 where he studied under Tura and Roberti, Lorenzo Costa moved first to Bologna, and then to Mantua, where he died in 1535.

At Bologna he worked for a long time with Francesco Francia, by whose superior talents and more definite ideas he was thenceforward influenced to a remarkable degree. Costa's frescoes and easel-pictures deal with the subjects of Court history and religion. These works are sometimes very engaging, owing to the astonishing atmospheric quality of their background landscapes. But his paintings suffer all too often from a frigidity and stiffness which might almost be called funereal. There is no doubt that he had a taste, as his *Garden of the Muses* in the Louvre proves, for solemn scenes of Arcadian peace. But this tendency very quickly leads to a lifeless style unless it is backed by adequate professional skill. In some of Costa's portraits, where there is less danger of this result, his colour and line are amazingly good.

COTES

Francis Cotes (1725-1770), who was born in London and spent all his life there, left a large number of portraits once as highly prized in England as those of Reynolds, whose style, in fact, they often recall. His pastel portraits rival those of Rosalba Carriera. Cotes's work was much admired by the fashionable English aristocracy of his day. He was one of the founder members of the Royal Academy.

COXCIE

Michiel Coxcie (1499-1592), who was born in Mecheln, first studied under Bernard van Orley. But a prolonged tour of Italy and the impact of Italian Mannerism eventually turned Coxcie into a rather feeble Mannerist along purely Raphaelesque lines. He proved himself to be an outstanding technician by his copy of Van Eyck's Ghent altarpiece, executed at the order of the King of Spain. Portions of this work are today to be found at Ghent, Berlin and Munich.

COYPEL

Antoine Coypel (1661-1722) was the son and pupil of **Noel** (1628-1707). In Paris, he derived much from Le Brun and some Roman painters. But his smaller studies reveal his admiration for Rubens. He occupies an important position in the history of French painting. His style was

L. CRANACH THE ELDER · PORTRAIT OF DR JOHANNES CUSPINIAN
23⅝" × 18". Winterthur,
Oskar Reinhart Collection

opposed to that favoured by the King, but was greatly admired by a younger generation of connoisseurs. The Duke of Orleans commissioned him to decorate a gallery in the Palais Royal and he produced one of the most Baroque ceilings in France. His style gradually became more popular in Court circles. In 1708 the King asked him to decorate the central part of the Chapel ceiling at Versailles.

COZENS

Alexander Cozens (1700-1786) was born in Russia and may have been the illegitimate son of Peter the Great and an Englishwoman from Deptford. After studying painting in Italy, he settled in 1746 in London. He was drawing master at Christ's Hospital and later at Eton and he wrote two curious books, *The Shape, Skeleton and Foliage of Trees* (1771) and *The Principles of Beauty relative to the Human Head* (1778). In his work Cozens reveals an experimental attitude which makes him of exceptional interest today. His pictures are almost all in monochrome wash, and he often used a method of composition which he described as 'Blot-drawing'. He made casual blots of sepia or Indian ink on paper and used them as a basis for a composition to be completed by brush or pen. The strange and compelling drawings Cozens produced by this method depict the grandeur of the wild scene he had known in Italy. There are collections of them in the British and Victoria and Albert Museums.

John Robert Cozens, Alexander's son (1752-1799) was a topographical artist but he imbued his exquisite, pale, nostalgic drawings of Italian mountain landscape and architecture with a poetry which raises them far above mere topography. Turner said that Cozens' oil painting, *Hannibal in his March over the Alps*, which has since vanished, taught him more than any other picture.

CRANACH

One of the greatest of German painters, Lucas Cranach the Elder, was born at Kronach in 1472 and died in Weimar in 1553.

L. CRANACH THE ELDER
MADONNA AND CHILD
24″ × 16¾″. *Munich, Alte Pinakothek*

The earliest record of his life, relates to his travels in the Danube Valley, begun about 1500, when he was twenty-eight. During this period of intellectual excitement he produced the two *Crucifixions* of the Vienna Schottenkirche and Munich. They are both decidedly macabre works, almost in the style of Grünewald. At this time he also painted four portraits, the finest being *Dr Cuspinian*, now in the Reinhart Collection at Winterthur. The *Rest on the Flight*, at Berlin, is also to be ascribed to this period. This picture became the most popular of Cranach's works, and is regarded as his most 'German' production.

On his return in 1504 he was immediately summoned to Wittenberg by the Elector, Frederick the Wise, to become his Court Painter. Cranach lived there as an official until the autumn of 1508, executing, in addition to an enormous number of

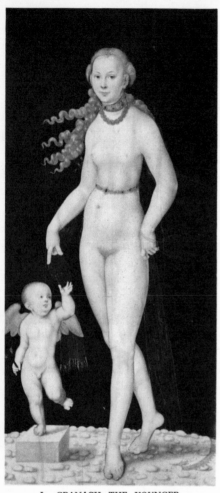

L. CRANACH THE YOUNGER
VENUS AND CUPID
78¾" × 39⅜". *Munich, Alte Pinakothek*

he produced countless paintings, once more of high quality, revealing a fresh delight in depicting figures, interiors and landscape. They include the fine Torgau altarpiece, quite in the homely Flemish style, the Dessau altarpiece for the Prince, with its large-scale figures resembling those in a group-portrait, the Vienna *Holy Family*, which might be a gathering of Cranach's cousins and grandchildren—it contains a self-portrait—as well as the *Expulsion of the Money-changers*, with its comic rendering of indignation, at Dresden, and its new, Rembrandtesque type of Christ. Finally, he painted the so-called 'Breslau Madonna', which has remained one of the finest German pictures of the Virgin.

But the most surprising result of Cranach's visit to Flanders was his discovery of the secular nude. In 1509 he was responsible for the first naked Venus in the history of northern European painting, now at Leningrad. The figure makes a rather singular and awkward impression. A second, later version, now in a private collection at Munich, strives to reproduce the symmetry of Dürer's *Eve*. It conveys aristocratic grace and has the head of a woman of rank. The features are identical with those of the two Marys in the *Holy Family* and of the Madonna with Christ of 1515. Cranach did not, accordingly, introduce any erotic element into his treatment of the nude at this time.

Changes in this respect and others came about between 1525 and 1530. Wealth and honours, including public eulogies in verse, fell thick upon him. He, the son of a Kronach painter—probably the name was originally Sunder—had become a patrician, a councillor, several times mayor, an intimate friend of Luther and of the Elector, a land-owner and the proprietor of a dispensary and printing-works. The new Elector Frederick the Magnanimous, acted like a minor Renaissance ruler. Cranach's eldest son **Hans**, who died in 1537 on a journey to Bologna, was now grown up and even the second son, **Lucas the Younger,** who died in 1586 at Weimar, could already help in the studio, where many others were by this time employed.

drawings, certain religious works and portraits which reveal Cranach's new outlook as a courtier. Year by year they grew less imaginative and weaker in impact.

The Elector then sent him to the Netherlands on the staff of an embassy to the Court of the Emperor Charles V. He returned in the spring of 1509, full of his new experiences. Until about 1520/25

Pictures issued from it in a steady stream. A report of 1533 certifies that Cranach's workshop had sent out 120 replicas of the portraits of two Electors. Paintings of Venus, by now of an erotic character and growing gradually more and more degenerate, were also being delivered. Examples are to be seen at Frankfurt, Rome and Munich (that in the latter city being by Lucas the Younger). They culminated in the frankly ribald *Old Man in Love with a Courtesan*. Dozens of bad copies of this work have given Cranach a still worse reputation for this sort of thing.

He himself, however, continued to turn out excellent and in fact important pictures. Throughout his life he never ceased to produce portraits. Those entitled *Squire Jörg* at Leipzig, *Luther's Daughter* in Paris, *The Mayor of Weissenfels* in Berlin, *A Saxon Gentleman* at Cologne, *Henry the Pious*—destroyed during the war—*Sibylle von Cleve* at Weimar, *Dr Schöner* in Brussels, *Geiler von Kaiserberg* and *H. Melber* at Munich render Cranach the equal of Dürer and Holbein in this field.

CREDI

Lorenzo Credi, who was born in 1459 and died in 1537 in Florence, named himself Credi after his first known ancestor, a goldsmith. Although Lorenzo's life coincided with the period which saw the advent of Leonardo, Michelangelo, Raphael and Giorgione, he seems not to have noticed the critical innovations they introduced. He began his career as an apprentice in Verrocchio's studio and worked on there, after reaching maturity, until that master's death. He never changed the style he had been taught, or rather had hammered into him. His Madonnas, Annunciations, Adorations and Saints show no trace of personal inspiration or inner compulsion to paint in that particular way and no other. It is impossible to feel that Credi was bound by nature to be a painter. Salvini calls him 'monotonous'. Gronau observes: 'He never freed himself from the conception of form he had adopted as an apprentice.'

Yet his pictures—for example, his *Venus* and *Madonna with Two Angels* at Florence, his *Adorations* in Berlin and Venice and his *Madonnas* in London and Paris—are often very fine, entirely in the manner of Verrocchio. It is impossible to distinguish between the hands of the two artists when considering Credi's altarpiece in the Cathedral at Pistoia.

His work represents average Italian *quattrocento* painting at its best, technically outstanding, but impersonal and reduced to a formula.

CRESPI

As a pupil of Cignani, Giuseppe Maria Crespi (1665-1747) continued the development of the once famous school at Bologna of the Carracci, who were followed by Albani and Cignani. But the old academic style of Bologna had already been modified in Cignani's work, by a new note reminiscent of Poussin's manner. In Crespi's best pictures this novel vision comes out quite clearly. In contemplating the attractive chiaroscuro of his already Rococo handling of dancing figures or such a subject as the *Woman Looking for Fleas* in the Uffizi Gallery, the spectator is instantly reminded of the Venetian masquerades and views of Guardi and Longhi. Here Crespi looks forward to the great painters of the succeeding age in Venice and forgets Baroque Mannerism. He renews the former cheerful freedom and charm of Bolognese painting. But in other pictures, on religious and mythological themes, he reverts to the older convention. His series of the *Seven Sacraments* at Dresden was inspired by a personal experience. On entering a church he had noticed a single brilliant shaft of light falling through the darkness to illuminate the figure of a penitent. All seven of the series in question retain the 'impressionist' vision thus suggested.

CRIVELLI

Though Carlo Crivelli was born in Venice (1430/35), his family was probably from the Marches Province of central Italy, whither he returned at the end of the 1460s, staying there for ten years. He then

A. CUYP
RIVER SCENE WITH CATTLE
18" × 29". London, National Gallery

went back to Venice, where he died in 1495. He seems to have been trained mainly in the Paduan tradition, for his first pictures—for example, his *Pietà* in Berlin—closely resemble Squarzione's. Later on the influence of Vivarini is perceptible. Nevertheless, Crivelli's work is unmistakable and of marked individuality. It suggests majolica, with its definite contours and lack of depth, or coloured ivory reliefs lavishly adorned, to disconcerting and unconventional effect, with garlands of flowers and fruit. Even the enamelled, garishly lit figures in relief of his *Pietà* at Boston are surmounted by an arch festooned with fruits, while his *Madonna Enthroned* at Milan is entirely surrounded by an ornamental bower of flowers, fruit and brocade. Berenson has justly remarked of Crivelli's pictures that they tempt the observer to handle them. A particularly admirable and characteristic work is his *Annunciation* in the National Gallery, London, which has one of the finest collections of his paintings, including the famous Demidoff Altarpiece.

CROME

John Crome (1768-1821) was born in Norwich of poor parents. After having worked as an errand boy to a doctor, he was apprenticed at the age of fourteen to a painter of coaches and inn signs. Crome is known to have painted three inn signs, 'The Two Brewers', 'The Guardian Angel' and 'The Sawyers'. The boy began

very early to paint landscapes, and he was noticed by Mr Thomas Harvey of Catton, who had a good collection of pictures, including works by Gainsborough, Wilson and the Dutch masters. Crome was allowed to study these pictures, and he made a copy of Gainsborough's *Cottage Door* and was especially attracted by the paintings of Hobbema. Harvey also found Crome employment as a drawing master, and later he taught at the Norwich Grammar School, where George Borrow was among his pupils. Crome used to teach out of doors. He was a successful teacher and his landscapes were much admired. In 1803 he founded the Norwich Society of Artists, which held exhibitions from 1805 onwards and of which Crome became President in 1808. Except for a visit to France in 1814, Crome rarely left the neighbourhood of Norwich and his work is above all inspired by his own locality. The outstanding qualities of Crome's painting are breadth and majesty, a grand simplicity of design and feeling for atmosphere. To the tradition of the Dutch painters Crome added the power of generalisation. The three National Gallery pictures, *Mousehold Heath*, *The Poringland Oak* and *Moonrise on the Marshes of the Yare*, show this great painter at his best. He is also well represented at the Castle Museum, Norwich.

CUYP

The name is also spelt Cuijp. Aelbert Cuyp (1620-1691), the most important of the three painters so called, was born and died in Dordrecht. He was trained by his father, **Jakob Gerritz** of Dordrecht (1594-1651), by whom some fine landscapes, coloured in the free style of Abraham Boelmart are extant, and also certain subtly and neatly designed portraits. Jakob Gerritz could teach his son nothing more. But it was enough to enable Aelbert to become a good painter and produce the fine work entitled *Boy with Falcon*, now in a private collection at Amsterdam. But a surprise was in store for the father. His son turned out to be a really great artist. Aelbert's eminence dates from the moment he saw his first picture by Jan van Goyen. It freed him from Bloemart's ideas about colour, dominated by reds and blues, and led him to develop his own kind of vision of a Dutch evening, with its golden-yellow clouds above the Dordrecht meadows and canals. He never tired of representing the magical effect of such lighting on dull greens and pale golds, either in a simple landscape or one diversified with herds or crossed by streams bearing boats or sailing-vessels. His urban views and rare studies of still-life are also admirable. Works by him are to be found in nearly every large gallery.

The third member of this family, **Benjamin Gerritz** (1612-1652), was Aelbert's uncle, his father's stepbrother. Born and dying in Dordrecht, he proved to be a remarkable character. It might have been

expected that he would have the same sort of career as his brother Jakob. On the contrary, he left several puzzles for posterity to solve. In his pictures of peasants, riders and 'Holy Nights' the influence can be discerned not only of Rembrandt, but also of the boorish Ostade. A small panel entitled *Groom with Horse*, in the Alte Pinakothek at Munich, is completely bewildering in its demoniac energy. It might have been painted by Goya.

D

DADDI

Bernardo Daddi is referred to in Florentine documents between 1320 and 1350. But very little is known of his life. There is no proof, nor is it likely, that he was ever a pupil of Giotto. He must, of course, have regarded the latter as an innovator

B. DADDI
THE ANNUNCIATION
17¼″ × 27⅞″. Paris, Louvre

and guide. But Daddi's pictures bear just as much relation to those of the Sienese Pietro Lorenzetti. Vitzthum believes that a colleague of Giotto's, the 'Master of Saint Cecilia'—a work in the Uffizi Gallery—determined the style of Daddi's early pictures and may have trained him.

He was an important painter of the generation which succeeded that of Giotto and Duccio. His frescoes in Santa Croce, Florence, depict tall and robust figures, already shown, at this early date, in movement, accompanied by gestures. The colour, however, is still cautiously restrained and monotonous in the orthodox manner. Yet the small private altarpieces which he seems to have been fond of painting after 1330 indicate a sudden and bold turn in the direction of novelty. The word, however, did not of course mean, in 1335, anything like what would today be considered sensational. At that period the least attempt to shake off the sanctified fetters of ecclesiastical prescription would require courage and imagination. Daddi's altarpieces are relatively small in scale. He evidently took a hitherto unprecedented pleasure in completely covering vacant surfaces, for the first time, with figures and other incidental forms, so as to compose a 'picture'. His colour, too, changed, providing Christ with a gleaming mantle of ultramarine blue and the Virgin with a pink robe, while the earth is just beginning—but only just—to give a hint of green.

Daddi's altarpieces and panels are to be found, among other places, in Berlin, Altenburg, Florence, London and New York.

DAHL

Michael Dahl (1656-1743) was a Swedish painter who worked chiefly in London. He was born at Stockholm and was a pupil of Klocker (Ehrenstahl). He studied in France and Italy, visited England in 1678 and settled there in 1688. He was a conventional portrait painter, but his aptness in conforming to the fashionable requirements of the day brought him considerable success at the Courts of Queen Anne, George I and George II. His *Charles XI of Sweden* is in the Royal Collection at Windsor, and the National Portrait Gallery has his *Queen Anne, George II, Addison* and *The Duchess of Marlborough*.

G. DAVID · THE ADORATION OF THE KINGS
(Detail) 48½″ × 65⅜″. Munich, Alte Pinakothek

DALEM

Little is known of the life of Cornelis van Dalem (c. 1535-1575), an Antwerp guild-master. But he taught a pupil as important as his own teacher was unimportant. After examining Dalem's pictures, it is difficult to believe that he taught Bartholomäus Spranger.

Dalem is still unfortunately much neglected today, partly because so very few of his works have survived. He was uncompromisingly and exclusively devoted to landscape, in which he reached a high standard. One of his finest paintings, *Landscape with Farm*, signed and dated 1564, is at Munich. The apparently deserted homestead, the dark stump of willow beside it and the ruins in the background, dim in the chill evening twilight, compose a picture strikingly described by Ernst Buchner as an 'anticipation of the melancholy scenes of decay illustrated by the German Romantics'.

DALMAU

Luis Dalmau worked in Spain between 1428 and 1460, during the period when the Netherlands had a far greater influence on Spanish art than Italy. At that time Barcelona, where Dalmau lived, was still a centre of Spanish culture. Barcelona also contains the only one of his works which is signed and dated; a picture of the Councillors of Barcelona adoring the Virgin and Child. The influence of the altar at Ghent is unmistakable. In 1431 Dalmau became the King's Ambassador to Flanders.

DANCKERTS

Hendrik Danckerts (1629-1679) was born at The Hague. He was trained as an engraver, studied painting in Italy and finally settled in England about 1668. He received commissions from Charles II for topographical paintings which are now at Hampton Court. He also engraved portrait plates of Charles II. He returned to Holland in about 1679 and died at Amsterdam. Danckerts is mentioned by Pepys who ordered four panels from him for his dining-room.

DARET

Born at Tournai c. 1400, **Jacques** Daret is named in contemporary records as an apprentice, in 1418, under the then highly esteemed local master, Robert Campin. It was the quest for information concerning Daret's career that led art historians, about the turn of the last century, to clues which have now identified Campin with the famous 'Master of Flémalle'. It is clearly evident from Daret's works that he was trained by that important artist. Nevertheless, there are notable differences between them. The Flémalle master's invariably somewhat striking and singular female countenances are never found in Daret's pictures. The latter preferred faces of a conventionally symmetrical type. His colour is also much livelier. Campin's meadows are a dull green; Daret's suggest sap. Their graphic representations of distance are surprisingly similar. But those of Campin are rather depressingly coloured, while Daret often relieves his by a touch of vermilion in the roof of a house.

As many dates relative to Daret's career have been recorded, it proved possible to identify his most important work, the altarpiece at St Vaast, beyond a doubt. Sections of it are now in Berlin, which possesses the *Visitation* and *Adoration*, and in New York, which has the *Nativity* and the *Presentation in the Temple*.

Daret lived most of his life at Tournai. He was only absent for a few years on assignments of some magnitude at Lille, Bruges and Arras. In 1468 his name is mentioned in the ducal archives of Burgundy for the last time.

Jean Daret (1613-1668) settled in Aix-en-Provence in 1637 after spending some time in Italy. He decorated many churches and houses with work that is strongly

Bolognese in character. Some of his pictures show the influence of Caravaggio. There is a fine self-portrait in this manner in the Hermitage at Leningrad.

DAVID, GERARD

Born at Oudewater in 1460 and dying in Bruges in 1523, Gerard David had already been forgotten eighty years later by Van Mander, who only refers briefly to hearsay about him. It was not until the end of the nineteenth century that arduous stylistic and documentary research revived his reputation. Many more than fifty of his works have now been identified, enabling him to be ranked as one of the best of the

older Dutchmen. When these painters of the Late Gothic School are discussed, the name of Gerard David usually closes the illustrious series leading from Van Eyck through Van der Weyden, Bouts Geertgen, Van der Goes and Memling.

Dutch by birth, he was probably trained by the distinguished master Ouwater before moving to the richer environment of Bruges. He may have worked for a time in Memling's studio, the latter being then the most eminent and popular painter in the city. When the German artist died David succeeded to his position, finding, apparently, that fame, fortune and personal appreciation came easily. Wealthy merchants, the municipality and the Church at once became his patrons. He maintained a large studio all his life. By this means his works were multiplied. They become towards the end very hard to distinguish from those of his assistants. During a visit to the rising centre of Antwerp, which no doubt attracted him from a business point of view, he met that city's most important painter, Quentin Massys. But this promising encounter came too late in David's career to influence his work.

It is open to question, however, whether he would have been interested in Quentin's innovations. David was a typical traditionalist in colour and design, a deliberate and imperturbable worker. His art was the product of a long succession of great painters of the past, though unfortunately it was not a product in the mathematical sense of multiplication. It was merely a cross-section or summary of their labours. Friedländer once observed of him that he made up for his lack of originality by his refinement and careful workmanship.

A certain irresolution seems characteristic, not only of David himself, but also of the figures in his paintings. There is a

MANUEL DEUTSCH · ST ELIGIUS AS A GOLDSMITH
47⅞″ × 34¼″. Winterthur, Reinhart Collection

race of weariness about the extreme regularity and uniform type of their features. Whenever they show some slight sign of feeling it suggests a sense of loss, or of fading memories.

David's best pictures are preserved in Bruges, which has one of his chief works, a vaulted altarpiece, Rouen, Paris, where there is another masterpiece, the *Wedding at Cana*, Munich, London, and the United States. The *Adoration* at Munich has little relation to David's other work, being based on a composition by Hugo van der Goes.

His art as a miniaturist still awaits adequate study. In this field he was one of the most important and widely influential painters of his time. (Ill. p. 84.)

DAVID, JACQUES LOUIS

As an artist living in the age of transition between the Rococo and Modern periods, Jacques Louis David cannot be given the space, in an Encyclopaedia of Old Masters, which would be his by right in a history of painting in general.

He was born in Paris in 1748 at a time when he would normally have been a Rococo painter. In fact, it was only by chance that instead of attending Boucher's studio he was taught by Joseph Vien, later Director of the Academy, who had already abandoned the Rococo for the Italian Classic style. It was thus that David joined the counter-Rococo movement and became, himself, the most important revolutionary artist in the French painting of his day. He also became a political revolutionary, in so far as a born opportunist can do so. He painted Napoleon as devotedly as he had the murderous members of the Convention and Marie Antoinette in the tumbril.

His talent was prodigious. It is not in any individual picture, but in his work as a whole, that his character is found to lag behind his gifts. He came to be a painter of importance, but not one of the first rank. Through his pupils, Ghérin and Ingres, he exercised a decisive influence upon the succeeding generation. He died in exile at Brussels in 1825.

DOLCI · ST CECILIA
(Detail) 36⅜″ × 35⅞″. *Dresden, Gemäldegalerie*

DE LA HIRE

Laurent de la Hire (1606-1656), who was born in Paris, was one of the founders of the French Academy in 1648. He was a pupil of Lallemand. Influenced at first by Primaticcio, he later became one of the more distinguished of the immediate followers of Vouet. Unfortunately, many of his decorative paintings are lost and his reputation has suffered undeserved eclipse. One of his best works is the *St Peter healing by His Shadow* in the Louvre.

DESIDERIO

Little is known of Desiderio, also called 'Monsù'. He was born c. 1580, and was perhaps of French or Belgian nationality. He settled in Naples and painted curious and compelling architectural perspectives of classical and Gothic ruins crumbling and toppling as though convulsed by earthquakes. Desiderio is represented at Budapest and Vienna. *St Augustine and the Child*, a moonlit landscape of tottering ruins strangely like the work of John Martin, is in the National Gallery, London.

DESMARÉES

Georg Desmarées was a Swede by birth; he was born in Osterby in 1697. His first teacher was his uncle, Meytens, in Stockholm; his second, who had a greater influence on him, was Piazetta, a Venetian. He worked for two years in Venice and Rome before he went to Germany. After staying for short periods in Augsburg and Nuremberg he became Court Painter at Munich and remained there for forty-six years, with two intervals in Bonn, until his death in 1776. Art historians, therefore, number him among the German rather than the Swedish painters.

Desmarées was a typical Rococo portrait painter. The art of portraiture was less effete at that time than those of historical or *genre* painting, and Desmarées' pictures are still elegant, charming, gay where the pastel colours of the ladies are concerned, decorative in the *bel air* of the gentlemen. The greater part of his works are to be found in museums in South Germany and in the private collections of old families.

DESPORTES

Born at Champigneul in 1661 and dying in Paris in 1743, Alexandre François Desportes, was trained in the latter city, as a child, by an animal painter who taught him the rudiments of the art. Desportes very soon found himself obliged to continue his education on his own account. That he did so in close contact with nature is agreeably evident from his later pictures of animals and hunting scenes, flowers and fruit.

But he owed his appointment as Court Painter to his portraits. As a visiting star —the expression may be legitimately employed to indicate the Court Painters who were sent from time to time to perform at the Courts of other sovereigns— he spent two years, from 1695 to 1696, at the Court of the Polish King in Warsaw.

No particular significance is now attached to the pictures of Desportes. They are technically accomplished, historically quite interesting and pleasant to contemplate. His designs for Gobelins tapestries are more important. His portraits show the influence of Mignard, who is definitely superior to him in this field. Desportes is represented in nearly all the national galleries, the largest collection of his works being in the Louvre.

DEUTSCH

Niklaus Manuel Deutsch was born at Berne in 1484 and died there in 1530. He was of humble parentage, had scarcely any education and does not even appear to have received any tuition in painting yet he became the governor of a canton and a member of the Town Council of Berne. It is odd, therefore, that he should have been financially so hard pressed. He was continually resorting to glass-painting, decorative work, sketches and portraits to make a little money. On the other hand he bought a house in the most expensive part of the town. In his capacity of cantor governor he held conferences in which he showed equal ability as a speaker and as a clever conciliatory diplomat, was the author of rabid anti-clerical writings, and took part in the campaign in Lombardy.

It would be quite mistaken to conclude from these biographical details that Manuel Deutsch was merely a Sunday painter. He has a definite place as an artist of the early German Renaissance in the history of painting at the turn of the century. It is interesting, and slightly touching also, to see him striving in his painting to follow the new style of Dürer and Baldung. Some of the experimental pictures he painted at this time, such as his *Pyramus and Thisbe* at Basle, are quite daring. In many of his paintings (*The Beheading of St John the Baptist* and *The Judgment of Paris*, Basle), there is something of the dramatic character of the carnival plays that he himself composed.

Nearly all Deutsch's pictures, which are often painted on both sides of the panel are in Switzerland. Among them is a self-portrait painted towards the end of his life, a weary, resigned face. (Ill. p. 86.)

DEVIS

Athur Devis, one of the most delightful painters of conversation pieces, was born in Preston in 1711 and died at Brighton in 1787. He was a pupil of Pieter Tillemans, but was little influenced by him. Devis introduced a note of poetry into the conversation piece with his stylised figures, feeling for light and sense of repose. Among his numerous pictures may be mentioned *The Children of Peregrine, 2nd Duke of Ancaster* (Collection of Viscount Rothermere), *Mr and Mrs Van Hartels and their Son* (Collection of Viscount Bearsted) and *Lady in a Park* (National Gallery, London).

DOBSON

William Dobson (1610-1646) was born in London, and probably studied under Francis Clein, the Manager of the Mortlake Tapestry Works. He was later apprenticed to Robert Peake, a young painter and picture-dealer, and in about 1635 he became an assistant of Van Dyck. On Van Dyck's death Dobson was made Serjeant Painter to Charles I, who sat to him. He imitated Van Dyck's extravagance and lived for a while in state, but the Civil War had begun and Dobson was soon involved in financial difficulties and was imprisoned for debt. He died soon after his release.

Dobson was by far the most gifted of Van Dyck's followers, showing great originality in both composition and colour. One of his most remarkable portraits is *Sir Richard Fanshawe* in the Fanshawe Collection. Another striking work, *Endymion Porter*, is in the National Gallery, London.

DOLCI

Carlo Dolci (1616-1686) closes the tradi-

DOSSO DOSSI · CIRCE
(Detail) 70⅜″ × 69⅜″. *Rome, Villa Borghese*

tion which had lasted three centuries, of Florentine painting. Its decline is only too evident in his work, in comparison with which the generally admitted sentimental decadence of Guido Reni seems positively ferocious. But such was the tendency of the age. Dolci was highly esteemed in his day. When he went so far as to paint an *Apotheosis* based on the style of the great Angelico, it was widely believed that he had rivalled the older master. Since he matured early, beginning to paint at fourteen and living to be seventy, it will be readily understood how he came to produce so much.

The most notable of his technically accomplished but affectedly mawkish works are *Poesy* in the Corsini Palace at Rome, *St Cecilia* and *Ecce Homo* in the Dresden Gallery and *St Andrew in Prayer* in the Pitti Palace, Florence. A *Madonna and Child* is in the National Gallery, London.

In his portraits, fortunately, he had no opportunity to lay bare the sufferings of

G. DOU · REMBRANDT'S MOTHER
28⅜″ × 22¼″. Amsterdam, Rijksmuseum

of religious and mythological themes when he used oils. But in his frescoes, which are to be taken much more seriously, he surpassed both Albani and Reni. Examples are to be found in the Grottoferrata Abbey, in the church of Sant' Andrea della Valle, Rome, and in the San Gennaro Chapel at Naples Cathedral. Even here he remains, of course, a child of his time and its educational system. But he approaches his subjects with considerably more sincerity than might be expected. He avoids theatricality and is particularly adept in the distribution and filling of space along classical lines, with no trace whatever of Baroque extravagance. It was probably this very feature of his style that made him unpopular in his own day. Rubens, however, spoke of him as the only Italian of his generation whose name would endure.

Nevertheless, Domenichino was given plenty of work, the Carracci with their useful connections, helping him to obtain commissions. His best-known picture is *Diana Hunting* in the Villa Borghese, Rome.

his soul. These works are accordingly a marked improvement on the rest. A few are really admirable. (Ill. p. 87.)

DOMENICHINO

Domenico Zampieri (1581-1641) was nicknamed Domenichino by his fellow-citizens at Bologna, where he was a contemporary of Albani. He accompanied the latter to the studio of Calvart and then to the Academy of the Carracci. Thereafter the two men separated, Albani settling down as a popular and wealthy member of the community, while Domenichino wandered southwards through Italy for thirty years, visiting Rome and Naples. Disappointment and lack of recognition dogged his footsteps. In Naples, where he died, he was actually hated.

Domenichino, together with his coevals, Albani and Reni, is the chief representative of Bolognese Baroque. Naturally enough, he was an eclectic artist, resembling Albani very closely in the prettification

DOMENICO DI BARTOLO

Several frescoes by Domenico di Bartolo Ghezzi (c. 1400-c. 1446) are to be found in his native town of Asciano in Tuscany, including an important work in the Scala Hospital. His few easel-pictures are preserved at Siena, where he died, at Perugia and in the United States. He may be regarded as helping in a modest way to set the pace of the Renaissance. The new spirit appears in his narrative gift, his enjoyment of the life of his time and his realistic depiction of common types such as the imperious and the oppressed beggars and cripples, each in their individual aspect. Piero della Francesca was influenced by him.

DOMENICO VENEZIANO

(*See* VENEZIANO)

DOSSI

Giovanni di Niccolo Luteri (born c. 1480/
90) was probably called Dosso Dossi from
his birthplace, a village near Mantua.
He seems also to have used this appellation
as a Christian name. The association with
Mantua is proved by the frescoes he
painted for that Court. But he lived nearly
all his life at Ferrara, where he died in
1542.

Active in the High Renaissance period,
Dossi restored Ferrarese art, which had
become somewhat stereotyped, to the main
stream of contemporary style. According
to Vasari, he had studied under Costa.
But during his middle years he shook off
the latter's influence, not only outwardly,
but also inwardly. In 1518 he visited
Rome and Venice. His encounter with
Giorgione and Titian changed his earlier
style, which had been academically conventional and naturalistic, out of all
recognition. His colour became deep and
luminous, his drawing more loose and
flexible, his vision uncompromisingly
romantic. He was encouraged to take this
line by another great man whom he met at
this time, the poet Ariosto, a romantic
like himself. The two men remained
friends for life.

Dossi's many frescoes at Ferrara,
Mantua and Pesaro are today for the most
part destroyed or in poor preservation.
But they are not his best work. His oil
paintings, which came to maturity later,
appeal to ourselves for the same reason as
they influenced all the painters who
flourished at Ferrara after Dossi. He
followed Titian in imparting personality to
the human face and Andrea del Sarto in
his treatment of movement and line. His
landscapes are even more romantic than
Giorgione's, often thrillingly so, with their
glittering cliffs and seashores, as in his
Circe at Rome, or deep, dark forests, as in
his *Rest on the Flight* at Florence. Salvini
observes that 'his highly impressionable
imagination took fire, by preference, from
the marvellous'. It ranged from the wonders of nature to those of human life. A
picture in the Uffizi Gallery represents the
preparation of a love-charm. (Ill. p. 89.)

Dosso's brother **Battista** was concerned
in the production of certain frescoes at
Trento. He outlived Dosso by eleven years.

DOU

Gerard Dou, who was born in Leyden in
1613 and died in 1675, came by a round-
about way to practise his art. His father
sent him at the age of ten to learn the trade
of a glazier and subsequently took him
into his own workshop. The boy was
undoubtedly most unlucky, for it was a
serious matter in those days for a prosperous craftsman to change his son's trade
and start him all over again as an apprentice. In 1628 Dou's father passed the lad
on to a young painter of twenty-two
whom he considered quite a good work-
man. This young man's name was
Rembrandt.

But Rembrandt, in whose studio Dou
worked until 1631, had little influence in
determining his bent for small, detailed
and elaborately finished *genre* paintings.
Dou chose such subjects as the *Young
Mother* at The Hague, *Evening School* at
Amsterdam, the *Dropsical Patient* in Paris,
the *Old Woman at a Window* in Vienna
and the *Storeroom* in Berlin, as well as
female cooks and market-women and
doctors' visits. The *Poulterer's Shop* in the
National Gallery, London, is a typical
piece. Dou's picture of Rembrandt's
mother, only about eight inches square, is
preserved in a glass case at Berlin.

DUCCIO

Duccio di Buoninsegna was born in
Siena in 1260. He was invited to paint an
altarpiece for Sta Maria Novella, Florence
(the *Rucellai Madonna*), in 1285, after the
establishment of peace between Siena and
Florence. He died in Siena in 1339.

The art of Duccio reflects the conflict
between the Byzantine tradition and the
new narrative tendency in Italian painting.
His work combines the formal elements
of the Byzantine mosaics with a new
gentle, exquisite sense of colour and a

vivid response to the Franciscan Gothic spirit of the age. It was due to Duccio's great example that the Sienese clung to the formal elements of Byzantine technique for some time after they had been abandoned by the Florentines under Giotto's influence.

Duccio's first famous work, the *Rucellai Madonna*, was formerly attributed to Cimabue, though modern critics ascribe it unanimously to Duccio. The work is characterised by a free calligraphic line which is new in painting. The National Gallery triptych reveals the first stage in the humanisation of the Madonna in Italian painting. The Virgin and Child in the centre panel are no longer rigid frontal images; they are concerned with one another: the child plays with the mother's veil and the mother looks down at him. Duccio's masterpiece is the altarpiece painted for the Cathedral of Siena and now in the Opera del Duomo, Siena. The work was commissioned in 1308. It shows a *Maestà* (Madonna and Child enthroned, surrounded by saints and angels) and on the back are twenty-seven scenes from the life of Christ. In these narrative panels there is little left of Byzantine iconolatry; they form the prototype for the Gothic narrative art of the whole Sienese school and reveal an astonishing combination of design and dramatic power.

DUGHET

Gaspard Dughet, called Poussin (1615-1675), was born in Rome of French parentage. He was the brother-in-law of Nicolas Poussin, whose name he assumed. Gaspard was a landscape painter, strongly influenced by Nicolas and also by Salvator Rosa, whom he resembled in his preference for the wilder and more dramatic elements of nature. There has been a tendency until quite recently to underrate Gaspard. He derived his fine sense of form from Poussin, but he developed an original style which is seen at its best in the Palazzo Colonna frescoes and the landscapes in the National Gallery, London, and at Holkham. He was of importance in the development of landscape painting, both in France and England. He had a rare gift of straightforward naturalism which makes him the true precursor of the Barbizon School.

DÜRER · THE ADORATION OF THE KINGS
40" × 45⅝". Florence, Uffizi

UJARDIN

orn in Amsterdam in 1622, Karel
ujardin died at Venice in 1678 during a
urney to Italy, which he certainly did
ot undertake for artistic or business
asons, but probably on account of dis-
tisfaction with his marriage. Houbraken
ports that he had been forced into it
d was not happy with his wife.

He had already visited Italy in his youth.
is strong reds, yellows and blues come
om that source, as well as the light that
athes his figures. He combined these
ements very successfully with what he
d learnt from Nicolas Berchem. His
ndscapes, with their animals, herdsmen
d travellers, especially those, like the
ick Goat at Munich and the *Stirrup Cup*
: Amsterdam, which tell a story in *genre*
yle, with conspicuous figures in the
reground, are fine paintings, unmistak-
ly his own. Their typical features are the
owerful but fastidiously lyrical colouring,
ending without fussiness from one pass-
;e into another, and the rustic, sunlit
:enes depicted under transparent skies.
ujardin also composed some good but,
ddly enough, somewhat mannered por-
aits, of which examples are to be seen
London at the National Gallery, the
allace Collection and the Dulwich
allery.

UMOUSTIER

orn, apparently, in Paris in 1560, and
ying there in 1603, Etienne Dumoustier,
ith his nephew, **Daniel,** is the best-known
the many painters named Dumoustier.
e was Court Portrait Painter to four
ngs and was given a warm welcome at
e Imperial Court in Vienna when he
d his brother, **Pierre** arrived there on
ave of absence from their posts.

His work has not yet been thoroughly
vestigated. Very few pictures are cer-
inly known to be his. Some idea of his
yle can be obtained by reference to
rançois Clouet, though it must also be
orne in mind that the Dumoustiers were
chiefly draughtsmen and etchers.

DÜRER · PORTRAIT OF A YOUNG MAN
11¼″ × 8⅜″. Munich, Alte Pinakothek

Etienne was no great colourist. His
painting is far from ostentatious. But it is
extremely sincere and neat.

DÜRER

The great German painter, engraver,
etcher and draughtsman was born at
Nuremberg in 1471, the third of eighteen
children of a goldsmith. Albrecht Dürer
was taught his father's craft, but his own
predilection was for painting, and at the
age of fifteen he was apprenticed to
Michael Wohlgemut. From 1490 to 1494,
after completing this apprenticeship, Dürer
travelled in Germany, though no exact
details of his wanderings are known. He
was back in Nuremberg in 1494, when he
married Agnes Frey. We learn from his
correspondence that he was in Venice for
some months in 1494-1495 and that he
returned there in 1505, possibly to assist
with the decoration of the German Merchants' Hall of Exchange. Up to that time

Dürer's work had been essentially Gothic in character and full of a northern intensity; his contact with Italian artists broadened his vision and gave him new freedom of technique without working any real change in the moral and intellectual earnestness of his outlook. Between 1512 and 1519 he worked under the patronage of Maximilian I and in 1520, after the Emperor's death, he visited the Netherlands. He spent the last seven years of his life uneventfully at Nuremberg, where he died in 1528.

Dürer is the foremost artist of the German School. His work springs from a union of science and fantasy such as is also to be found in Leonardo's art. In his early twenties he was already launched upon the copperplate and wood engrav-

ings in which he has no superior. It w particularly in his wood engravings th Dürer was vital and unique, in his gran eur of conception, fertility of inventio and skill in execution. His woodcuts f the Apocalypse, issued in 1498, proclai the artist's genius in this medium, but the are surpassed by the remarkable sets f the *Life of the Virgin*, the *Great Passi* and the *Little Passion*, all issued in 151 but executed earlier. Here the torture fancy of the early group is replaced b spaciousness, serenity and an even great certainty of accomplishment. The heig of his achievement is represented by th grand apocalyptic engravings of 151 1514 the famous *Melancolia, The Knigh Death and the Devil, Adam and Eve* an *The Prodigal Son.*

Dürer lifted the art of engravir on metal and wood to a new plan As a painter, it was with h remarkable topographical wate colours that he broke fresh groun The well-known watercolour Innsbrück, now in the Albertin is the first portrait of a town in th history of painting, and it al shows a delicate perception light which no one before Dür had attempted to render with suc precision. Dürer's oils are unusu and subtle in colour, but the preserve the detailed craftsma ship of his engravings and nev achieve the glow and sereni which Dürer had admired Venice in the work of the agein Giovanni Bellini. His most in portant pictures include T Madonna with the Siskin (1506 Portrait of a Woman (1506), Po trait of a Man (1507), Hieronym Holzschuher (1526) (all at Berlin Portrait of his Father (149 (National Gallery, London), Ada and Eve (Madrid), Self-portra (1500), the Paumgartner Alta piece (1498), Jakob Fugger (1520 The Four Apostles (1526) (all Munich), and The Virgin an Child (1503) (Vienna).

Dürer was the author of thre

DÜRER · PORTRAIT OF HIERONYMUS
HOLZSCHUHER · 19¼″ × 14⅜″. *Berlin, Staatl. Museen*

orks on geometry and perspective, anat-
my, and fortification.

USART

ornelis Dusart of Haarlem (1660-1704)
as the chief pupil and closest friend of
driaen van Ostade. He painted similar
:enes of peasants outside their cottages,
atherings for music or for drinking,
rd-parties and quarrels. His colour is
ore lively than Ostade's, but the attitudes
his figures are often awkward and
inatural. Dusart, however, has a more
teresting claim on our attention. On
stade's death he inherited his pictures,
me of which had been left unfinished.
usart completed and signed them. It is
erefore no wonder that they contain a
umber of excellent passages.

UYSTER

illem Cornelisz Duyster (1598/9-1635)
elonged to the group of young painters
Amsterdam which included Codde,
mon Kick and Dirk Hals, the first artists
specialise in the rendering of purely
ale parties of smart, dashing officers. In
uyster's pictures the militia ensigns, in
eir full-skirted, cream-coloured uniforms,
ashed silken sleeves and exuberantly
idulating headgear, lounge somewhat less
solently in their chairs than they do in
ick's versions. Their behaviour appears
ss noisy than that represented by Dirk
als. They sit at tables puffing their pipes
playing tric-trac, while individuals,
nspicuous in the foreground, pose for
e 'camera', staring out of the canvas, as
the case of The Hague *Officer*, with the
oomy eyes of footpads. These single
ures are usually placed in front of others,
ıly vaguely discernible, in the back-
ound. They seem to be positively
vertising the brilliant handling of paint
d the rich hues of their clothing. Many
Duyster's pictures—for example, the
imp at Munich—were long supposed
be by the great Terborch. *Soldiers
arrelling* and *Players at Tric-Trac* are in
e National Gallery, London.

DYCK

Born at Antwerp in 1599 and dying in
London in 1641, Anthony van Dyck came
from a prosperous home. He lost his
mother at an early age and, being a seventh
child, was 'spoilt' as a family favourite.
He matured quickly and was generally
regarded, for his exceptional intelligence,
as a prodigy. He must have been extremely
handsome at that age. Later self-portraits
prove that he was quite conscious of the
fact. Their narcissistic expression is unmistakable. The features are aristocratic-
ally pale as alabaster, the eyes sentimental,
the mouth sensual, the smile that of a Don
Juan. Such an appearance, together with
his rapid professional success and the
women who swarmed round him, provided material for the legend of a life of
orgy and passion. But there is probably no
foundation for this view. In Van Dyck's
short career he produced many hundreds
of pictures. Anyone who has worked to
that extent knows that twenty-four hours
are never enough for the day's toil.

He appears in the records of the
Antwerp Guild of St Luke as an apprentice to Hendrik van Balens as early as
1610, at the age of only eleven. A portrait
of an unknown man has survived which
bears Van Dyck's monogram, together
with the date 1613 and the note '*aetatis* 14'.
Accordingly, he was not only mixing
colours and cleaning brushes at that time,
but actually painting. The boy was really a
prodigy. At sixteen he set up on his own
account. The contemporary writer Bellori
reports that Van Dyck was then studying
under Rubens. But this statement is
refuted by Van Puyvelde in his authoritative work on the artist.

In 1620 Van Dyck was invited to
London by the Earl of Arundel. It was
the first step in his independent career,
inspiring in him that inordinate ambition
which later became notorious. But he
failed to achieve immediate success. Six
months later his English competitors forced
him to leave the country. He then resolved
to go to Italy. He began by working in
Genoa, where he studied Rubens and
Titian. He was also deeply impressed by

the excess of sentiment in the paintings of Guido Reni. Van Dyck's first important religious paintings and portraits date from this period. On his return to Antwerp in 1627 he continued to produce portraits, but also embarked upon a series of magnificent biblical scenes. In 1632 his triumph was assured by another invitation to London, this time to the Court of Charles I, who settled an annual pension of £200 on him, presented him with two houses and gave him a knighthood. The King's dazzling magnanimity endowed the English, to their amazement, with a truly royal painter who had the manners of a nobleman. The pictures he produced during the next two years are both technically brilliant and show

striking psychological insight. Their over whelming impact resembles that of a grea personality on the stage. The high spirits o the artist as he worked, his intoxicatio with his own skill and delight in exercisin it are most evident.

In 1634 he paid what was intended to b a short visit to the Continent in order t attend to certain financial business. Bu the honours there conferred upon him the ceremonies with which he was wel comed and the commissions he receive prolonged his residence abroad for a yea Landing for the third time in England i January 1635, he remained in that countr for the next five years.

It was a period of intense 'commercia activity. Contracts poured in upon hin He would often only sketch a portrai though with due care, or even simply th face and hands, either leaving the finishin touches to his assistants or rapidly dashin them in himself. During these 'Englisl years there was really nothing left of th original Van Dyck, the student of Ruben and admirer of Titian and Giorgione, bu a virtuoso, who could have painted wit his eyes shut. In reality, as an artist, h was going downhill.

In 1639 he married a lady of the Cour whose portrait he is quite groundlessl supposed to have painted in his *Cel Player*, now at Munich. A year later th threat of civil war, in which Charle eventually lost his throne and was execute obliged Van Dyck to leave England. A Antwerp where Rubens had just died, th idea of succeeding to that artist's positio must have occurred to him. He wa received with much ceremony. But th grandiose plans which he submitted to th Regent and subsequently to the King c France were not accepted. He sudden found himself practically ignored, growin all the more restless and agitated, person ally, in consequence. It is also probabl that he was already seriously sufferin from venereal disease at this time. I November 1641 he returned, with onl five servants, to rejoin his wife in Londo where he died, in spite of all the King doctors could do, three weeks later. He w buried in Old St Paul's Cathedral.

VAN DYCK · KING CHARLES I
90¾″ × 82¾″. Paris, Louvre

All the great galleries possess works by Van Dyck. His splendid early paintings include the series of apostles' heads and studies for them, mainly in Bavarian galleries, the self-portraits at Munich and Vienna and the *Silenus* at Dresden. Just before his first visit to London he painted the brilliant portrait of Cornelius van der Geest, now in the National Gallery, London.

To his second period, of works produced in Italy and after his visit to that country, belong such fine pictures as the two versions of the *Mocking of Christ* at Berlin and Madrid, the two *Sebastians* at Munich and in the Cook collection formerly at Richmond now in the United States, the portraits of the Marchese Spinola at Berlin and New York, that of Cardinal Bentivoglio in the Pitti Palace, Florence, of Maria von Wassis at Vienna, of 'Giustiniani' at Berlin, the *Rest on the Flight* at Munich and many other portraits, especially the splendid *Charles I on Horseback* in the National Gallery, London. The later *Rest on the Flight*, now at the Hermitage Museum in

VAN DYCK · THE REST ON THE FLIGHT
53¾″ × 82¾″. Munich, Alte Pinakothek

Leningrad, and the Antwerp *Lamentation* are also outstanding works.

E

EARL

Ralph Earl (1751-1801) was born in Worcester County, Massachusetts. As early as 1775 he painted a *View of the Town of Concord*, believed to be the first historical picture by an American painter. The canvas has the straightforward simplicity of a primitive painting and Earl had indeed started his career as an itinerant artist, like so many of the American primitive painters. But in 1778 Earl sailed for England and visited Benjamin West, and at least had his advice if he did not study under him. He returned to America in 1785. His work had gained academic status, but still retained, especially in his portraits, a strong, simple sense of design and colour.

ECLECTICISM

The word comes from the Greek *eklegein*, to pick out, choose or gather, and is applied to the manner of those artists who compose their works from chosen elements in the style of other artists and epochs, striving to combine them in a manner free from excess. Eclecticism is a phenomenon which frequently occurs in both the early and declining stages of a culture. Early Christian artists, for instance, conscious of the ancient cultures which had preceded them, worked in an eclectic-manner until a peculiarly Christian style was gradually evolved. A typical example of eclecticism as an expression of the final stages of a civilisation occurs at the end of the Italian Renaissance in the mid-sixteenth century. The Italian *Eclectice* were led by the brothers Carracci (q.v.) at Bologna, who founded the first European school of art in opposition to the mannerism apparent in Michelangelo's late works and generally prevalent in sixteenth-century painting. The Carracci tried to combine the drawings of Raphael, the chiaroscuro of Correggio, the nobility of Michelangelo with all the outstanding features of the greatest Renaissance masters to produc a final perfection in painting. Among th followers of the Carraci were Guido Ren Domenichino and Sassoferrato. The resu of their eclecticism was often a set, lifeles style which sometimes degenerated int sentimentality or empty rhetoric.

EECKHOUT

Gerbrand van den Eeckhout was bor in Amsterdam in 1621 and died there i 1674. He studied under Rembrandt at very early age and became the latter favourite pupil. He began his independer career in 1640. He painted entirely in th style of his idolised master and immed ately received many commissions f portraits from wealthy patricians an corporations. Rembrandt being at that tin highly esteemed in Amsterdam. Eeckhout early portraits and pictures on biblic subjects bear an astonishingly close r semblance to Rembrandt's work. The can be no doubt that even today mar paintings regarded as inferior but undi puted productions by Rembrandt are i reality by Eeckhout.

Like all Rembrandt's other pupil Eeckhout gradually began to go his ow way, with disastrous results. He continu ally increased the size of his design stressed his contrasts and weakened h gestures, while his colour grew steadi greyer. He rarely succeeded at a later tin in producing works of such significar colour as he had achieved under Ren brandt's guidance. He painted interio which sometimes show the influence Terborch, religious and historical subjec and portraits. His *Wine Contract* is in th National Gallery, London.

EHRENSTAHL

David Klocker was a German painte born in Hamburg in 1629. He studied i Amsterdam, went to Sweden in 1652 an was shortly afterwards knighted Ehrenstahl. He remained in Stockholm until his death in 1698, occasionally visiting Germany, Paris and London. Called the 'father of Swedish painting', Ehrenstahl was the founder of a new tradition in Swedish painting, training young Swedish artists in his studio. He became Court Painter to Charles XI and was the principal portraitist of the Swedish aristocracy, but he also painted Swedish landscape for the first time. The decorative swags and putti he was fond of introducing into his pictures were copied by Burchard Precht, a cabinet-maker who designed furniture for the Royal Palace. Ehrenstahl's work can be seen at its best in the National Museum, Stockholm.

ELSHEIMER

Adam Elsheimer was born at Frankfurt in 1578 and died in Rome in 1610. After studying under the unimportant painter Uffenbach he moved south. He stayed some time in Munich, then crossed the Brenner Pass into Italy, stopping for a while at Venice, where he found temporary employment in the studio of Johann Rottenhammer. In 1600 he reached his ultimate destination, Rome. He seems to have soon settled down in the city, making friends among the German and Dutch colonies. He was intimate with Paul Brill, the eminent landscape painter, and made the acquaintance of Rubens during the latter's stay in Rome in 1601. Elsheimer's intellectual development was by then complete. He had become a master. It is interesting to find that his meeting with Rubens had some effect on the latter's style, though none on Elsheimer's own. His Netherlandish tendencies, further

A. ELSHEIMER · JOHN THE BAPTIST PREACHING
16″ × 22″. Munich, Alte Pinakothek

emphasised under Brill's influence, were already evident when he left Frankfurt, as can be seen from his fine *John the Baptist Preaching* at Munich. The study of Caravaggio had opened his eyes to the problems of light and naturalism, while at the same time increasing his distaste for anything approaching pathos. He much preferred the discreet satirical detail. Paradoxically enough, melancholy men—and Elsheimer died a victim to melancholia—often show this trait. It was entirely by his own efforts that he achieved his highly characteristic masterpieces, depicting scenes at night.

They are small easel-pictures or etchings on the usual themes of the time. Mary, Joseph and the Child are represented encamped at the edge of a distant forest, where shepherds have lit a fire. Or else shadowy figures flee through the night in picturesque, ghostly confusion, while Troy burns behind them, as in a work at the Munich Pinakothek. One is reminded of Albrecht Altdorfer's night-piece in the Uffizi Gallery and recognises the old problem of German painters of 100 years before, now again, after long neglect, under examination.

Important works by Elsheimer are to

C. ENGELBRECHTSEN · THE CROWNING WITH THORNS
15¼″ × 16¼″. Berlin, Staatl. Museen

painter's own somewhat extrava
gant notions of Renaissance splen
dour. How he came to develo
this style is uncertain. It is alread
fully formed in his survivin,
works.

They deal exclusively wit
religious subjects, are of onl
moderate size and extremel
colourful. The outlines are ofte
difficult to follow. But their com
plexity has a charm unusual a
this period.

His paintings are rarely me
with. Two rather large altarpiece
of the Crucifixion are at Leyde
and Utrecht. Single panels are t
be found at Aachen, Amsterdam
Antwerp, Berlin, Dresden, Ghent
Vienna and some private collec
tions in France and England.

be seen in Munich, Berlin, Dresden,
Frankfurt, Florence and London.

Shortly before his death the Dutch
painter Pieter Lastman arrived in Rome,
met Elsheimer and was deeply impressed
by his pictures. This event had an important result. On Elsheimer's death
Lastman took his paintings to Amsterdam,
where later on he taught Rembrandt.

ENGELBRECHTSEN

Cornelis Engelbrechtsen (also spelt
Engelbrechtsz) was born in 1468 in
Leyden and died there in 1553. Nothing
is known of his life except the meagre
information provided by Mander, to the
effect that he was a respected citizen and
maintained a studio where the most
important pupil was Lucas van Leyden.
Mander also states that Engelbrechtsen
was the unconscious originator of the so-
called 'Leyden Style'. It consists, briefly
summarised, so far as Engelbrechtsen is
concerned, merely in an obscure conjunction of Gothic mentality with the

ERRI

The brothers, **Agnolo** and **Bar
tolomeo** degli Erri were active a
Modena after 1450. Until recently it wa
supposed that their most outstanding work
produced in common, was the *Coronatio*
triptych at Modena. But this painting i
now ascribed to Agnolo alone. Its composi
tion, surprisingly enough, is wholly Gothic
The frame is also of grotesque Gothi
design. But as soon as the picture i
closely examined, the painter is found t
have belonged entirely to his period. Th
style of both brothers recalls that of Cossa
Their tonal values even resemble those o
Piero della Francesca, whose works the
probably saw in the neighbouring city o
Ferrara.

A fine Madonna by Agnolo is preserve
at Padua and another by Bartolomeo a
Strasbourg. An important *St Vincent* b
Bartolomeo was recently discovered in th
Seminary at Modena.

ESTENSE

Baldassare Estense was the natural sor
of Niccolo d'Este III, Duke of Ferrara
He was born at Reggio in the province o

Emilia towards the end of the fifteenth century. The date of his birth is not known and the man himself is something of a mystery. As late as the nineteenth century one of his works disappeared. This loss would not have been so serious if the picture had not been the only one duly authenticated. It represented the young poet Strozzi and was signed in full: 'Baldassares Estensis Nob. pix. anor. 36 1499.'

It is clear that he painted from choice, not from necessity, for his membership of the princely House of Este was always acknowledged. He studied in Milan, where his presence at the Court is mentioned as early as 1461. He stood high in the favour of the Sforza family, who were most reluctant to allow him to return to Ferrara. In the eighties and nineties of the century he occupied the remunerative post of commander of a fortress at Reggio. He died at Ferrara in 1504.

The delicate task is now being undertaken of trying to identify pictures by Baldassare on the sole evidence of records, descriptions and historical data. Works

which may be his are constantly turning up. Documents refer to over fifty portraits and frescoes by him. The *Death of the Virgin*, in the private collection of Prince Massari, was believed by Adolfo Venturi to be an altarpiece mentioned in contemporary papers. Two extremely interesting paintings are preserved in the Alte Pinakothek at Munich. One of them is a most remarkably composed portrait of an aristocratic family, restrained in colour and conveying an impression of arrogant severity. The other, representing a boy, is excessively intellectual in style, almost in monochrome. The sitter's attributes prove it to have been a portrait offered by the young Hungarian Prince Corvinus to the Sforza family during his courtship of some feminine member of the dynasty. Attempts are being made to reconstitute Baldassare's work on the strength of these and a few other paintings.

After the highly revealing exhibition of Ferrarese painting held in 1933, R. Longhi's meticulous researches, positively resembling those of a professional detective, enabled him to assemble an interesting group of pictures possibly by Baldassare.

EVERDINGEN

Allaert van Everdingen was born in Alkmaar in 1621 and died in Amsterdam in 1675. He studied under Roelant Savery and Pieter de Molijn. The influence of the former, who was an animal painter, can only be traced in Allaert's drawings, while the attractive landscapes of Pieter de Molijn had no chance to make an impression on him. For at nineteen Everdingen had been enchanted by a visit to Scandinavia, with its deeply fissured fjords and romantic mountain gorges clothed in dark oak forests, its storm-tossed pines and the forms of deer and elk looming up through dissolving mists on the rocky heights.

Thenceforward he painted surging breakers and the wooded ravines of the north, just as he had seen them, with elks on the rocks above. Examples of such pictures are to be seen at Brunswick. They were the first to introduce this

BALDASSARE ESTENSE · FAMILY GROUP
44¾″ × 36″. *Munich, Alte Pinakothek*

subject into Dutch painting, influencing, among others, the great Jacob Ruysdael. Everdingen's work is especially well represented in Brunswick, Dresden, Amsterdam and Berlin, where his *Castle on a River* is in purely nineteenth-century romantic style, as well as in Munich, Paris and Vienna.

Allaert's brother **Cesar** (1617/21-1678) resided permanently in Alkmaar, only visiting Haarlem, The Hague and Amsterdam occasionally. His work, in complete contrast with Allaert's, consists of portraits and mythological scenes, very smoothly realised. The supple figures are very effectively lit and deeply coloured, their movement being depicted in Mannerist style. They throng the foreground of his large-scale canvases. Very well painted, but somewhat over-emphatic, these pictures at the first glance suggest a Fontainebleau Jordaens. The best of them are the *Bacchus with Two Nymphs* in Berlin, *Diogenes in Search of a Man* at The Hague and the portraits at Alkmaar, Amsterdam and Brunswick. There is a particularly charming portrait of a girl in the latter city.

EXPERTISE

This word is the technical name given to the data provided by an expert on any particular painting. The document constitutes a kind of official certificate of good standing for the picture and serves it, if the expert has a good reputation, in somewhat the same capacity as an international passport serves a traveller.

A properly qualified expert will always be objective and brief in his statements. He will rarely permit himself any aesthetic judgment and will never refer to market prices. The *expertise* must explain exactly what the picture looks like, what its period is, whether it is an original, who painted it, whether it is signed and if so whether the signature is old and whether it is genuine, in the artist's own hand, and finally, whether the work has been studied in the original or only from a photograph.

A model *expertise*, handwritten on the back of a photograph of the picture, would for example read: 'The painting illustrated on the back hereof is in oils, transferred to canvas from wood. It measures $51\frac{1}{4}$ ins. in height by $32\frac{1}{4}$ ins. in width. A strip 1 in. wide has been fastened to each of the sides. I have studied the picture in the original. I consider it an important work bearing the genuine signature of Lucas Cranach the Elder and executed about 1518. It is the earliest representation known to me of the subject of *Venus and Amor* painted by Cranach after that of 1509 now in Leningrad. Brunswick, 29 June 1936. (Signed). Prof. Dr Eduard Flechsig.'

The *expertise* is also made use of at sales, in inheritance valuations and in insurance assessments.

EYCK

With the brothers Van Eyck, Flemish painting began its career with, so to speak, a flourish of trumpets. It at once reached the heights. This fact alone suffices to give them—primarily **Jan**—their exceptional rank, historically speaking, as artists. Such is also the reason why research has ever since been preoccupied

J. VAN EYCK · DETAIL FROM THE MADONNA AND THE CHANCELLOR ROLIN

with the elucidation of their activities. **Hubert** in particular remains to this day a very shadowy figure. Study of the brothers is, of course, by no means confined to purely professional research. For Jan's pictures are among the rarest and most precious in the world.

There is no documentary evidence, incidentally, of blood relationship between the two men. The name Eyck, which Jan used in signing several of his paintings, refers to a place called Maaseyck, where one of his daughters lived as a nun. But he is also mentioned as 'the painter Van Tricht', a reference which would connect him with the adjacent town of Maastricht. This question, however, is of little importance compared with those relating to Hubert. It is remarkable, for example, that no mention is made during the fifteenth and sixteenth centuries of a presumably famous artist named Hubert van Eyck though Jan is

J. VAN EYCK · THE MADONNA AND THE CHANCELLOR
ROLIN · 26⅜″ × 24⅜″. *Paris, Louvre*

often referred to. Furthermore, at the beginning of the last century, when overpainting was removed from the Ghent altarpiece, an inscription in Jan's hand was revealed which may be approximately rendered: 'The painter Hubert van Eyck, greater than all before him, began the difficult work which Jan, the second in the art, completed.'

The statement implies that it was Hubert who was really the genius. But we are too well acquainted with Jan's works to accept such a view. At the time of his brother's death fraternal affection may have induced Jan to believe Hubert the better artist. But Jan's development proves the contrary. Hubert was undoubtedly a great man in his own right. Puyvelde writes that he was a genius who unfortunately remained obscure. But his work was simply that of a pioneer. In addition to parts of the Ghent altarpiece, especially the middle section, he may be credited with some of the miniatures in

the so-called Turin Book of Hours, the New York *Crucifixion* and *Resurrection*, the *Women at the Tomb* in the Beuningen Collection, Vierhouten and the Berlin *Crucified Christ*. These are all paintings of importance. Hubert died at Ghent in 1426.

Jan was probably born 1380/90, and his name is recorded for the first time in 1422, when as Court Painter to John the Pitiless, Bishop of Lüttich, whose palace he decorated with pictures now lost. In 1425 Jan was appointed Court Painter and Gentleman of the Bedchamber to Philip, Duke of Burgundy. He was of course in no sense the latter's valet, but his trusted and intimate friend, ranking among the highest of the Court officials. He was often in England, Spain and Portugal on private business for Philip. He could come and go as he pleased at Court. He ate at the Duke's table and the Duke himself visited him. Philip also stood godfather to one of Jan's children and allowed him a staff of highly efficient servants, who wore Court livery.

J. VAN EYCK · JAN ARNOLFINI AND HIS WIFE
33″ × 22½″. London, National Gallery

Jan was on familiar terms with philosophers and scientists, consorted with kings and Moorish caliphs, and could almost be described as playing the *Rosenkavalier* to the Duke's future wife. He lived the life of a nobleman and painted like one.

His pictures fascinate the spectator, in the first place, by their air of quiet self-possession and composure. In order to appreciate the magnitude of his achievement, it is necessary to remember that before his time painters had great difficulty in communicating their ideas, tormented as they were by the problems of rendering movement, perspective, natural appearances, colour and detail. In Jan van Eyck's work these problems seem no longer to exist. The handling shows no evidence of strain. To take a single instance, one never dreams of referring to his 'imitations' of nature. The faces of his personages reflect their moods with extreme sensitivity. His perspectives are indicated with the ease of a modern artist. Recession in depth from the cosy warmth of the foreground interiors is rendered with a charm, and to an extent, which could have been contrived by no other painter of the day, even in Italy. Each foreground detail, whether chandelier, carpet, convex window or brocade, sparkles like a small gem. Yet none detaches itself from the picture as a whole, which remains as harmonious as an individual melody. His colour is of unprecedented splendour. Yet its dazzling beauty of tone is at once modified when the eye is led beyond such passages to the face, for example, of the Infant Christ or that of the Chancellor Rolin in the painting of the Madonna executed for that formidable personage, who is represented kneeling expectantly, gazing with half-closed eyes, in most reluctant humility, at the Child. The Virgin holds the Boy in her outstretched arms, with the absent expression of one lost in a mystic dream. But the Child, as He raises His hand to bless the Chancellor, directs upon him a weary and suffering look, like that of an old man. The three figures are surrounded on all sides with every conceivable effect of brilliant illumination, while all the loveliness of earth is manifest beyond the open door.

This picture is preserved in the Louvre. Equally famous are the *Canon van der Paele Madonna* at Bruges and the portrait of Arnolfini and his wife in London. The Ghent altarpiece is in the church of St Bavo in that city. In 1934 the lower left wing, representing aristocratic riders, was stolen, and has never been recovered.

Further masterpieces by Jan van Eyck include the small, early *Madonna of the*

Nave, in Berlin, the Dresden *Madonna with Saints*, the Melbourne *Ince Hall Madonna*, the *Lucca Madonna* at Frankfurt, the *Annunciation* at Washington and the magnificent portraits of Arnolfini (Berlin), Jan de Leeuw (Vienna), a goldsmith (Hermannstadt), a turbaned man (London) and Jan's wife, Margarethe, at Bruges, where the artist died in 1441.

Some of his paintings bear the inscription ALS IK KAN, written in his own hand. These words are said to refer to a Flemish proverb, *As I can, but not as I would.*

F

FABER

Conrad Faber of Frankfurt (1500-1553), whose name is also recorded as Conrad von Creuznach, was eventually recognised as the author of the so-called Holzhausen portraits. He had previously only been known as a mediocre draughtsman and military engineer. But he is now proved to have been an excellent portraitist. His works are nearly all half-lengths, with the sitter posed against landscapes usually of a routine character, but quite attractive. The artist did not pay much attention to the mood or general mentality of his subjects, confining himself to external impressions. He never depicts scoundrels, magnates or groundlings, but deals only with amiable characters in good society. Few of his pictures are known. But, as it happens, he is represented in Dublin and in the Metropolitan Museum of New York.

FABRIANO

Gentile da Fabriano was probably born (1370/75), as his name indicates, at Fabriano. He died in Rome in 1427. Nothing is known of him until 1408, when he arrived in Venice. A century later Sansovino saw a great fresco by him in the Doges' Palace, representing a sea-battle, as well as two altarpieces in Venetian churches. But after another century every trace of his work in Venice had disappeared. The Doges' Hall had been burned down and the altarpieces had vanished.

Fabriano was already celebrated during his Venetian period. He drew a pension and had the right to wear patrician dress. It is not clear how he came to lose this position. In 1414 he was at the Court of Brescia, where he met the Pope and was invited to go as Court Painter to Rome. But at this time the Pope had his hands full with unrest in the city and Fabriano, instead of complying with this invitation, travelled in 1420 to the brilliant and alluring centre of Florence. There he executed the works which have survived to testify to his eminence. They include the *Adoration* he painted for Strozzi, the fabulously wealthy rival of the Medici, which is now in the Uffizi Gallery, and the triptych of the Guaratesi family, one part of which is in that Gallery and another in London. In 1425 he produced a fresco, the *Madonna with Notaries*, famous in its day but now destroyed, for Siena, and also decorated Orvieto Cathedral with another fresco of the Madonna. Then, at last, he turned south to Rome, where in six months he painted a series of frescoes dealing with St John, a Madonna and a portrait of the Pope. All these works have now been destroyed. The Pope obtained nothing more from Fabriano, for the artist died within the year.

Kreplin called him a 'meteor that came and went, a brilliant and isolated figure in the Italian art of his day'. This remark calls attention to the really most extra-ordinary circumstance that Fabriano, who was born a whole generation before Masaccio and lived at the same time as Starnina, Lorenzo Monaco and even Agnolo Gaddi, affords a brief glimpse, as by a flash of lightning, of the full glory of the future Renaissance. Immediately after-wards the curtain descended again. The vision was forgotten. The painful efforts to transcend the Gothic style were re-newed.

The work in which Fabriano heralds the Renaissance stands in astonishing con-trast with other paintings of his day. These suggest, in their 'Adorations', the biblical phrase, 'Now it happened in those days that a command went forth'. But in Fabriano's picture of this subject the words we mentally hear might be: 'Once upon a time a wonderfully handsome Prince was riding to the city with knights

and squires, horses and hounds, falcon and dromedaries, across hilly country among groves of olives. The horses wer gorgeously caparisoned, advancing in rank of four, with the Prince in his golden rob riding a white palfrey in the midst of them But the long procession did not find wha it was looking for in the city. So it travelle on from castle to castle till at last it halted The knights and pages dismounted i joyful excitement, for the Prince, whos gilt spurs a squire hastened to remove, ha come to his destination. It was not a palace, but a ruin. He met no princess, bu only a serving-wench with a new-bor Boy.'

An equally fine painting, though not i the same Renaissance style, is the Londo *Virgin of the Triptych*, while the Orviet fresco of the Madonna is a notably bol work. This picture is in very poor con dition. But one feature of it is astonishingl

GENTILE DA FABRIANO · THE ADORATION OF THE KINGS · *120" × 112¾". Florence, Uffizi*

vident: the infant Christ is represented with an unprecedented xpression of hearty laughter, directed straight at the observer.

Fabriano's earlier works, however, are all in the Late Gothic style. The *predelle* (q.v.) of the Milan *Coronation* are composed wholly in the spirit of Starnina. The feeling conveyed is one of melancholy and self-torment, the setting extremely simple. The Berlin *Virgin* still looks very like a production by the Gothic artist Allegretto Nuzi.

FABRITIUS

Carel Fabritius is the most shadowy figure in Rembrandt's circle. The little we know of his life suggests that it was tragic. The date of his birth is doubtful, but was probably 1614. He was killed in 1654, at the age of about forty, in the explosion of a powder magazine at Delft, which also destroyed such of his works as were in his house at the time.

C. FABRITIUS · MAN IN FUR CAP AND CUIRASS
28″ × 24½″. London, National Gallery

Fire, too, caused the loss, in 1864, of a large group-portrait. Accordingly, only about half a dozen of his pictures survive, of which four are considered masterpieces. They comprise the extremely vivid *Sentinel* at Schwerin, a self-portrait as good as a Rembrandt at Munich, another at Rotterdam and The Hague *Goldfinch*. The latter is a most remarkable little picture, quite unpretentious, of a brightly coloured finch sitting on its perch against a bare wall. The bird is not painted as if it were an ornament or a plaything. Nor is it a 'study'. It is a 'portrait', from the life. The effect is altogether exceptional. The style is almost as free and matter-of-fact as a portrait by Frans Hals. And yet it not only implies a sensitive delight in the painter, but also a profound sense of the kinship of all living creatures.

According to Hoogstraten, who was his fellow-pupil, Fabritius studied under Rembrandt in 1640/41, while still living in his native city of Amsterdam. He was anything

but an imitator of his master, making no use, for example, of the typical Rembrandt red and deep shadow. If Fabritius had not died so young, he would have developed an entirely individual manner.

It appears that his reputation stood high in his lifetime. But during the next 250 years he was quite forgotten. It was not until the works of the great Jan Vermeer were rediscovered at the end of the nineteenth century that those of Carel Fabritius also came to light. For Vermeer had been his pupil.

Carel's contemporary and namesake, **Barent** Fabritius, was also a member of Rembrandt's circle. Active in Amsterdam and Leyden between 1650 and 1672, he is now regarded, on the evidence of recent documentary research, as Carel's brother. Barent's style remained dependent on Rembrandt's throughout his life. Reproductions of Rembrandt's work by him are still extant. He was an excellent colourist, but less assured as a draughtsman. His pictures, dealing almost exclusively with biblical themes, resemble Eeckhout's more than those of any other master.

FAKES

Works of art have at all times been forged, very seldom innocently, i.e. for the sheer pleasure of imitation. Usually the intention was fraudulent. Albrecht Dürer, for instance, was obliged to obtain an Imperial decree declaring the imitation of his woodcuts and engravings a criminal offence. They were at that time being deliberately forged by dealers for profit. There was no question in this case of a lack of understanding of or respect for the principles of copyright. By 1500 such naïvety had long been a thing of the past. In 1523, when Ottaviano dei Medici requested Andrea del Sarto to make as close a copy as possible of Raphael's portrait of Pope Leo X, the painter suspected that a forgery might be intended. Accordingly, he took care to place his private symbol in an inconspicuous position on the canvas. He had guessed rightly. Ottaviano had been ordered by the Pope to send Raphael's original to Gonzaga, Duke of Mantua. But the Florentine, instead of doing so, sent del Sarto's copy to the Duke. The fraud was not discovered till Vasari detected it some years later.

The art of faking has flourished ever since the Rococo period. At that time it was the petty princes and the newly created nobles whose love of display afforded hitherto unprecedented scope for the forgers' activities. Today demands from rapidly enriched American millionaires are on such a scale that even such long-established centres of faking as Rome, Florence, Vienna, Madrid and Paris often despair of producing enough 'ancient' jewellery, furniture, weapons, works of craftsmanship, bronzes, sculpture and paintings to satisfy their customers. According to a celebrated witticism, 'Rembrandt painted 800 pictures: 1,200 of them are in Texas'.

Europeans are just as much victimised as Americans, though the former usually get off more cheaply. Even the more modest, prudent and knowledgeable buyer is sometimes trapped. Junk-shops and so-called 'forced sales' are particularly rich in items ascribed to the wrong artist or not genuine 'antiques'. The argument that faking is not worthwhile in the case of a low-priced article is often fallacious. In Paris at the turn of the century it was possible to buy miniatures on ivory by the highly esteemed Viennese painter Füger at absurdly cheap rates. The manufacture of them cost very little. The small ivory plates were sensitised to take photographs of works by Füger. The image was then coloured by hand, sprayed, polished and framed in the style of the original.

But such precise faking is not always necessary. Even a slight manipulation of the signature may be profitable. If the dot over the 'j' in 'jp' is removed the initials on a seascape by Jan Peeters become 'JP', those of Jan Porcellis, whose works are worth double the price of the other's. Again, if the Christian name in 'Constantin Netscher' is erased, the signature will be read, with any luck, as that of the more important father, not the son. The picture can then be sold at exactly ten times the price, even if some surprise happens to be expressed at its inferior quality.

Such frauds, however, are relatively insignificant. A forger aiming at higher profits does not shrink from painstaking scientific study over a period of years on end. Each new method of detection is countered by a process of equal subtlety.

The most interesting case in this connection is that of Han van Meegeren whose forgeries came to light during a political trial at Amsterdam in 1945. In defending himself against the then serious charge of having sold to Hermann Göring during the war, a national treasure of the greatest value—to wit, a painting by Jan Vermeer of Delft—Van Meegeren confessed that all the works believed to be Vermeer's which had been 'discovered' between 1935 and 1945 had been painted by himself. A curious feature of the case was the strenuous resistance offered by the owners of the pictures in question to the arguments of the experts. But their attitude is intelligible enough in view of the weakness of human nature. No one likes to admit that he has been deceived, especially in paying over such enormous sums. Van Meegeren declared in court that his agents had sold, among others, the following works painted by him in the style of Vermeer and bearing a forgery of the latter's signature: for the *Head of Christ* he had been paid 400,000 gulden, for *Jacob's Blessing* 1,275,000 gulden, for the *Woman Taken in Adultery* 1,650,000 gulden (by Göring) and for the *Foot-washing* 1,250,000 gulden (by the Dutch Government). He said that he had often worked for more than a year on one picture. He had been in the habit at first of buying cheap canvases dating from the time of Vermeer and removing from them such passages of colour as he did not need for his own operations. He ground his own colours in accordance with ancient prescriptions and processes. He even procured lapis lazuli from England to enable him to reproduce Vermeer's original blue, a gram of it costing him about £10. He used, like Vermeer, brushes made of badger's hair, for the wrong sort of bristle might otherwise subsequently be found adhering to the canvas and thus reveal the fraud. The completed picture was submitted to a special drying process in an oven, so as to give it the cracked, fissured and damaged appearance characteristic of old paintings. Then it was varnished with a solution resembling as closely as possible that employed in Vermeer's period. Thereupon it was ready for 'discovery'.

Nevertheless, Professor Coremans of Brussels was able to demonstrate, after exhaustive tests, that Van Meegeren had made certain technical mistakes. This evidence substantiated the judgment of a number of experts whose unerring eyes had already convinced them, without further research, that these pictures could not possibly be Vermeer's.

Laymen felt inclined to ask whether, in

H. VAN MEEGEREN
CHRIST AND THE WOMAN TAKEN IN ADULTERY
(Fake in the style of Vermeer van Delft)
38⅞″ × 35¼″. Dutch State possession

these circumstances, Van Meegeren, considered purely as a painter, had not at any rate proved himself to be the equal of Vermeer. But such an 'objective' view of the matter involves a fallacy. People like Van Meegeren are highly talented technicians who only differ from ordinary copyists in their ability to contrive an ingenious new combination of the stylistic features and methods of organisation used by the old masters and still available for exploitation. Such imitators resemble gifted and sensitive actors capable of playing, without being, Hamlet, though only so long as they are able to refer to Shakespeare's text. The sculptor Alceo Dossena, who in 1927 voluntarily disclosed the secret of his magnificent forgeries, may perhaps be regarded as something more than a mere fraud.

FERRARI

A great number of Italian painters of this

name are known. Few rise above mediocrity and most do not even reach that level. But two may be mentioned.

Gaudenzio Ferrari (1470-1546) was born in Valduggia, soon left for Milan and died in that city. He was much influenced by Bramantino and Luini. His pictures are very rare outside northern Italy. His *Annunciation* in Berlin is a fine but shallow piece of decoration, with large-scale figures and a lavish display of silk and velvet. His more imaginative work in fresco is preferable.

A certain **Francesco Bianchi** Ferrari, who died at Modena in 1510, probably taught Correggio. The elongated, lean figures in Francesco Bianchi's paintings, with their haggard aspect, are reminiscent of Cosimo Tura and Ercole Roberti.

FERRER

(*see* BASSA)

FETTI

D. FETTI · THE GOOD SAMARITAN
28″ × 17¼″. *New York, Metropolitan Museum*

Domenico Fetti was born in Rome in 1589 and died in Venice in 1624, probably in consequence of a youthful indiscretion. He modelled himself on Caravaggio, but the impression made on him by Rubens, when the latter visited Rome, long remained operative, as in the *Assumption of the Virgin* at Munich. Until about 1618 Fetti's figures and canvases were on the large side, the forms being powerfully moulded by means of light and shade. They always tell some kind of story, as they do in the pictures of Caravaggio and and Rubens.

This style was much in favour at the Court of the Gonzaga family at Mantua, whither Fetti was invited in 1613. He was most generously entertained there. But in 1621 a trifling dispute arose between him and the Duke, in consequence of which the painter abruptly left for Venice. The real reason may have been that he did not find Mantua particularly amusing. The Gonzagas in vain entreated him, on several occasions, to return. But he stayed away

until his death. It is usual to maintain that it was Venetian life and the Venetian style of painting which caused Fetti's break with Caravaggio. But it is more likely that he had a presentiment of his early death, lending a more elegiac note to his work. His canvases grew smaller. He became deeply interested in landscape and the play of light in nature. There is a new zest in the drawing of detail. Many of his pictures, even during the Mantuan period convey an almost Germanic type of feeling, illustrated by *Elias and the Angel* in Berlin.

FIORENZO

Fiorenzo di Lorenzo (c. 1440-1521 in Perugia) painted exclusively religious subjects. Two duly authenticated works at Perugia have in the course of time enabled others to be identified which prove that Fiorenzo, though not an important painter, could produce small-scale paintings of great charm and invariably high competence. He must have been a good teacher, a fact which is itself a contribution to history. Perugino, Pinturicchio and Signorelli, all high-ranking painters, probably studied under him. His own stylistic affiliations are with Verrocchio and Ghirlandaio. An *Adoration* in the Pinakothek at Perugia, believed by Vasari to be Perugino's, is today ascribed to Fiorenzo and Pinturicchio in common.

FLEGEL

Born at Olmütz in 1563 and dying in Frankfurt in 1638, Georg Flegel at first painted landscapes. But on his travels in the Rhineland he came in contact with Flemings of the so-called Frankenthal School (see *Schoubroeck*), probably worked with them for a while and finally turned his whole attention to still-life composition. He became the most remarkable representative of a sort of 'New Realism', such as was practised in modern times about 1925. His themes are exactly the same as those to which Alexander Kanold was devoted—for example, the *Still-Life with Toby Jug* at Cologne and the *Table with Victuals* at Stuttgart. They are given a rare charm by the contrast of agreeable colouring with prosaic conception. Actually, in those days, Flegel's style amounted to no more than enlargement and isolation of the accurately observed incidental passages of still-life inserted by the older Dutch masters in their religious pictures. It was not until a generation later that tonal and compositional methods were applied to still-life studies in the works of Pieter Claesz and Heda.

FLINCK

Govert Flinck was born at Cleve in 1615 and died in Amsterdam in 1660. He studied under Lambert Jacobsen at Leeuwarden. In 1632 he moved to Amsterdam, working there with Rembrandt until about 1635. His productions during the next eight or ten years bore such an astonishing resemblance to those of his great master

that for centuries many of them were taken to be Rembrandt's. But today the great difference between these zealous and clever imitations and the deep psychological insight of genius is very evident.

In the last fifteen years of his life Flinck 'went astray'. It is possible to take a less lenient view of his behaviour. An amiable but somewhat weak and timid character, Flinck was unwilling to be drawn into the atmosphere of boycott and distinctly unpleasant agitation that surrounded Rembrandt. 'Before the cock had crowed once', he thrice artistically denied his former master and forsook him for the smooth representative style of the portraitist Van der Helst, just then the city's favourite painter. Flinck was no worse an artist than Helst. But the label of imitator still sticks to him. His portrait of Rembrandt painted in 1639 is in the National Gallery, London.

FLORIS

Frans Floris de Vriendt was born c. 1516 and died in 1570 in Antwerp. He studied at Lüttich, apparently under Lambert Lombard, for a time. He seems to have imbibed from Lombard the absurd notion that, in Friedländer's phrase, 'to erect dazzlingly bright marble halls is to restore the beauty of antiquity'. A prolonged visit to Rome, where he saw Michelangelo's frescoes in the Sistine Chapel, sent him spinning—the word is certainly not too strong—out of his course. His *Last Judgment* at Vienna is utterly nonsensical. The scene is not one of 'Judgment', but of an indoor battle. The same can be said of the *Fall of the Angels* at Antwerp. These pictures epitomise the false view of humanism and classicism taken by certain Flemings in the sixteenth century. Floris would be forgotten today if he had not been rescued from oblivion by activities which he carried out entirely against his will. He, the great classicist, was forever being plagued to paint portraits. He complied with these demands, but took no trouble whatever over the work. The portraits, accordingly, turned out to be original, dashingly vigorous productions, of pioneering significance in their brush-work and colour organisation.

FONTAINEBLEAU

The palace near Paris to which the French kings moved in the sixteenth century from the castle of Chambord has given its name to a whole period of French painting. Francis I called in two Italians, Rosso and Primaticchio, to decorate the rooms at Fontainebleau. He did not suspect that in so doing he would be changing every aspect of artistic activity at the French Court for nearly three generations. Primaticchio was the leading spirit, later joined by Niccolo dell' Abbate, in developing a Mannerist style of decoration, believed to be antique because it depicted Odysseus, Roman pastoral scenes and slender nudes in the character of Diana,

SCHOOL OF FONTAINEBLEAU (c. 1550)
DIANA AS HUNTRESS
76¾" × 53¼". *Paris, Louvre*

for which two charming royal mistresses smilingly agreed to pose.

Highly typical representatives of the School of Fontainebleau were Jean Cousin the Elder (c. 1490-1560), the Younger (c. 1522-1594), Antoine Caron (q.v.), Ambroise Dubois (1543-1614) and François Quesnel (1543-1619), who was born in Edinburgh, where his father worked for a while as Court Painter, and died in Paris.

The advent of the great Poussin at the beginning of the seventeenth century finally extinguished the Fontainebleau style, by then already moribund. It fell to its lowest in public estimation in the middle of the nineteenth century.

FONTANA

Prospero (1512-1597) and **Lavinia** Fontana (1522-1614) were father and daughter. They represent the last phase of Bolognese Mannerism, committed simultaneously to archaism and extremely rapid and stylish handling. Prospero's altarpieces often look almost like industrial products.

He was invited to France by Primaticchio, head of the School of Fontainebleau (q.v.), but soon returned to Bologna on grounds of health.

Lavinia found favour with the Carracci, went to Rome and acquired a high, though exaggerated, reputation as a portrait painter among wealthy patrons. Unfortunately, she is not represented, in galleries outside Italy, by her pleasing portraits, but only by her very weak religious pictures. She died in Rome.

FOPPA

It was really not until modern times that the permanent influence of Vincenzo Foppa on the whole of Lombard painting in the second half of the fifteenth century was recognised. It is unlikely that he meant to found a school. But the sheer quantity of his production during an exceptionally long life eventually gave definite direction and unity of style to the feeble and hesitant work of his contemporaries in the province. Lombardy was

hen very isolated from the main stream of
development. But it was already slowly
becoming aware of problems in painting
to which Foppa's pictures provided solu-
ions. His own style was derived from
Pisanello through Jacopo Bellini—Foppa's
St Peter Martyr at Milan is thoroughly
Venetian—and Mantegna.

He aimed at novel chromatic effects—
for example, grey tones in flesh and often
garish local colour. His attempts at a
monumental style did not employ the rigid
archaism of former provincial painters,
but were contrived by showing his figures
engaged in common tasks, the attitudes
being naturalistic, while the facial expressions alone conveyed a stony solemnity.
Foppa's work is above all distinguished by
its silvery tone and advanced understanding of atmospheric effects.

He was born at Bagnolo near Brescia
in 1427, moving in 1456 to Pavia. He also
painted frescoes in the Cathedral at
Genoa and worked for the Dukes of Milan.
At the age of sixty-three he returned to
Brescia, where he died in 1515/16. By 1500
his influence had been superseded by that
of Leonardo.

Outside Italy Foppa's works are preserved in Berlin, London and British and
American private collections.

FOUQUET

Jean Fouquet, who was born c. 1420 at
Tours and died there c. 1481, was regarded
in his lifetime as the greatest painter in
France. In the sixteenth century he was
still remembered, Vasari discusses him as
'Foccare'. But by 1757 Louis XV did not
know who had painted the portrait of his
ancestor Charles VII. When he ordered the
picture to be sent from Bourges to Paris
he described it as 'the portrait of our
royal ancestor in the aforesaid Sainte
Chapelle'. By 1840 the work had become
quite anonymous, being known as a
'Greek picture' and sold for 450 francs.
Today it is the pride of the Louvre and
its author, Jean Fouquet, the pride of
France.

The task of identifying his easel pictures
had to begin afresh in modern times. For
only his miniatures, i.e. book-illustrations,
were documentarily attested. These are of
exceptional quality, quite in the spirit of
the traditional Book of Hours. They have
enabled a round dozen of paintings by
Fouquet to be duly authenticated. The
portraits of Charles VII and his Chancellor, Juvenal des Ursins, hang in the
Louvre. That of the Chancellor makes the
somewhat impersonal impression of a
typical donor's portrait. But the discon-
solate King is represented on a Gothic
scale, with a characteristic elaboration of
the background that recalls Van Eyck's
portrait of the Arnolfini couple. Pictures
of equal merit are the *Man with Wine-glass*
in the Louvre, now considered to be almost
certainly by Fouquet, and the *Man
Putting Out His Hand* in the Liechtenstein
Gallery at Vienna.

A donor's portrait in Berlin represents
Estienne Chevalier, the King's Lord High
Treasurer, and his patron saint. A similarity of character has been so magnificently rendered by the painter in the two
figures that they seem to be those of
brothers whose gentle and humane dis-
positions make an immediate appeal. The
other wing of the diptych, representing the
Virgin and Child surrounded by cherubs
in red, is in Antwerp. The picture has since
become famous. The unusual form of the
head of the Madonna was modelled on
that of Agnes Sorel, the King's mistress.
The strange, archaic beauty of the painting
as a whole has nothing Flemish about it.
The effect is entirely French.

Little is known of the life of this great
artist. But it seems clear that he had studied
Flemish painting, especially that of Jan
van Eyck. He also visited Italy. But his
encounter with Fra Angelico, which it is so
tempting to suppose may have been a
collision between two fixed stars, appears
to have left no trace upon the style of
either painter. Fouquet remained, in
Friedländer's words, a 'sober, objectively-
minded artist with the refined taste in
design and the virtuosity, but also with the
stylistic limitations, of the book-illustra-
tor'. (Ill. p. 114.)

J. FOUQUET · AGNES SOREL AS THE MADONNA
36¼" × 32¾". *Antwerp, Musée Royal des Beaux Arts*

FRAGONARD

Jean-Honoré Fragonard was born in Grasse in 1732 and died in Paris in 1806. He was the son of a glover. In the French Rococo period his father's trade appears to have been as surprising a source of high talent as the cobbler's trade in the time of Hans Sachs.

Fragonard's gifts were discovered, while he was still a notary's clerk, by Boucher. The latter at first recommended him to Chardin. But he afterwards took him into his own studio, believing he had detected a kindred spirit.

Nowadays Fragonard's name is connected by most people with Boucher-like scenes of an erotic character, suggesting the alcove. But this view of him is too one-sided and does not do him justice. He had of course, as a product of the Rococo age and the Paris of Louis XV, every opportunity for the kindling of his imagination. Moreover, he had ambitions to cut a

figure at Court, though, oddl enough, he was not particularl successful in doing so. But th content of his erotic pictures is c less importance than their hig professional quality, his brilliar brushwork, developing that Rubens almost to the point c impressionism. He certainly ad mired both Rubens and Rem brandt. It was not, however, th exuberant female figures of th former, but his dynamism ha sensuousness that attracted Fra gonard, whose charming *Bather* could not have been conceive without the example of Ruben' playful nereids. Fragonard als painted wonderfully fine pre-im pressionist domestic scenes—fc example, the *Pastry-cook* and *Gar den Washing* at Amiens—as we as religious pictures and som good portraits. There can be n doubt that at his best he surpasse Boucher. He was prevented fror succumbing to Mannerism b several journeys to Italy, durin which he met the serious-minde H. Robert and studied the Venetians.

The French Revolution put an end t Fragonard's creative activity. But thi result appears to have been due to person shock rather than interference from other for he enjoyed the protection of Jacque Louis David at this time.

Masterpieces by Fragonard are pre served in public and private collections i France and also in London, Madrid an Leningrad. The frescoes he once painte for Mme Dubarry are in Washington.

FRANCESCA

The name is sometimes spelt 'dei Fran ceschi' in documents. Piero della Francesc was born in Borgo San Sepolcro, Tuscan in 1416/20 and died there in 1492.

No more than a dozen works by hir survive, not because many have been los but because he only painted a few othe in his life of seventy years. He took sixtee years to produce his *Madonna of the Cloa* ltarpiece and another fifteen ver the San Agostino altarpiece. These facts are interesting. But is contemporaries were apt to dmire such pertinacity less in he case of painters than in that f writers. Consequently, Piero's ame was regarded as that of a provincial, not to be compared with that of the great masters, Fra Angelico, Uccello, Ghirlandaio, products of the brilliant international centre of Florence. He was remembered as a mathematician and an author for some time after his death. Then oblivion descended upon him for three centuries. During that period the classic homes of art were invaded by swarms of tourists. Venice, Milan, Florence and Rome were full of pilgrims. But no one thought of visiting the village of Borgo San Sepolcro or the sleepy, isolated little town of Arezzo, where Piero's masterpiece was slowly decaying on the interior walls of the church. It was not until the end of the nineteenth century that his works were again discovered, whereupon his reputation immediately rose higher than ever before. Today he is regarded as one of the greatest painters of all time.

L. Venturi writes, in a passage which cannot be bettered: 'He appeals more than any other Italian painter to modern artistic sensibility. For the present century's tendency to abstraction finds its strongest support in the restrained, contemplative vision characteristic of Piero's work, an effect he always prefers to any display of action. Realism and abstraction attain a uniquely even balance in his art. Masaccio creates a monumental painting full of moral energy, in which the world is dominated by God Incarnate and His disciples, working their miracles. Piero, on the other hand, creates a monument of contemplation, in which the current of life seems to flow with the deliberation of eternity.'

Piero's unique quality is most clearly

J. H. FRAGONARD · BATHERS
(Detail) 25⅝″ × 32″. Paris, Louvre

expressed in the Arezzo frescoes illustrating the *History of the Cross*. The fourteen scenes depicted either cover an entire wall or decorate small Gothic arches. The narrative of the events connected with the Cross is not so much told as arrested at certain points. The figures concerned in it have a royal presence. Their grandeur is not due to any splendour of attire or even to their sacred character. It is derived from the singular dignity with which they hold their postures and gaze down from the walls upon the intent spectator below. Their expressions are amazingly varied and yet similar. They afford us no clue to the world in which they live and appear insensible and self-absorbed. When the personages are represented as supposing themselves unobserved, as in the *Death of Adam* or the *Restitution of the Cross*, with its kneeling group of citizens, they have an aspect of eternity, as if their actions were obligatory for all time. The effect is awe-inspiring.

The same spirit, though rather warmer and more intimate in effect, is evident in the fresco of the *Resurrection of Christ* at Borgo. Piero's third masterpiece is the diptych in the Uffizi Gallery. One wing portrays the half-length figure of Federigo da Montefeltro, the other his wife, Battista Sforza. Both faces are in full profile. The impression conveyed is fascinating. One cannot imagine that the people of the Early Renaissance ever looked otherwise than in this picture. The back of each wing shows a lumbering triumphal chariot being driven through a broad, magnificently painted landscape.

Two *Nativities* by Piero have been preserved. The great picture at Milan was completed about 1485, twenty years after the Arezzo frescoes. The colour is powerful, warm and plastically organised. The familiar scene is presented in the artist's characteristic monumental style. But on this occasion the effect is only 'beautiful', not eerie and disturbing. There is a

PIERO DELLA FRANCESCA · THE VIRGIN
(Detail from 'The Nativity')
49¾″ × 48½″. London, National Gallery

definite loss of tension in the London *Nativity*, a fragment in which the group of angels is still rendered in Piero's former manner and the attitude of the man with lifted hand has a noble solemnity, yet the kneeling Madonna appears in the last analysis as no more than a girl of flesh and blood. The type to which her features conform and their specific charm were never repeated later in Italian painting. In his old age the artist had grown humbler and more grateful for his success. He smiles in this work for the first and only time.

A threequarter-length *Virgin and Child with Two Angels* and a *Scourging of Christ* are at Urbino and a conventional decorative fresco depicting a prayer to St Sigismund at Rimini. The early works St *Jerome with a Founder*, *Baptism of Christ* and *Madonna with Cloak*, are preserved in Venice, London and Borgo respectively. The San Agostino altarpiece formerly thought to be lost, was recovered in 1941, when Meiss identified three saints as parts of it in London, New York and the Poldi-Pezzoli collection in Milan. Longhi the eminent authority on Piero della Francesca, succeeded in recognising the *predella* (q.v.) in a *Crucifixion* in New York. Six years later Clark discovered Piero's *St Augustine* at Lisbon.

The artist is first mentioned in 1439 as assisting Domenico Veneziano with certain frescoes in Florence, since destroyed. He was much influenced by both Veneziano and Uccello. In 1442 he was appointed a member of the Borgo parish council. The contract for the Arezzo frescoes was signed in 1447. Some two years later he was decorating apartments in the palace at Ferrara with frescoes no longer extant. He was at Rimini in 1451. The Arezzo frescoes were completed in 1466. He moved to Perugia in 1468 to escape the plague then raging in Tuscany. In the following year he was at Urbino. In his old age he is said to have gone blind and devoted himself entirely to mathematical and scientific studies.

FRANCESCHINI

Marcantonio Franceschini (1648-1729), a

PIERO DELLA FRANCESCA · THE QUEEN OF SHEBA ADORING THE HOLY WOOD
142⅜″ × 298¾″. Arezzo, S. Francesco

Bolognese painter and the most popular follower and favourite pupil of Cignani, continued the traditions of the school of Albani, the only direction in which any further development was possible at the time. In this special field, that of large-scale decoration, Franceschini can still be studied with pleasure. In his church frescoes at Bologna, for instance, he revelled in deep tones of blue and red, the colours most admired by Baroque painters, and in startlingly foreshortened renderings of conventionally graceful, lightly posed figures in restless movement.

FRANCESCO DI GIORGIO

Francesco di Giorgio was born in Siena in 1439 and died there in 1502. He abandoned painting for architecture and engineering in 1477. He had by then introduced new and up-to-date features into Sienese painting, such as an improved luminosity, more energetic movement, secular pomp and a predilection for architecture. Plain surfaces and static figures grow less and less characteristic of the Sienese school after his time. In predella (q.v.) landscapes his style was more lyrical, sometimes positively romantic, attracting the approval of Leonardo da Vinci. Most of the religious pictures and small mythological scenes by Francesco di Giorgio are to be found at Siena and Florence, as well as in private collections in England and France. His *St Dorothy* is in the National Gallery, London.

FRANCIA

Francesco di Marco di Giacomo Raibolini (1450-1517?), a Bolognese, called himself Francia in honour of his teacher, a French goldsmith referred to in documents as

'Franze'. It appears that Raibolini did not give up goldsmith's work for painting until he was thirty-six, unusually late in life for a Renaissance painter. Vasari maintains that he was self-taught, which is possible. It may also be that Francia had not thought of painting until he met Costa at Bologna in 1485. A year later he is mentioned in the guild registers for the first time as a painter.

In his new profession he soon achieved as much fame as he had enjoyed while a goldsmith. He produced altarpieces and memorial portraits in great quantity. They are to be found today in nearly all the large galleries, even outside Italy, as, for example, in Chantilly, London, Paris, Leningrad, Berlin, Dresden, Munich, Vienna and the United States. Francia's style is based on those of Bellini and Cossa. His excellent portraits—for instance the beautiful *Scappa* in the Uffizi Gallery —owe much to Perugino.

When once his work has been attentively studied, it is relatively easy to recognise. He never changed his manner. He aimed above all at the production of 'beauty', of beautiful, calm, somewhat lifeless figures, beautiful background landscape, beautiful, monotonously extended passages of flat colour in garments and beautiful, very simple composition. The sum total of all this 'beauty', unfortunately, verges upon vacuity. Vasari, with his love of gossip, undoubtedly came near the truth—for the story sheds a positively startling flood of light upon Francia's character—in alleging that the artist never succeeded in realising an ideal with which he was one day suddenly confronted in the art of Raphael. On examining the technique of the latter's *St Cecilia*, Vasari goes on, Francia suffered a heart attack and dropped dead.

The frequent over-estimation of this painter is due to the harmonious effect of his figures. They pose no problems. But, unfortunately, they also fail to arouse interest.

FRANCIABIGIO

Francesco di Cristofano Bigi, according to Vasari, was born in Florence in 1482, where he died in 1525 at the age of forty-two. As he studied under Albertinelli, who was the same age as himself, he seems to have made a late start in his profession.

All histories of art warn their readers against over-estimating Franciabigio. Salvini calls him a mere eclectic and imitator. Gronau says he should never be rated higher than he deserves. Hausenstein dubs his art 'effeminate'. It almost seems as though one ought to be ashamed of taking an interest in him, in the same way as connoisseurs of music find people who

FRANCIA · THE MADONNA AND CHILD AND TWO ANGELS · *25⅝" × 19⅜". Munich, Alte Pinakothek* enjoy Puccini rather a nuisance. It is certainly true that Franciabigio's borrowings are obvious. His flowing, luminous passages are derived from Andrea del Sarto with whom he collaborated for a considerable time, as in the Chiostro dello Scalzo and Poggio a Caiano frescoes. He also owed much to Raphael and Fra Bartolomeo. Yet his pictures are genuinely his own. They come from the same source, in which dark, glowing colour is combined with the velvety brown tinge used by Leonardo to suggest antiquity. Deep harmonies are thus evoked in Franciabigio's paintings.

His portraits are indisputably outstanding. They are to be seen in Florence, Berlin, Vienna, London and Paris. His *Bathsheba*, painted in 1523, in competition with Pontormo and Bacchiacca, is at Dresden. The Uffizi Gallery possesses his Raphaelesque *Madonna at the Well* and the Pitti Palace his *Calumny of Appelles*. At Turin there is an *Annunciation*, in Vienna a *Holy Family* and at Munich a *Virgin and Child* by this artist.

MASTER FRANCKE · THE NATIVITY
(*From the Thomas Altarpiece*) 39⅝″ × 35½″. Hamburg, Kunsthalle

FRANCKE

The name of Meister Francke is only mentioned once, in a brief sixteenth-century note of his responsibility for the St Thomas altarpiece at Hamburg, where he was living shortly after 1400. Whence he came, how long he lived and what his real name was are still unsettled questions. The surname 'Francke' is a characteristic later corruption. The altarpiece dates from 1424. Consequently, the artist was probably about fifteen years younger than Meister Bertram. This assumption is supported by his style, which is more lively, elaborate and dramatic than that of the older master, pays greater attention to perspective and especially to architecture, and is also richer in colour. But Bertram and the Bohemian School presided at the birth of these works. Flemish influence is also traceable. The artist may have been born in Flanders. Francke, however, is a master in his own right. At this period no one else in Germany rivalled the splendour of his colour, the variety of movement in his figures and their typical contrasts in the expression of restless malice and sedate piety. His art represents an important advance. Bertram would not have been able to paint so gorgeously arrayed and inflexible a figure, anticipating the manner of Bouts, as that of the High Priest in the *Scourging* at Hamburg. The dramatic and emotional features of Francke's pictures are no longer dictated by ideas but by direct observation.

Few of his works are extant. There is a *Man of Sorrows* at Leipzig, a St Barbara altarpiece at Helsinki, and another *Man of Sorrows* at Hamburg, which also possesses the St Thomas altarpiece, comprising among other scenes the beautifully tranquil version of the Nativity here illustrated.

FRANCKEN

Frans Francken the Elder was born at Herenthals in 1542 and died in Antwerp in 1616. He belonged to a numerous family of Flemish painters, with many ramifications. He and his son were the most famous of them. The elder Francken studied under Frans Floris, whose light touch he unfortunately lacked. The pictures attributed to him are somewhat ponderous and at first chromatically weak, though they acquired strength and depth of colour later on. They include three altarpieces at Antwerp, a *Christ Carrying the Cross* at Dresden and at Brunswick a miniature *Adoration*, painted on copper, with hundreds of tiny figures. He seems to have treated mainly biblical themes. Much of his work has been lost. **Frans Francken the Younger** (1581-1642), his pupil, was more successful. His best paintings are to be found in Antwerp and Vienna. Works by him were for long wrongly ascribed to his father, owing to his habit of signing them 'Old Frans', as Frans the Elder had signed his pictures, after his own son had begun to paint. Innumerable pictures by Frans the Younger have been preserved. They are mostly small and depict biblical or mythological scenes in the *genre* style of the seventeenth century, though with advancing years his handling grew broader, looser and more colourful. His figures are like those of a 'little Rubens'. The third Frans (1607-1667) was in fact nicknamed 'Rubens-Francken'.

FREDI

Born at Siena, c. 1330, Bartolo di Fredi was one of the masters of the brilliant early period of Sienese painting. It is known that he was for some time associated with Andrea Vanni (c. 1332-c. 1396), who may perhaps be placed in the same category. Fredi's work is mentioned for the last time in 1397. He seems to have died at Siena shortly after 1400.

His pictures are confined to exploiting the discoveries with which his great Sienese predecessors, Pietro and Ambrogio Lorenzetti and Simone Martini, had already astonished the world. Many critics are inclined to agree with Vitzthum in believing that Fredi 'far outstripped his models in realistic detail and narrative skill, though without ever really mastering the treatment of mass'. But comparison with the vigorously realistic and animated *Entombment* of Simone Martini in Berlin or the smooth flow of narrative in Ambrogio Lorenzetti's *Good Government*, both a generation older than Fredi's work would seem to relegate him to the second rank at most. His biblical frescoes at Siena and in San Gimignano are his best surviving work of this kind. The small altarpieces and little panels shaped to a pointed arch, many of which are in private collections and one, *St Anthony Abbot*, in the National Gallery, London, have far more of the charm which all the early Primitives (q.v.) exercise upon us today.

FREMINET

Martin Freminet of Paris (1567-1619) was a product of the Fontainebleau tradition. After 1603 he resided at the Palace, succeeding Dumoustier as Court Painter. But his style bears little relation to that of the old Fontainebleau school. A prolonged tour of Italy had revealed new ideals to him, those of Caravaggio and Parmigianino. They are only too evident in his biblical and mythological scenes, but unfortunately deprived of life and thoroughly artificial. Freminet's best works are his frescoes in the Chapel of the Holy Trinity at Fontainebleau.

FRESCO

This word is often used today to signify any kind of wall-painting. It was originally used by the Italians of paintings executed upon damp, fresh (fresco) plaster, which needed entirely different and much more rapid methods of work than those developed later for dry surfaces. Frescoes excavated at Knossos show that the process used by e Cretans was essentially the same as that ractised later in Greece, Rome, and nedieval and Renaissance Italy. The escoes of the Italian Renaissance have een studied in greater detail than those f other periods and many technical ccounts exist by contemporary writers, ne best-known among them being Cennino Cennini. The cartoon was drawn on ne wall and the plaster applied in sections ccording to the amount of work to be done or the day. The Renaissance painters ppear to have initiated certain departures om the original technique. The Minoan orks scarcely ever show traces of joins uch as are necessarily produced by the rocess just described, where the area of ny one section of plastering is limited by ne amount of work which can be accomlished in one day. Michelangelo's frescoes the Sistine Chapel, for example, show ne joins very clearly. It is thought that ne work of antiquity was either executed y a group of painters instead of by one ndividual or that some lost procedure nabled the workers to treat the plaster so nat it would retain its moisture for longer eriods. Renaissance painters further introuced the use of *secco*, touching up dried escoes with pigment ground in egg, curd, r other binding medium, and adding small uantities of lime or lime-water to the olours. It is the addition of lime which as imparted to Italian frescoes their pale, nalky tone. *Fresco secco*, the technique of xecuting entire paintings in secco, is ainting on a dried lime-plaster wall with igments ground in an aqueous binding aterial. The finished, dry lime-plaster all is saturated with lime-water the night efore painting, and in the morning it is ain soaked with as much lime-water as it ill absorb. The painting is executed on nis moist surface as in true fresco, but the olours, instead of being ground in ater, are mixed with a solution of asein. In *fresco secco* the colours must be ainly applied.

RIES

orn at Freiburg in 1465 in Switzerland nd dying in Berne in 1518/20, Hans Fries studied under Heinrich Bichler, the best master in a country at that time undistinguished in painting. But more important influences on Fries were a journey to Basel, where he may have met Dürer, and a further trip to Ulm. He thus came to know Flemish work, on which his later pictures—highly prized by his contemporaries—were based. But a trait all his own is the sly humour illustrated, for example, in his *Last Judgment* at Munich. In this painting, filled with his characteristic slender-limbed, lofty-browed little nudes, one suddenly realises that the innumerable resurrected souls are not actually being borne aloft by the hands of angels, but seated, happily smiling, with their hindquarters protruding, on the angels' arms. Fries has a vivid narrative gift, showing a typically medieval vigour in the gestures represented. He is as devout a Christian as he is ready to laugh delightedly, on occasion, at any excess of 'holiness'. His colour sometimes recalls that of Burgkmair. His chief works are to be found at Basle, Freiburg, Zürich, Nuremberg and Munich.

FROMENT

The records of the Court of King René of Anjou state that Nicholas Froment (fifteenth century) came from Uzès in Provence. But his works are only known to us from Avignon (q.v.) documents.

Two pictures only are authenticated. The rest seem to have perished in the troubles of the time. The extant paintings, both altarpieces, are in such utter contrast with each other that if they were not attested in writing it would be difficult to believe they were by the same hand. The *Raising of Lazarus* at the Uffizi Gallery shows strong Flemish influence. The drawing is painfully concerned with interior perspective. The figures gesticulate awkwardly. In the *Burning Bush* at the Cathedral of Aix-en-Provence the artist has undergone a complete metamorphosis. This is an outstanding work, painted in a confident, idiosyncratic style, wholly French in inspiration. A lifetime of experience must have elapsed between the

two productions. Froment's draughtsman
ship and sense of colour are now perfecte
Tenderness of feeling and a gent
melancholy are evident. The portrai
of the King and Queen, as donors, on th
wings of this altarpiece, surmounted b
glowing red canopies, are unforgettabl
as likenesses alone. With this wor
Froment acquires a place among the mos
important masters of the second period o
Avignon brilliance.

FRUEAUF

Rueland Frueauf the Elder was probabl
born at Salzburg in 1440/50 and died i
1507 in Passau, where his main outpu
appears to have been concentrated. H
was for long only a name to art historian
The first of his works to be identified we
four panels of the Passion at Vienna
until then labelled simply, in accordanc
with their signature, as by the 'Mast
R.F. of Vienna'. Four panels in the chur
at Grossgmain and altarpieces in Pragu
Venice, and Budapest are also by Frueau
As an artist of Gothic severity, intense
devout, he conceived his didactic painting
strictly in terms of persons. He was alwa
ready to omit a passage of landscape o
some other incidental feature in order t
throw into greater relief the one essenti
gesture he required from any particul
figure. He carried this practice to extrem
in his *Resurrection of Christ* at the Munic
Pinakothek.

FÜGER

Born in Heilbron in 1751 and dying i
Vienna in 1818, Heinrich Füger intende
to be a scientist. He only painted 'at od
moments' until certain influential patror
persuaded him to give up his scientif
studies. One of the admirers of his ear
portraits was Lavater, the physiognomi
and mystic, who told Goethe about hin
In 1774 Füger moved to Vienna, whe
he was appointed director of one institu
tion after another, thus adopting a care
which has never yet done an artist ar
good. His large-scale pictures seldom ri

N. FROMENT · THE BURNING BUSH
(*Wing. Reduced in height*)
111¼″ × 36″. Aix-en-Provence, Cathedral

ove the level of academic classicism.
t his illustrations to Klopstock's *Messias*
interesting. They aroused much com-
nt at the time. He also painted, until his
ht deteriorated, very attractive minia-
e portraits, for preference on ivory.
ey often suggest the ideal of a con-
nporary English gentleman.

Füger did in fact paint Englishmen. His
trait of Lord Nelson is in the National
rtrait Gallery, London.

ULLER

ac Fuller was born towards the end of
first decade of the seventeenth century,
ssibly of Jewish parentage. He is said
have studied in Paris under the en-
aver François Perrier. Returning to
gland, he painted portraits and murals.
e died in Bloomsbury in 1672. Fuller is
interesting painter in that he was
nost entirely uninfluenced by Van
ck. His self-portraits in the Bodleian
brary and Queen's College, Oxford, and
the National Portrait Gallery, London,
d his *Matthew Locke* in the Examination
hools, Oxford, reveal an original style
great vigour. Fuller also painted altar-
ces for Wadham and Magdalen, Oxford.

URINI

ancesco Furini (c. 1600-1646), a Floren-
e painter, was exceptional in producing
arms of female nudes. Polite society in
orence appears to have had an astonish-
g capacity for absorbing such works.
ders were placed in a perpetual stream
Furini's gleaming, languishing beauties,
nted in rather oppressive tones. Eventu-
y he ceased altogether to turn out
thological and biblical scenes with
eral figures and concentrated entirely
on half-length nudes.

One day he became a parish priest. It
uld be impossible to notify a change of
art more abruptly. Thenceforward he
ly accepted commissions for pictures
ating to his new occupation. In his last
nner, which somewhat resembles that
Guido Reni, he deals with purely

religious themes and also painted a few
frescoes.

FUSELI

Born Johann Heinrich Füssli at Zürich in
1741 and dying as Henry Fuseli in
London in 1825, this artist came of a very
good family and was given an excellent
education in every way. His worthy
fellow-citizens, including the famous
author, Bodmer, a constant visitor to the
house, would certainly have been disgusted
if they could have foreseen the painter's
future.

In consequence of violent attacks made
by Fuseli on the provincial government,
he fled to Germany in 1763. In Berlin he
zealously studied theology, only to abandon it, the following year, in favour of a
new obsession. After travelling in England
and Italy, where he met Wincklemann,
Jacques Louis David, and Mengs, in 1778
he finally settled down in London as a
painter. Becoming popular in English
society, he contrived to obtain a good deal
of lucrative work as a painter, critic,
lecturer and author.

He was a friend of Blake, who influenced him, and was associated with the
production of the Boydell illustrations to
Shakespeare's plays. He was made a Professor of Painting and Keeper of the Royal
Academy, and was buried next to Reynolds
in St Paul's Cathedral.

Fuseli's pictures, of which the most
popular is the *Nightmare*, in a private
collection at Basle, are much concerned
with scenes of ghostly horror and terrifying dreams. He was also fond of classical
fantasy. Milton's *Paradise Lost* alone
inspired him to produce forty-seven
gigantic paintings.

FYT

The name is also spelt Fijt. An Antwerp
painter, Jan Fyt (1611-1661) studied under
Frans Snyders and like him painted
animals and still-life. Fyt was born to
wealth. Prosperity proverbially attracts
prosperity. In his lifetime his fame was
exaggerated. But modern criticism is less

J. FYT · STILL-LIFE
WITH HOUNDS
*78" × 122¾". Munich,
Alte Pinakothek*

enthusiastic. He himself was actually obliged to take legal action against forgery of his work, which commanded enormous prices.

His subject-matter is derived entirely from Snyders. But his composition is more ornate and fussy, his brushwork more lively, and his colour richer in contrast. He was fond of large still-life studies related to the chase, nearly always pro-vided with the typical feature of a hou in the act of scenting or two hou jostling to sniff at the dead game spr out on a table. Sometimes a snarling with ruffled fur, is shown stalking, just in Snyders's pictures, among the ot items presented.

Fyt's pupil, Pieter Boel (1622-167 imitated his master, also depicting c on the prowl.

ADDI

Renaissance times the life of Taddeo
ddi (c. 1300-1366) was already shrouded
legend. He inherited some of the
lected glory of the venerable Giotto.
The earliest date on any of his pictures
1334. It appears on the triptych in
rlin. Gaddi's first works still clearly
dicate his loyalty to Giotto. But he
adually began to introduce new elements
his own, which afterwards characterised
whole school of his followers. Giotto
d only one aim, that of conveying his
rong personal reaction to sacred themes.
ıt Gaddi came in the course of time to
treat further and further from the
ortrayal of emotion. The pleasure he took
overcoming architectural difficulties and
ilding up imposing symbolical scenes
entually led him to take an intellectual
ew of his task. Giotto was content to
nfine his main effects to the foreground.
ıt Gaddi's masterpiece, the S. Croce
escoes at Florence, depicting the Virgin's
sit to the Temple, shows three colon-
des set at angles to one another and a
scending stairway in three stages. Small,
rge, and medium-sized figures seem to
e intermingled. The eye, in its search for
finition, is led to note faces and gestures,
nes and the artist's indisputably subtle
eatment of architecture. The intimacy of
iotto turns to decoration in Gaddi's work.
But, oddly enough, Gaddi's style, in his
d age, reverted quite noticeably to that
Giotto, as, for instance, in the Uffizi
ſadonna and the S. Croce Museum
fectory frescoes at Florence. The latter
nstitute a long frieze depicting the Last
upper, the structural formality of the
ble and figures being combined with
ovel iconography, especially striking in
ıe case of Judas, who is represented, not
wicked, but as pitiable in his isolation,
eing seated with no one on either side of
m for some distance.
Taddeo's son, **Agnolo,** continued his
ther's style. But Agnolo's colour is
righter and clearer, his drawing looser
ıd more lively. He has been unde-
ervedly ranked below Taddeo. More
recent critics consider his less rigid and
forceful manner as indicating, not simply
a decline from Giotto's, but the initiation
of a new, courtly, 'international' style.
Taddeo had died at Florence in 1366.
Agnolo, born about 1333, died a wealthy
man, with extensive commercial and
banking interests, in 1396, also at Florence.
His *Coronation of the Virgin* is in the
National Gallery, London.

GAINSBOROUGH

Thomas Gainsborough was born in 1717
at Sudbury, Suffolk. His father was
Postmaster at Sudbury and his mother was
an amateur painter of flower pieces.
Gainsborough showed talent in drawing
and painting very early, and at the age of
fourteen he was apprenticed to a silversmith in London. He was discovered by
the French illustrator and engraver,
Hubert Gravelot, who conducted an art
school in London, and in 1742 he became
Gravelot's pupil and assistant. Through
Gravelot Gainsborough met Hayman and
possibly Hogarth and other painters of his
circle. By 1745 the young painter was
established in a studio of his own but in
less than a year he was back in Sudbury.
Shortly afterwards he married a girl called
Margaret Burr, about whom little is
known except that she had an income of
£200 a year. They set up house at Ipswich
and Gainsborough began painting portraits
of the neighbouring gentry as well as
landscapes. One of his earliest patrons was
Philip Thicknesse, Lieutenant-Governor
of Landguard Fort. At his suggestion and
furnished by him with introductions,
Gainsborough moved to Bath at the end of
1759. His success there as a portrait
painter was immediate. When the Royal
Academy was established Gainsborough
was made a foundation member on the
invitation of Reynolds. In 1774 Gainsborough settled in London. With Reynolds,
his rival as a portraitist, his relations were
strained, although Reynolds had bought
Gainsborough's *Girl with Pigs* and had
declared him to be the best landscape
painter in Europe. Some days before his

GAINSBOROUGH · THE MORNING WALK
94⅜″ × 71⅞″. London, National Gallery

tendency of the age was again
naturalistic painting, and alrea
in the background of *Henee
Lloyd and His Sister* (Fitzwillia
Museum) and *The Artist with I
Wife and Child*, which may ha
been influenced by Wattea
Gainsborough had begun
evolve that feathery, flowing, ar
ficial landscape by which he
best known. After he moved
Bath and became acquainted wi
the work of Rubens, his brus
work grew swifter and lighter ai
he developed still further a high
stylised form of picturesque lan
scape. Not only his finished pi
tures but · most of his landsca
drawings were made in the studi
the designs being composed fro
broken stones, pieces of coal ar
cork, moss and clay. Even at t
height of his success as a portra
painter Gainsborough was unab
to sell more than a few of his lan
scapes and when he died his hou
was stacked with them. *The Ma
ket Cart*, National Gallery, is
typical late landscape.

The impressionistic brushwoi
the grace, the incredible lightne
of touch and silvery colour whic
distinguish Gainsborough as
landscape painter are still more in eviden
in his portraits. They also convey a feelii
of intimacy and a high sense of individuali
springing from a romantic interest in t
difference between one face and anothe
Gainsborough catches the most revealii
expression of his sitters, but he never giv
us a still-life copy of their features as, fe
instance, Zoffany did.

Gainsborough is well represented in t
National Gallery. Among his masterpiec
are *The Painter's Daughters*, 1759, *S
William Blackstone* and *The Mornii
Walk* (National Gallery), *The Counte
Howe* (Kenwood), *Mrs Sheridan and M
Tickell* (Dulwich) and *Mrs Robinsc
(Wallace Collection).

GARBO

The work of Raffaellino del Garbo, wl

death in 1788 Gainsborough wrote a
celebrated letter to Reynolds asking to
see him. Speaking of their meeting afterwards in his Fourteenth Discourse, which
was an obituary of his rival, Reynolds said
that if any little jealousies had subsisted
between them, they were forgotten in
those moments of sincerity.

Gainsborough's avowed predilection was
for landscape painting. His early mastery
in this field is shown in *Mr and Mrs
Andrews* and in the National Gallery
Cornard Wood. In these pictures as in all
his early landscapes Gainsborough based his
style on that of Wynants and other minor
Dutch painters whose work he could have
seen in many private houses in East
Anglia. The enchanting landscape background of *Mr and Mrs Andrews* is astonishingly truthfully observed. But the whole

is born c. 1470 in Florence and died
ere in 1524, was thought to be well
iderstood until documentary research
vealed information about a certain
iffaello Bartolommeo di Carlo and one
iffaello di Bartolommeo di Capponi in
dition to the original Raffaello di Barto-
mmeo del Garbo. Since then the
iestion whether these references indi-
ted one, two, or three painters has not
en settled. Some of the pictures con-
rned closely resemble those of Filip-
no Lippi and Botticelli. Others clearly
iow the influence of Pinturicchio and
erugino. Vasari mentions only one
affaellino. Gronau also believes there was
ily one. Bode thinks there were two,
erenson three.
Nothing in the pictures themselves
intradicts the assumption that they are
i by Raffaellino del Garbo. As a pupil of
ilippino Lippi, he had direct knowledge
: the artistic heritage of Botticelli. His
ialky greyish-greens, as in his *Pietà* at
lunich, are harder and colder than
otticelli's and his emotions are less
rident. But that is all. The fact that the
vo artists can be compared in this way
roves how discreetly del Garbo em-
loyed Botticelli's technique of expression
id also his palette, as can be observed in
ie former's *Virgin with Sebastian and
lndrew* in Berlin. Raffaellino later assisted
inturicchio with frescoes in the Vatican.
fter this date his softer, brownish tone is
oticeable. Pinturicchio was one of Peru-
ino's colleagues.
Del Garbo's works are relatively rare.
s they so closely resemble Botticelli's,
iey are conspicuously hung in galleries.
Ie is represented in the National Gallery,
.ondon.

iAULLI

Jicknamed Bacciccio, Giovanni Battista
iaulli was born at Genoa in 1639 and
ied in Rome in 1709. He won the favour
f the great sculptor Bernini, who obtained
or him his first commissions for portraits
1 Rome and at the Court of Modena.
t is greatly to be regretted that so many of
is portraits have been lost, for Gaulli

was one of the best of the Italian Baroque
portrait painters. His pictures, which in
his last period echo to some extent those
of Van Dyck, show no trace of Mannerism.
They are lifelike, facile, and clever, the
cleverness being shown especially in his
portraits of Bernini in the National
Gallery, Rome, and of Cardinal Leopoldo
Medici in the Uffizi Gallery. His many
extant frescoes, particularly those decorat-
the ceiling of the church of Il Gesù in
Rome, represent the first step taken along
the line of development leading to
Tiepolo.
Gaulli, strangely enough, is little known
today outside Italy. It was not always so,
for the King of Portugal gave him a title of
nobility on account of one of his pictures.

GEERTGEN

This name means nothing to most people
today. But it is one to conjure with among
connoisseurs of Dutch fifteenth-century
painting. They feel a particularly tender
affection for Geertgen's clumsy diffidence,
his fumbling sensitivity and robust, yet
childish, sentiments. No more striking
illustration of this captivating feature of
his character could be found than the
bearded, long-nosed male figure which
constantly recurs in his paintings and
probably represents the artist himself.
Sometimes he is shown as a shock-headed
grave-digger, pathetically zealous and
devout, burying the bones of St John. Sometimes he stares in wide-eyed, silent veneration, rather than grief, at the dead Christ.
Sometimes he appears as one of the Three
Kings or as John the Baptist, in melancholy,
perplexed solitude, his head resting on his
hand and his big bare feet crossed at an
awkward angle.
Friedländer writes: 'Affectation and
sentimentality are entirely absent. The
effect is caught with such ingenuous objectivity that it borders on the comic.' The
masculine shyness always discernible in
Geertgen's pictures is most attractive. His
female figures are modesty itself, the flat,
oval treatment of their faces rendering them
so chaste of aspect as to appear unreal.
These slightly comic men and ethereal

women lend a serene, immaculate air to his works. Geertgen, moreover, was a great painter. His beautiful glowing colours are bathed in a tranquil light which had been missing from Dutch pictures since the time of Jan van Eyck.

Little is known of his life. He obviously came from Leyden and died in Haarlem c. 1490. Mander (q.v.) knew no more of him than that he was twenty-eight when he died. He studied under Ouwater and is said to have served an apprenticeship in book illustration at Bruges in 1475. He certainly saw the work of Dirk Bouts and the Monforte altarpiece of Van der Goes, now in Berlin. But his own style remained that of

a thorough northerner. He moved Haarlem, where he was appointed offici painter to the Knights of St John, wit whom he lived, as 'Geertgen tot Sint Jans for the rest of his short life.

His works include a *Lamentation* an *Legend of the Bones of St John*, these bein authenticated masterpieces at Vienna, *Holy Family* on a large scale, recallin Ouwater's style, at Amsterdam, a *Ma of Sorrows* at Utrecht, a small, nocturn scene of the *Nativity* in London, a *Virg and Child* at Milan and another in Berli an *Adoration* at Prague, a *John in Solitu* in Berlin and three or four other pictur not quite certainly his.

GEERTGEN · ST JOHN IN THE WILDERNESS
16¾″ × 11¼″. *Berlin, Staatl. Museen*

GELDER

This Dordrecht painter's frien Houbraken, has transmitted son account of his life to posterit Aert de Gelder (1645-1727) described by him as a cheerfu even-tempered, and pious bu critical and shrewd personag who bore his affliction of squin ing, which occasioned some cru jests, with resignation. His mo attractive feature was his devotio to Rembrandt.

Gelder belonged to a prominen family, his father being one o the directors of the West Indi Company. After studying und the well-known theorist an painter Hoogstraten, Aert move about 1661 to Rembrandt's studi in Amsterdam. Rembrandt had b that time become unfashionabl But Aert took no notice of h unpopularity. Without giving u his own idiosyncrasies—the slap dash drawing, the thick impast and other somewhat boisterou methods of attracting a spectator attention—the younger man adop ted Rembrandt's style and con tinued to employ it, in oppositio to the taste of the day. Conse quently, he grew steadily poore Eventually he had to sell h house. It would certainly hav pleased this good-natured artis

he could have foreseen the later success
his work. For the time came when
s pictures were believed to be by Rem-
andt and commanded corresponding
ices.

In his lifetime his reputation was merely
ovincial. But his true worth has now for
ng been recognised and he is represented
nearly all the big galleries.

ENGA

irolamo Genga of Urbino (c. 1476-
1551) was one of those minor 'universal
niuses' who thrived so well in the atmo-
here of the Renaissance. He painted
sel-pictures and frescoes, decorated
teriors, organised festivals, planned forti-
cations and worked as an architect. His
rsatility, accordingly, rivalled Leon-
do's. But his pictures, unfortunately, did
ot.

He studied under and assisted Signorelli,
ccentuating still further the latter's rigid
yle. Genga's *Aeneas* at Siena and *Cupid
ound* in the National Gallery, London
lustrate this tendency. It was somewhat
laxed under the influence of Perugino,
hom he joined about 1500, and Raphael,
hom he met at Perugino's studio. The
ape of the Sabine Women* at Strasbourg is
a example of his looser manner. It gradu-
ly improved in grace of execution, but
ll more and more into the convention of
a extraordinary structural symmetry,
arried to extremes in his *Disputation of
e Fathers of the Church on the Immaculate
onception* in Berlin, a work at the same
me of the greatest possible fascination.
[e could never entirely suppress his gift
or decorative exuberance.

For most of his life he was employed
y the Court at Urbino, where many of
is frescoes have survived. A typical
eature of them is the frequency with
hich sham architecture is represented.
Senga was in fact really important as an
rchitect.

GENRE

his word, meaning genus, mode or
ustom, is applied to the kind of picture
vhich represents unidentified but typical
ersons engaged in common, unexacting
but characteristic tasks. Terbrugghen's
Tric-trac Players, for instance, is a *genre*
picture. But if a painting represented
Napoleon playing chess with Bernadotte,
it would not fall into this category, since
it would have been painted for the sake
of introducing a historic figure and the
game, though unimportant in itself, would
here have a special significance. *Genre*
painting flourished, in particular, in the
Netherlands during the seventeenth century, when it was practised by Jan Steen,
Teniers, Brouwer, Metsu, Dou and
Ostade. Vermeer of Delft was also a *genre*
painter, a fact which proves that the
highest level of pure art can be reached by
this sort of picture, where the trivial
theme is of no consequence whatever.

GENT, JUSTUS VON
(*see* JUSTUS)

GENTILESCHI
Born in Pisa in 1562 and dying in London
in 1637, Orazio Gentileschi went to Rome
at the age of seventeen, where he soon
received his first commission for frescoes.
Some of these paintings—those, for example, at San Niccolo in Carcere—have
unfortunately been damaged. They prove,
nevertheless, that the artist must have been
one of the first to abandon Mannerism.
About 1600 he fell completely under the
spell of Caravaggio. In 1626 Charles I
invited him to London and gave him a
pension of £500 a year. The painter's
reputation reached Spain. Philip IV
ordered from him a *Finding of Moses*, now
in the Prado. Hermann Voss writes:
'Though his naturalism would be incon-
ceivable without reference to Caravaggio,
the emotional element in Gentileschi is
entirely different, being tempered to a
delicately elegant lyricism sometimes
touched with effeminacy.' His style forms
a link between that of Caravaggio and that
of Elsheimer.

His most popular work is an *Annunciation* at Turin. The contrasting notes of
naturalistic reporting and idealistic tenderness lend great interest to his *Rest on the
Flight* at the Louvre. It is unfortunate

O. GENTILESCHI · THE LUTE PLAYER
57⅞" × 52". Vaduz, Liechtenstein Gallery

power of rendering detail h
resembles Hilliard. A great ma
pictures are attributed to hi
among them several portraits
Queen Elizabeth. The only ful
authenticated works are the po
traits of Elizabeth Cherry, Lac
Russell and Sir William Russe
dated 1625, at Woburn, the po
trait of William Camden in tl
Bodleian Library, Oxford, and tl
remarkable *Head and Shoulders*
a Dead Man, dated 1607, in tl
Kröller-Müller Collection, ne
Arnhem.

GHIRLANDAIO

The name of Domenico del Ghi
landaio calls to mind the mo
brilliant period of Florenti
painting. His contemporari
could say, with Ulrich von Hutte
in Germany, 'It is a pleasure t
be alive.' The Renaissance ha
not yet reached its zenith. Tl
age still retained something of tl
cool, fresh atmosphere of earl
morning.

that the size of his pictures necessitates
their relegation to the larger rooms of
galleries.

His daughter **Artemisia** was born at
Rome in 1597 and died in Naples after
1651. In the latter city, after working in
Florence, she acquired an important
influence, of the same kind as her father's,
on Neapolitan painting.

GHEERAERTS

Marc Gheeraerts (1561-1635) came to
England from Bruges at the age of six with
his father, also called Marc and also a
painter. **Marc Gheeraerts the Elder** was
well known in his own country as a painter
and designer. Portraits of Queen Elizabeth
and Burghley attributed to him are in the
National Portrait Gallery. But Marc
Gheeraerts the Younger is a much more
interesting artist. Despite his Flemish
origin, he is the first painter to express an
unmistakably English spirit in portraiture.
His work is informed with a gentle poetry,
and in the delicacy of his workmanship and

Ghirlandaio, who was born in Florenc
in 1449 and died there in 1494, signed h
chief works 'Bighordi Grillandai'. He wa
the son of a goldsmith and wreath-make
named Bigordi and studied under Baldc
vinetti, though Verrocchio had a fa
greater influence on his style. The fre
quency with which the artistic ancestr
of the later Florentines can be traced bac
to these two men is quite unaccountabl
Ghirlandaio very soon became famous—
was not until later that the reputations c
Botticelli and Leonardo far outstripped hi
own—first acquiring fame for his frescoe
He was quite unable himself to cope wit
all his commissions and so set up a larg
workshop. Its existence has unfortunatel
made it difficult for posterity to distinguis
his own work from that of others whom h
employed and thus isolate it from th
indifferent contributions of his collabor
ators. His personal style is most evident i
the frescoes of the Sassetti Chapel in S
Trinità at Florence, depicting the life o
St Francis, and in the Tornabuoni frescoe

f the life of the Virgin in S. Maria Novella, Florence. In these scenes he combined biblical elements with features typical of everyday life in Florence, which greatly attracted his contemporaries. But these narrative and anecdotal passages would fail to hold our attention today if they were not so splendidly painted in so forthright and chaste a manner. The simplicity and strictness of his composition are rather wooden in effect and there is little feeling to be traced in the faces of his figures.

D. DEL GHIRLANDAIO · PORTRAIT OF AN OLD MAN · 20¾" × 18¾". *Paris, Louvre*

And yet they seem 'laid up in lavender'.

Ghirlandaio also painted a series of frescoes in San Gimigano, Pisa and Rome. In the latter city he collaborated in the decorative work begun at the Sistine Chapel in 1481. It was not until 1508 that the ceiling was painted by his pupil, Michelangelo. Relatively few of Ghirlandaio's easel-pictures have been preserved. Some are in the Uffizi Gallery.

The altarpiece of the *Virgin in Glory* at Munich can only be in part by Ghirlandaio. But the *Old Man with His Grandson* in the Louvre is a masterpiece. The pretty little boy in this picture, affectionately embracing his grandfather, who is disfigured by a boil on the nose, only sees the old man's tender smile, not his repulsive ugliness. The effect is intensely moving.

Ridolfo del Ghirlandaio (1483-1561) was Domenico's son. He was taught by his father's brother, David, a painter of little distinction. Ridolfo's style was made up of elements taken from Fra Bartolommeo, Raphael and Leonardo; it is heavy and lacks genuine inspiration. But Ridolfo had a happy gift for portraiture. The quality of his work is best shown by the two Uffizi pictures of scenes from the life of St Zenobius. His *Procession to Calvary* in the National Gallery, London, contains an interesting portrait of Piero di Cosimo.

GIAMBONO

Michele Giovanni Bono (active 1420-1462), called Giambono, was born in Venice and was perhaps a pupil of Jacobello del Fiore and a follower of Gentile da Fabriano. The *Virgin and Child* in the Palazzo Venezia in Rome, with its background of Venetian damask, showed the influence of Gentile. Giambono also painted the St Chrisogorus in SS. Gervasio and Protasio, Venice, the standing figure of a Pope, now in the Civic Museum, Padua, and a *St Mark* in the National Gallery, London, all decidedly Gothic in style.

GIORDANO

The Neapolitan painter Luca Giordano (1632-1705) was one of the most famous Italian artists of his time. His personality, even more overwhelming than his productions, so dazzled his contemporaries that they were unable to detect his entire lack of creative ability. Naples, Rome, Florence, Venice, Bergamo and Genoa were awestruck by him. The Pope loaded him with honours. Charles II invited him to Spain, where he remained from 1692 to 1702. He bequeathed to posterity mythological, biblical, allegorical and historical paintings, altarpieces and battle-scenes, still-life pictures and portraits. He painted in oils, fresco, tempera and pastel. The fresco he produced for the dome of San Martino at Naples only took him forty-eight hours. The number of his works is estimated at 5,000. Posse writes that he was 'a typical virtuoso, but lacked artistic integrity. He imitated the styles of Ribera, Veronese, Titian, Tintoretto, Bassano, Raphael, Guido Reni and even Dürer, Rembrandt and Rubens, to the point of downright forgery.'

There is a 'Raphael' by Giordano in the Prado, a 'Ribera' at Berlin and several 'Lucas van Leydens' and 'Dürers' in the United States. It is only necessary to inspect one of these works to realise that the gifts of a craftsman of genius were wasted in this way.

GIORGIONE

The mystery surrounding Giorgione's life and work has not been dispelled to this day. The fact would not be so strange in the case of a Gothic painter. But it is quite inexplicable in that of a man of the Renaissance. For the age was historically self-conscious and articulate to a marked degree. Giorgione was one of the most puzzling and shadowy, and yet one of the greatest, painters who ever lived.

His full name is not mentioned in any document. Vasari and Aretino in their later publications call him 'Giorgione', i.e. 'the great George'. His friends referred to him, in Venetian dialect, as 'Zorzi'. He came from Castelfranco. But the year of his birth is unknown. Probably it was 1478. His arrival in Venice and appearance at the studio of Giovanni Bellini, who ruled the painters of the day like a Doge, caused something like the excitement of a stupendous natural phenomenon. He seemed a tremendous fellow full of wildly revolutionary and romantic ideas. Within ten years he changed the whole aspect of contemporary painting. Breaking with all tradition, he was the first artist to praise painting for its own sake. He shocked Venice by his frescoes in the German Merchants' Hall. No one could understand

them, as they had no 'subject'. Today they only exist in a fragmentary state and in engravings. Nor could anyone comprehend his enigmatic *Tempest* or his strange landscape of the *Three Philosophers*, which looks as if it might mean something, but in the end reveals nothing but its own endless fascination. Giorgione gave his amazed contemporaries, for the first time, an art unfettered by any prescribed terms of reference. It was art for art's sake.

Giorgione's pictures have in fact no subject: they do not portray incidents and they are not illustrations. They are records of the artist's romantic sensibility. He created ideal landscapes with figures which recorded his personal reactions to the world he knew. Two centuries were to pass before a similar lyrical, romantic attitude was reflected in the art of Watteau.

We know next to nothing of Giorgione's character. But oral tradition has preserved the legend of his boisterous adventures, his singing and dancing, and his love-affairs. A document dated 25th October, 1510, refers to the property left at his death, of which we have no other intimation. The plague was raging in Venice at the time. Giorgio of Castelfranco probably died of it.

GIORGIONE · THE TEMPEST
31¼″ × 28¾″. Venice, Accademia

His works constitute a complete iddle for posterity. Half a century go books about him might contain s many as thirty or forty reproductions of pictures attributed to im. Any work which to some extent suggested his style was claimed as his by its proud possessor. Many in fact bore the helpful signature 'Zorzo'. But this plentiful supply of dubiously authenticated works has melted away under the tests applied by modern research. Very few are now regarded as genuine. Some idea can therefore be formed of the value of each individual item. Such a painting as the *Three Philosophers* at Vienna would be bought by the United States at any price. Venice possesses the *Tempest*, Berlin the *Portrait of a Young Man*, Castelfranco the altarpiece of the *Virgin Enthroned*, Dresden the *Sleeping Venus* and Paris the *Fête Champêtre*.

GIOTTINO

Some scraps of information relating to a certain 'Giotto di Maestro Stefano, called Giottino', active between 1324 and 1369, have enabled several frescoes and panels to be ascribed to this artist. But quite a different painter, about whom there is also some documentary evidence, appears in Vasari's *Lives* as Giottino. This is one 'Maso Fiorentino, called Giottino'. Vasari thus makes one person out of two.

Some modern experts believe there were two; others only one. In either case the work in question is that of an outstanding disciple of the great Giotto di Bondone. The paintings now grouped under Giotto's name, viz. the *Crucifixion* and *Nativity* in the Strozzi Chapel of the Cloister of Sta Maria Novella, Florence, show him to be close to Giotto in dramatic power and plastic quality.

GIOTTO

Born at Colle di Vespignano c. 1266 and dying in Florence in 1337, Giotto di

GIORGIONE · PORTRAIT OF A YOUNG MAN
$23\frac{1}{4}'' \times 18\frac{5}{8}''$. *Berlin, Staatl. Museen*

Bondone was gratefully and vividly remembered by Italians, for 150 years after his death, as a man of the 'Dark Ages' who had created Western painting and opened their eyes to a new vision. Lorenzo de' Medici set up a bust of him in Florence Cathedral. That was something the ordinary citizens could understand. They thronged to attend the ceremony and gazed upon the monument as if it were that of some old king or saint. Even so enlightened a representative of the Renaissance as Vasari does not hesitate to couple the name of Giotto with that of God. 'Through the grace of Heaven', he writes, 'Giotto alone, though born at a time of incompetent masters'—he ignores Cimabue—'resurrected the dead body of art and raised it to such a perfection that it could be called excellent. It was truly the greatest of miracles that so coarse and bungling an age

GIOTTO · THE BAPTISM
(Fresco.'Detail) 92" × 100". Padua
Arena Chapel

could attain to such creative skill, in the person of Giotto, that the art of painting, of which people at that time knew little or nothing, once more came to take a definite part, through him, in our lives.'

Giotto's high reputation is by no means due to his historical position alone, as might be assumed by those who have never inspected his works with the attention they deserve. Such an examination at once proves that he would have been a great painter if he had been born 100 years later. The difficulty of recognising the archaic beauties of his style is intelligible enough. Sometimes, on being suddenly faced with reproductions of details taken from his paintings, one cannot believe that one has ever seen them before. For example, one may be looking, from roof-top level, at the back of a Cross sloping forwards and downwards above the wall of the house. The object is brick-red against a clear blue sky. The struts and ropes holding it in position are visible, for they are the necessary supports, in a profane view, for such a symbol. Nothing indicates that the crowd in movement below it is paying any attention to the crucified figure on the other side of the Cross. This detail is so emphatically presented as to be positively expressionistic. The fresco from which it is

taken is at Assisi. Again, a female figur is shown framed in a stone doorway, a though at the moment of stepping int public view. The head is bent far back, th mouth wide open, as if uttering a soundles scream, the clenched hands tearing at th clothing about the neck. The woma appears to be suffocating. Beneath thi picture, which is in the Arena Chapel a Padua, Giotto inscribed the title, Ange

The impression made by his work as whole is no less majestic. His object wa to display the permanent pattern o humanity's reactions to experience a exemplified in stories from the Bible, whic he naturally regarded as of universa application. He illustrated, therefore, th feelings inherent in astonishment, hesita tion, anger, terror, devotion, parting, meet ing and humiliation. He omitted everythin inessential, reducing landscape and archi tecture, for instance, to mere suggestions The historical significance of Giotto is tha he freed painting from the rigid Byzantin convention. Every one of his pictures i dramatic. Their grandiose effect, far mor striking than any which the 'excite Mannerists could contrive 250 years late arises from the silence in which the scene proceed. No one speaks. The action is all important. No cries are uttered. Sufferin is dumb. Grief is expressed only, as in the *Meeting of Joachim and Anna* at Padua, by a dark mantle drawn across the face as the figure turns away. Prolonged contemplation of the great Madonna altarpiece at the Uffizi Gallery is required before the full force of the expression on the features of the Virgin can be realised. It conveys neither the impassivity of Cimabue's Madonnas nor the innocent girlishness of Fra Angelico's nor the haughty, unapproachable egotism so often depicted by Piero della Francesca. The steady gaze of Giotto's Virgin is that of critical, expectant concentration. One feels that she will remember, at the Day of Judgment, all those who have made application to her. Dante bears witness to the deep impression received by Giotto's contemporaries from his frescoes and altarpieces. The poet, who probably met the painter at Padua, mentions him in the *Divine Comedy*.

Little is known of Giotto's life. He was the son of a peasant. Cimabue is said to have found him drawing as he watched his flock and to have taken the young shepherd into his studio. He very soon became famous, obtaining the most important commissions. His chief works are to be found at Assisi, Padua, Florence and Berlin. Frescoes and panels are preserved in Florence, panels in Berlin. Like many great Italian painters, he was also an architect. The campanile of the Cathedral at Florence was designed by him. He was granted the contract, which he did not live to complete, three years before his death.

GIOVANNI DA MILANO

Giovanni di Jacopo di Guido should really be called, not 'da Milano', but 'da Caversago', from his birthplace near Como. Certain documents in fact mention him by this name. He is first referred to in 1350 as an immigrant apprentice painter at Florence and for the last time in 1369 as a Vatican artist. But he seems to have spent most of his life in Florence.

He is still regarded as the 'foreign' painter among the Florentines of his day. It is clear that he was not influenced by them. They were already adherents of Gaddi's school, while he remained faithful to the strict Sienese style and that of Giotto. His devoted studies of facial expression, clothing and animals also seemed 'foreign' to the Florentines.

His chief works, many of which have apparently been lost, are his *Pietà* in the Uffizi Gallery, his frescoes at Santa Croce, Florence, and his altarpiece at Prato. Berlin possesses a wonderfully fine drawing of the Crucifixion. Drawings dating from this period are extremely rare. None of Giotto's, for example, is known, and only one by Taddeo Gaddi, in London. Berlin has a single drawing by Agnolo Gaddi.

GIOVANNI DI PAOLO

Giovanni di Paolo di Grazia was born c. 1403 in Siena and died there c. 1483. Little is known of his life. Though a pupil of the eminent Sassetta and living at a time when the Renaissance spirit had long been operative, Giovanni di Paolo, surprisingly enough, painted some of his pictures in a Gothic style stubbornly unaffected by all subsequent development. Yet other paintings appear purely eclectic, recalling the manners of a number of his contemporaries. His *Annunciation*, for instance, and *Expulsion from Paradise* are based on work by Fra Angelico. He is accordingly to be judged as a Late Gothic artist. In his *Flight into Egypt*, at Siena, sunlit contours are simply outlined in gold. In the *Rescue from Shipwreck in a Storm*, at Philadelphia, ship, wreckage and figures, including that of the Saviour, are distributed in surrealist fashion, constituting a flat pattern, free from perspective and space composition. Both these works have great charm.

GIRTIN

Thomas Girtin was born in Southwark in 1775, the son of a brush-maker. He was apprenticed to a drawing master named Fisher and afterwards to Edward Dayes, and at eighteen he was already an accomplished topographical draughtsman. He met Turner at the house of Dr Monro, the amateur painter and collector, and the two young men worked side by side copying drawings in the doctor's collection. Girtin travelled all over England making drawings, and in 1801 he went to Paris. The next year he was dead of an affection of the lungs. Girtin's fame rests on his watercolours. He developed the watercolour technique so that instead of consisting, as it had done hitherto, of line and wash, it could compete in strength and depth of tone with oil. Many of Girtin's watercolours are naturally purely topographical, but others, such as the noble *Kirkstall Abbey*, are sensitive records of moods and emotions rather than of place, and show Girtin to have been one of the earliest painters of romantic landscapes, the precursor of the great nineteenth-century romantics, Turner and Constable.

GIULIO ROMANO

The real name of this 'Giulio from Rome' was Pippi. He was born in that city in 1499 and died in Mantua in 1546. He remained on intimate terms with Raphael until the latter's death in 1520, living in his house, studying under him, assisting him with his Vatican frescoes and probably even with his easel-pictures, such as the *St Margaret* and *Joanna of Aragon* in the Louvre. He inherited Raphael's property.

In 1524 Duke Federigo Gonzaga invited him to Mantua. The invitation was eagerly accepted. For meanwhile Aretino's sonnets, with illustrations by Giulio of a hitherto unprecedented indecency, had appeared and seemed likely to create a scandal. The wrath of the Pope, in fact, came to a head shortly after Giulio's departure, bursting in full force upon the unfortunate copper-etcher, Marcanton. But by that time Giulio was safely in Abraham's bosom at Mantua. The Duke appreciated his painting and architectural designs, loading him with honours and gifts. It was during this period that Giulio produced most of his surviving works, including some excellent portraits and innumerable frescoes which were admired by Rubens himself.

Giulio's colour, in his later years, bore less and less resemblance to Raphael's, often resorting to highlights of blazing red accompanied by black shadows. But ancient Roman life and sculpture continued to exert the influence they had acquired over him in his youth.

GOES

The document stating that Hugo van der

H. VAN DER GOES · THE
PORTINARI ALTARPIECE
*(Centre panel) 101¼″ × 121⅞″.
Florence, Uffizi*

Goes was born at Ghent does not record the year of his birth. It must have been about 1400. In 1467 he was appointed a master of the local guild, the witness to his appointment, a certain Josse van Wassenhove, being none other than Justus of Ghent. In the following year Van der Goes took a very modest part in the provision of decorations for the wedding of Charles the Bold at Bruges. But by 1469 his reputation already stood high. In 1475 he was working at his world-renowned altarpiece for the Florentine commercial agent, Portinari. But a year later he had entered a monastery. His reasons for taking this astonishing step are still obscure. It is probable that he already suspected the onset of the insanity which eventually overtook him.

At first, however, he lived in very worldly style at the monastery, that of the Red Cloister, near Brussels. He

H. VAN DER GOES · THE PORTINARI ALTARPIECE (*Detail*)

visited Louvain to act as arbitrator in the question of the town's indebtedness to the widow of Dirk Bouts, who had recently died. Money was owed to her in respect of Bouts's unfinished series of panels for the municipal Courts of Justice. Van der Goes also received important visitors at the monastery, including the future Emperor Maximilian. But by 1482, when the artist died, his mind had already given way.

The melancholy fate of this great master, whose body was 'possessed by demons and the Devil' and destroyed, while the pure lustre of his works lived on, made a deep impression at the time. Men were already conscious of the idea expressed by Max Friedländer in our own day. He observed that if we were told that Memling's mind was affected we should have no reason to draw any conclusions from the statement. But in the case of Van der Goes, he added, the tension evident in his works appears so great that

his mental collapse may be regarded as the snapping of it, a consequence of creative strain. Alternatively, his genius might be considered a result of his diseased condition.

The tension referred to by Friedländer as characteristic of Hugo's pictures is entirely different from that, for example, of vigorous movement in Michelangelo's works or the oppressive accumulation of suppressed emotion in those of Dirk Bouts. It is to be found in the dualism clearly discernible in the opposed groups of figures typical of all his chief productions, as, for example, in the famous Portinari altarpiece at the Uffizi Gallery, depicting the Adoration of the Shepherds. On one side the artist represents the group of those who will never be accused and have no need to fear. It includes the Virgin, the Infant Christ, the angels and the symbolic irises. There is less material emphasis in their forms, which are ascetic and coloured in transparent, cool tones. On the other side Van der Goes shows the group to which he felt himself to belong. They are thick-blooded, darkly coloured, unsteady on their feet, representing the naïvety and fervour of an ignorant rabble in comparison with the Divine purity. The adoring and the adored are no longer, in Van der Goes's works, a single big family. The elect seem utterly separate from the rest, unless the tiny Child Himself provides the link between His group and that of the rude shepherds, showing their teeth in uncouth grins of delight.

When this element has once been detected in a picture by Van der Goes, it will be recognised as the source of a constant feeling of anxiety in his works. Such a feeling would be merely a supplementary, purely intellectual con-stituent of his art and would not be sufficient in itself to prove him a great painter, if his productions were not at the same time so wonderfully impressive as sheer painting.

His composition and realistic draughts-manship, and to a less extent his singularly cool range of colour, exercised a powerful influence on his successors. The Italians themselves, when the Portinari altarpiece arrived in Florence, were fascinated by the work of the ill-fated Flemish master. A similar spirit informs his Berlin *Nativity*. Its note is repeated in the tumultuous entrance of the shepherds, caught in the act of snatching off their caps. A third important work, the Mon-forte altarpiece, also at Berlin, is difficult to place chronologically. The style is remarkably unassuming, tranquil and conservative. Its somewhat ironic melan-choly was carried a stage further by Geertgen. There is another *Nativity* at Wilton House and a Madonna altar-piece at Frankfurt. His earliest work, the *Fall* and *Deposition* diptych, is at Vienna, his latest, the *Death of the Virgin*, at Bruges. Puyvelde notes of this picture that the apostles 'look like men in the grip of hallu-cination and nightmare'.

GOLTZIUS

The fame of Hendrick Goltzius, born at Mühlbrecht, near Venlo, in 1558 and dying in Haarlem in 1617, can hardly be imagined today. When the Emperor Rudolf II gave orders for a picture by Goltzius to be procured, the imperial agent reported that neither love nor money could obtain one.

And yet it was not until 1600 that Goltzius turned to painting. His renown had in fact begun while he was still only etching on copper. The reason why he took up painting is unknown. It may have been simply vanity. He had just returned from a prolonged tour in Italy. He began by experimenting with small paintings on copper and ended by composing large allegorical and mythological scenes with figures in the pretentious Mannerist style. His touches of red are characteristic. As a painter he had no influence. But many painters, among them Cornelis van Haar-lem (q.v.) profited by association with him, for he was a highly cultivated, judicious and gifted man.

GONÇALVES

The greatest of Portuguese painters, Nuno Gonçalves, is first mentioned in documents during the period 1450-1471. A century later he is referred to by a chronicler as having been an 'eagle'.

Gonçalves was a truly great painter. His St Vincent altarpiece at Lisbon is far superior to all other productions of his time in Portugal and Spain. The six large panels in oils, somewhat resembling frescoes, show King Alfonso and Henry the Navigator praying to their patron saint. They are closely surrounded by a crowd of personages whose figures occupy the entire background, so that not an inch of landscape is visible. But all the pride of the Renaissance is anticipated in the faces and forms represented, from the dignity and self-assurance of the scholar to the careless squalor of the poverty-stricken. The colour is so sumptuous that at the first glance one might suppose that the artist had studied Hugo van der Goes. But this view would be mistaken. The spell cast by Gonçalves is due to elements of a wholly different nature, purely Portuguese.

The St Vincent altarpiece is authenticated by documents and signed by the artist. But unfortunately no conclusive evidence has yet been found of his responsibility for other works.

GOUACHE

This French word denotes a watercolour in which the paint has been thickened by a substance. The colours do not, therefore, mingle and flow into one another, with transparent effect, in the ordinary way. On the contrary, one colour is laid over another, completely covering it, as well as, of course, the entire painting surface, whether paper, woven material or ivory. The technique is therefore closely related to that of oils, though the matt surface of the painting in gouache, on the other hand, resembles that of a normal watercolour. In tempera painting the colours are also held in solution in this way, but are not, as in gouache, opaque. Gouache was frequently used by the Old Masters for preliminary sketches.

GOVAERTS

Abraham Govaerts of Antwerp (1589-1626) painted a great many, mostly small, landscapes. They are to be found in nearly all European galleries, though sometimes unjustly confined, 'for lack of space', to the basement. The style of Govaerts is derived from that of Coninxloo, though he was later more influenced by that of Jan Brueghel. The landscapes are painted in tones of deep green, usually representing faintly-lit, thick woods, with a view into the distance. A horse-drawn cart, some resting peasants or a traveller attacked by robbers may be added. But sometimes Govaerts places in his superbly painted glades a tiny fairies' chariot, with a fairy queen and red-legged swans.

GOYA

Francisco José Goya y Lucientes was born at Fuendetodos in Aragon in 1746 and died in Bordeaux in 1828. It was not until modern times that he was regarded as an Old Master. To our fathers he seemed almost as up-to-date as themselves. A whole series of his pictures may be compared with those of much later periods. His impassioned *Execution of the Rebels* appears more modern than Manet's restrained *Execution of Maximilian*. His impudent *Nude Courtesan* at Madrid looks later than Manet's respectable *Olympia*. His expressionist *The Old Men* might have been painted more recently than Van Gogh's *Potato Eaters*. He is the last of the Old Masters, the first modern artist. His work foreshadows the whole course of painting for 100 years after his death.

But the historical position of a painter can at most render him interesting and significant. He can only be regarded as great on the strength of his purely pictorial qualities. Goya passes his test. The portraits of his middle period have a beauty, assurance, refinement of colour and psychological subtlety that bring him close to Velasquez in this field. He represented his brother-in-law, Bayeu, a commercially successful painter, in masterly fashion as a vacant-faced old man who had made

GOYA · SELF-PORTRAIT
18⅞" × 16". Madrid, Prado

nothing of his life, the very image of joy-lessness. This portrait is in the Prado. That of the Surgeon-General Queralto at Munich has an incomparable nobility. The portrait of Countess Solana-Carpio in the Louvre is harmonious in design. But the underlying sentiment is one of scorn for human pretension. The standing figure has the look of excessive gentility given by Terborch to his paintings of individuals. The woman's birdlike, garish adornments resemble those of a tragedy queen. Goya's feelings are indicated even more emphatic-

GOYA · KING CHARLES IV AND HIS FAMILY
(Detail) 112″ × 134⅜″. Madrid, Prado

ally in his masterpiece, the large picture of the royal family of Spain, its pitiable king and his hysterical consort, looking like strolling players in their grease-paint.

His important pictures of dramatic action are late works, beginning about 1798. The malicious group-portrait belongs to about the same period. Goya had by that time recovered from a serious breakdown, both physical and mental. In his wild, dissolute youth, he had painted tamely. Now, tamed himself and resentful of the base conduct of mankind, he became an artistic rebel. When he began work, after the recovery of his health, on the Florida frescoes, today so famous, at Madrid, he climbed the scaffolding as if storming a barricade. These wall-paintings, the finest he ever did, were dashed off in three months. He made use of his thumbs and of sponges soaked in colour as well as brushes. His last works also comprise, in addition to the great drawings, his *Execution of the Rebels*, at Madrid, his scenes from common life and in particular the weird paintings, of a sinister beauty, with which he decorated the walls of his country house. They include *The Old Men* and the *Witches' Sabbath*, now in the Prado. Goya was the most demoniac in inspiration of all painters. It only failed him when he sank to insincerity and pot-boiling. The failure was then absolute. His *St Francis Exhorting the Unrepentant Dying Man*, at Valencia, resembles a hypocritical, moralising piece by Fuseli.

Goya was trained at Saragossa by José Luzan. But his models were Velasquez, Mengs and Tiepolo, the two latter artists being at Madrid from 1761 onwards. Mengs obtained him commissions for tapestry designs to be used in the State factory. One of these, *Under the Sunshade*, is preserved in the Prado. Goya painted them entirely in the spirit of Tiepolo. The first contracts for frescoes came to him through his brother-in-law. In consequence of stabbing affrays and offences against morality, he fled to Italy, allegedly with a troupe of circus performers. The works he painted in Italy have disappeared. In 1771 he returned to Spain, where he undertook portraits and ecclesiastical commissions. In 1792 he fell ill and became completely deaf. His detestation of Napoleon and scorn for the Spanish Government drove him, though he had meanwhile been appointed Court Painter, into retirement at his country house. In 1824 he visited France, returning for a short while to Madrid in the summer of 1826. He then remained in voluntary exile at Bordeaux until his death.

GOYEN

Jan van Goyen was born at Leyden in 1596. His father, who wished him to become a craftsman, apprenticed him at the age of ten to a glass-painter. In addition to fetching beer and tobacco, sweeping the floor and rocking cradles, the boy also apparently learnt to draw. He served three 'masters' in this way. Only the fourth allowed him anywhere near an easel. At twenty Jan paid a visit to France, where no doubt he realised that the best thing he could do would be to resume his apprenticeship. He was able to do so, the father being still willing to pay for his lessons. The ensuing year was decisive, for Jan's new teacher was none other than the important landscape painter, Esaias van de Velde. The pupil made rapid progress. In 1634 he settled at The Hague, where life was easier. He would have become a rich man if he had not speculated in tulips and fallen a victim to unscrupulous scoundrels. He made another mistake, though it was one we may be grateful for. He painted too many pictures, over 1,000. They were all equally good and prices fell. So he died poor in 1656, leaving his son-in-law, Jan Steen, to inherit a great many canvases, children and difficulties.

Goyen's first pictures are ponderously realistic in drawing, like those of his teacher, Van de Velde. The colour, too,

J. VAN GOYEN · LANDSCAPE WITH OAKS
35⅞" × 44¼". Amsterdam, Rijksmuseum

is conventional. But from about 1630 onwards one masterpiece succeeds another. The drawing grows less and less obtrusive and colour all-important. The greyish-green tones of the earlier pictures and the blended tints of sunny gold in the late landscapes are laid on direct, almost in pre-impressionist style. Nothing but pure landscape is conveyed in his best work. The atmospheres of evening or of early morning, riverside or downland views, as well as subjects taken from village life, alternate with wintry scenes. Goyen is one of the finest landscape painters Holland has produced. He is well represented in the National Gallery, London.

GOZZOLI

The son of a peasant, Benozzo di Lese Gozzoli was born in Florence in 1420 and died at Pisa in 1497. His father apprenticed him to Lorenzo Ghiberti. The boy's talent must therefore have been remarkable, for Ghiberti was at that time the most celebrated of sculptors. Shortly after 1444 Gozzoli abandoned sculpture and bronze-casting for painting. He entered the studio of Fra Angelico. Such plain statements may well stagger a twentieth-century reader when he reflects on the great names they introduce and the glory conferred upon the period by these illustrious artists.

Innumerable frescoes by Gozzoli survive in Rome, Orvieto, Montefalco, Perugia, San Gimignano, Pisa and Florence. The most famous is the *Journey of the Magi* in the private chapel of the Riccardi-Medici palace at Florence. Gozzoli never again achieved the richness of colour and splendid drawing, the dawnlike freshness, of this wonderful work, constituting a sparkling overture to the great drama of the Renaissance. Some of his easel-pictures, such as his *Madonna* and *Resurrection of a Dead Boy*, both at Berlin, are in fact naïve and lacking in invention. Few of his smaller works have been preserved. The nearer they approach the theme of the Riccardi fresco, the more successful is the treatment, as, for example, in the enchanting *Rape of Helen* in the National Gallery, London.

GRAF

Urs Graf was born at Solothurn c. 1485 and died in Basle, c. 1527/8. He was for ever on the move, a blustering soldier of fortune who drank hard and beat his wife, but an incorrigible jester whom everyone liked. More than once, on the occasion of some festival, popular clamour demanded his release from prison. For he was always being locked up.

He produced mostly drawings and illustrations. Only two of his paintings have survived, though he undoubtedly executed others. His two extant pieces, *St George and the Dragon* and *War*, are both at Basle. Graf owed much to Hans Baldung. But his style is less balanced, more slapdash and fanciful than Baldung's.

GRANACCI

Francesco Granacci was born in Florence in 1477 and died there in 1543. He began his career in the studio of Domenico Ghirlandaio, where he met a fellow-apprentice named Michelangelo Buonarroti and formed a lifelong friendship with him, though the two men were utterly dissimilar. In 1508 Michelangelo took Granacci with him to Rome to assist in the execution of the Sistine Chapel frescoes. Though the influence of Ghirlandaio, several of whose altarpieces Granacci finished after his teacher's death, always pervades his work, he did not accept it uncritically. He modified it sometimes by reference to Michelangelo, sometimes to Fra Bartolomeo or Lorenzo di Credi. Owing to this inconsistency of style, it is often difficult to identify his pictures. He was a man of many parts. Consequently, he was well known in a city so fond of pageantry as Florence.

GRANDI

It was formerly supposed that 'Ercole Grandi' was born about 1462. But he died in 1933. The latter date is not a typographical error, but, if you like, an abuse of language. In 1933, during the great exhibition of Ferrarese masters, it was discovered that the 'Ercole Grandi' mentioned in certain documents was identical with Ercole Roberti. Longhi, in his monograph on the Ferrarese School, cut out Grandi's name. The pictures which had been previously distinguished, in laborious and somewhat arbitrary fashion, from those of 'Grandi's' double, were then ascribed, or at any rate some of the most important of them, to Ercole Roberti.

GREBBER

Frans Grebber (1573-1649), a Haarlem painter, though much in demand for portraits and militia groups in his lifetime, is now regarded as of little importance, except as the teacher of Saenredam and Sir Peter Lely. He moved in prosperous circles, knew Rubens and Goltzius, and was consequently able to give his son Pieter a good start.

Pieter Grebber (1610-1652) is a much more significant artist. He freed himself from the academic style of his teacher, Goltzius, by tireless study of nature, including the nude. His large mythological and symbolic paintings show the influence of Rubens and in particular of Jordaens. But the style of his portraits is softly sentimental, with a special tenderness for pretty, hazel-eyed, exotic faces.

GRECO

Domenico Theotokopouli, called El Greco, was born at Candia in Crete c. 1541. He subsequently travelled through Venice into Spain. Though widely believed to be one of the most baffling of painters, he is not so in reality. A close examination of Tintoretto's *Christ Lulling the Storm* (see illustration under *Tintoretto*) proves that all the features of El Greco's style now regarded as expressionist were already present in the picture by the Venetian, with whom it is certain that El Greco at one time worked. Allowance must also be made for the impact on Greco of the ecstatically overwrought atmosphere of mysticism at Toledo. The Catholic Counter-Reformation was then at its height in Spain. The Church was reacting against the chilling blasts of Luther and Calvin by an excessive heightening of Catholic ardour. It welcomed, accordingly, every type of support for mysticism and the exaltation of the supernatural. It approved, for example, the elongated debility of El Greco's ecstatic figures, his dramatic landscapes, echoing Genesis, his colours recalling those of lightning and the unnatural, 'at the ninth hour' illuminations of his pictures. It is highly probable that the Spaniards of that time found El Greco's paintings less sensational than they appeared in the nineteenth and twentieth centuries. Modern tendencies in painting are partly responsible for the enormously high reputation, no doubt exaggerated to some extent, at present enjoyed by El Greco. In fact, he is once more being welcomed by persons in a state of ecstasy, though this time it is the principle of abstraction which they adore.

There is, of course, no question of the magnitude of his achievement. His work is equally important in landscape, portraiture and narrative painting. His most fascinating landscape, the *View of Toledo* in New York, looks as though Toledo, the creation of man, had been poured like molten lead into the excavated creation of God, and reduced to lifeless torpor in the process. One of Greco's best portraits, the *Grand Inquisitor Guevara*, is also preserved in New York. A second version is at Winter-

thur. Toledo possesses the *Burial of Count Orgaz*, a masterpiece, and Madrid a *Portrait of a Nobleman*, a *Resurrection* and a *Stripping of Christ*. A second version of the latter picture is at Munich. *The Dream of Philip II* hangs in the Escorial and a *Madonna* in Washington. Among other works in the National Gallery, London, are *Christ Driving the Traders from the Temple*, which clearly shows Tintoretto's influence, and the *Agony in the Garden*. The Greek collector, Reeder Niarchos, owns a *Pietà*.

But it should not be forgotten today that El Greco painted weak pictures, especially at the beginning of his career. The *Healing of the Blind Man* at Dresden is an example of this inferior work.

Little is known of his life. He is supposed to have studied under Titian, certainly collaborated with Tintoretto, paid a brief visit to Rome in 1570 and left that city for Toledo, where by 1577 he is recorded to have obtained citizenship. The cool-headed Philip II, who did not

EL GRECO · PORTRAIT
32⅜″ × 26⅜″. *Madrid, Prado*

EL GRECO · TOLEDO
48¾″ × 44¼″. New York, Metropolitan Museum

like him, only commissioned him once. Greco's patrons were prelates. He died at Toledo in 1614.

GREENHILL

John Greenhill was one of the most important English-born painters of the latter part of the seventeenth century. He was born about 1644 at Salisbury and the earliest known example of his work is a portrait of the Mayor, John Abbott, which hangs in the Guildhall there. Greenhill came to London in 1662 and entered Lely's studio. He died young in 1676. Despite his youth and the influence of his master, Greenhill's work is highly individual and purely English in temper. Two of his finest portraits are *Sir James Oxenden* in the collection of Lady Capel Cure and *Captain Clements* at Greenwich Hospital.

GREUZE

Jean Baptiste Greuze was born at Tournai in 1725 and died in Paris in 1805. He originated a type of unsophisticated girlish prettiness, with models wearing neat frilled dresses and caps. They have the fresh complexions of girls of good family, but the sly glances of less than innocent housemaids as they pout, simper and preen themselves These canvases date from the period of transition between the Rococo style and that of 'sensibility'. They have retained a certain picturesque charm to this day.

At one time, however, Greuze had a different aim. He wanted to achieve fame as a 'great'—that is to say, in his view, a historical—painter. When he moved to Paris after serving his apprenticeship at Lyons, he started by producing *genre* pictures in the former Dutch style. They proved a success. Year by year his reputation in this field increased. He then turned from imitating the old Dutch masters to develop his own style of smooth, enamel-like, sentimental and anecdotal illustration. Of these touching scenes of invalid fathers and paternal curses Diderot observed that they were 'exquisitely elaborate'. Meanwhile, Greuze was industriously painting his own wife's pretty little head, the girlish features that were later to become famous. No one who has ever inspected them will be surprised to hear that Madame Greuze's repeated infidelities eventually obliged the artist to divorce her.

The revolution put an end to his popularity. He died in poverty.

GRISAILLE

The literal meaning of this French word is 'grey'. When used of painting it refers to a work in oils or tempera—never to a drawing—executed exclusively in grey tones. In the late Gothic period the outer sides of the wings of altarpieces were sometimes in grisaille, as, for instance, in the works of Jan van Eyck and Dirk Bouts. By this procedure the altarpiece acquired sculptural features and the wings, owing to their lack of colour, were subordinated to the central effect.

GRÜNEWALD

Research has hitherto failed to throw any considerable light upon the shadowy figure of the painter and 'hydraulic engineer', Mathis Gothart (c. 1475-1520). Only a century after his death Sandrart had hardly anything to say of him. The few hints and references in documents subsequently discovered have added little to Sandrart's information. The latter calls him 'Matthäus Grünewald, also known as Matthäus von Aschaffenburg'. Some records mention Mathis Nithard Gothart of Würzburg. He himself signed his work MG.

In 1501 Mathias Grünewald, as he is now named, is mentioned in the records of Seligenstadt, near Aschaffenburg. From 1508 to about 1525 he was at Mainz in the service of the archbishop. He can be traced at Frankfurt in 1526 and in the following year far away at Halle on the Saale. There he painted the great Erasmus-Mauritius panel, now in Munich. Sandrart states that he had an unhappy life.

His few surviving works are among the most thrilling ever produced by the Christian spirit of the West.

Stylistically he remains unique, though efforts have been made to argue that he must have studied the remarkable Jan Polack, as well as Hans Burgkmair and possibly Hieronymus Bosch. Such attempts have little importance. Grünewald is an isolated figure in an age of disciplined, 'reasonable' painters like Dürer, Cranach and Holbein. His Isenheim altarpiece consti-tutes a final, 'unreasonable' mani-festation of formidable power.

His style is one of expressionist fervour, yet neither mystical nor ecstatic. The statements made are too clear and deliberate to justify any such description. The *Crucifixion* on the outer side of the Isenheim altarpiece has a terrible, realistic sobriety, conceived in the stern and gloomy spirit of archaic tragedy. The inner side of the altarpiece, with its incomparable play of colour, includes an *Annunciation* in which the Virgin adopts a writhing posture, a *Concert of Angels before the Madonna* and a *Resurrection* which is truly 'brighter than a thousand suns'. In none of these works is there any sign of dizzy exaltation, but only of such ardour as inspired Van Gogh to his strenuous endeavours to render brilliant sunlight.

MATHIAS GRÜNEWALD · THE ISENHEIM ALTARPIECE
(*The 'Resurrection'. Wing reduced in height*) 107⅞″ × 97¼″. *Colmar*

145

Grünewald never reached this level again. The altarpiece in question, today at Colmar in Alsace, represents his supreme achievement. But even in so tranquil and typical a picture of saints as the Mauritius panel at Munich, with its ebony and gold tones, Grünewald seems a painter from another world in comparison with Dürer in his versions of the Apostles or Pacher in his depictions of the Fathers of the Church. In the Munich panel the banner of pure orthodoxy is raised.

Other surviving works by Grünewald include a *Crucifixion* at Basel, a *Lamentation* at Aschaffenburg, a *Christ Carrying the Cross* and another *Crucifixion* at Karlsruhe, *Two Saints* at Frankfurt-am-Main and sections of the Maria Schnee altarpiece at Freiburg and Stuppach. In the *Mockery of Christ* at Munich the humiliation of Jesus is shown in an unprecedented and appalling manner. He sits with a clumsy bandage forcibly clapped over His eyes as though it were a bucket. The thought perpetually recurs that behind the bandage He must be weeping. A newly discovered painting in Munich, the attribution of which is not undisputed, but which is certainly elaborate enough in background to suggest Grünewald, represents the *Head of an Ecclesiastic*.

GUARDI

While Canaletto and Tiepolo acquired European fame, Francesco Guardi (1712-1793) was considered an industrious and amiable old painter, but not one to be taken very seriously. He was not elected to the Academy until near the end of his life and it was left to posterity to recognise his true stature.

As a Venetian he stood at the close of the Rococo period, the conclusion of a whole age of freedom and sovereignty enjoyed by the city. Four years after his death Venice became the capital of an Austrian province. Indefatigably, as if he felt bound to hand down former traditions, Guardi painted his impressions of Venice, his affectionate memories of her and his appreciation of the spectacle offered by her

gay, swaggering gallants. He did not see the city as a panorama, like Canaletto, but in intimate detail, full of the fragrant homely charm of a small town. He set down his views, distant prospects and scenes of action either in unpretentious lusciously flowing passages of brushwork like those of Corot or else in rapid flick of colour, short, nervous touches such a Magnasco employed. He often merely suggested his capricious figures, in 'short hand'. He never adopted a ceremonious attitude. He was too modest a man and too much of a pure painter to do so. Even his pictures of the pageants organised by Venice in honour of the Tsarevich show no sign of respectful formality. The artist' eye saw nothing in the Crown Prince and other dignitaries but dots and dashes Guardi is worlds away from any suspicion of anecdotal art. As a pure painter and nothing if not a colourist, he always looked for 'motives', never for a 'subject'.

His religious pictures have fallen into neglect, though they can still be seen in Venice, Trent, Pasiano, Roncegno and Grado. They do not show him at his best But this fact is more to his credit than otherwise. It is obvious that in these case the 'subject' forced itself too obtrusively on his attention. It restricted and embarrassed him, imposing a sense of obligation on his work. But he had to paint such pictures in order to earn a living. A small *Madonna and Child*, however, conceived as a *genre* study, is delightful. The picture is in a private collection in France.

Guardi was trained by his brother **Giovanni Antonio** (1698-1760), who had a higher reputation than Francesco in Venice. His pictures are excellent. But he was no genius. One of the sisters married Tiepolo.

Paintings by Francesco Guardi are today preserved in all large galleries and collections. They have seldom come on the market since he became popular in the United States.

GUERCINO

Giovanni Francesco Barbieri (1591-1666) is known in the history of art by his

ickname, Il Guercino
la Cento, 'the squint-
ng fellow from Cen-
o', a town near
'errara. He died at
Bologna, where he was
losely associated with
he Carracci circle,
hough the opposing
nfluence of Caravag-
io on his work is
qually evident. He
probably studied the
atter at Rome during
he years 1621-3 while
ngaged on his master-
piece, the *Aurora*
resco at the Villa
Ludovisi and the
lmost romantically

GUARDI · THE GRAND CANAL, VENICE · *19¼" × 29⅜". Washington, Nat. Gall.*

motional *Night* fresco. He returned
o Bologna in 1642 by way of Piacenza,
vhere he painted more frescoes. In
he former city he achieved a high reputa-
ion.

But the extremely accomplished and
mpassioned frescoes at Rome remain his
est work. His oils are very uneven.
Many of the smaller, unpretentious pic-
ures, such as the *Pleasures of Summer* in
the Uffizi Gallery, show a surprising vein
of poetry. But he was unfortunately also
capable, after undergoing the influence of
Guido Reni in 1625, of such works as
St Peter Raising the Dead in the Pitti
Palace, Florence, which shows no trace
of his former delight in the well-propor-
tioned human figure, the drawing being
confused and the tones repeatedly at
variance with nature.

H

HALS

Frans Hals was born at Mecheln in 1580 and died in Haarlem in 1666. He left a superb artistic legacy to posterity, for his works seem to prove that he experienced the whole range of human feelings, from the most exuberant vitality to the bitterest resignation. Yet his life was utterly uneventful. There is no documentary evidence that he ever enjoyed life in so hearty and masterful a fashion as Rembrandt did, nor that he ever, like Rembrandt in his old age, stamped through the streets as if he were King Lear in exile. The plain truth is that Hals lived on charity. He stood smiling, cap in hand, ready to receive his share, when the cart sent round by the municipality to distribute turf among the poor, as winter fuel, passed his house. The last of the dramatic legends formerly current about Hals was disposed of by Bredius some years ago. It had been alleged that the artist had cruelly beaten his first wife to death. But Bredius proved that the culprit was another Frans Hals.

The life of Hals can be very briefly summarised. In 1591 his father moved from Antwerp to Haarlem, where Frans soon began to study under Mander. An academic style, imitative of Italian humanism, was then already being industriously cultivated at Haarlem, though Hals's pictures show no trace whatever of it. An old list of his works ascribes a landscape and several religious pictures to this period. But these are no longer extant. His earliest dated picture, the *Banquet of the Civic Guard of Archers of St George* painted in 1616, when he was thirty-six, proves him to have been already a master at that time. He then had a high reputation in Haarlem for portraiture. By 1633 his large picture of the *Cloveniers Arquebusiers*, now in Haarlem, had made him known outside Holland. Yet he was still not making much money, for he was careless and unbusinesslike. He had married for the second time and soon had no less

FRANS HALS · PORTRAIT OF WILLEM CROE
18½″ × 13⅜″. Munich, Alte Pinakothek

than twelve children. All the same, i is not easy to understand why he wen bankrupt, though he was never highly pai and never a fashionable artist like Van de Helst. The snobs, as we should call ther today, placed no orders with him, fo neither he himself nor his works could b described as 'smart'. The nearer hi painting approached genius in its increas ingly broad and summary handling, th fewer customers he obtained. By 165 he had been compelled to mortgage hi entire property. Soon afterwards h applied for relief as a pauper.

The disorder of his life stands in com plete contrast with the unmistakabl steady development of his painting. H was interested in human beings and trie at first to represent them in such characteristic extrovert attitudes as those of laughter, amusement, singing, play-acting and speechifying. The *Junker Ramp* in New York, *Hille Bobbe* in Berlin, the *Gipsy Woman* in Paris, the *Laughing Cavalier* in London and the *Toper* in Amsterdam exemplify this tendency. But Hals soon noticed that human character could also be expressed in other ways. He became more and more interested in the psychological aspect of Rembrandt's portraits. Indifferent to the taste of the public, he developed a technique that flouted it, slashing in his heads as though the brush were a sabre. He grew content with less and less variety of colour, finally confining his palette to brown, grey, black and white.

Some 200 portraits of individuals, including the *Descartes* in the Louvre, and eight large portraits of groups have survived. In the latter his mastery is equalled only by that of Rembrandt. But Hals must be allowed the primacy of having developed, so to speak, the vivid 'snapshot' from the formal 'school group'. He devoted the highest compositional skill to representing moments of 'relaxation', practising and stylising his efforts till in this field too he came to realise what long experience teaches, that the less is usually the more. In 1664 the female supervisors of the old men's home in which he lived as a pauper charitably commissioned him to paint a group of them. He immortalised the complacent, ugly old creatures in a work, now at Haarlem, which is worlds away from his earlier portrait-groups of Company officers. His line was by then tremulous with age. But the picture expresses the frosty wisdom of the evening of life.

The most important of his larger pieces are preserved in the Haarlem museum called after him. But a quarter of them are already owned by the United States.

Seven of his sons became painters, of whom only one is worth mentioning.

Claes Hals (1628-1686) painted scenes of peasant life in the style of Molenaer. They have no particular distinction. On the other hand his rare lowland views are decidedly fine. They resemble Jacob Ruysdael's.

FRANS HALS · THE BANQUET OF THE CIVIC GUARD OF ARCHERS OF ST GEORGE IN HAARLEM (*The 1627 version*) · 71⅝" × 103". *Haarlem, Frans Hals Museum*

Dirk Hals (1591-1656), Frans's younger brother by eleven years, is still esteemed for his 'Cavalier' scenes. He may be characterised in much the same way as Codde (q.v.).

HAYMAN

Francis Hayman (1708-1776) was born in Exeter, came early to London and played a considerable part in the politics of the art world of his time. He was intimate with all the London artists, among them Hogarth, Laroon, Highmore and Samuel Scott, and he was probably the master of Gainsborough. Hayman was one of the original Royal Academicians, and was Librarian of the Academy from 1771 to 1775. Hayman passed his youth in painting scenery for theatres, and later had some success as a painter of portraits and conversation pieces. There is a well-known example in the National Portrait Gallery, showing the artist in his studio painting Sir Robert Walpole.

HEDA

One of the most important Dutch painters of still-life, Willem Claesz Heda of Haarlem (1594-1682) lived at the very time when a striking change occurred in the treatment of such subjects. The great decorative pieces were being replaced by the so-called 'monochrome collation', in which the beauty of ordinary household objects was rendered with truly Van Eyckian fervour. The citizens of Haarlem had already been attracted by the simplicity of the paintings of Pieter Claesz. Heda developed this restrained style to its full maturity. He represented few items. The remains of a sweet course, an almost empty wine-glass, fragments of nutshells, a pewter pot and a charred clay pipe were all he used, composed so as to form an obviously pyramidal design on the strictly horizontal surface of a table. The effect was not that of a set collation, but of a backward glance at a simple meal just concluded. The suavity of texture was never again achieved until Chardin repeated it. Heda's palette was restricted to golden-yellow, brown, grey and a subdued white.

In his gamut of tones he played melodies of an engaging melancholy.

HEEM

Jan Davidsz de Heem was born at Utrecht in 1606, and moved to Antwerp at the age of thirty. Though he returned to his native city for a few years later on, he spent most of his life in Antwerp and died there in 1684. At that time the frontiers of Holland in the north and Flanders in the south were widely separated. De Heem's movements between the two countries no doubt largely account for his peculiar style. His first still-life studies—for example, the *Violin and Books* at The Hague—reproduce the tone values of Pieter Claesz and Heda. De Heem then developed into a flower-painter, clearly influenced by the Fleming Daniel Seghers, though his Dutch vision, familiar with the shadowy paintings of Rembrandt, prevented him from adopting Segher's deliberately unemotional manner and his frequently Baroque detail. In this way De Heem made the best of both worlds. His flowers are exquisitely and meticulously drawn, in the loveliest colours. They are either arranged in tasteful glass bowls, which reflect the windows of his studio, or hang in bunches against a neutral background, from which they stand out like great, flashing, many-coloured gems. He also derived from Antwerp his fondness for a refined, Baroque, consequently somewhat theatrical type of still-life, introducing at times a large lobster in order to provide a luminous passage of vermilion. He is regarded as an important painter today.

His son, **Cornelis** de Heem, born at Leyden in 1631 and dying at Antwerp in 1695, was trained by his father and, like him, painted mainly flowers and still-life. His very numerous works are in general confused and overcrowded in composition. Nor are they improved by his incidental touches in the taste of the period. But some of his flower pieces are in every respect equal to those of his father.

HEEMSKERK

Not so very long ago, Maerten van Heemskerk, who was born at Heemskerk in 1498 and died at Haarlem in 1574 was regarded as an Italianate producer of religious pictures, hardly worth a place in the second rank of sixteenth-century Dutch artists. His St Lawrence triptych, now at Linköping in Sweden, is an overloaded, eclectic work, utterly lacking in outstanding features. His *Momus Finding Fault with the Works of the Gods*, at Berlin, is also chaotic and fussy. He lived for several years in Italy, where it seemed that a false conception of art had stifled his talent.

But a more favourable view is now taken even of his pictures of Roman antiquities. His versions of ruins and the Colosseum are really landscapes. A completely different estimate of the artist has been prevalent ever since he was proved to have painted the splendid, typically Dutch portrait, with its golden tones and sweeping brush-strokes, of *Anna Codde at the Spinning Wheel*, now at Amsterdam, its companion portrait, *Pieter Bicker*, also at Amsterdam, and the large *Family at the Breakfast Table*, preserved at Kassel. The influence of Heemskerk's friend and master, Scorel, is certainly discernible in this picture, which is his last. But it is a fine achievement, brilliantly composed, with effective colour and detail. The basket, loaf and jug on the table would alone constitute a still-life of high quality.

A certain **Egbert** van Heemskerk, who was born in 1634 at Haarlem and died in London in 1704, is known for his numerous scenes with witches, his *genre* paintings and farmhouse interiors in a style suggestive of that of Jan Molenaer and a less-talented Brouwer.

HEES

The landscapes of Gerrit van Hees, who died in Haarlem in 1670, are still occasionally regarded as early works by Jakob Ruysdael or Hobbema. Graphically they are excellent, presenting dark, massive

J. D. DE HEEM · FLOWERPIECE
40¾″ × 33⅝″. Munich, Alte Pinakothek

forms silhouetted against an overcast sky, with the contrasting feature of a brightly lit stretch of road leading to labourers' cottages among bushy trees. But on further scrutiny one begins to lose interest in these productions. They seem derivative, petty and uninspired. Hobbema, by comparison, conveys a sense of height and freedom, whereas Hees is always earthbound.

HELST

Bartolomeus van der Helst (1613-1670) was the son of a Haarlem innkeeper, who would nowadays be described as the proprietor of a small hotel. The first lasting impression received by Bartolomeus, as a boy of sixteen, was that of the eighty oil-paintings of his father's collection being carried out into the street by a bailiff and subsequently removed, with all the rest of the furniture of the house. The father must therefore have been a man of some culture, though unfortunately not successful in business. The son retrieved the family fortunes with ease. For he it was who replaced the ruined and despised Rembrandt as the leading painter in Amsterdam. But there is no need to attach any particular blame to Helst on that account. He was never associated with Rembrandt and owed nothing to him as an artist. Helst had been trained by Nicolas Elias and was one of the Amsterdam Guild founders in 1653. His groups of civilians or militia and his portraits of individuals are more sensitive than those of his teacher and more ostentatiously brilliant in the display of gorgeously gleaming silks or the neutralisation of a black robe in chiaroscuro. For he had, of course, seen Rembrandt's pictures. He would also occasionally give his models the swaggering pose, hand on hip, affected by Frans Hals. The fashionable society of Amsterdam delighted in his technically expert, extremely lifelike portraits, so precisely indicative of middle-class urbanity.

Helst made a great deal of money. Yet he must have had bad luck, for he died, at Amsterdam, in debt. Once more a Helst collection was stacked on the pavement, ready to be carted away. Two fine portraits by Helst are preserved in the National Gallery, London.

HEMESSEN

Almost nothing is known of the life of Jan Sanders van Hemessen, who was born near Antwerp c. 1500 and died probably at Utrecht c. 1575. At one time art historians were much concerned with him, as he was believed to have been identical with the unknown and puzzling 'Brunswick Monogramist'. But he was eventually quietly restored to the position to which the works he actually painted entitled him. It may be briefly indicated by suggesting that he may have aimed—see his *Roysterers* in Berlin—at the effects which Pieter Aertsen subsequently produced. But Hemessen also painted half-length figures in a vigorous, somewhat clumsy style, recalling similar work by Mabuse or Marinus van Reymerswaele. Like Aertsen, Hemessen was one of the first great realists of his day.

Jan van Hemessen had a daughter, **Katharina,** also an excellent painter (1527/8-after 1566). She married Christian de Morico, a musician, and went to Spain with Mary of Hungary in 1556. Several signed pictures exist, mostly female portraits; there is one of Katharina herself, dated 1548. Two signed portraits, one of a man, one of a lady, are in the National Gallery, London.

HERLIN

The most important and influential of a large family of South German painters, Friedrich Herlin is mentioned for the first time in 1459, in the archives of Nördlingen. He seems to have died by 1499, for in that year his name ceases to appear in the records of the Inland Revenue Office, an omission then as now a sure sign that he was dead. His chief productions, altarpieces at Rothenburg, Bopfingen and Nördlingen, are proudly inscribed in his own hand: 'Friederich Herlein, painter at Nördlingen, made this work.' Herlin's great talents are most strikingly evident whenever he relies entirely on himself, as happened if he did not consider the reverse side or outer wing of an altar-screen important. In the Nördlingen altarpiece the *Women Founders in Their Pews* have the shy delicacy of aspect characteristic of Konrad Witz. But in the main sections of the screen Herlin felt obliged to imitate the Flemish masters. He provides an awkward but delightful translation of the styles of Robert Campin and Rogier van der Weyden into the Swabian idiom.

HERMITAGE MUSEUM

The former Imperial Gallery at St Petersburg became the National Gallery when the city was renamed Leningrad. The Hermitage Palace, as it is still called, is among the most important of the world's galleries. An atmosphere of secrecy has surrounded it since the 'Iron Curtain' descended in 1917. The treasures of the

REMBRANDT · THE ANGEL LEAVING TOBIAS
17¼" × 20¾". *Paris, Louvre* (*See* Highlights)

tion and Titian's *Venus with Mirror*. The American multimillionaire Mellon (q.v.) bought the entire consignment and presented it to the National Gallery at Washington.

HERRERA

The personality of Francisco Herrera, who was born at Seville in 1576 and died in Madrid in 1656, must have been decidedly odd. At any rate, his reputation for eccentricity spread considerably faster than his renown as an artist. In his youth he had been a coiner, a fact which says a good deal for his talents as a draughtsman. At a later date his versatility, boldness and realism as a painter were highly praised. But to modern eyes his work seems coarse rather than realistic, and superficial rather than bold. His best productions are the *genre* studies, such as the *Blind Musician* in a private collection at Vienna and the *Idiot* at Avignon. For a short time he taught Velazquez.

HESDIN

The French painter Jacquemart de Hesdin is named for the first time in the Court archives of the Duc de Berry at Bourges in 1384. By the end of the fourteenth century he had become the most important of book-illustrators, only later superseded by the brothers Limburg. He died in 1409/10. He produced so-called 'Hour Books', devotional manuals of the calendar type, which the Duke piously collected. The Paris *Grandes Heures* and *Petites Heures*, in particular, are duly authenticated works by Hesdin. The ornamental decoration and the paintings themselves are extremely attractive, though clearly surpassed by those of the Limburgs owing to a certain simplicity and Gothic intensity of feeling characteristic of the latter. A striking feature of Hesdin's style is a strong Sienese influence, especially perceptible in the representation of architecture.

Hermitage are only known at first hand by the older generation of travellers and experts. The rest of the Western world is only acquainted with them through books and occasional loans. Whenever the Soviet Union consents to the temporary release of a few items, the effect is that of a peep into some treasure-chest in a fairy tale. No connoisseur ever neglects such opportunities. In the autumn of 1956, for example, some of the wonderful Rembrandts in the Hermitage were sent to Amsterdam for exhibition during the celebrations of the 350th anniversary of the artist's birth.

Only once has the collection been the subject of sensational news. In 1930, when the Government urgently needed foreign currency, twenty-one of the Hermitage pictures were offered for sale. They included Raphael's *Alba Madonna*, Botticelli's *Adoration*, Jan van Eyck's *Annuncia-*

One of these precious gems of book-making has recently been acquired from the Rothschild Collection in Paris by the Metropolitan Museum of New York. Though it dates from Hesdin's period, it has not yet been proved to be his work. It contains 224 pages of parchment and 148 illustrations.

HEYDEN

Jan van der Heyden was born at Gorin-chem in 1637 and died in 1712 in Amsterdam. He was one of the most important Dutch painters of townscapes. He created a new category of picture which owed nothing to any previous model or fore-runner. Such an achievement is rare in the history of painting.

He is sometimes called the Canaletto of Holland. But this comparison is a super-ficial one. Heyden's spirit and style are in reality quite different from Canaletto's. The former's significance is based on his architectural and street scenes. He did not cultivate 'tone-values', but reproduced what he saw realistically. Each individual stone of a house or leaf on a tree is shown separately. The atmosphere is so pre-cisely rendered that a meteorologist could register the state of the weather, the season and the time of day from it. Canaletto never attempted such effects. He simply painted the golden beauty of his city.

The astonishing result in the case of Van der Heyden's works was that his uncompromising attention to detail invari-ably produced a true 'picture', coherent and thoroughly professional. His vision never flinched. He could paint an immense, desolate square as well as a street in the form of a single dark outline against light, or again a row of houses fanning out in dazzling sunshine or a picturesque canal. Everything he produced was 'neat'. His more rustic, suburban subjects are slightly less successful, though they are at least equal in quality to the Saxon Belotto views. The constantly repeated assertion that Adriaen van der Velde painted his figures for him remains unproved. Hey-den's pictures did not change in any way after Adriaen's death. In any case, a num-ber of pencilled figure studies by Heyden are extant.

He was also a first-rate and duly appre-ciated engineer. He invented a new kind of street illumination and the first hose for fire-extinguishing.

HIGHLIGHTS

Highlights play an important part in both chiaroscuro and naturalistic painting. In a chiaroscuro picture such as Rembrandt's *The Angel leaving Tobias* (p. 153) high lights emphasise the drama and illuminate the principal figures in the composition there is no attempt to simulate the effects of nature. In a representational picture however, such as Hals' portrait of Willem Croes (p. 148), the highlights on the stretched skin of the knuckles of the hand holding the gloves have been put in by the painter exactly as they were in nature in order to enhance the realism of the image.

HIGHMORE

Joseph Highmore was born in London in 1698. He painted many portraits, but is best known for his narrative pieces. The most celebrated of these are the twelve charming illustrations to Samuel Richard-son's *Pamela*, which are divided between the National Gallery, London, the Fitz-william Museum, Cambridge, and the Melbourne Gallery. Highmore died at Canterbury in 1780 and was buried in the Cathedral 'in the body of the church and wrapped in sheep's wool', according to the register.

HILLIARD

Nicholas Hilliard was a miniaturist whose portraits had no equal in the work of English artists of the day in either accom-plishment or grasp of character. He was the oldest of the seven children of Richard Hilliard, a goldsmith, and was born in Exeter in about 1547. Nicholas himself was actively engaged in the goldsmith's craft throughout his career. Possibly by 1558 he was in London, and when he was no more than eighteen he painted a portrait

J. VAN DER HEYDEN
A CANAL IN AMSTERDAM
14¾″ × 18″. *Paris, Louvre*

of Mary, Queen of Scots. In 1572 he painted a famous portrait of Queen Elizabeth (National Portrait Gallery). The freshness and delicacy of his work captivated the Queen and Hilliard remained high in her favour until her death in 1603. He was made limner to Elizabeth, and James I confirmed him in this post. Hilliard died in 1619. He based his style on that of Holbein and he also made a close study of Dürer's engravings. Among Hilliard's many well-known miniatures are *A Youth leaning against a Tree among Roses*, *A Man against a Background of Flames*, *Alice Brandon* (the artist's wife), *Richard Hilliard* (the artist's father), and *Self-Portrait, Aged 30*, all in the Victoria and Albert Museum.

HOBBEMA

Meindert Hobbema (1638-1709 in Amsterdam), first 'discovered' in the nineteenth century, is now regarded as one of the greatest of Dutch landscape painters. But he led the most wretched life imaginable. He was brought up in an orphanage. He mismanaged, for all his pains, the sale of his pictures, the friendship of his teacher, Jacob Ruysdael, being apparently of little use to him in this respect. In the end he practically gave up painting, for at last even he had a great stroke of luck. He married a serving-wench whose relations with the cream of society were so marvellously effective that she was able to get him appointed a municipal employee. The patient, dreamy fellow obediently laid his palette aside and spent his time, for the next twenty years, in broaching oil and wine casks. Then at last he painted one more picture, *The Avenue Middelharnis*, today in the National Gallery, London. It is the only one of his works which immediately strikes the eye as unusual, owing to the avenue of slender poplars leading in a straight line to the background, to which the brick-red of the distant houses lends a cheerful touch of colour. His other landscapes are in general quite conventional, the subjects being invariably slightly undulating designs of bushes, relieved by the addition of a brook, a cottage or a mill. He is fond of massive trees crowned with dark foliage, through which a little light filters to give a higher tone to his forest glades. His favourite colours are strong greens, yellows and browns. His drawing tends to gnarled effects which reinforce his expression of the kind of romanticism popular

HOBBEMA · THE AVENUE,
MIDDELHARNIS, HOLLAND
40¼″ × 55½″. *London, National Gallery*

with simple souls. The small figures in his paintings, only introduced for the sake of perspective, are unfortunately by no means masterly in execution. They would be disturbing if the landscape relied on brilliance and perfection of detail for its effect. But this is not the case. Hobbema was incapable of producing a 'tasteful' work. He could only supply a heartfelt vision. As the age did not care for that sort of thing, he died forgotten, and was buried at the public expense in a pauper's grave.

HOGARTH

William Hogarth was born in Smithfield, London, in 1697, the son of an impecunious schoolmaster who had come from Westmorland. At the age of fifteen he was apprenticed to a silver-plate engraver. He then learned to engrave on copper and began to design bookplates, showcards and illustrations. In 1720 Hogarth started work as an independent engraver, producing two sets of illustrations to Butler's *Hudibras*. In his spare time Hogarth worked under Sir James Thornhill, with whose daughter he eloped in 1729. The story of his life is a record of ceaseless toil with brush and graver. He died in his house in Leicester Fields on 10th October, 1764, and was buried in Chiswick Churchyard.

Hogarth began his career as a painter with small conversation pieces, such as the *Family Group* in the National Gallery, London, and the *Wanstead Assembly*.

He then turned his attention to the series of progressive moralities with which he made his most personal contribution to his art, *The Harlot's Progress* (1731; in a private collection), *The Rake's Progress* (1735; Soane Museum), and *Marriage à la Mode* (1745; National Gallery, London). These were followed by *Calais Gate* (1719; National Gallery, London), *The*

HOGARTH · THE SHRIMP GIRL
25″ × 20″. *London, National Gallery*

March to Finchley, and *Four Pictures of an Election* (1755; Soane Museum). Among Hogarth's portraits some of the best known are *Lord Lovat* (1746; National Portrait Gallery), *William James*, in the Worcester Museum, Mass., U.S.A., and his *Self-Portrait*, the famous *Shrimp Girl* and *Hogarth's Servants*, all in the National Gallery, London.

Hogarth always had difficulty in selling his pictures, but he made engravings of his 'modern moral subjects' especially to bring them within reach of a large public, and these were a great success. In 1741, when the original paintings for *A Harlot's Progress, A Rake's Progress, Strolling Actresses in a Barn* and *The Four Times of the Day* were still in his studio, Hogarth decided to sell them personally by auction. He sold all his pictures and made £427, the equivalent of about £3,000 today.

No English painter before Hogarth had attempted to make any comment on the established order of society. By depicting and criticising the life about him in his serial pictures, Hogarth reformed English painting, dominated at the beginning of the eighteenth century by the imitators of Kneller, and gave it a truly national character. It is thus in his didactic works that his originality and importance most reside. But Hogarth's powers as a pure painter are apparent in passages in all his works and are strikingly revealed in the sparkling *Shrimp Girl*, which Whistler declared to be the best portrait ever painted by an Englishman, in *Hogarth's Servants* and in the enchanting *Wanstead Assembly*.

HOLBEIN

Hans Holbein the Younger was born at the end of 1497 or the beginning of 1498 in Augsburg, and died in London in 1543. This level-headed, critically-minded painter would probably have wished his

life to be written in sober, factual terms. There is no evidence that he was ever interested in the acquisition of honours or that he was impressed by flattery. He might have said: 'Everyone longs for what he does not possess. Some long for immortality; others for money. I long for money.' His longing went unappeased, for he never grew rich. The proceeds of the

H. HOLBEIN THE YOUNGER · PORTRAIT OF THE MERCHANT GEORG GISZE · *38⅜″ × 33⅛″. Berlin, Dahlem Museum*

sale of his property in London after his death only realised just enough to provide for his two illegitimate English children. His wife had been living alone in Basle, with her children, for the previous ten years. She inherited a single trunk. For a clear-thinking, sensible man, Holbein left a remarkable amount of disorder and trouble behind him. One begins to wonder whether this estimate of his character is correct. His works are incomparable models of objectivity. Perhaps he himself was just the opposite.

It was in his father's studio that the

younger Holbein came in contact with the spirit of the Renaissance, as well as with many other complicated and exciting phenomena. For **Hans Holbein the Elder** (c. 1465-1524) was not only an eminent but also a remarkably brilliant painter. The son, impressed by the Renaissance works he saw all around him— he had moved to Basle with his brother Ambrosius in 1515—painted the strangely artificial side view of *Christ Entombed*, the crudely Italianate *Last Supper* and the *Entombment*, which resembles a work by one of the pseudo-classic German painters of the early nineteenth century, known as 'Nazarenes'. This picture is at Basle. None of these productions can honestly be called masterpieces. But the lad had not yet grown into the cool, detached personality he was afterwards to become. On the contrary, it seemed for a short while as though a greater sincerity, cordiality and mildness would be found in him. He painted Erasmus of Rotterdam, who had come to see him, as a gentle, preoccupied scholar. This portrait is now in the Louvre. The *Meyer Madonna* at Darmstadt is full of typical German middle-class feeling and the portrait of his wife with her two children, at Basle, is really beautiful. Many connoisseurs believe it to be the best picture he ever painted.

Meanwhile, on Erasmus's advice, he had already paid one brief visit, from 1526 t[o] 1528, to England. Basle, then in the firs[t] picture-hating throes of the Reformatio[n] was offering him fewer and fewer oppor[-] tunities. When in 1532 he returned, th[is] time for good, to England, he took th[e] astonishing step of abandoning all h[is] former enthusiasms. He arrived as [a] changed man, a cool, unemotional observe[r] of life. The cause of this alteration in h[is] character is unknown. He was received i[n] London with open arms. His powerf[ul] patrons included the Chancellor, Si[r] Thomas More, Henry VIII himself an[d] the then world-famous corporation of th[e] Hanseatic merchants. Thenceforward Hol[-] bein paid only occasional short visits to h[is] native land during the journeys he under[-] took to paint portraits of the King'[s] prospective wives.

During the last ten years of his shor[t] life—he probably died of the plague— Holbein painted the series of portrait[s] which have rendered him the equal in th[e] field of Dürer, Rembrandt, Hals, Velasque[z] and Titian. But his style was unique, no[t] resembling that of any of these grea[t] artists. The language of his portraits is tha[t] of a judge or member of a jury. No glim[-] mer of an indulgent smile or ordinar[y] human fellow-feeling is discernible. Bu[t] this very feature of his work is fascinating for Holbein possessed uncannily shrew[d]

HONDECOETER
A COCK FIGHT · 44″ × 57⅞″
Munich, Schleissheim Gallery

insight into human nature. It is obvious, however, that he took no interest in the basic traits which Rembrandt dredged up from the uttermost depths of his sitters' characters and represented so vividly, as 'extenuating circumstances', in his portraits.

Holbein also produced frescoes and the famous *Danse Macabre* series of drawings. His chief works include *Archbishop Warham*, *The Astronomer Kratzer* and *Anne of Cleves* at the Louvre, *Jane Seymour* at Vienna, *Georg Gisze* in Berlin, the *Ambassadors* and *Christina of Denmark* in London, *Charles de Morette* at Dresden, *Prince Edward* at Washington and *Henry VIII*, the latter having only survived as a contemporary copy, preserved in Rome. A self-portrait, in miniature, is in the Wallace Collection, London.

HONDECOETER

Gillis, Gysbert and Melchoir de Hondecoeter represent three generations of animal painters, three stages of stylistic development and three degrees of immorality. **Gillis** (1575-1638), who spent his life at Amsterdam, just qualifies for the latter distinction. His paradisal studies of animals, associated with the patriarch Noah or Orpheus, are extremely attractive little paintings, derived from those of his teacher, Savery, and from Coninxloo. Gillis's son and pupil, **Gysbert,** born in Amsterdam in 1604 and dying at Utrecht in 1653, enlarged the scale of animal painting, often making his fowls express human emotion in the Mannerist style. His close observation of nature is very evident. Gysbert's son and pupil, **Melchoir,** born at Utrecht in 1636 and dying in Amsterdam in 1695, is accounted one of the greatest of the Dutch animal painters. In his case the statuesque forms his father had painted are endowed with life. Cocks fight, birds of prey swoop on the farmyard, peacocks spread their trains and song-birds warble. There is more space in his pictures and they are more freely composed than his father's. The centre of interest is stressed by highlighting. The landscape as a rule provides no more than a dim backcloth for

the whirling kaleidoscope of glistening hues in the birds' feathers. His dead birds are also admirable, though depressing in the same artistically deplorable fashion as are those conventional 'moated grange' pictures in which cattle are put on show for the spectator. Fortunately, Melchior's representations of dead birds are mostly to be found in the castles to which they naturally belong.

HONTHORST

Gerard van Honthorst was born at Utrecht in 1590. He studied under Bloemart, then went to Rome for ten years, after which he returned with a high reputation as a painter and lived alternately at The Hague and Utrecht, opening a successful art school in the latter city, where he eventually died in 1656. At the end of the 1620s he paid a short visit to England at the invitation of Charles I. In London he painted a decoration in Whitehall, portraits of Charles I and Henrietta Maria and the portrait group of George Villiers and his family. The Queen of Bohemia's children became his pupils. His success continued to his death.

Though so popular in his lifetime, he was little remembered subsequently, until in modern times both he and Terbrugghen, the two distinguished artists who brought Caravaggio's revolutionary style from Rome to Holland, were rediscovered. But while Terbrugghen was recognised as a startling predecessor of Vermeer and the cultivation of pure colour, no such appreciation was accorded to Honthorst. He had in fact concentrated too exclusively on Caravaggio's lighting. Though he undoubtedly made most elegant use of this extraneous effect, he remained so absorbed in it that he never really, so to speak, came to the surface in his pictures.

His many *Nativities* and entertaining scenes by candlelight, with their musicians and carousing, flirting figures, which caused him to be nicknamed in Italy 'Gherardo of the Night', are rendered with very great skill. There is always some touch or other in them, a bread-platter, a brightly-lit hand or a girl's face, delightful enough to cut out and keep for its own sake. His best picture,

A Visit to the Matchmaker, is at Utrecht. His works play an important part in art history, because they contributed to Rembrandt's experience of pictorial light and shade.

HOOCH

Pieter de Hooch, who was born at Rotterdam in 1629 and died in Amsterdam c. 1684, was the son of a bricklayer. The number of talented sons who emerged from humble, sometimes very poor, homes in this period is strikingly large. They grew up in bare, dark rooms, living on dry bread and turnips, in the midst of squalor and indigence. At sixteen or seventeen they suddenly realised their powers. At twenty-five they had already become admired masters.

Pieter de Hooch was apprenticed to Berchem at a very early age. He began by copying his teacher's style. But after meeting Palamedesz he turned to the production of guardroom scenes. In 1654 he moved to Delft, where his style suddenly became that now regarded as characteristic of his work. For thirteen years he painted the new vision that had been revealed to him. It was that of the domestic idyll in the snug security of some sunlit chamber, with the typical Hooch recession in depth, and only a faint suggestion, through the window, of the world 'outside'. In the room a matron or a maidservant carries out, with modest satisfaction, some household task, or walks busily and happily through the little walled garden with a child at her side.

Two friends, again, may be seated over a jug of wine in some cosy Delft backyard while the clean red brickwork's deep note stands out against green foliage and the clear evening sky. The more humble the bliss depicted the more admirable is the effect of these works. Some of de Hooch's masterpieces are almost as fine as Vermeer's. The latter's colour may be richer, but de Hooch's appeal is more intimate.

In the 1660s, while he was still not yet forty, his longing to communicate such visions weakened. He moved to the international centre of Amsterdam, where his impressionable spirit underwent other influences. His interiors grew smarter. Marble chimney-pieces and pillars excluded the former warmth and intimacy. His colours became as cold and desiccated as the hearts of the dwellers in this elegant world, glimpsed by the bricklayer's son through a window, across a hedge. He was repelled and chilled by

P. DE HOOCH · A DUTCH GARDEN COURT
24⅞″ × 18¾″. Amsterdam, Rijksmuseum

The *Courtyard of a Dutch
ouse*, dating from his best
riod, is in the National Gallery,
ondon.

OOGSTRATEN

amuel von Hoogstraten of Dor-
echt (1627-1678) studied for a
me under Rembrandt. But his
rviving portraits and *genre* pic-
res do not indicate that he was
important artist, though his
ick Woman at Amsterdam is not
r behind the work of Jan Steen.
his old age he composed a
eatise on painting. But this pro-
uction is of less interest than
s passionate study of optics.
ne of its fruits is the *Peepshow*
the National Gallery, London,
here effects of perspective are
tained with astonishing skill.
iles, two chairs and a dog are
inted partly on the wall and partly on the
or, a table entirely on the floor.

IOPPNER

hn Hoppner was born in London in 1758
d died there in 1810. He became asso-
ated with the royal family at an early age,
being appointed to the choir of the
ing's Chapel. He was even rumoured to
a natural son of George III. Consequ-
tly, his career began under the most fav-
rable auspices. After some not parti-
ularly arduous training at the Academy,
became a popular society portrait
inter and regarded himself as a duly
alified successor to Reynolds. But in
ct he fell a good deal short of this
osition, for he was by no means a genius.
certain dryness and superficiality in his
ork are combined with undeniable brilli-
ce and harmony in the field of colour. If
had taken more trouble with his draw-
g, this feature of his work would be even
ore conspicuous.

IOUBRAKEN

s a historical painter and portraitist

W. HUBER · THE AGONY IN THE GARDEN
23⅛″ × 26¾″. *Munich, Alte Pinakothek*

Arnold Houbraken, who was born at
Dordrecht in 1660 and died in Amsterdam
in 1719, is not considered important. He
rendered, however, great service to posterity through his biographies of artists.
His *Great Dutch Men and Women Painters*
was published in 1718.

HOUCKGEEST

Born at The Hague c. 1600 and dying at
Bergen op Zoom in 1661, Gerard Houckgeest was the first of the famous Delft
painters of interiors. Hesitant attempts had
been made before his time, as by Peeter
Neeffs (c. 1578-1659) at Antwerp, to represent church interiors. But these efforts were
on the point of being abandoned as not
worth while when Houckgeest and Saenredam of Amsterdam simultaneously raised
this form of art to a high level. Houckgeest
started by producing pictures of dull, un-
wieldy, rectilinear churches which would
hardly have ensured him posthumous fame.
But about 1650, when he had just left Delft
for his country estate near Bergen, a decisive development in his style took place.
Suddenly his rigid façades, dismal colouring and dwarfish figures disappeared. The

pictures grew bright as a summer morning. The figures acquired plasticity. His organisation of space became interesting in its division by diagonal rows of massive columns. Dark panels, banners and coats of arms reflected the play of light. Many of these works are so admirable as to approach the quality of those by the great Saenredam.

HUBER

Wolf Huber, who was born at Feldkirch in the district of Allgäu, Bavaria, between 1485 and 1490, and died at Passau in 1553, was one of the most striking figures among the group of painters headed by Altdorfer. He stopped at Passau on a journey down the Danube, settled in the town and became Court Painter to the local Prince-Bishops. The other Passau artists opposed him. But they could not impede his career, and he was soon famous far beyond the frontiers of the country. His delicate sense of colour is particularly evident in his large-scale figures and lavish draperies reflecting a dim, fluorescent light, as in his *Mount of Olives* at Munich. At the same time, like a true romantic painter, he had a taste for irony and caricature. His praying Christ is rendered with fine sensitivity. But the artist's mischievous irony immediately catches the eye with his snoring disciple. Huber could be even more disturbing in the details of such crowded canvases as the Vienna *Erection of the Cross*, where it is impossible to avoid the impression of something comic as well as tragic about the hoisting process. But when he suppressed such tendencies, especially if his great gifts as a landscape painter were thrown into the scales, as in his *Mourning for Christ* at the parish church of Feldkirch, a peculiar beauty resulted, recalling the work of Hans Baldung. Huber's pictures are few. His wonderful drawings of landscape are much more numerous. (Ill. p. 161.)

HUDSON

Devonshire born and destined to become the teacher of Reynolds, Thomas Hudson (1701-1779) died at his Twickenham hunt-

ing lodge, to which he had retired whe the rising fortunes of his former pup threatened to put an end to his career as a only moderately talented portraitist. It w an amiable gesture. His portraits are sour work, tastefully coloured and good lik nesses. But all he really did at the conce of the masters was to turn over Reynolds music for him.

HUGUET

Jaume Huguet, the last important repre sentative of the old Catalan tradition painting, was active, on documentary ev dence, between 1448 and 1492 and died Barcelona. At this period Catalonia ha finally lost its political independence ar was about to be united with its hate neighbour, Castile. Huguet can only l understood in the context of the stubbor conservatism of his country. The older l grew, the more old-fashioned his sty became. His figures are on a large scal

J. VAN HUYSUM · STILL-LIFE
31⅝" × 23⅝". London, Wallace Collection

rm is almost ignored. The drawing is
ffly realistic, the outlines being really
ly 'filled in' with colour, often so
ightened with gold as to approach the
'ect of relief. Yet these productions
uld perhaps have been quite impressive
Huguet had not deliberately over-
corated his altarpieces. His chief works
e to be found at Barcelona, Vich and
rrasa.

UYSUM

n van Huysum, who was born in
nsterdam in 1682 and died there in 1749,
veloped Dutch still-life painting (see
ghers) to its highest point of virtuo-
y. His pictures of flowers and fruit can
examined centimetre by centimetre for
e eye to dwell with delight, time after
ne, on the dew of a blossom, the filigree
of veins in leaves, the glassy whiteness or
blue tinge of grapes, the porcelain of tiny
snail-shells and the powdered wings of
butterflies. His favourite colours are
golden-yellow, bright, creamy-red and
cool, bluish green. The father, **Justus** van
Huysum (1659–1716), also of Amsterdam,
had used backgrounds as dark as those of
de Heem. Jan made them light, initiating
an entirely new range of high tones,
characteristic of the Rococo period. He
painted direct from nature. In the spring
he would leave a picture unfinished, to
wait for a certain flower to bloom in the
autumn. Regarded during his lifetime as
one of the greatest painters in the world,
he would often receive over 1,000 guilders
for a picture. But in fact, from a purely
pictorial point of view, he is much inferior
to such artists as Jan Davidsz de Heem. His
Italianate landscapes are of no importance.

I

CONOGRAPHY

ancient Greece iconography meant the
eparation of descriptive lists of works of
t or, in modern terminology, catalogues.
ut in the technical language of art his-
rians the word now has a different mean-
g. It refers to the formality of treatment
hich came to be applied, especially in
rly painting, to subjects sanctified by
adition. Late Gothic Italian painters, for
:ample, almost invariably represent the
Iadonna seated on a throne with high
ms which resemble masonry. This prac-
ce would be described as peculiar to
onography. The representation of the
aditional attributes of the saints is also a
ature of iconography. Today the conno-
tation of the word has been extended to
cover more modern conventions. When
Tintoretto for the first time relegated the
table of the Last Supper to the background
of a picture instead of placing it in the foreground and accordingly rendered the chief
figure, that of Christ, on a small scale, he
broke the rules, so to speak, of iconography.

Iconology is a new branch of the study
of art, concerned with the systematic
investigation of iconography.

ILLUSIONISM

The attempt in painting to create as nearly
as possible by means of perspective, foreshortening and chiaroscuro an illusion of

visual reality. The term is particularly applied to the extreme effects achieved by baroque painters. The painters of ceilings in the churches of Rome and Naples excelled in the rendering of endless celestial perspectives. First attempted by Correggio in Parma, this type of decoration was developed by Pozzo in Rome, and was finally carried all over Europe by Tiepolo, who worked in both Germany and Spain. In England it was introduced by Rubens in his painting of the ceiling of the Banqueting Hall, Whitehall, and carried on by Thornhill in his decorations at Hampton Court and the Painted Hall at Greenwich.

IMOLA

Innocenzo Francucci da Imola was born at Imola c. 1494 and died in Bologna c. 1550. He was a pupil of Francia. At Florence he worked for some years in the studio of Albertinelli, thereby not exactly improving his style of composition. It was also in Florence that he saw Madonnas by Raphael and graciously reproduced them, for our benefit, in his own works—for example, his *Madonna with Saints* in Berlin. His pictures represent little more than rows of large-scale, unrelated figures, conforming with the ecclesiastical convention in design and colour. It would be more fitting to call such Italian painters 'minor masters' if it were not for the enormous extent of their canvases.

Primaticcio, destined to acquire such importance in relation to the Fontainebleau School, was trained by Imola.

ISENBRANT

Known to art historians as a respected and prosperous Bruges painter, Adriaen Isenbrant (c. 1485-c. 1551) painted an altarpiece, *Our Lady of the Seven Sorrows*, now in the church of Notre Dame in that city. It is his chief work. But it cannot be denied that his small panels are much more attractive. At this date the Bruges painters seemed to have lost their way and inspiration was at a low ebb. But Isenbrant escaped the capricious influences brought

A. ISENBRANT · THE REST ON THE FLIG[
19¾″ × 13⅝″. Munich, Alte Pinakothek

to bear on him, while Bruges sank slow[to the level of a provincial town, by a fir[adherence to the standard of Gera[David. The latter may, indeed, ha[trained him.

Isenbrant's figures bear a positive[monotonous resemblance to those [David, which are themselves all rath[alike. But the former artist sets them [darkly glowing landscapes, so that his litt[Madonnas, with their downcast eye[seem to be seated, as in his *Rest on t.[Flight* at Munich, in a grotto by Leonard[Isenbrant's interiors also suggest dim[lit warmth. They are occupied by Davidi[figures of melancholy aspect, relieved by [occasional touch of admirable red. Th[language is that of a gentle murmur [farewell. An altarpiece in St Saviou[church at Bruges is ascribed to Isenbra[His *Magdalen in a Landscape* is in th[National Gallery, London.

JACOMART

Jacomart, whose real name was Jaume Baço, was born in Valencia c. 1413 and died there in 1461. King Alfonso of Aragon, who had patronised Dalmau and sent him to study the works of the great masters in Flanders, despatched Jacomart to Naples, the capital of his Kingdom of the Two Sicilies.

At Naples Jacomart came in contact with early works of the Italian Renaissance, which influenced his own later productions. The chief of these are the St Anna altarpiece at Jativa and that of St Martin at Segorbe. Such slight traces of Italian style as Jacomart introduced into his Valencian manner soon disappeared, giving place to a predominantly Dutch tendency.

JANSSENS

Abraham Janssens of Antwerp (c. 1575-c. 1632) produced large mythological, religious and allegorical pictures in a smooth, naturalistic style. The marginal figures of cupids and satyrs reveal a certain quiet humour. But the chief figures show an effort to blend the classical Italian nude with that of Rubens, in which endeavour Janssen's temperament only allowed him to achieve a kind of agreeable languor. His surprisingly successful effects are obtained by graceful draughtsmanship and luminous colour. For a time he was regarded in Antwerp as a serious rival to Rubens.

Hieronymus Janssens (1624-1693), also of Antwerp, was known, owing to the characteristic element in nearly all his paintings, as Janssens the Dancer. He painted countless scenes of social occasions, centred as a rule on a smartly dressed young couple on the point of leading off the dance. These works attract the spectator more on account of the pleasure with which he repeatedly recognises this curious idiosyncrasy than for any special pictorial merit.

Of the life of the most important of the Janssens, Pieter Janssen Elinga, little more is known than that he was a Dutchman living in Amsterdam in the second half of the seventeenth century. He painted admirable interiors which sometimes, as in his *Woman Reading* at Munich, approach the quality of Pieter de Hooch's. He was fond of the effect of light descending from a lofty window, though he treated it more softly and sentimentally than did Hooch. His dark still-life studies, reminiscent of Kalf, have a refined simplicity.

JEAURAT

A successful climber of the steepest academic ladders, the Parisian, Etienne Jeaurat (1699-1789), was nevertheless—the conjunction is practically obligatory today—a good painter. His scenes of everyday life in Paris, the *Carnival*, the *Arrest of Prostitutes* and the *Street Riot*, in the Carnavalet Museum, Paris, have much of the grace of Chardin. It is a pity that Jeaurat's pictures are so fussy, for he had the ability to approach Chardin's 'pure' style still more closely. The portraits—for example, that of Voltaire—are first-rate. But his fortunately rare historical paintings, with their beating of the big drum, are appalling.

JOHNSON

Cornelius Johnson (1593-c. 1604) was the son of a Fleming, but was himself born in London. He painted James I and Queen Anne of Denmark, and Charles I. Johnson started in the Elizabethan tradition, but his style changed after Van Dyck came to England. His *Charles I* in particular shows the influence of the great master, and his *Lady Fanshawe* is a frank imitation of Van Dyck. Nevertheless, Johnson's portraits are characterised by a personal, grave, poetic quality. He went to Holland in 1643 and his work lost all sense of poetry and became dull and commonplace. An example of this last period is *Apolonius Veth* in the National Gallery, London.

JORDAENS

Jacob Jordaens, the greatest Flemish painter of the seventeenth century after Rubens and Van Dyck, was born in Antwerp in 1593 and died there in 1678. He was trained, not by Rubens, as is often said, but by Adam van Noort. It was not until much later, when Jordaens had long been a master, that he came to know Rubens personally, and relieved him of certain commissions which Rubens himself could not carry out owing to pressure of work, but was willing to hand on to an artist of proved excellence. Their first meeting probably took place in the 1630s. Jordaens had by that time painted quite a number of important pictures, was married, owned a house—which still exists—in the fashion-able Hoogstraat and was Dean of the Guild of St Luke. His small studio had become a workshop and the first student he had registered in 1620 had been joined by a swarm of pupils and apprentices. When the Spanish Infante entered Antwerp as Regent in 1635, some of the gigantic pictures and decorations carried in the triumphal procession came not only from Jordaens's workshop, but from his own hand, for he was indefatigable in production. Thenceforward his fame increased by leaps and bounds. In 1639 the English King for long could not make up his mind whether to employ Rubens or Jordaens on the decoration of Greenwich Palace. The death of Rubens in 1640 saved Charles the trouble of coming to a decision. Jordaens's pictures for Greenwich have since disappeared.

J. JORDAENS
MELEAGER
AND ATALANTA
*61¼″ × 48¾″. Munich,
Private Collection*

But by this time he was considered
e leading painter of Flanders. In
e 1650s he joined the Protestant
urch. But this step did not pre-
nt the Catholic authorities from
ntinuing to employ him on the
ost important contracts, nor the
tist from supplying them with
agnificent paintings neither less
or more 'Catholic' than before. For
rdaens was never in his heart of
earts so typical a religious artist as
e Church believed him to be, nor
typical an allegorical one as the
ghteenth century suspected, nor,
ally, so typical a mythological
inter as the nineteenth century
pposed. Neither a pious legend nor
mythological scene attracted him
r its own sake. In reality he was
terly indifferent to both subjects.
tellectual preoccupations play no
rt in his work. Feeling is more
portant. But everything is subor-
nated to visual impression. He was
either a born storyteller nor an in-
rpreter. Form and line alone had
e power to charm him and he was intoxi-
ted by colour. This is the key to our ap-
reciation of his work. It is quite untrue that
e was a kind of Rubens. He was too big a
an, too devoted to his art and too strong
personality to be a 'kind' of anything.
e could paint heads which combine the
erits of Rubens and Frans Hals and
vent colours in which Rubens and
aravaggio might have collaborated. There
as only one effect he could not achieve.
e could not add such expression to his
ictorial values as enchants the student of
ubens, deeply moves him in a work by
embrandt or suggests nobility of spirit in
Velasquez.

His early works are unmistakable on
ccount of their abnormally strong colour.
hey dealt mostly with subjects, such as
atyr Visiting a Peasant, as in pictures at
russels, Munich and Cassel, and Meleager
nd Atalanta, exemplified at Antwerp,
Madrid and a private collection in Munich.
He continued to treat such themes in his
iddle period, though with somewhat less
btrusive colour. At this time he painted

J. JORDAENS · MOSES STRIKING THE ROCK
83¼″ × 72″. Karlsruhe, Kunsthalle

some of his *Beanfeasts*, to be seen in
Brussels and Leningrad, unfortunately
signing, however, certain inferior productions of his studio. *Like Father, Like Son*,
of which versions exist at Antwerp and
Munich, and *The Fruits of the Earth*, preserved at Brussels and Dresden, also date
from this stage of his career. In his last
years his colour darkened and grew more
subdued.

Throughout his life he painted religious
subjects. The most important of these
works were executed in his middle period.
They include the fine *Adorations* at New
York and Stockholm, the splendid *Moses
Striking Water from the Rock*, at Karlsruhe,
the *Tribute to St Peter* at Copenhagen and
Holy Families in London and San Francisco. His best group-portrait, representing
himself with his wife and daughters, is in
the Prado. It is a most robust specimen of
the middle-class spirit in painting, that of
which Leo van Puyvelde has observed:
'Jordaens had a wonderfully sound sense of
impartiality and is always so thoroughly
honest.'

JOUVENET

Known as the 'Great' and the 'Carracci of France', Jean-Baptiste Jouvenet owed his nickname to the bombastic tendency of his age. He was in no sense 'great'. Born at Rouen in 1644 and dying in Paris, in 1717 he began by painting mainly religious and mythological subjects derived from Poussin. At a later stage the influence of Rubens is beyond doubt, though Jouvenet added a not uninteresting naturalistic element of his own to his ecclesiastical works. It is evident in his physical types and still-life items. His style developed from that of Le Brun and eventually acquired much prestige, his only rivals being the Coypels (q.v.). Jouvenet executed large decorative works, such as the ceilings of the Parlements of Rennes and Rouen, the chapel at Versailles and the Invalides.

JUAN

Juan de Flandes, a rather mysterious Spanish painter, died at Palencia in 1519. Nothing is known of his origin or his life. He is only referred to as 'Juan de Flandes' at the time of his death. He was undoubtedly Flemish by birth. His style is purely Dutch, except for the occasional appearance in his works of Moorish types and typical Spanish landscape. His chief productions are the altarpiece executed for Palencia Cathedral and thirty small panels for an oratory, representing episodes from the life of the Virgin and of Christ. Most of these panels are today in Madrid, London and Vienna. Juan de Flandes has been greatly praised for his colour, his realism and the elegance—though this verdict is questionable—of his drawing. But if his works had been found somewhere in Belgium, unsigned, they would probably have been simply regarded as average produc-

tions of the first few years of the sixteen century.

JUSTUS OF GHENT

This was the name by which Josse va Wassenhove was known abroad in his lat years. Little has been recorded of his lif He left Antwerp for Ghent in 1464 and w evidently highly esteemed as a painter that date. About 1470 he seems to ha been invited to the Court at Urbino. any rate he suddenly left Ghent and nev saw his native land again. In 1473 the nam of Justus of Ghent appears in the Urbir archives for the first time and a year lat for the last time. This fact, however, do not mean that he was already dead. The is just as little mention of the Spania Pedro Berruguete, his collaborator in tl decoration of the palace. Justus execute three important works, an *Adoration* no in New York, an altarpiece of the Cruci xion at St Bavo in Ghent and the docu mentarily attested *Last Supper* at Urbin But it is not yet clear what part he took the production of pictures at Urbino, particular twenty-eight portraits of famo men preserved at that city and in tl Louvre and four allegories, of which tho in Berlin were destroyed during the wa Others are in London.

His remarkable ability is seen at its be in the Crucifixion altarpiece of 1464. great many ingredients from the past, co tributions from Bouts, Campin and hou book designs, are mingled in this strikir composition, to form a brew later decante by Van der Goes. Broken colour and lo tones are conspicuous. The remote distan is splendidly painted in three stages colour perspective, presenting in miniatu the scenes of common life which Justus friend, Van der Goes, subsequently tran ferred, on a large scale, to the foregroun

KALF

Willem Kalf, who was born in Amsterdam in 1622 and died there in 1693, was one of the most important painters of still-life in the late seventeenth century. His life is little known. But one fact is repeatedly mentioned. He is said to have been a man of exceptional culture and learning. Even in the absence of this statement the circumstance could have been deduced from

lusciously coloured pots, brooms, barrels and baskets of vegetables shine in the darkness, Kalf might be taken, at a glance, for a distinguished pupil of Rembrandt.

KAUFFMANN

Angelica Kauffmann was born at Chur in Switzerland in 1741 and died in Rome in 1807. She matured at a remarkably early

W. KALF
STILL-LIFE
23¼″ × 28⅜″. Paris, Louvre

the refined taste of his pictures. Their composition could not well be more economical. The colour is at first subdued to a single tone, as in the works of Pieter Claesz and Heda. Later, under the influence of Rembrandt, it becomes deeper and richer. A glowing Rembrandtesque gold, a touch of darkly gleaming red drapery and the sparkling lemon-yellow or the milky white of a faience vessel stand out against a background which time has now dimmed till it is nearly black.

In his rare kitchen interiors and dusky corners of a courtyard, where victuals and

age. Like most prodigies, however, she never fulfilled the high expectations which her talent had aroused. The truth is that she was no more than a very gifted crafts-woman of refined taste with a lively imagination, a typical feminine product of the 'age of genius'. Her large canvases, such as the *Death of Leonardo da Vinci* and *Nathan the Wise before David*, are romanticised essays in classicism. Her portraits are effeminate versions of the English style. With Antonio Zucchi, Angelica was the most prolific of Adam's collaborators. She worked at Syon House, Kedleston

Hall and Harewood House. These decorations are far more satisfactory than her weak portraits and compositions.

KEIRINCX

Alexander Keirincx was born at Antwerp in 1600 and died in Amsterdam in 1652. He painted a number of forest landscapes which are, surprisingly enough, to be found in almost all galleries, despite the alleged acute shortage of space. For it is quite clear that Keirincx was not an important painter. His early works are decidedly timid student's efforts in the 'English Garden' convention. The later pictures are much more attractive, with their soft and flowing, 'Dutch' colour. The style becomes light and graceful, as in the Hamburg *Landscape*, which recalls Goyen, or baroque and theatrical, as in The Hague *Forest Landscape with Figures*. Keirincx was in London in 1640/41, where he is often mentioned in the royal archives as 'Carings'.

KESSEL

Jan van Kessel of Antwerp (1626-1679) was trained by his uncle, Jan Brueghel II, under whose influence he produced tiny, meticulously rendered pictures of butterflies, beetles and birds. They were ignored for centuries, but are today collected with the greatest enthusiasm, especially in the United States. Kessel dispensed with composition in these little works. Part of their charm arises from the arrangement of his miniature jewels of colour in rows of five, ten or twelve at a time, as if on a blackboard. The larger flower and fruit pieces are either in the plain style of a work by Kalf or represent a somewhat loaded breakfast-table. In the latter case his skill begins to deteriorate.

The Amsterdam artist **Jan** Kessel (1641-1680) painted landscapes. His favourite views were those from a hill across a broad plain with strips of fields running in all directions, the pallid silhouette of a town on the horizon and a great expanse of cloudy sky. Sometimes trees, meadows and roofs are touched with particles of light

in a manner recalling the work of Verme? of Haarlem. Jan Kessel's *A Torrent in Mountainous Landscape* is in the Nation Gallery, London.

KETEL

Cornelis Ketel was born at Gouda in 154 and died in Amsterdam in 1616. He was man of far-reaching humanist ideals an a distinguished portrait painter. His meri were really only re-discovered in th present century, when the cleverness ar freedom of his portraits, with their occa sional substitution of finger for brus' could again be appreciated as productio? of a period of Mannerism and hostility portraiture. Strangely enough, he too remarkably little trouble over the con position of his group pictures, merely se ting his heads in a row from right to le? This man of high character suffered t? grievous affliction of paralysis during t? last six years of his life.

KETTLE

Tilly Kettle (c. 1740-1786) was born London and studied at the St Martin Lane Academy. From 1770 to 1778 ? worked in India, sending back pictures f? exhibition at the Royal Academy. He di? in Aleppo on his way to India for a seco? visit. Kettle was a portraitist who bas? his work on that of Reynolds, but who pictures are stamped by a strong feeli? for flat pattern and by a subtle range low tones which are entirely person? Represented in the National Galler? London, by *A Young Man in Fawn Coa* Two of his best works are *Rear-Admir Kempenfelt* at Greenwich, and *Eliza a? Mary Davidson* at Dulwich.

KEYSER

Thomas de Keyser (1597-1667), the lea? ing portrait painter at Amsterdam befo? Rembrandt's arrival, began by painting a stiff, rather old-fashioned style, which ? afterwards relaxed under the influence Hals and Rembrandt. He was at his best small, pleasing equestrian portraits, givi?

TH. DE KEYSER
PIETER SCHOUT ON HORSEBACK
34⅜″ × 17¾″. Amsterdam, Rijksmuseum

he citizens of Amsterdam the aspect of a Don Carlos. He also seems to have set the fashion for a type of picture, strikingly small in area, in which the restricted space was entirely filled by whole family groups, given interest by postures and surroundings which appeared to have been chosen by themselves. Certain mythological and biblical paintings by Keyser have also been discovered. But their only importance is their astonishing revelation of his secret addiction to bright colours and animated movement. Keyser's fine portrait of Constantin Huggens and his clerk is in the National Gallery, London.

KNELLER

Gottfried Kneller was a German, born at Lübeck in 1646, and he studied painting in Amsterdam under Ferdinand Bol. In 1672 he went to Rome, where Carlo Maratti was then the approved master, and to Naples and Venice. Kneller arrived in England in about 1674 determined to rival the careers of Van Dyck and Lely. He soon built up a vast practice, employing a great number of assistants. Ten ruling monarchs as well as Wren, Newton and Dryden were among his sitters. Kneller married an Englishwoman, Susannah Crane, daughter of the Archdeacon of Lincoln, was knighted as Sir Godfrey in 1692, became very rich and died at Twickenham in 1723. Most of the incredible number of his portraits were painted at extraordinary speed and show little insight into character, for Kneller's aim was seldom other than the purely material one of fulfilling the demands of fashionable patronage. He was nevertheless a very talented painter and one of his portraits at least is an inspired work. It is that of William Wycherley, painted about 1705, in the Sackville Collection. *The Marquess of Tweeddale* in the National Gallery, London, is also of fine quality.

KNIJFF

So excellent a landscape painter as Wouter Knijff, who was born at Wesel c. 1607 and died at Bergen-op-Zoom c. 1693, should be mentioned in any such work of reference as the present, though his pictures are extremely rare. He certainly left more paintings behind him than are recognised as his today, many being no doubt attributed to Jan van Goyen, whose style is very similar. Knijff's productions were mostly riverside scenes, which Hofstede de Groot observes may be distinguished from those of Goyen and Salomon Ruysdael by 'the houses extending towards the river bank, where they become too obtrusive, and by the monotonous steel-blue of their slate roofs'.

KONINCK

Until the nineteenth century, the biblical scenes, portraits and genre pictures of Philip de Koninck (1619-1688) could be seen everywhere. But today they are never mentioned. The productions in question were mediocre. It is difficult to account for the fact, since he was at one time Rem-brandt's pupil. His landscapes, however make him a great painter. They are quit unique for his period, being big, vigorou visions of enormous plains, watered by stream with gently sloping banks. Th eye loses itself in following the retreatin, echelon of parallels under a vast expans of sky. The clouds and the strips of san that penetrate the dull green vegetatio gleam faintly, in a tone of somewha tarnished golden-brown.

Salomon Koninck (1609-1656), also o Amsterdam, was probably a distant rela tive of Philip. He flourished at a time whe Rembrandt still enjoyed the greates esteem. Salomon could therefore have n hesitation in imitating so popular a styl He did his best, producing a number o genre-type portraits, punctiliously lifesize and some much more attractive littl biblical scenes, good enough to justify th continued retention of his name in galler catalogues.

KONRAD VON SOEST

This artist's father came from Soest. Bu the son, though generally known by thi name, lived and worked in the old West

PH. KONINCK · A LAND
SCAPE IN GELDERLAND
40″ × 58″. *London,
National Gallery*

halian town of Dortmund. He appears to have been born c. 1370 and to have died c. 1422. His chief works are an altarpiece at Bad Wildungen, dated 1404, and the remains of one at the Marienkirche in Dortmund. An important painter, he differed fundamentally from his Hamburg contemporary Francke, in expressing a tender lyricism most unusual at this early period. It is derived, as is at once evident on examination of the paintings, from book illustration. The beautiful, slender 'hour-book figures' in his foregrounds are especially typical of this style. French in their fastidious refinement, they represent not ordinary men, but great lords, deep in philosophic debate at the feet of the cruci-fied Christ. They show no signs of grief or hatred. It is no accident that on the side-panel representing the Whitsun gath-ering two of the disciples are reading books, one of them in the act of adjusting his scholar's spectacles. Konrad saw his-tory as an exquisite legend, a drama no longer agonising.

KULMBACH

The family name of Hans von Kulmbach, Suess, is documentarily attested, but for some strange reason fewer and fewer writers use it. He was associated with Albrecht Dürer—probably his actual assistant for a while. Born at Kulmbach in 1480, he was first apprenticed to Jacopo de' Barbari at Nuremberg, where he remained until his death in 1522. During the years 1514 to 1516 he sent three large triptychs to Cracow. There is no proof that he accompanied them himself. Overland routes, particularly those between Nurem-berg and Cracow, were by then so good as to present no difficulties to transport. Hans von Kulmbach, accordingly, must have had a wide circle of patrons. But his importance should not be over-estimated for that reason. Those who commissioned him were in fact former clients of Dürer and Veit Stoss.

The delicate refinement of his works often amounts to positively romantic feeling. It is colour, rather than invention

or draughtsmanship, that lends them life. Even his portraits, which show the artist's naïve timidity in the presence of his exalted sitters, exemplify the peculiar subtlety of his tonal values—for instance, that of the Margrave Casimir at Munich. His chief pictures are the Clothworkers' altarpiece in the Church of St Sebaldus at Nuremberg, designed by Dürer, the Cracow panels, of which those representing the *Last Supper* and the *Death of John* were regarded by Buchner as 'among the noblest of Nurem-berg paintings', and the *Adoration of the Kings* in Berlin, an unquestionably im-portant work suggestive, in the best sense, of the style of Dürer.

KUPETZKY

An age-old and honourable debate between Slavs and Hungarians as to the nationality of Johann Kupetzky is still undecided.

KULMBACH · MARGRAVE CASIMIR VON BRANDENBURG · *17″ × 15⅜″. Munich, Alte Pinakothek*

He was born in 1667 at Bösing near Pressburg, a German town at that time. Yet 'Jan' Kupetzky's pictures undoubtedly exhibit certain features which must be either Hungarian or Slav. He imitated Rembrandt's chiaroscuro, impasto and line. But all his models, in their shirts adorned with gay embroidery, look like the bol lords of the Puszta.

Kupetzky lived for long in Italy. The he visited Vienna and finally , in 172 Nuremberg, where he died as a success ful and brilliantly accomplished artist i 1740.

L

LAER

Peter van Laer (Bamboccio) was born near Haarlem before 1595 and died there before 1660. Before 1610 he went to Rome and became a pupil of Elsheimer. A contemporary in Rome, the historian Posseri, describes how in the cafés frequented by foreign artists it was customary for a newcomer to hold a *Festa del Battesimo* where he was given a nickname, and that at Van Laer's *festa* he received the name 'Bamboccio' owing to his Punch-like appearance. Bamboccio exploited the arts of Elsheimer and of Claude and Poussin as décor for his own observations of life in the streets of Rome and in the Campagna. These pictures of peasant, tavern and animal life were known as 'bambocciati' or 'bambochades'. The liveliness of Laer's observation made an inevitable appeal to the public and he enjoyed great success, which continued when he returned to Holland in 1639. His influence on Dutch art was considerable, for he initiated the whole school of Dutch low-life popular painting, while the picturesque elements of his art were specially developed by Wouwermans. According to an old tradition, Bamboccio committed suicide from chagrin at Wouwermans' rise to fame. Represented in the Louvre and the Uffizi.

LAIRESSE

Born at Lüttich in 1640 and dying in Amsterdam in 1711, Gerard de Lairesse was the chief representative in Holland of the 'enlightened' classicism which had been taught for a generation before his time at the French Academy. In his day the styles of Rembrandt and Frans Hals were already a somewhat painful memory, while the popular realism of such painters as Teniers, Ostade and Steen only interested a few collectors. Classical antique art was all the rage in fashionable Dutch society. Lairesse sedulously rang the changes on such subjects as the *Death of Germanicus*, now at Cassel, and *Seleucus*

Giving Up His Wife to His Son, of which there are versions at Amsterdam and Karlsruhe. In these works the most exalted personages, in the most exalted attitudes, perform all sorts of out-of-date actions for a high moral purpose among pillars or in Arcadian glades. The paintings are technically perfect and carried out in strong, cheerful colours. But Poussin, though Lairesse was inspired by him, had no such conception of antiquity. Lairesse's best works remain his rustic love-scenes.

His last twenty years were spent in poverty, for he had gone blind. But in this condition he dictated an exhaustive treatise on the art of painting, published at Amsterdam in 1712 under the title of *Het Groot Schilderboek*. Lairesse is well represented in the Dulwich Gallery.

LANCRET

Nicolas Lancret (1690-1743), the painter of the frivolous society of the Rococo period, was the son of a Parisian coachman and rose from these humble origins to participate in the elegant Court life of Versailles. While still a student, Lancret met Watteau at the studio of the *genre* painter Gillot and joined him as an assistant to Claude Audran. Watteau was older than Lancret, more mature and more of a genius. Lancret admired him so much that he determined to equal his achievement.

But the younger man's popular success in painting *fêtes galantes* led to a quarrel with his hero. At this distance of time it is easy to see the difference between the two arists. Lancret's pictures, which deal mainly with pastoral and theatrical life, are most agreeable. But they lack Watteau's melancholy detachment. They remain no more than illustrations of a formerly poor man's frank adoration of these exquisite beings, 'the most beautiful ever seen', as Voltaire used to call them. Frederick the Great possessed twenty-six canvases by Lancret. He is represented in the Louvre, the National Gallery, London, and the Wallace Collection, where *A Girl in a Kitchen* shows a different and more interesting side of his work.

LARGILLIÈRE

Nicolas de Largillière (1656-1746) was born in Paris, but went at an early age to Antwerp, where he was trained as a painter. In about 1674 he came to England as an assistant to Lely. He specialised in painting the still-life elements and landscape backgrounds of Lely's pictures. He returned to Paris in 1682 and remained there until his death, rapidly becoming the portraitist most patronised by the rich Parisian bourgeoisie, though he was also favoured by Louis XIV. Largillière became a member of the Académie Royale in 1686 and in turn Professor, Director and Chancellor. His work is characterised by rich colour and fluency of execution, and his conception of portraiture is more free and baroque than that of his immediate predecessors. In his use of oil he is the most painterly of all his generation. Largillière is well represented in Paris; there is a good self-portrait at Versailles. A *Portrait of a Man* is in the National Gallery, London, and *Louis XIV and His Heirs* is in the Wallace Collection.

LASTMAN

The Amsterdam painter, Pieter Lastman (1583-1633), was unlucky, not lucky, in having Rembrandt for a pupil. His name has ever since been mentioned in a slightly patronising tone, which he does not deserve. Before Rembrandt's time Lastman had already seen Caravaggio's pictures in Rome and guessed, from the chiaroscuro painting of his own friend Elsheimer, the direction in which further progress might

be made. On his return to Amsterdam in 1607 he made the experiment. By the time Rembrandt arrived at his studio in 1622 Lastman had long been painting 'early Rembrandts'—for example, the *Raising of Lazarus* at The Hague and *Susanna and the Elders* in Berlin, which is the obvious basis for Rembrandt's picture of the same subject.

The best-known works of this most admirable artist, which commanded high prices in his lifetime, include the *Sacrifice of Abraham* in the Louvre, *Orestes and Pylades* at Amsterdam, *The Baptism of the Moor* at Munich and *Ulysses and Nausicaa* at Brunswick.

LA TOUR

Georges du Mesnil de La Tour was born at

G. DE LA TOUR · ST IRENE WITH THE WOUNDED
ST SEBASTIAN · 64″ × 51⅜″. *Berlin, Staatl. Museen*

Vis-sur-Seille in 1593 into an aristocratic family long established in Lorraine, and died in Lunesville in 1652. It is strange that with such distinguished artistry so little should be known of his life. For 250 years his name was forgotten and his marvellous paintings were ascribed to anyone but himself. As late as 1926 his famous *Adoration of the Child*, now in the Louvre, was being advertised by Berlin art-dealers as the work of Honthorst. Today it seems incredible that La Tour's entire production, positively unique in style, should not have been immediately recognised on all sides. Nothing could be easier than to distinguish his candle-lit scenes from those of Schalcken or the few others who attempted such effects. His figures are large in scale. The general tone is a clear brick-red. The shadows in his rooms are not genuine chiaroscuro. Consequently, his outlines allow plenty of space for deployment of the most subtle gradations of colour. Of his chief works, the *Adoration*, *Joseph the Carpenter* and *St Mary Magdalene* are in Paris, *St Sebastian Mourned by St Irene and Her Women* is in Berlin, the *Denial of St Peter* and the *Angel Appearing to St Peter* are at Nantes, a *Nativity* is at Rennes and the *Woman with Flea* at Nancy.

Maurice Quentin de La Tour, the son of a trumpeter, was born in 1704 and died—mentally deranged—at St Quentin in 1788. The town was indebted to him for many benefactions and charitable foundations and did not neglect him in his affliction. The sensational success of an exhibition of works by Rosalba Carriera, which he had seen in Paris, caused La Tour to take up pastels. He eventually devoted himself entirely to portraits in that medium. They are today the pride of a few large galleries and private collections, for their exquisite, delicate technique and brilliant sense of character set them far above those of his contemporaries. About eighty-five of his pastels are in the St Quentin Museum. But the Louvre has his five full-lengths of Mme de Pompadour, and his portrait of Henry Dawkins is in the National Gallery, London.

LAWRENCE

Sir Thomas Lawrence was born at Bristol in 1769, the son of an innkeeper. He was extremely precocious. As a child he made drawings for the guests at his father's hostel, and by the time he was twelve he had a studio at Bath which was frequented by fashionable society. His youthful work was in pastel. Five years later Lawrence began to paint seriously in oils, and removed to London, where he was helped by Reynolds. His success was immediate. In 1791 he was elected an Associate of the Academy, and on the death of Reynolds in 1792 he was appointed Principal Portrait Painter to the King. In that year he also painted portraits of the King and Queen which were taken by Lord Macartney on his embassy to China and presented to the Emperor. Lawrence travelled all over Europe painting portraits of the great persons of the hour, the Emperors of Austria and Russia, Metternich, the Duc de Richelieu and Pope Pius VII, the last being one of his most brilliant works. Among English celebrities Lawrence painted Lady Blessington, Scott, Southey and Canning. Lawrence had astonishing facility and technical accomplishment, but was without profound insight into character. He died in 1830 and with him an epoch in English portraiture came to an end.

LE BRUN

Charles Le Brun (1619-1690) showed a most precocious talent very early and went to work first in the atelier of Perrier and then of Vouet. He completed his training in Rome, where he studied the work of the Baroque painters and of Poussin. Returning to France in 1646 he obtained several important commissions for decorations in the Hotel Lambert and the Château of Vaux. In 1661 he received his first royal commission and after that came under the protection of Colbert and received every post of importance in the artistic world. His reform of the Academy converted it into an institution with a virtual dictatorship in the arts and a fully equipped art school. He was also responsible for the

LE BRUN · THE
CHANCELLOR ON HORSEBACK
118" × 140". Paris, Louvre

complete decoration of Versailles and of Marly. He furnished cartoons for the Gobelins, his series including the *Months*, the *Elements* and the *Histoire du Roi*.

His immense output covered allegorical, historical and religious paintings, frescoes, Gobelins tapestries, designs for garden sculpture and furniture. But amidst the lumber of his bombastic baroque products a sincerely executed picture may occasionally be discovered which can immediately be recognised as far above the average and of real pictorial quality. Such a work is the *Chancellor Seguier on Horseback* in Paris.

LELY

Sir Peter Lely (1618-1680), also called Van der Faes, was of Dutch parentage and came from Soest near Utrecht. He studied under F. P. Grebber in Haarlem. He came to England in 1641 in the train of William, Prince of Orange. His portrait of Prince William and his bride, the daughter of Charles I, established him in the Royal favour and he was soon enjoying an extensive practice. Lely now abandoned his native Dutch style for that of Van Dyck, seen in such portraits as his *Sir Thomas Fanshaw* (1645), and *Sir Charles Lucas*. His talents came to maturity only after the Restoration. This period is epitomized by

his two celebrated series of portraits, the *Flagmen* at Greenwich Hospital, and the *Windsor Beauties* at Hampton Court. The latter are by no means penetrating interpretations of character and are occasionally gross in feelings, yet they show the artist as an unusually subtle colourist. On the other hand, some of the portraits at Greenwich, *Admiral Jeremy Smith*, for example—are masterly character studies, while the portraits at Ham House of Elizabeth Dysart in her youth and after her marriage to Lauderdale are fascinating revelations of a brilliant, ruthless personality.

LE MOINE

The name is also spelt Lemoyne. The Parisian François Le Moine (1688-1737) was one of the best fresco painters of his time. He produced extremely decorative work, not merely the frigid, absurdly pretentious ornamentation which the Court painters of the day turned out by the yard, but real 'pictures', though in the qualified sense imposed by such vast orders as that for the Versailles paintings of the *Labours of Hercules*, to cover more than 3,000 square feet. Some idea of the style of Le Moine's easel-pictures—for example, his *Omphale* in the Louvre, *Andromeda* in London and *Narcissus* at Hamburg—can be obtained when it is remembered that

L. LE NAIN
THE HAY CART
22⅜″ × 30¾″. Paris, Louvre

Boucher was taught by Le Moine and owed a great deal of his skill to him. A Venetian influence, through Ricci, and also some resemblance to Lancret's work, can be detected in Le Noine's pictures.

LE NAIN

The three brothers Le Nain remained forgotten until well into the nineteenth century. The character of the paintings of Louis scenes of common life in town and country executed at the height of the Baroque period, and the fact that the three men never married and lived together all their lives, suggest hermit-like existences in poverty and obscurity. But, strangely enough, the brothers were prosperous, well known, members of the Academy and quietly happy. The justly high esteem now accorded to them, however—to Louis in particular—dates from modern times.

Nothing is known of their training. And as they may have collaborated at times in the same paintings, which they signed only 'Le Nain', there is no clue on which to base an analysis of their styles.

Antoine, born at Laon and dying in Paris, painted in a manner resembling that of such Dutchmen as Avercamp. He produced portraits, miniatures and groups in the *genre* convention. He paid much attention to drawing, but little to modelling, showing a marked interest in the lower levels of society.

Louis was also born at Laon, in 1593. He died in Paris in 1648, two days after his brother. He had settled in the city by 1630, but is called in early sources 'Le Romain', indicating perhaps a visit to Rome. His work is large in scale and subdued in colour, forming a surprising parallel to the early productions of Velazquez. His affection for the anonymous, despised masses is much more pronounced than that of Antoine. In executing such pictures as the *Forge*, now at the Louvre, the *Milkmaid's Family* at Leningrad, the *Swineherd's Cart* in the Louvre and *Saying Grace* in London, Louis painted as if he were one of those he portrayed, not like an investigator from a different world.

Mathieu, born at Laon in 1607 and dying in Paris in 1677, aimed at pleasing everyone. He produced good portraits and *genre* works with a Flemish flavour. His figures belong to a higher social level than those of his brothers.

LEONARDO DA VINCI

Leonardo is regarded as the typical Renaissance man. He was inspired by the kind of curiosity about the physical world which ushered in the modern era of empirical enquiry and which led him to a knowledge of the structure of living organisms and the forces of nature unsurpassed by any man of his age. He devoted as much of his energies to scientific study as to art. He used the results of his scientific observations in his pictures and developed the art of light and shade to an extent even beyond that of Masaccio.

He was born in 1452, the natural son of a prosperous notary named Piero, from Vinci, near Empoli in Tuscany, and became a pupil of Verrocchio, the remarkable personality who played so important a part in the artistic life of his day, though his own works are not among its most significant. In Verrocchio's studio Leonardo participated in a *Baptism of Christ*, now at the Uffizi Gallery. It is the earliest surviving picture in which he took a hand. He painted the angel on the left and the romantic landscape behind that figure with its stretch of hills, lakes, shining mists and pools, anticipating the background of the *Mona Lisa*. The angel, while closely related to those of Verrocchio, yet conveys quite a different effect, not of innocent childlike grace, but of the 'unearthly beauty so often apparent in Leonardo's later works.

By 1472 he had learnt all Verrocchio had to teach him. But he continued to reside in the latter's house until about 1480. The two men were both exceptionally versatile, the elder kindling the imagination of the younger. They must have argued from morning till night about anatomy, perspective, sculpture, the flight of birds, crystallisation, God and the world at large. No doubt it was Verrocchio who revealed its wonders to Leonardo. In 1481 the latter received his first big commission. The monks at Scopeto ordered the *Adoration of the Kings* now in the Uffizi Gallery. The work is unfinished, being really only a preliminary layout in monochrome. The impression it makes is nevertheless extraordinary. Roberto Salvini observes that 'the figures flicker like the tongues of flames. But their spellbound, wavering movements are all directed to a single centre, that of the triangle of light composed by the group in the foreground.'

In 1482 Leonardo abandoned this work, accepting an invitation to the Court of the Sforza family at Milan, where he remained until 1499. He was already nearly forty but seemed to be fated to do nothing more than act like a player at several chess-boards at once, passing from one to another to make a single move that had the effect of a revelation, and then leaving the game he had almost won to remain unfinished while he turned his attention elsewhere. It was in

LEONARDO DA VINCI · THE MADONNA AND CHILD AND ST ANNE · 67¼″ × 52″. *Paris, Louvre*

Milan that he painted the subsequently world-famous fresco—today already half in ruins—of the *Last Supper* in the church of Sta Maria delle Grazie. In 1483 he had begun the *Virgin of the Rocks*, now in the Louvre. In this picture the whole personality of the artist appears for the first time. Here the visual curiosity of a studious, sceptical, analytical spirit has paradoxically produced forms that seem to drift in the uncertain twilight of a dream. Much lies hidden in his sensitive and unacademic use of chiaroscuro. Leonardo explained the matter in more illuminating —that is to say, more comprehensible— terms when he wrote: 'Notice the faces of men and women in the street at evening, in cloudy weather. They then assume a most charming and gentle aspect.' And 'very great charm of shadow and light is to be found in the faces of those who sit in doors of dark houses.' It was in this fashion that he painted, on his return to Florence, the *Mona Lisa*, renowned in Leonardo's time for its realism, and the wonderful *Virgin and St Anne*, both in the Louvre. A great fresco depicting the battle of Anghiari, begun in competition with Michelangelo, was left, like so many others, unfinished and has been reduced to fragments. In 1506 he again left Florence, first returning to Milan, where he was mainly occupied with engineering works and sculpture and did little painting. But he managed to set all the Lombard painters by the ears, turning them into 'little Leonardos'. Melzi, Luini, Boltraffio, Predis, Giampetrino and d'Oggione were thus transformed. In 1515 King Francis I of France invited him to settle at a castle near Amboise in Touraine, whither the faithful Melzi accompanied him. None of the works of these last years—for Leonardo died at the castle in 1519—has survived. Perhaps by that time this Faust-like devotee of learning had buried his dreams.

For most of Leonardo's pictures there exist many preliminary drawings. His painting represents only a portion of his contribution to art and science. His *Treatise on Painting* and *Notebooks* are of the utmost importance for an understanding of his genius.

LE PRINCE

Born in Metz in 1734 and dying at Saint-Denis-du-Port in 1781 Jean-Baptiste Le Prince was a great traveller, working in Italy, Holland, Finland and Russia. At St Petersburg he was greatly appreciated as a pupil of the famous Boucher, whom he imitated. The Tsarina hastened to give her private apartments in the Winter Palace a touch of Paris. In 1762 Le Prince returned to the French capital, still full of his experiences in Russia. He reciprocated the Tsarina's compliment by making the Russian style all the rage in Paris for some years. His most acceptable pictures are his designs for Beauvais tapestries.

LE SUEUR

Eustache Le Sueur (1616/17-1655) was born in Paris. His early work was strongly influenced by Vouet, as is shown by the eight paintings illustrating the *Hypnerotomachia Poliphilo*, a romance by Francesco Colonna, which Le Sueur executed in about 1637. These are to be seen in the museums at Rouen, Dijon and Le Mans, and in the Czernin Gallery, Vienna. A little later, under the influence of Poussin, Le Sueur's work became more classical in spirit. It also shows a new and personal religious feeling, which achieves its finest expression in the grave illustrations to the life of St Bruno, painted for the Charterhouse of Paris, 1645-48, some of which are now in the Louvre. In his last years Le Sueur's style was almost completely dominated by that of Raphael, although he never went to Rome and only knew Raphael's work from engravings.

LEYDEN

The career of the short-lived Lucas Hughensz van Leyden (c. 1494-1533) dazzled his contemporaries like the passage of a comet. Vasari's biography rates him above even Dürer. The admiration both of Vasari and of modern critics is due to the element of genius in his pictures, the unrestrained energy of his drawing and use of colour, his apparent facility. He had not quite reached his full stature in the earliest of his known works, the *Chess Players* at

L. VAN LEYDEN · A YOUNG COUPLE
10¾" × 12¾". Strassburg, Musée des Beaux Arts

Berlin. It is still reminiscent of his teacher, Engelbrechtsen. But in the *Card Players* at Salisbury he brought his style to maturity. This picture is a standing reproach to all who have tried to prove that painting is a 'mystery'. Here is the secret, one is tempted to say. Red planes are just brushed on in red and green in green. In other words, Lucas, in his best and most lively works, always allowed the picture-plane to remain a *plane*. The turning-point came in 1521, when he met Dürer, having travelled to Antwerp for the sole purpose of paying his respects to the master. He then began to study the engravings of the Italian Marcanton, for he was himself a copper-engraver of distinction. After this date the signs of genius in his work quickly began to fade. He imitated Dürer—for instance, in his *Last Judgment* altarpiece at Leyden. Eventually the 'comet' plunged to extinction in the great sea of Renaissance style copyists. Many people, no doubt, will prefer Lucas's late, more 'elgant' productions, in Dürer's manner. But at this point he begins to be one of a crowd. He was more significant while he was still a *Fauve*.

LEYSTER

Born at Haarlem in 1609 and dying at

Hemstede in 1660. Judith Leyster was one of the few women admitted to the painters' guild. It is assumed that she studied under Frans Hals, in whose style she painted for a while. The effective productions of Honthorst, with his candle-lit scenes and treatment of light in the manner of Caravaggio, also fascinated her for a considerable time. But her drawing was unsound. In her *genre* pictures and portraits the smile is often disagreeably distorted. At the age of twenty-five she married the distinguished artist, Jan Molenaer. Thereupon she added, and may well be forgiven for doing so, yet a third ingredient to the composition of her works, which were very small in scale. Her *Boy and Girl with a Cat* is in the National Gallery, London.

LIBERALE DA VERONA

The Verona artist Liberale della Biava (1445-1526/9) worked for a long time in Tuscany. He painted a great number of religious panels, which are to be seen in nearly all the larger galleries. His style derives partly from Antonello da Messina and partly from Mantegna and Matteo di Giovanni. It is so uneven, however, that Bernard Berenson on one occasion maliciously referred to Liberale's works as 'those weak and deplorable pictures with their stuffed puppets' and in the next breath to 'that wonderful work the *Pietà* at Munich' and 'his most enchanting picture, the *Dido* in the National Gallery'. During the last few decades interest in Liberale's painting has been increasing.

LIBRI

Gerolamo dai Libri, who was born in Verona in 1474 and died there in 1555, was strongly influenced by Domenico Morone, who perhaps trained him. He worked in accordance with strict rules, repudiating, in his religious pictures, all features not exclusively devoted to solemn celebration of e virtues of the saints. The only technical aim he wholeheartedly pursued was the attainment of a new and peculiar type of perspective, already tending to Baroque practice. His compositions are often of exceptional interest, exemplified in the *Madonna with Two Saints* at Verona, but would be more enjoyable if the contents were less orthodox and the spirit more amiable. His *Virgin and Child with St Anne* is in the National Gallery, London.

LICINIO

The name of Bernardino Licinio, born at Porcante, Bergamo, c. 1489, occurs in records up to 1549. But he does not seem to have died until about 1565, in Venice. Practically nothing is known of his life and development. Apart from a few eclectic religious works of no consequence, some two dozen of his portraits survive, indicating the influences of Giorgione and Palma Vecchio—for example, a female portrait at Munich and that of a man in London. Some of these portraits are very fine.

LIEVENS

Jan Lievens was born in Amsterdam in 1607 and died there in 1674. For a time his development ran parallel with Rembrandt's. He studied with the latter under Lastman. Both pupils acquired the 'Rembrandtesque' style about the same time, though Lievens seems to have led the way and in any case matured earlier. He painted fine pictures at this period of a more intellectual character and more assured than those of Rembrandt. They include the small portrait of Rembrandt's mother in profile, a work of exceptional promise. But in 1631 Lievens left Amsterdam for England, whence he proceeded to Antwerp, where he rapidly succumbed to the Flemish influences of Van Dyck, Teniers and Brouwer. On his return to Amsterdam in 1644 he had lost all traces of Rembrandt's manner. His style had become smooth and urbane, half French, half Flemish. A self-portrait is in the National Gallery, London.

LIMBOURG

Pol de Limbourg (c. 1380/90-c. 1416), in collaboration with his brothers **Jan** and **Hermann**, produced one of the most precious works of art in the world, the Hour Book—*Les Très Riches Heures*—of the Duc de Berry. It is now believed that the family name was really Malouel, the brothers being nephews of the painter Jean Malouel, born about 1360 at Geldern and dying in Paris in 1419. Very few of his works, unfortunately, have survived. Pol and his brothers were probably born at Lymborch, the present Limbricht, in the Dutch province of Gelderland. They were orphans. Jean Malouel saw to their education and also assisted them in their careers at a later date, for he himself occupied the

POL DE LIMBOURG · APRIL
(*From the* Très Riches Heures) 5⅜″ × 6″. *Chantilly, Musée Condé*

important post of Court Painter to the Duke of Burgundy.

Hesdin (q.v.) died in 1409. In 1411 the Limbourgs were appointed to succeed him at the Court of the great patron of art, Jean de Berry, in Bourges. The brothers had become book-illustrators, Pol having the greatest talent. His skill recalls that of Jan van Eyck and was far superior to that of his French contemporaries. The Duke loaded him with honours and gifts. Pol de Limbourg died soon after 1416. His brothers outlived him. The *Très Riches Heures* is his masterpiece, though he himself did not live to put the finishing touches to it. The pictures of the Months are the most famous of the collection. They are small works in tempera, of the greatest charm and refinement, painted in bright, glowing colours. The landscape drawing, the elegance of the attenuated figures and the splendour of their dress are gems of observation. The book is preserved in the Chantilly Museum. A second authenticated work, the *Heures d'Ailly*, is in the Rothschild Collection in Paris.

LIOTARD

Jean Etienne Liotard, who was born in Geneva in 1702 and died in 1789, was a most remarkable character. He had travelled widely and after spending five years in Constantinople adopted Turkish dress, retaining it on his return to Europe until a late marriage put an end to this eccentricity. His restlessness and ambition drove him from one court to another, from Vienna as far as London. He devoted himself entirely, after failing in other fields, to pastel portraiture and *genre* painting allied to portraits, as in his *Chocolate Girl* at Dresden. His Turkish scenes are interesting, but actually most unprofessional. On the other hand, he took very great care over his delightfully captivating portraits. Some of his miniatures in oils, after Watteau and Lancret, are charming.

LIPPI

Fra Filippo Lippi (1406?-1469) was the son of a Florentine butcher, Tommaso di

Lippi. Left an orphan while still a child he was taken into the care of the Carmelite and entered the Order at the age of fifteen He studied under Lorenzo Monaco an was a follower of Masaccio and was als influenced by Fra Angelico. The details c Fra Filippo's life are vague, but he pro bably left the monastery in 1431. Brown ing's poem, *Fra Filippo Lippi*, suggest that the standards and observances of th cloister sat uneasily upon the painter, an at an undetermined date he obtained re lease from his monastic vows and marrie a nun, Lucrezia Buti, who had sat to hir as a model and whom, according t Vasari, he had abducted. They had a child Filippino Lippi, who was born at Prato where Fra Filippo was engaged on th splendid frescoes in the Cathedral illus trating the lives of St Stephen and of S John the Baptist (1452-1464). Gentleness humanity, humour and an exquisitely re fined sense of colour, in which he was i advance of his time, characterise Fr Filippo's work. At the time of his death h was working in Spoleto on a second grea cycle of frescoes, *Scenes from the Life of th Virgin*, which he left unfinished. Typica works by Fra Filippo are in the Uffizi an the Louvre, and the *Annunciation*, S *Bernard's Vision of the Virgin* and *Seve Saints* are in the National Gallery, London

When Fra Filippo died, his son **Filip pino**, born in 1457, came under the guidance of his father's assistant, Fra Diamante. Ir 1472 he entered the workshop of Botticelli who exercised a most important influence on his work. It is not certain whethe Filippino went to Rome to work in the Sistine Chapel. In 1482 the Signoria of Florence commissioned him to paint one of the walls in the Sala del Publica and ir 1485 the *Madonna and Saints*, now in the Uffizi, for the Sala degli Otto di Pratico. From 1484 to 1485 Filippino was at work in the Brancacci Chapel. In 1486 he finished the *Vision of St Bernard* in the Badia, Florence. In 1487 Filippo Strozzi ordered from him frescoes of episodes from the lives of SS. John the Evangelist and Philip for Sta Maria Novella. Filippino only finished these in 1502, two years before his death. In 1504 he began the *eposition*, now in the Accadnia, Florence, which was later impleted by Perugino. Lippi as thus highly successful in his own day and he was loved as a an, so Vasari tells us, for his modesty and courtesy. The tendency of critics of our own time has been to underrate ilippino's stature as an artist. erenson, for example, describes is figures as 'unconvincing and ithout significance, because 'ithout tactile values'. However, Lippi is, at his best, a strikingly riginal artist with an extremely nusual sense of colour and pattern and an ability to express variety of moods ranging from the mysticism and almost Oriental spirit of contemplation of the great National Gallery, London, altarpiece *The Virgin and Child ith SS. Jerome and Dominic* painted for the Rucellai Chapel, Florence, to the gaiety of the *Worship of the Golden Calf*, also in the National Gallery, London.

FRA FILIPPO LIPPI · THE VIRGIN ADORING THE CHILD · *50¾″ × 46¾″. Berlin, Staatl. Museen*

LISS

The name is also spelt Lyss. Liss was born at Oldenbourg in Schleswig-Holstein c. 1600 and died in Venice in 1629. A visit to Rome at an early age led him, after encountering Caravaggio's works, to take up the study of light, to the extent, almost, of becoming an 'open-air' painter (cf. *The Inn Porch* at Kassel). In 1621 he moved to Venice, where he met Fetti. He found in the latter's style the first real revelation of his own inclinations. Sandrart reports that he drew a great deal from the nude at our Academy in Venice'. During the next few years he produced many vigorous, broadly painted works in the spirit of Rubens, such as the *Toilet of Venus* in the Uffizi Gallery, the *Finding of Moses* at Lille and the *Soldiers and Girls Revelling* at the Viennese Academy. His *Judith and Holofernes* is in the National Gallery, London.

LOCHNER

When the Cologne councillors, some seventy years after Lochner's death, proudly showed his *Adoration of the Kings* to the visiting celebrity, Albrecht Dürer, they could tell him nothing more about the artist except that he had come to Cologne from Meersburg on Lake Constance and died in the poorhouse. Modern research has added two important dates to this information. Stefan Lochner is mentioned in the Cologne archives for the first time in 1442 and for the last time in 1451. But the years of his birth and death are still unknown.

His beautiful paintings can be identified with fair certainty. The finest and most numerous of them are at Cologne. They include the altarpiece of the *Adoration of the Kings* in the Cathedral, the *Virgin of the Rose Bower*, the *Nativity*, a Madonna

LOCHNER · THE VIRGIN IN THE ROSE GARDEN
20″ × 16″. Cologne, Wallraf Richartz Museum

altarpiece, a *Last Judgment* and four panels representing saints. Other works are at Darmstadt, Frankfurt, Nuremberg and Munich.

Lochner is most commonly thought of as depicting scenes with 'fair and gentle' Madonnas, delicate, dreamy figures, the contours of which seem almost to melt into their surroundings. But this is a one-sided view. It is true that he continued the Cologne style developed twenty years before by the great 'Master of St Veronica', refining it and imbuing it with tender feeling and a kind of lyricism derived from book illustration. But he was also capable of passion. He could raise his voice, as in his *Last Judgment*, like a Fleming. When he expressed tender and delicate emotion, he was not being vaguely sentimental. His Madonnas do not suggest hymns played on the harmonium, but medieval love-ballads

to the music of a spinet. He is re[p]resented in the National Galler[y] London.

LOMBARD

Lambert Lombard was born [at] Lüttich c. 1506 and died the[re] c. 1566. At first he frankly a[nd] honestly imitated Mabuse and h[is] early pictures show the latter['s] influence. But later he visite[d] Rome, a place with which, as [a] learned humanist, he was alread[y] familiar at a distance. He came [to] the conclusion that the Italia[n] painters were not making near[ly] enough of their wonderful gift[s] He showed them—he, a Dutch[man]—what he meant on his retur[n] in 1538 to his native land and th[e] society of pupils, such as Flor[is] and Goltzius, who thought as h[e] did. Thenceforward his picture[s] were full of marble halls, baths an[d] senators in whirling togas. Th[e] effect was sumptuous, but mis[s]leading. The visions thus conjure[d] up by Lombard came to an en[d] with his own work and that o[f] Floris. We may be grateful fo[r] the fact. Friedländer observes [:] 'Never in any circumstances can one expec[t] much of a result when a Dutchman take[s] it into his head to give up the study o[f] nature.'

An excellent self-portrait is preserved a[t] Lüttich. Its quality and technical standard[s] are so high that it has recently been attri[[] buted to Frans Floris. There is a copy a[t] Kassel.

LONGHI

Pietro Longhi (1702-1785) was a contemporary of Guardi, and, like him, [a] Venetian. He produced hundreds of small-scale illustrations of life and activities in the reception-rooms and markets, along the promenades and during the carnivals and duck-shooting expeditions of Venice. He did not work in the same style as Guardi, for he had been trained at Crespi's hool in Bologna. Apparently he had seen onochrome engravings of the pictures of hardin and also of Boucher's *genre* aintings. If so, much in his development ould be explained. His compositions are ss significant and elaborate than theirs. is figures are usually rather puppet-like, hile his colour is not in the least like hardin's, being cool, flat and somewhat arsh.

His son, **Alessandro** Longhi (1733-313), who also lived in Venice, was a ortrait painter.

ORENZETTI

he brothers Pietro and Ambrogio Lorenetti are regarded not only as two of the ost important Sienese painters of the fourenth century, but also among the greatest all Italy. They should really be no less ell known than such artists as Ghirlandaio, Iurillo or De Hooch, of whom everyone as heard. Ambrogio in particular is easy appreciate and understand, though Pietro less so.

Both were born between 1280 and 1290 nd died, probably of the plague, in 1348 Siena. In 1348 the formerly flourishing ity was like one vast cemetery. Pietro's tyle is clearly derived rom those of Duccio nd Giotto. It never uite loses its archaic lavour. But Ambrogio s less conservative. He nay perhaps, therefore, ave been the younger f the two brothers. ietro's pictures are ery reticent. He prefers rigid outline, tradiional colour and a cerain passivity to any ort of 'incidental' comnunication. Ambrogio, n the other hand, is a estful and imaginaive illustrator. Typical aintings by Pietro are is *Deposition*, treated as conomically and conrapuntally as a work by

Giotto, and his *Madonna and Child*, a fresco at Assisi, where the Virgin's expression, as she gazes upon her Son, is that of an aristocratic mother, awe-inspiring in its acceptance of coming affliction, yet conscious of helplessness in the face of the Child's impending fate. The effect of this blue-and-gold composition is unforgettable.

Ambrogio's frescoes entitled *Good and Bad Government*, in the Palazzo Pubblico of Siena, constitute his masterpiece. There is nothing breathtaking about them. They are panoramic paintings of great beauty and imaginative variety, harmoniously composed narratives of changing scenes enacted by slender, naturalistic figures in manycoloured garments. The settings are the houses of ordinary citizens or charming, grassy meadows and gardens which anticipate Brueghel's landscape backgrounds. These works are as memorable as Pietro's. But the colours—red, grey, dull green and brown—are those of normal life.

A few religious panels by both the Lorenzettis survive, at Siena and Florence. These works are naturally all much alike, as each brother had to satisfy current taste in complying with the orders of an average client.

A. LORENZETTI · GOOD GOVERNMENT
(*Detail: Going to the Hunt*) *Fresco. Siena, Palazzo Pubblico*

LORRAINE

Claude Gellée, called Lorraine, was born at Nancy in 1600 in poor circumstances and was trained as a pastry-cook. At the age of twelve he went to Rome in that capacity and was employed by Agostino Tassi, a landscape painter who taught the young pastry-cook to paint. In 1625 Claude returned to France and worked with Deruet, painting architectural backgrounds for him, but two years later he was back in Rome, never to leave the city again. He died there in 1682.

We know very few details of Claude's life or the dates of his early paintings, and no great artist has inspired so little literature. Poussin lived in Rome at the same time as Claude for nearly forty years and never mentions him, though we have reason to believe that they met. Our scanty knowledge is based on a short biographical note by a fellow painter, Sandrart, who accompanied Claude on his early painting expeditions. From Sandrart we know that Claude both drew and painted from nature, especially his distances. This is of the greatest interest, as it is quite contrary to the usual practice of the old masters. Claude's drawings from nature show a sensibility to natural phenomena which place him apart at once from the Mannerists Brill, Elsheimer and Domenichino on whom he based his style. Many of these sketches might be the work of the Impressionists, especially in their sense of light. They have infinite variety, poetry and freshness. The drawings were admired and imitated by the early English watercolourists, particularly by Alexander Cozens. A second group of Claude's drawings consists of finished preparations for paintings with the motives carefully adjusted for their compositional effects. The drawings in the *Liber Veritatis* were records made after paintings, probably in an attempt to guard against fraud.

In his pictures Claude subordinated his knowledge of nature to a poetic conception of landscape and to his special feeling for light and atmosphere. He conformed to an underlying scheme of composition which seldom varied. It involved a dark foreground mass on one side of the picture, a middle distance with some large central feature such as a clump of trees and two further planes, the second being the luminous distance for which Claude has always been famous. His wonderful effects of recession are the result of his sure sense of tone.

Claude was appreciated in his own day and has always been the object of much devotion. He achieved the fullest expression of his genius in the works of his late middle and old age. He is well represented in most national collections, particularly in the National Gallery, London. The following pictures may be specially mentioned: *The Temple of Apollo* (Palazzo Doria, Rome), *Acis and Galatea* and *The Flight into Egypt* (Dresden), *The Times of the Day* (Hermitage), *The Marriage of Isaac and Rebecca* and *Cephalus and Procris* (National Gallery, London), and *Pegasus* (Holkham Hall).

CLAUDE LORRAINE · A SEAPORT AT SUNSET
39" × 51". London, National Gallery

LOTTO

Lorenzo Lotto, who was born

Venice, c. 1480 but led a wandering life and died at the monastery of Loreto in 556, was virtually rediscovered by Berenson. For his date, Lotto's works are somewhat unexpected, not because a cursory glance reveals anything specially unusual about them, but because his portraits, for example, though vaguely reminiscent of those of Titian and Palma Vecchio, present certain odd peculiarities when closely examined. They convey no effect of detachment or summary judgment. The spectator realises, sometimes uneasily, that Lotto, whose philanthropy was of the anxious, positively self-tormenting type, was in the habit of automatically lending his sitters his own personality. They often have expressions which they would certainly not wish to have made public or, in Berenson's phrase, they 'look as if they were begging for sympathy'.

The artist's many other paintings, mostly of a religious character, vary a great deal. They are frequently bizarre, but always full of poetry, and of high pictorial quality. He was acquainted, incidentally, with the work of Dürer. The altarpiece of St Lucia at Jesi is one of his most interesting productions. Among several works in the National Gallery, London, the *Family Group* and *A Lady as Lucretia* are outstanding.

LOUVRE

In 1546 King Francis I of France ordered a new building to be erected on the site of the ancient Parisian hunting-lodge popularly known as the *Louverie*, or meeting-place for wolf-hunters. Subsequent generations enlarged the size of the edifice until in 1868 it attained its present dimensions. After the Revolution the former palace became a museum. The name *Louverie* was contracted into *Louvre*.

LUINI

Born at Luino on Lake Maggiore c. 1480, Bernardino Luini probably died in Milan

LUINI · MADONNA AND SLEEPING CHILD
(*Detail*) 36¾″ × 29¼″. *Paris, Louvre*

in 1532. He studied under Borgognone and painted in the style of this master and of Bramantino some biblical scenes and a few frescoes of no great importance. But on Leonardo's appearance at Milan in 1506 Luini fell wholly under his spell, to an extent seldom encountered in the history of art. He proceeded to paint Leonardo's subjects, Leonardo heads, the Leonardo smile and the Leonardo chiaroscuro. But the more obscure, reticent and abstruse elements in Leonardo's style were rendered by Luini's dexterous, feminine touch intelligible to everyone. The latter's productions might be called a cheap, popular edition of Leonardo's. Most of the big galleries own pictures by Luini. They are quite admirable works, if their vacuity is discounted. Among paintings inspired by Leonardo they reach about the same standard as those by Predis and Melzi. They are much better than Giampetrino's paintings.

M

MABUSE

This name is the Flemish form of Mau-
beuge, where Jan Gossaert was born
c. 1478, and was applied to this artist,
who died at Middelburg c. 1533/6, by his
contemporaries.

Mabuse was an important painter. He
occupies a special position in the history
of Dutch painting, being generally described as having brought from Italy, in
the train of Philip of Burgundy, the cult
of the nude in art, represented in the
antique style. But this statement is a
half-truth. His attention was certainly

MABUSE · JACQUELINE DE BOURGOGNE (?)
14¾″ × 11¼″. London, National Gallery

drawn to the painted nude in Italy. But he
took little interest in such studies. His
own treatment of anatomy remained purely
artificial. It was not the living body but its
plastic quality which attracted him after
his visit to Rome. He would have been

better pleased with a collection of statue
by Praxiteles than with any model
flesh and blood. Characteristically, h
always had a few engravings by Düre
within reach. He sacrificed light, colou
and psychological content to the achieve
ment of sculpturesque effects.

His pictures, accordingly, seemed to h
contemporaries the last word in modernit
and sophistication. The brilliance of h
technique, too, increased his reputatio
His portraits in particular—for exampl
that of Jean de Carondelet in the Louvre—
are most captivating. But the emphati
sculptural contours of his Madonnas ofte
make a strange impression and the nude
in his mythological scenes carry his obses
sion with the statuesque to excess.

MAES

At the age of sixteen, Nicolaes Maes, wh
was born at Dordrecht in 1632 and die
in Amsterdam in 1693, was apprenticed t
Rembrandt. A highly gifted, somewha
melancholy and serious lad he left th
studio five years later as a 'master'. Hi
admirable *genre* pictures, set in plainl
furnished interiors, are inspired by Rem
brandt, but lack the latter's feeling fo
atmosphere. Maes, however, lends a
intensely vivid quality to such momentar
situtations as that of a peasant woma
saying grace at a humble meal—thi
painting is at Amsterdam—or of an ol
woman peeling an apple as she sits at he
spinning wheel (Berlin). His *Young Seam
stress*, in a private collection at Edinburgh
is another example of such works. At th
end of the 1650s, like Flinck, Lievens an
so many others, he took the step, whethe
deliberately or by chance, of forsaking th
unpopular Rembrandt and attaching him
self to Van der Helst, who preferred th
Flemish manner. Thenceforward Mae
painted mainly portraits in a 'smart'
pretentious and tasteless style.

Dirk Maes or Maas (1659-1717) wa
not related to Nicolaes. This Haarlem

N. MAES · GIRL AT A WINDOW
49¼″ × 36⅜″. Amsterdam, Rijksmuseum

ainter, like his friend Huchtenburgh, depicted battles. He showed much more originality in his gaily animated *Horse Fairs*.

MAGNASCO

Alessandro Magnasco (1667-1749), who worked in Genoa, was one of the most remarkable of the later Italian painters. His pictures are often small and always

shadowy. They are painted in light, delicate, hesitant touches, representing scenes from the lives of ordinary citizens, soldiers, gipsies, strolling players, nuns and street-singers. The emphatic chiaroscuro resembles Rembrandt's. The 'shorthand' treatment of the figures was later exploited by Guardi. Magnasco's works are still greatly underestimated. They often convey a grotesque, Daumier-like effect, the coquetry of a Watteau turned gipsy or the spectral quality of Goya. The source of Magnasco's style remains a complete mystery. His mediocre Milan teacher cannot be held responsible for the development of this rare genius.

MAINARDI

Born at Gimignano c. 1460 and dying in Florence in 1513, Sebastiano Mainardi became Ghirlandaio's brother-in-law and worked in his studio. His contributions to several of Ghirlandaio's frescoes are recognisable and duly attested. He also painted a number of easel-pictures of great merit—for example, his Berlin *Madonna and Child*, the Pisa *Madonna of the Rose*, a *Madonna* and *Portrait of a Girl* in London and the portrait of a young man in Berlin. After Ghirlandaio's death in 1495, Mainardi's style lost its inspiration, growing harder and coarser.

MANDER

A lover of history, Karel van Mander (1548-1606) both painted and wrote it.

MAGNASCO
A SCENE DURING
THE INQUISITION
*17⅞″ × 33″. Vienna,
Kunsthistorisches Museum*

His pictures are forgotten. But his *Schilder-Boeck* (Book of Painters), published in 1604, is immortal. In these biographies of painters he transmitted to posterity everything known in his time about those who acquired eminence between 1366 and his own day. He is not always reliable. But he is often the only authority able to throw any light on the darkness in which research still has to grope in the case of many works. He might be called the Vasari of the north. He was born at Meulebeke in Flanders and died in Amsterdam. He taught, among others, Frans Hals.

MANNERISM

A phenomenon which occurs when the artist is more preoccupied with form and technique than with subject or idea. It is likely to appear in the declining stages of a culture. Though examples of Mannerism can be found throughout the history of art as the name of a style, the word is applied principally to Italian painting outside Venice from about 1520 to the end of the High Renaissance in 1600, the beginning of the Baroque period. Michelangelo is associated with Mannerism, and in his tondo of the *Holy Family* (Uffizi), painted about 1501, the remarkable twist in the figure of the Virgin foreshadows the typical Mannerist attitudes; it anticipates the elaborate S-shape, the *figura serpentina* which played an important role in sixteenth-century Italian art and was admired in the writings of the time. Similar figures, though less extreme, occurred after this date in Raphael's work. The developed Mannerist style appeared in the work of Raphael's pupils in Rome, headed by Guilio Romano, and in Florence in the work of the pupils of Andrea del Sarto, Rosso,. Pontormo and Bronzino. Parmigianino, an important Mannerist painter, began his career at Parma, and combined the influence of Correggio with that of the Roman Mannerists. The style of these painters is eccentric and highly self-conscious; their figures are curiously elongated; they have a languid grace and frequently make empty gestures and adopt

meaninglessly complicated poses, as Bronzino's *Venus, Cupid, Folly and Ti* (National Gallery, London) in order to into an involved composition, which generally assymetrical. There is a conscio straining for effect through distortion proportion. The favourite Mannerist cc ours, as far as it is possible to generalis are shades of lavender, rose and lemo which give a cold, intellectual, metall atmosphere to their pictures. The Mai nerists excelled in portraiture; their elega style was admirably suited to the portray of their sophisticated sitters. Bronzino a Parmigianino were outstanding portrai ists. Important Italian Mannerist pictur include *Vertumnus and Pornona*, Pon ormo's fresco in Poggio a Caiano, Vil Medicea; *Moses defending the Daughters Jethro* (Uffizi) by Rosso; *A Young Sculpt* (Louvre) by Bronzino; *Cupid carving h Bow* (Vienna), *The Vision of St Jeron* (National Gallery, London) and *Portra of a Girl* (Naples) by Parmigianino; an *Laocoon* (Palazzo Ducale, Mantua) b Guilio Romano.

MANSUETI

The years of the birth and death c Giovanni di Niccolo Mansueti are n known. But he is named in Venetia records between 1485 and 1527. He spe his whole life in the studio of Genti Bellini, loyally assisting him with h easel-paintings. Nor can he be blamed fc appropriating not only the brushes, bu also the style of his master. His exclusivel religious compositions resemble brownis engravings and look as hard as tin. The have the character of *predelle* (q.v.), bu are unfortunately large in scale. *A Symbol Representation of the Crucifixion* is in th National Gallery, London.

MANTEGNA

Andrea Mantegna, one of the great stylisti innovators in painting, was born at Isola d Carturo, near Vicenza, in 1431 and die at Mantua in 1506. At the age of ten h was adopted, probably as an orphan, b Squarcione, who maintained a large studi

Padua at the time. The University manists were frequent visitors at Squarﾠ▬ne's house. Consequently, Mantegna, ﾠile still a child, became acquainted with e heritage of antiquity and the profesﾠﾠrial idealisation of ancient Rome. He ver lost his affection for the 'great' period classical art. But his feeling for it was ﾠite different from that of the later ﾠssicists. His knowledge of the life of tiquity was far too superficial to involve m in concentration upon its details or ﾠtual historical events. He was vividly ﾠare only of its individuals, such forceful aracters as Cato and Caesar. His vision Niobe mourning for her children reﾠlted in the Milan *Dead Christ*, the ﾠure of a murdered consul, with nothing ﾠhatever Christian about it. It was some ﾠch attitude, perhaps, that initiated his ﾠylistic development, though it is clear ﾠat the process itself proved long and ﾠmplex. In any case, the utterly different ﾠews of Squarcione were certainly not sponsible for those of Mantegna. Nor ﾠd Squarcione's style of painting any ﾠfluence on him. Mantegna's works derive ﾠmistakably from those of Andrea del

Castagno, Uccello and Donatello, all three of whom he could have seen in his youth at Padua or Venice. It was these artists who suggested the sculptural modelling of his figures, his incisive line, his treatment of landscape in geological layers, his stressed gestures and tragic use of colour. The *Dead Christ* has an exceptional severity, even for Mantegna. But it is a good example both of his brushwork and the kind of pictures he had in mind. He was the first to introﾠduce Gothic devotional fervour into northﾠern Italy. His *Madonna and Sleeping Child*, at Berlin, is one of the most disciplined, but deeply felt, representations of this subject. It resembles an ancient Roman gem carved with the figures of a patrician mother tearlessly mourning the fate of a son under sentence of death.

The frescoes painted by Mantegna in 1457 in the Eremitani Church at Padua, which were almost entirely destroyed during the war, and those of 1474 in the Camera degli Sposi at Mantua, suggest that he was acquainted with the work of Piero della Francesca in the neighbouring city of Ferrara. Mantegna's paintings are imﾠpressively monumental. But they are

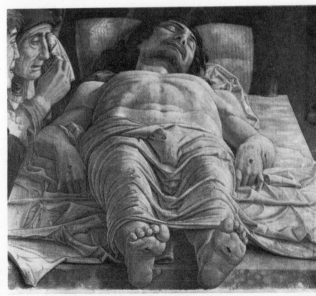

MANTEGNA
THE DEAD CHRIST
27¼" × 32¾". Milan, Brera

MANTEGNA · ST GEORGE
(Detail) 26⅜″ × 12¾″. Venice, Accademia

more relaxed and cheerful than Piero's, with exquisite individual passages of colour.

His influence on the whole practice of painting, above all in northern Italy, was immense. In 1454 he had married one of the sisters of Giovanni Bellini, thus entering upon still closer relations with Venice, where Bellini remained for long under his spell. In 1459 Mantegna moved from Padua to Mantua, settling at the Court of his admirer and patron, Ludovico Gonzaga, who actually conferred upon him, if the records available are correctly interpreted, the title of Count. In 1466 and 1467 the artist was welcome with much ceremony at Florence and Pisa. In 1488/9 he was received in Rome by Pope Innocent VIII.

Mantegna's most important easel-paintings include the Louvre *Crucifixion* and *Madonna of Victory*, the London *Agony in the Garden*, the San Zeno triptych at Verona, the portrait of Cardinal Mezzarota at Berlin, the Uffizi *Adoration* triptych and portrait of Cardinal Carlo Medici, the *St George* at Venice and *Death of the Virgin* in the Prado.

MARATTI

Born at Camerino in 1625 and dying Rome in 1713, Carlo Maratti first achiev recognition and success about 1650, af seeing paintings by Correggio and Gui Reni, which brought about a compl revolution in his style.

Modern criticism finds his religious p tures excessively baroque in manner, tl is to say, emotionally and compositiona overloaded, with an agitated line and cleve calculated colour that lack motivation. I portraits, on the other hand, are in su prisingly good taste, as for example I *Portrait of a Cardinal* in the Natior Gallery, London.

MARIESCHI

Michele Marieschi who was born in Veni in 1696 and died there in 1743 probab paid less attention to the inspiration of I Muse than to the promptings of his ov opportunism in his production of views Venice based on those of Canaletto. B Marieschi sometimes reproduces atmo pheric colour with amazing fidelity. I laid many a cuckoo's egg, which still mak a remarkable impression, in Canaletto nest and, especially, in that of Bellotto.

MARMION

Documentary research long ago reveal the name of Simon Marmion. But until tl early twentieth century none of his wor had been discovered. It is only in mode times that trustworthy characteristics his style are beginning to be noted, wi the result that more and more of his pi tures are now being identified on tl strength of his exceptionally fine book illu trations, preserved in Leningrad, Brusse Louvain and London.

Though it seems that Marmion was bo at Amiens c. 1435/45 and would accor ingly be French by birth, he belongs artis ically to Flanders, where he worked ar received the training which formed h

tyle on that of Dirk Bouts. He was active
n Lille, Bruges and Valenciennes, and
ied in the latter city in 1489.

The earliest work which can be attri-
uted to him with fair certainty is the
t Bertin altarpiece in Berlin, some
mall parts of which are preserved in
ondon. Contemporary evidence supports
his ascription. Stylistic criticism based on
his production gives to Marmion, among
ther important panels, a large *Crucifixion*
t Philadelphia, a *Discovery of the Cross* in
Paris and a *St Jerome with Founders* at
Philadelphia. Even when Marmion's style
esembles that of Bouts most closely, it
nakes a gloomier, more monkish impres-
ion. Bright as are the tints in Marmion's
miniatures, he never introduced into his
panels any of the beauty of Bouts's colour.

MARSHALL

Ben Marshall (1767-1835) was the
most able follower of Stubbs as a
painter of horses. Like Stubbs,
Marshall was fascinated by ana-
omy and painted horses with
every visible muscle and tendon
strongly emphasised. After beginning as a portrait painter,
Marshall established himself at
Newmarket. The pictures he produced there of horses, often with
trainer, jockey or groom, are not
only interesting as animal paint-
ngs; they show great feeling for
he dramatic light of the heath
landscape of Newmarket, and are
of startling severity. Most of
Marshall's pictures are in private
collections.

MARTINI

Nothing is known of the early life
of Simone Martini, who was born
at Siena in 1280/85 and died in
Avignon in 1341. He seems to
have worked for a time at the
Royal Court of Naples, for in
1315 he was still drawing a salary
there and is recorded as having
been ennobled. In 1320 he must

have returned to Siena, for shortly afterwards he supplied Orvieto with an altarpiece and the Town Hall of Siena with a
great fresco of the *Virgin Enthroned*, still
in situ. In 1324 Martini married the sister
of the young painter Lippo Memmi, whom
he thenceforward occasionally employed to
assist him (see *Memmi*). The wonderful
fresco at the Palazzo Pubblico, Siena, in
honour of the victorious commander
Guidoriccio, dates from 1328. At about the
same time Martini produced his masterpiece, the Assisi frescoes. The Uffizi
Annunciation was painted for the Cathedral
at Siena in 1329. Ten years later Martini
was sent on ecclesiastical business to
Avignon, where the exiled Pope was living.
After carrying out his task, Simone, accompanied by his brother, stayed on at Avignon

SIMONE MARTINI · THE ANNUNCIATION
(Centre panel) 106″ × 122″. Florence, Uffizi

for the rest of his life. He was celebrated in two poems by Petrarch, who was also attached to the Papal Court at the time. Martini's works in France cannot, however, be dated with any certainty.

He may have been trained by Duccio. At any rate he grew up completely imbued with the latter's spirit and gives no hint, in his early pictures, of his future greatness. His small *Christ Carrying the Cross*, in the Louvre, is conceived in Duccio's manner, the only novelty being the introduction of brilliant colour. Martini did not produce the great innovations which have given him an international reputation until comparatively late in life. He was already fifty when he painted the *Annunciation*.

The conception of this work has been compared, somewhat daringly, with that of an Indian miniature. It is true enough that the scene bears some resemblance to a mimetic ritual dance. Once the comparison has been made one is continually reminded of it in examining Simone's later pictures. Consequently, no surprise whatever is felt at the presence of flute and lute players in

MASACCIO · ST PETER AND ST JOHN DISTRIBUTING ALMS (*Detail*) · *92″ × 60¾″*.
Florence, S. Maria del Carmine

one of the artist's famous Assisi frescoes, that in which St Martin is shown receiving the accolade. Martini was not particularly interested in the treatment of perspective, landscape and anatomy, problems which would have fascinated Duccio. He was concerned with a different kind of beauty, that of a scene rendered with serene poetic fantasy. Even the striking effect of display achieved by the extensive dimensions of his *Condottiere Guidoriccio* fresco is not in the least encumbered by historical detail. The rhythmic oscillation of its line suggests a sonnet written on the wall by his friend Petrarch. It was the unfettered graphic freedom and lightness of his line that Martini bequeathed to the next generation. He may be regarded as the actual founder of the Avignon School (q.v.).

MASACCIO

Tommaso di Giovanni Guidi Masaccio ('big Maso'), the son of a notary, was born at San Giovanni Valdarno, near Florence, in 1401, and died in Rome in 1428. He is said by Vasari to have been trained by Masolino. At any rate the two men worked together for years. They were closely associated until Masolino, who was born in 1383 at Panicale and died at Florence in 1447, left for Hungary in 1427. The friendship is rather unaccountable. Masolino was, indeed, a highly accomplished painter. But his admirable surviving works, including Madonnas at Munich and Bremen and the charming frescoes in the Baptistery and Collegiate Church at Castiglione d'Olona, Milan, suggest a quiet conservatism. Essentially a Late Gothic painter, he must have thought the works even of Gentile da Fabriano unprecedentedly daring. It seems strange that such a man should have been attracted by the heroic vigour of Masaccio. Perhaps the difference of temperament and the unvarying awe with which, according to tradition, Masaccio was regarded, caused Masolino to abandon the last work they undertook in common, the Brancacci Chapel frescoes, and accept an invitation to Hungary.

Masaccio's work initiates Italian Renaissance painting with resounding effect.

MASACCIO · THE ADORATION OF THE KINGS · 8⅜″ × 24¾″. *Berlin, Staatl. Museen*

The interest of his achievement lies in the fact that it does not derive from immediate predecessors and the tentative forecasts of such artists as Gentile da Fabriano, thereby taking but a single step forward, but positively returns once more, in detail, to the ideas of Giotto. It follows that he set no store by the refinements which had long since been adopted and did not regard them as an appropriate vehicle for his own conceptions. Gentile da Fabriano would undoubtedly have considered the Brancacci frescoes formally retrogessive. But in point of fact Masaccio's revival of extreme simplicity in the treatment of form was for him the only way to concentrate the attention of the spectator, undistracted by dazzling feats of virtuosity, upon absolutely unprecedented stylistic innovations, such as the rendering of the human figure, not as a legendary form outside time and space, but as a recognisable person, resembling those of contemporary life. His fresco in S. Maria di Carmine, Florence, *The Sick Man Healed by Peter's Shadow*, is not in the least like the usual biblical illustration. It depicts power in action. The effect of actual physical presence and the exercise of a spiritual force universally applicable rather than confined to a single miracle is so strong that the subject of the picture might be 'The great emperor passes by and the veterans throw away their crutches and fall in once more behind him.'

It is not feasible to give a verbal description of Masaccio's methods in thus lending acts continuous validity and unveiling the depths of the human spirit. He scarcely ever indicates facial expression. He relies almost entirely, like Piero della Francesca and Michelangelo at a later date, on bodily attitudes and the significance of movement. He was able to suggest curiosity by a slight turn of the head, terror by an abbreviated lift of the hand and the grandeur of a saint by half-closed eyelids. The greatness of his art is shown at its best in the frescoes he painted in collaboration with Masolino in the church of Santa Maria di Carmine, Florence, at the orders of the silk merchant Brancacci. Masaccio was personally responsible for *Peter Baptising, The Healing Shadow*, the *Expulsion from Eden*, the *Tribute Money, Peter and John Giving Alms* and, in part, for *Peter Invoking the Holy Ghost*. Four other areas were painted by Masolino and five by Filippino Lippi. Masaccio's fresco of the *Holy Trinity* in S. Maria Novella, Florence, is of less outstanding quality.

The solemnity of Giotto and the anticipations of the momentous impact of Michelangelo are naturally less evident in Masaccio's easel-paintings. He collaborated with Masolino between 1423 and 1425 in the famous Uffizi *St Anne, the Virgin and Child*, the two latter figures being by Masaccio alone. In 1427 he produced an altarpiece for Pisa. Its cornice was the *Crucifixion*, on a gold ground, now in the Naples Museum. The discreet, beautifully coloured *predelle* (q.v.) are in Berlin. Even in so small a *predella* as that of the *Adoration of the Kings* in Berlin, which is only 8¼ in. high, the unusually powerful effect of the two lordly, swaggering 'human' figures, those of the founders, who intrude upon the legendary scene, is most conspicuous. The London *Madonna and Child*, which formed the central panel of the Pisan altarpiece, is a work of superb quality. It entirely repudiates the idea of maternal charm, glorifying, instead, in its massive forms, the human creature thus brought helplessly to birth.

MASO DI BANCO

This artist is mentioned in Florentine records between 1320 and 1346. Vasari (q.v.) identifies him with Giottino. But this view is refuted by the fact that Maso died about 1350, whereas Giottino's name occurs long after that date. Maso's chief works are his five frescoes in the Bardi Chapel at S. Croce, Florence. His art can be described in the same terms as that of Giottino (q.v.). The fact is not surprising, for both were pupils of Giotto. Maso's pictures may perhaps be regarded as more dramatic, more attentive to perspective and more colourful. He was one of the most important Florentine painters of his time.

MASOLINO

(*See* MASACCIO)

MASSYS

Quinten Massys also signed his nam Metsys and Matsys. He was born a Louvain in 1466 while the great Dir Bouts still held the post of municipa painter there, and died in Antwerp in 153 as the most eminent master in that city He was the son of a blacksmith and accord ing to Van Mander exercised that trad himself until, 'for love of a girl of good family', he became a painter. It is clea from this report that by 1500 the ol social hierarchy no longer prevailed an 'artists' were already considered persons o some distinction. A new age was begin ning. For while Geertgen at Maarlem Hieronymus Bosch at Hertogenbosch an Gerard David in Bruges were still paintin like men of the fifteenth century, Massy had already initiated the preliminar tremors of the avalanche of the Renais sance and of humanism which he an Mabuse were eventually to release, thu obliterating the surviving features of th previous era.

Q. MASSYS
A MONEY CHANGER
AND HIS WIFE
28⅞″ × 27¼″. *Paris, Louvre*

In the picture by Massys entitled the *Virgin and Child with Lamb*, at Posen, the composition of the three figures is copied very closely from that of Leonardo's *St Anne, the Virgin and Child*. But Massys seems to have subsequently shaken off the effect upon him of this first impact from Italy, for he never showed such conspicuous signs of it again. He remained conservative in his technique and subject-matter. His colour is discreet and highly professional, often somewhat glassy. His composition is strikingly simple. In his Antwerp *Entombment* the mourners stand in an almost serried rank behind the prostrate body of Christ. In the Brussels St Anne altarpiece the central figures are grouped like those of a school photograph. Both these works are masterpieces, as is also the Louvre *Money-changer and His Wife*, formerly in the possession of Rubens. In this first important painting by Massys of a purely *genre* character the figures are presented strictly full-face, both in the same inclined attitude, while the counter and shelves run exactly parallel. This peculiarity is not always so evident in his works, for they vary considerably. But they all give the impression that he composed with difficulty. His naïve determination to distinguish his good and evil figures is most noticeable. The latter are grotesque caricatures. The former, including, of course, the real persons who sat for his portraits, have a look of melancholy and characteristically humanist resignation. Massys had fine taste and a special sensitivity in the delineation of anatomical planes, faces and skin. But unfortunately he made little use of this faculty, even enveloping his Infant Christs, eccentrically enough, in long garments.

He painted a number of outstanding, highly individual and intensely sensitive portraits, of which important examples are preserved at Frankfurt, Oldenburg, Vaduz, Chicago, Rome, which has that of Erasmus of Rotterdam, and Longford Castle, where there is a portrait of Peter Gillis (Aegidius).

Of his sons, who were both most admirable painters, **Cornelis** (c. 1508-c. 1580) was at his best in landscape, while **Jan** (c. 1509-1575) produced mainly *genre* pictures in his father's manner.

MASTER OF THE AACHEN ALTARPIECE

It is unfortunate that this Cologne painter can only be named as the author of an altarpiece at Aachen. He was trained in the Flemish School and had adopted a restless and capricious style of Mannerism. He must have been active shortly after 1500 and shows decided traces of the Antwerp mode, his figures, for all their delicacy, being alluringly full and soft. The features of his Madonnas are provided with every sort of enhancement. They are surrounded by a great variety of flashing, glittering and gleaming points of light, emanating from silk, reflected from marble, or in the dewy, pearly sheen of dangling glass beads and the glow of jewels. The colours are dazzling. This artist's Munich *Virgin and Child with Angelic Musicians* is one of the most attractive Madonnas produced at the time. A *Crucifixion* by him is preserved in the National Gallery, London.

MASTER OF THE AIX ANNUNCIATION

The Annunciation altarpiece in the church of St Magdalen at Aix, the wings of which are preserved at Brussels and Vierhouten, one fragment being at Amsterdam, presents one of the great puzzles of Late Gothic painting. Many historians of art have conjectured that this important work, which shows clear traces of the influences of Konrad Witz and Van Eyck, was executed by Jean Boyer, Court Painter to King René of Provence about 1450.

MASTER OF ALKMAAR

The chief works of this Alkmaar artist consist of seven panels illustrating charitable acts. These paintings, formerly in the church of St Lawrence at Alkmaar, are now in Amsterdam.

The narrative technique is naïve and calculated to appeal to simple piety. The scenes take place in the streets of Alkmaar, the squares of the city looking as though constructed from a child's box of bricks. The style resembles that of fifty years before. It seems as if the painter had made full-size copies of the tiny glimpses through a window provided by the bygone Master of Flémalle. But this archaism has great charm.

An *Adoration* triptych at The Hague is of interest to the historian of manners. Few other works by the Master of Alkmaar survive.

MASTER OF THE BARTHOL- OMEW ALTARPIECE

This work, now at Munich, once belonged to the Carthusian Monastery at Cologne, which also owned many other paintings by the artist. The attempt has accordingly been made to prove that he may have been a monk. But there is not the slightest reason to suppose so. On the contrary, he seems to have left his native city of Cologne as a young man and to have worked for several years in the Netherlands, possibly at Antwerp. He died shortly after 1500. Ernst Buchner conjectures that he may actually have been a Dutchman.

There is no mistaking his style. He was a brilliant technician, his colours being so deep and glowing as to lend his smaller pictures—for example, his capricious renderings of the Madonna—something of the sparkle of jewellery. There is a bizarre element in the invention of such incidental features as ornaments, clothing and style of headgear. In the Bartholomew altarpiece the total effect is positively Spanish, reminiscent of Bermejo. One cannot help feeling that the artist had an ironical turn of mind. His figures have an outlandish grandeur and the composition is nearly always extravagant. It is hard to believe that his work ever stimulated any depth of devotion. The paintings are rarely met with. The artist seems to have formed no school. His *SS. Peter and Dorothy* in the National Gallery, London, is a characteristic work.

MASTER OF FRANKFURT

This artist is so called on account of two works he painted for Frankfurt churches, the *St Anne Altarpiece* and *Mount Calvary*. But it is known today that he was not a German. He lived, except for one visit to Frankfurt, at Antwerp, where it is possible to trace his activities. A self-portrait dated 1496, with a note of his age at the time, enables the year of his birth, 1460, to be calculated. He was an excellent painter. His religious pictures, of which over fifty are known, show the influence of the schools of Ghent—for example, of Hugo van der Goes—and of Antwerp. He often borrows directly from Quinten Massys. A number of good portraits are also extant, in which he evidently prided himself on a marked display of naturalism. In the middle of a double portrait of himself and his wife, in a private collection at Brussels, a fat bluebottle appears to have alighted.

MASTER OF THE GARDEN OF PARADISE

The world-renowned picture at Frankfurt of the Virgin and Child enjoying blissful relaxation, with saints and angels, in a small garden is unusually intimate in feeling. It is supposed to have been painted shortly after 1400 by an Upper Rhineland master.

MASTER OF THE GLORIFI- CATION OF THE VIRGIN

In addition to the large picture at Cologne from which this artist derives his provisional name certain other works have been attributed to him on stylistic grounds. He was obviously a Cologne citizen and lived in the second half of the fifteenth century. He knew the works of the great Dutchmen and perhaps also those of the Avignon masters. But in many respects he remained spiritually akin to Lochner, as in his *Saints with a View of Cologne*. He was a painter of considerable importance.

MASTER OF THE FEMALE HALF-LENGTHS

This provisional description is applied to an artist active in the Netherlands, probably at Antwerp, shortly after 1500. He produced a very great number of half-length figures of women, most of them being given the attributes of sanctified Magdalens. In other words, the painter was no doubt unconcerned with any particular legend. He merely wished to depict a series of charming girls wrapped in meditation, reading, writing, playing musical instruments or even on occasion impersonating the Virgin. They all have the same graceful, somewhat lifeless aspect, the same hair-style and the same silken garments. Despite a certain monotony of appearance and mood, these elegant works are highly attractive. The best of them is unquestionably that at Vienna known as *Three Ladies Making Music*. One of the rarer scenes with full-length figures, in an Italianate landscape, representing the Adoration of the Kings, is at Munich. This master is a favourite with private collectors. (Ill. p. 205.)

MASTER OF LIESBORN

This master painted the screen of the high altar at Liesborn, near Münster, towards the end of the fifteenth century. He was undoubtedly a Westphalian by birth, though his work shows a strong Dutch influence. This element, however, seems to have reached him through Cologne, where Flanders-trained painters, such as the Master of the Life of the Virgin, were active at the time.

The Master of Liesborn, of whom unfortunately practically nothing is recorded, painted in a strikingly refined, grave and tranquil style. Stange observes that 'he had no such pronounced style as Koerbecke or the Master of the Life of the Virgin, his talent being rather for decoration. The characterisation of his figures presents very little variety and never any special depth.'

Separate portions of the Liesborn altarpiece are now preserved in London and Münster. London also has a very charming *Annunciation* and Soest a large *Crucifixion*.

MASTER OF THE LIFE OF THE VIRGIN

The master responsible for the Munich panels representing the life of the Virgin has regularly grown in general estimation, though intensive research has not yet been able to dissipate the mystery of his anonymity. Very many of his works are known today. It is abundantly clear that he once maintained an important studio. He lived at Cologne during the second half of the fifteenth century and may be regarded as the greatest of the masters active at that period in the Lower Rhineland.

Stylistically, his work derives from that of Dirk Bouts. He continues the latter's tradition so unmistakably that he is assumed to have been an actual pupil of that artist. His introduction of the manner of the great Louvain master into the Rhineland influenced a whole generation of painters. The panels of the Life of the Virgin, of which one is in London and seven in Munich, are among the finest proofs of his capacity. They are above all outstanding in their production of the illusion of space. The dewy freshness and grace of the drawing combine with the subdued tones of colour typical of the Cologne school to lend an enchanting tenderness and delicacy to the scenes depicted. The extremely slender figures lack the hortatory significance of those of Bouts. Yet they suggest an admirable modesty and reserve, though apparently living the lives of ordinary middle-class people in the Rhineland.

There are further important panels by this master at Cologne and a Crucifixion altarpiece, with a portrait of the founder, Nikolaus Cusanus, at Cues. (Ill. p. 202.)

MASTER OF THE LYVERSBERG PASSION

The altarpiece sections formerly in the Lyversberg Collection are now to be found at Cologne and Nuremberg. The style of the unknown artist responsible for them immediately recalls that of the famous Master of the Life of the Virgin. Both painters lived at the same time during the fifteenth century in Cologne and may even have been trained together in Flanders. The Lyversberg Master was evidently an industrious pupil. His pictures, which clearly show the influence of Bouts, contain some fine passages. But he had never learnt to compose, lacking the requisite visual imagination. His painting is good in itself, but suffers from a failure of constructive intelligence.

MASTER OF MOULINS

It seems almost inexplicable today that this important fifteenth-century painter, one of the best ever born in France, should have been confused, in the nineteenth century, with Hugo van der Goes, at times even identified with him. The latter fate actually overtook the Autun Nativity, which has only certain superficial compositional affinities with the work of Van der Goes, no doubt familiar enough to the Moulins master. The latter's human types may bear some chance resemblances to those of Goes, for example the portraits of the Portinari children. Yet they are essentially different, having high foreheads and a refined dignity of expression, full of painful experience, with a precocious solemnity even in the childish faces. The temperament of the Moulins master is, moreover, a complete contrast to that of Van der Goes. In the former's work all gestures are restrained, not, as in the case of Memling, owing to a native passivity, but through a distaste for ostentation. One has the feeling that the painter himself must have been an aristocrat, capable of taking part in public ceremonies without vulgar display. The attitudes of his praying donors and of his Madonnas convey this suggestion. The older the artist grew, the more pronounced

MASTER OF THE LIFE OF THE VIRGIN
THE BIRTH OF THE VIRGIN (*Detail*) · 33½″ × 41¾″.
Munich, Alte Pinakothek

his style became, with its significant external characteristics, in his figures, of a slightly hooked nose, deeply furrowed upper lip and sidelong glancing, somewhat prominent eyes. About a dozen of his pictures survive. They were always highly regarded. His masterpiece is the altar screen of the Virgin in Moulins Cathedral. The Louvre *St Magdalen with a Donor* exhibits, with incomparably beautiful effect, the contrast between the saint's aristocratic refinement and the positively fawning devotion of the ugly countenance, touching in its humble humanity, of the donor.

The suggestion has recently been made that the Master of Moulins produced sculpture as well as paintings. He is thought to have been responsible, among other works, for the ducal tomb at Nantes, which the decorative figures strikingly resemble those of his paintings. If this theory is correct, the name of the Master of Moulins is known. For the Nantes sculptor was no other than Jean Perréal, called 'Jean de Paris', mentioned after 1485 as the highly esteemed sculptor and painter, though no paintings by him have yet been found, accredited to the Courts of Charles VIII and Louis XII. Perréal died in 1530.

MASTER OF THE POLLING PANELS

These pictures, formerly in the conventual church at Polling and now at the Munich Pinakothek, were probably executed by Gabriel Angler. Two of the paintings, an *Innunciation* and a *Nativity*, belonged to an altarpiece depicting the life of the Virgin. Eight others, illustrating the foundation of the monastery by Duke Tassilo, formed the wings of a cruciform altarpiece. Gabriel Angler can be traced as active at Munich between 1434 and 1482. Unaffected by the 'universal painting' of his day—to coin a phrase on the analogy of 'universal literature'—Angler produced naïvely realistic works, exceptionally beautiful in colour and conveying the effect of a popular ballad. (Ill. p. 204.)

MASTER OF ST GILES

A painter trained in the Netherlands who worked in France in about 1500 and who is named after two works in the National Gallery, London, *St Giles and the Hind* and *The Mass of St Giles*. He seems to have been slightly influenced by the styles of Hugo van der Goes and Gerard David. The *Mass* represents an incident in the relations between Charlemagne and St Giles, and depicts the monuments and furnishings of the Abbey Church of St Denis as they were at the end of the fourteenth century.

MASTER OF ST SEVERIN

The unknown Cologne artist responsible for the panels formerly in the church of St Severin and today distributed between Munich and Cologne lived shortly after 1500. Close study of his works reveals a number of most unusual stylistic features. The general impression is of Dutch training, great luminosity, crowded composition and a fixity of expression, an absent-minded look in the faces of his figures, as for example in his *Christ Before Pilate* at Cologne. On the other hand, the technique employed and the effect conveyed by his *Mourning for Christ* at Munich are so enigmatic as almost to recall the work of Mantegna and Liberale.

MASTER OF ST VERONICA

The artist responsible for the splendid and delicately executed pictures of *St Veronica* at Munich, the *Madonna of the Peaflower* at Nuremberg and the *Madonna of the Vetch* at Cologne lived in the latter city a generation before Stephan Lochner. He is

MASTER OF MOULINS · ST MARY MAGDALEN WITH A DONOR · *21¼"×16". Paris, Louvre*

the first recognisable master of the famous Cologne School and its 'sensitive' style. It is interesting to remember that at the beginning of the present century the authenticity of his pictures was disputed. A considerable number of experts held them to be forgeries dating from the Romantic period, for in the course of cleaning a certain altarpiece painted in the style of the Veronica Master the over-corrosive liquid used for the purpose revealed an underlying picture of very early date, though of no importance. It was therefore supposed that a mistake had been made in ascribing the top painting to an Old Master. The authorities of the Wallraf-Richartz Museum at Cologne took down the pictures of the Veronica Master and put them in store. But when Wilhelm von Bode (q.v.) heard of the occurrence he offered the Cologne Museum a large sum for one of the paintings which had been taken down. This offer led to a revision of the previous judgment. The panels were re-examined. It turned out that Bode had been right. The top painting was really by the Veronica Master. His fine work had been destroyed in favour of a still earlier one, which the Master had considered so poor that he had overpainted it.

MASTER OF THE POLLING PANELS · GOING TO THE HUNT (*Detail from a wing of The Crucifixion*) *Size of wing 107¾″ × 34½″. Munich, Alte Pinakothek*

MASTER OF THE URSULA LEGEND

This artist, who lived at Cologne in the second half of the fifteenth century, was for long identified with the Master of S Severin. But modern criticism is now better able to perceive the typical stylistic features which the Master of the Ursula Legend was alone in borrowing from Hugo van de Goes, and especially from Geertgen. He may even have been a pupil of the latter, for it is not certain whether he was born in the Rhineland or in Holland.

The charm of his pictures is derived chiefly from their colour and tone-values, in which he already showed the greatest mastery. His chief works, dealing with the legend of St Ursula, were formerly in the church of St Severin at Cologne, but are now to be found not only in Cologne, but also at Nuremberg, Bonn, Paris, Magdeburg and in private hands.

MASTER OF THE VILLENEUVE PIETÀ

The uncommonly beautiful and impressive painting known as the *Pietà of Villeneuve-les-Avignon* is now in the Louvre. It dates from about 1460. It must have been the artist's masterpiece, for no other picture of comparable quality from the same hand is known. Chronologically, the work belongs to the second of the two periods in which the School of Avignon (q.v.) flourished. One of the most eminent authorities on the School, the Abbé Requin, believes the painting to have been executed by the Avignon artist Pierre Villatte, who came from Limoges and was slightly younger than Charonton (q.v.), a painter celebrated at the time, with whom he collaborated in the Chantilly *Cloaked Madonna* altarpiece. If the Abbé's assumption is correct, Villatte must be regarded as one of the great French artists.

MASTER OF THE VIRGO INTER VIRGINES

The Amsterdam painting entitled the *Virgin Among Virgins* is the work of a master by whom over a dozen other pictures have so far been discovered. But his identity still eludes the most intensive research. He must have lived in the second half of the fifteenth century, perhaps near Gouda or Delft, where woodcuts in a similar style have been found. He may be identical with the painter known as the Master from Delft, who executed a triptych now in the National Gallery, London. His extraordinarily interesting, though aesthetically disconcerting, pictures are unmistakable. The features of his personages, including the Virgin's, are of a waxen pallor, with much of the hair shaved off the forehead, so that they present an eerily cadaverous appearance. These masklike faces are forced into such distorted expressions of suffering as to convey a shocking, positively spectral effect. The artist commands a subtle palette of broken colour. But he employs it only on clothing and accessories. He takes no interest in landscape, which is often rendered in a modern, abstract style. A secretive, devouring passion characterises the work of this important, unconventional master.

MASTER OF THE WINTER LANDSCAPES

Active in the first half of the seventeenth century, this artist was obviously Flemish. It is thought today that he may have been a certain Gysbrecht Leytens, whose works have hitherto remained unknown. Leytens was born at Antwerp about 1585. His pictures, which are among the best winter landscapes, painted about the year 1600, have a great deal of originality. His ghostly trees and type of composition are unmistakable. There is more variety and assurance, but hardly more atmospheric quality in the productions of Joos de Momper. The special attraction of the Master of the Winter Landscapes is his sly propensity for making the spectator

shudder at the oddity of nature. His paintings are very rare. (Ill. p. 206.)

MATTEO DI GIOVANNI

It is remarkable that this important artist, who was born at Borgo San Sepolcro c. 1430 and died in Siena, in 1495, should be so little studied. Even critics acquainted with the works of Sassetta and Neroccio have no idea of those of Matteo. He underwent many influences, culminating in that of Mantegna in the latter's post-Padua phase. But such indications are so faint as to be only just recognisable. His chief aim was to carry over the poetic tradition of the older masters into Renaissance times, associating the charmingly tender and subtly expressive art of Siena with new elements. A typical work by Matteo is the London *Madonna of the Girdle*, where the over-lifesize, hovering figure of the Virgin revives the former poetic conceptions of the Madonna and the idea of 'silent devotion',

MASTER OF THE FEMALE HALF-LENGTHS
THREE LADIES MAKING MUSIC
16″ × 13¼″. Vienna, Harrach Collection

MASTER OF THE WINTER
LANDSCAPES · THE FLIGHT
TO EGYPT · *30⅞″ × 47⅞″.*
Paris, Private Collection

while the pious recipient, as he grasps the girdle, rushes forward with the admirable impetuosity of a figure by Pollaiuolo. The dual impression is thus created in Matteo's work of holiness as identical with melancholy and of the vehement longing of humanity for salvation as dramatically expressed in the dash of a starving man for a crust. It is therefore precisely Matteo's hesitant acceptance of the Renaissance and the divided loyalties of his spirit that account for the great attraction of his style.

MAULBERTSCH

Though the best-known Viennese painter of the age of Maria Theresa, Franz Anton Maulbertsch was not an Austrian. He was born in 1724 at Langenargen, Lake Constance. But he soon left his birthplace for Vienna, where he occupied many important professional posts, acquired European fame and eventually died in 1796.

His reputation, though now considerably modified, has stood the test of time. It rests upon the important frescoes he executed for churches, palaces, libraries and monasteries. He left only a few canvases, to be seen at the Baroque Museum, Vienna. The decisive influences on his style were those of the Venetians Piazzetta and Pittoni and of Carlone. He used the free Late Baroque idiom, never adopting that of the Rococo period. He remained impetuous and vehement scorning all frivolity

and insincerity. He aimed at the buoyancy of Rubens, the ideals of Tiepolo and the chiaroscuro of Rembrandt. But the achievement of so ambitious a programme proved rather too much for his capacity.

MAURITZHUIS

This building at The Hague was erected (1633-44) as a residence for Count John Maurice of Nassau and is now one of the principal art galleries in Holland. Most of the Dutch painters are included in the collection, outstanding masterpieces being *The Anatomy Lesson of Professor Tulp,* one of more than a dozen pictures by Rembrandt; and Vermeer's *View of Delft* and *Head of a Young Girl.* The gallery also contains a fine *Descent from the Cross,* by Rogier van der Weyden, portraits by Rubens of his first and second wives, Isabelle Brant and Hélène Fourment; and *Eve Offering Forbidden Fruit to Adam,* by Rubens and Savery.

MELOZZO DA FORLI

There is still much uncertainty, in spite of the most industrious research, as to the life and works of this artist. His activity at the Court of Urbino is only attested by a single reference in a poem. The question whether any painting by him survives at Urbino remains unanswered. In the nineteenth century most of the Palace frescoes were ascribed to him. But since then many of these productions have been identified as by Justus of Ghent (q.v.).

The duly authenticated extant pictures by Melozzo are enough to warrant his importance. Though born at Forli in 1438 and dying there in 1494, he spent at least ten years in Rome, where he executed a number of frescoes still preserved. These have for the most part now been removed and distributed between the Quirinal and the Vatican. His reputation stood high in his lifetime. But he was soon forgotten. There is no evidence whatever about his training. But it is tempting to believe that he may have been associated at an early age with Piero della Francesca, for it is scarcely possible to derive his style from any other source. But he only took from Piero what suited his own taste. He transformed Piero's statuesque monumentality into one of movement. The *Grocer's Assistant Grinding Pepper*, for example, at Forli, looks like a snapshot of one of Piero's figures in a frenzy. He also gave Piero's simple devices for representing space an element of perspective, as seen from a lower level, or foreshortened. Even his angels, as in the Vatican frescoes, whether they carry a palm-frond or a lute, are depicted in hurried, urgent postures. The beauty of his line is often quite intoxicating. In a certain sense he anticipated Mannerist attitudes.

MELZI

Francesco Melzi was the favourite pupil of Leonardo da Vinci, as well as his intimate friend, constant companion, heir and, after Leonardo's death, the 'Keeper of the Holy Grail'—in other words, the writings, diaries and drawings of the master. Melzi is described by his contemporaries as an amiable, sensible man of very good family. He was already old when Vasari visited him in connection with the preparation of Leonardo's biography.

Melzi was born at Milan in 1493, where he attached himself to Leonardo, accompanying him to Rome and also sharing his voluntary emigration to France. He returned to Italy in 1519 with Leonardo's will and bequests, dying at Milan shortly

after 1566. He does not seem to have painted much, for he was well-off and did not need to sell his work. He must also have been extremely busy in connection with Leonardo's other interests, such as his literary and scientific studies. Melzi's chief painting, *Vertumnus and Pomona*, executed in Leonardo's style, is preserved at Berlin.

MEMLING

Hans Memling's exaggerated reputation began in the early nineteenth century. At that date the Dutch primitives were entirely neglected. Memling was the only one of these early painters whose gentle lyricism and emotional passivity had any affinity with the spirit of the Romantic period and could, in Friedländer's phrase, 'pass the portals where aesthetic prejudice stood guard'. Since then more light has been thrown on his personality and his works have been thoroughly studied. It is possible to declare that he was an attractive painter, whom no doubts, passionate feelings or yearnings could torment and whose achievement was very great. And yet among artists of the first rank he seems the least eminent.

The name is more correctly spelt Memlinc. He came from the Mainz district and it seemed a fair assumption that he was born c. 1433 at the village of Mömlingen. But according to recently discovered documentary evidence his birthplace was Seligenstadt, near Aschaffenburg. He died in 1494 at Bruges, where he had been a guild-master and citizen ever since 1465. It is generally conjectured today that he had previously lived at Brussels, working with Rogier van der Weyden. At Bruges, which at that period prior to the silting up of the harbour, was still a flourishing city, Memling soon came to be highly regarded. He was considered one of the most outstanding portraitists of the day and a particularly successful painter of Madonnas. He gradually acquired a kind of patriarchal status in the city, a position inherited, after his death, by Gerard David.

Memling's portraits, which are nearly

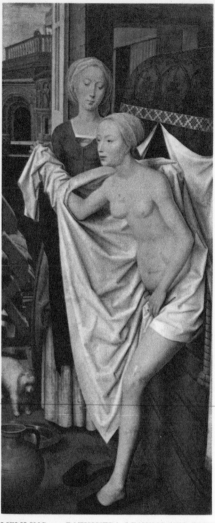

MEMLING · BATHSHEBA LEAVING HER BATH
$56\frac{5}{8}'' \times 33\frac{7}{8}''$. *Stuttgart, Staatsgalerie*

Sybille Sambetha and *Martin van Nieu-wenhove*, both at Bruges. They also have plenty of animation. But Memling does not seem to have been acquainted with or capable of recognising traits of character other than those he possessed himself.

The atmosphere of his religious pictures is equally tranquil. At times the wind rises a little, as in his *Deposition* and *Mourning Women* at Granada, obviously inspired by Hugo van der Goes. His retable of the *Virgin with Saints* at Bruges even shows traces of real greatness. But elsewhere his handsome Madonnas and all the biblical figures associated with them have the vaguely smiling, unconcerned faces of dreamers. Even in a scene of such bloody violence as the martyrdom of the virgins led by St Ursula, decorating St Ursula's Shrine at Bruges, the action proceeds on both sides with the greatest equanimity and religious devotion. Memling's colour, too, has a quietly harmonious effect.

Other important works by this artist include the *Seven Joys of Mary*, an elaborately varied composition at Munich, the Turin *Man of Sorrows*, the New York *Annunication*, the Madrid *Adoration* altarpiece, the altarpiece of the Virgin, with a self-portrait, at Chatsworth, the Floreins altarpiece at Bruges and the delightful *Bathsheba* at Stuttgart.

MEMMI

Lippo Memmi, named in Siena records between 1317 and 1347, was the brother-in-law of the great Simone Martini, with whom he has always been associated, owing to the fact that he was allowed to add his signature to Martini's on the *Annunciation* in the Cathedral at Siena. In this picture Memmi was responsible for the two saints depicted on the side-panels. The San Gimignano frescoes, which he painted in collaboration with his father, are almost exact copies of the work of Martini. Several of Memmi's diminutive panels of the Madonna, only 8 or 12 in. high, but

all half-lengths and may be found today in galleries all over the world, are somewhat tiresomely alike, at any rate during his best period. But many of them are unquestionably of exceptional beauty—for example, the *Man with a Medal* at Antwerp, the *Young Man* in New York, host attractive, are preserved in Berlin.

MENGS

Hardly any trace now survives of Anton Raphael Mengs's former international reputation. He was born at Aussig in 1728 and died in 1779 in Rome, where he met Winckelmann, from whom he imbibed enthusiastic admiration for antiquity and in uncompromising hostility to Rococo art. It was in this sense that Mengs's extraordinary influence on all subsequent European painting was exercised. In the course of time, particularly during his long residence in Rome, his pronouncements on art came to be regarded as infallible. It was he who, while Court Painter in Madrid, gave Goya his first commissions for Gobelin tapestry designs.

Mengs's laborious pictorial essays in classical narrative are now forgotten. Only his portraits are still appreciated. Those in the Prado are superior to any extant by him in Germany. His debt to Velasquez in this field is obvious.

R. MENGS · MARIA LUISA OF PARMA
19¼″ × 15¼″. Madrid, Prado

METROPOLITAN MUSEUM, NEW YORK

This, the leading museum in America, was founded in 1870, opened to the public in 1871 and has rapidly expanded by means of gift, purchase and bequest. Among the many collections of old masters which have enriched the museum may be mentioned the Benjamin Altmann Collection of Dutch masters presented to the Museum in 1913, which includes examples by most of the seventeenth-century Dutch painters, among them a large number of Rembrandts and Hals' celebrated Hille Babbe; and the Michael Friedsan Collection of early French and Flemish pictures, including six decorative panels by Hubert Robert, painted about 1784 for the Château de Bagatelle, The Mendicants by Le Nain, and examples by Fragonard and Boucher. Among the oustanding masterpieces in the Museum's collection are Veronese's Mars and Venus; a Hunting Scene by Piero di Cosimo; three panels by Botticelli showing the Miracles of St Zenobius, the fourth of which is in the National Gallery, London; a remarkable series of paintings by Pinturricchio from the palace of Pandolfo Petrucci, Siena; Tintoretto's Miracle of the Loaves and Fishes; Goya's Nightmare, Marie Louise, Princess of Parma, and Don Tiburcio Perezi; Bruegel's Harvesters; Venus and Adonis and The Holy Family by Rubens; and Van Dyck's Earl of Arundel and His Grandson.

METSU

An excellent minor Dutch master comparable with Mieris, Brekelenkam, Dou and Maes, Gabriel Metsu was born at Leyden in 1629 and died in Amsterdam in 1667. He was first trained by his parents, who were both painters. Thereafter, it is supposed, he studied under Gerard Dou. The style of Metsu's early work is, however, much more reminiscent of that of Jan Steen. He depicted scenes in bedrooms, people eating and drinking, doctors' visits, women spinning at small bow-windows and maids in the kitchen. These popular subjects derived their charm in some cases from the rendering of atmosphere, in others from the jewel-like tints employed. In the case of Metsu, who after 1657 lived at Amsterdam, the main attraction is the extreme elegance of his execution and his ultimately Rembrandtesque handling of atmosphere. His chief works include the *Poultry Seller* at Dresden, the New York *Visit to a Woman in Childbed*, the Leningrad *Oyster Eaters*, The Hague *Musicians* and the *Sick Woman* at Berlin. There are good examples of his style in the National Gallery, London, and in the Wallace Collection.

MEULEN

Born at Brussels in 1632 and dying in Paris in 1690, Adam Frans van der Meulen worked in the studio of Pieter Snayers. He made only a poor living with his battle-pieces until he decided to migrate to France, where he worked in the Gobelins Factory and became a member of the French Academy.

In the course of time he devoted himself wholly to military subjects, accompanying the French armies and illustrating their battles and sieges, as well as the districts through which they marched—for instance, in his *Winter Landscape* at Aschaffenburg and *St Germain* at Hamburg. He also painted encounters between their marshals—for example, *The Duke of Lorraine Meeting Turenne*, at Minneapolis. He executed many portraits of the King, including a diminutive equestrian representation of great charm, preserved at the Hermitage.

MICHELANGELO

He himself invariably signed his name with the spelling Michelangiolo. Born at Caprese in 1475 and dying in Rome in 1564, Michelangelo di Ludovico Buonarroti was well connected, his father being

G. METSU · THE MUSIC LESSON
26¾″ × 21⅜″. New York, Metropolitan Museum

Mayor of Caprese and Chiusi and the family tracing its descent from the Counts of Canossa, though this claim was not supported by any documentary evidence even in Michelangelo's own time. His life has been meticulously investigated for centuries by historians, men of letters, doctors and psychoanalysts. But in every age it has been differently interpreted. He has sometimes been regarded as a 'giant' at other times as an 'unlucky genius'. When it became the fashion to equate genius with insanity, he was described by W. Lange-Eichbaum as an 'advanced depressive, an inordinately conceited paranoid and hypochondriac psychopath'. The fact is that if the cheapest edition of common humanity is regarded as the norm, every genius must certainly be considered 'abnormal'. The agitation and strain affecting the nerves of such a man as Michelangelo, to the point of breakdown, may be deduced from the gloomy lines he once composed:

'I stand bent double like David with his sling——'

another short poem refers to the sensitivity from which he took refuge in his art:

Gentle and hidden is the fountain,
compassionate the source,
from which my sufferings flow.'

A different side of Michelangelo's character, known to us from hundreds of extant letters, shows him to have been capable of cool calculation. He undertook intricate financial transactions, aimed at wealth and achieved it. He was also an unusually shrewd judge of political affairs. This gift enabled him on two occasions to escape the mortal dangers consequent upon the fall and then the restoration of the Medici dynasty in Florence. He knew everyone and consorted with Popes, princes and diplomats. His affections, moreover, were insatiable and ardent. The versatility evident in so full a life has always commanded the admiration of all who have studied it.

He painted pictures, carved statues, cast bronzes, designed and erected buildings—the dome of St Peter's, Rome, is his work—and wrote poetry. Only three documentarily attested painted works by him have survived. These are the Roman frescoes in the Sistine and Pauline Chapels, the latter consisting of a *Conversion of St Paul* in poor preservation and a *Crucifixion*, and a circular panel of the *Holy Family*, in tempera, at the Uffizi Gallery. The *Entombment* (first recognised as by Michelangelo by Cornelius and Overbeck) and the *Madonna and Child with St John and Angels* at the National Gallery, London (perhaps Michelangelo's earliest picture, painted c. 1494), have also been ascribed to his hand. With these works Michel-

MICHELANGELO · THE HOLY FAMILY
Diameter 48". Florence, Uffizi

angelo, like Giotto and Masaccio before him, revolutionised the painting of his day and caused confusion among the next generation of artists. He was the chief initiator of classical Mannerism (q.v.), the influence of which began with the Sistine frescoes.

After attending high school, he studied under Domenico Ghirlandaio. Then, in 1489, he turned to sculpture, entering the studio of Bertoldo. A year or two later he was admitted to the school established by Lorenzo de' Medici and began to acquire a reputation. It was founded by turns upon his achievements in sculpture, painting and lyric poetry, increasing first in one then in another of these fields. But it was his sculpture—in particular, his *David* and the Bruges *Madonna*—which caused him to be summoned to the Vatican in 1505. At this period he had already painted the *Holy Family*, called the Doni Madonna from the patron who commissioned it, and produced a cartoon, now lost, for the picture of the *Battle of Cascina* intended as a counterpart to Leonardo's

211

proposed fresco of the *Battle of Anghiari* in the Town Hall. But neither fresco was ever completed. In Rome Michelangelo at first devoted himself entirely to sculpture. In 1506 he returned to Florence. In 1508 Pope Julius II ordered him to execute frescoes on the ceiling of the Sistine Chapel at the Vatican. By 1512 the work was finished. The nine principal fields of the ceiling were enclosed by symbolical figures and supported by Biblical personages occupying the lateral fields and architectural framework. The main fields depicted nine scenes, of which the most famous, the *Creation of Adam*, is a typical specimen of Michelangelo's power of conception.

In 1533 Pope Clement VII ordered him to decorate the end wall of the Sistine Chapel with a representation of the Last Judgment. The fresco was completed, with long intervals between the stages of work, by 1541. During the next nine years the artist executed, with considerable difficulty—for he had fallen into a gloomy and depressed state of mind—the two Pauline Chapel frescoes. He does not appear to have used a brush subsequently. From some of his designs, the paintings for his patrons were carried out by Pontormo. Others never reached the stage of paint.

Even Michelangelo, like other painters, had a long line of predecessors. His early circular picture of the *Holy Family* is clearly much indebted to Signorelli. His frescoes, however completely original in style they may appear, reveal a monumental tendency derived from Masaccio—for example, in the *Expulsion from Eden* of the Sistine Chapel. The unique element in his art comes from his unquestioning faith in the expressive power of the human body, his untiring devotion to the glories of the nude, his confidence in his capacity to represent the world by his representation of mankind.

MIEREVELT

Michiel van Mierevelt, who was born in Delft in 1567 and died there in 1641, was one of the earliest Dutch representatives of the 'new age of portraiture', in which humanist Mannerism had been succeeded by preoccupation, once more, with th middle classes and contemporary life an personalities. At a later date the perio culminated with the portraits of Fran Hals, Terborch, Rubens and Rembrand When Mierevelt began to paint, othe pioneers, such as Pickenoy, Ravesteyn an Keyser, had just been born. He was there fore active at a very early stage of the retur to portraiture, though his work gives n inkling of the fact. The characteristic Del tone-values are already evident in hi pictures. Initial harshness and rigidity ar replaced in his best period by a mellow luminous style, the play of brilliant light o flesh and delight in white materials, suc as tulle and lace. Most of his portraits ar half-lengths in semi-profile against neutral background. He is represented i the National Gallery, London, and th Wallace Collection.

MIERIS

Frans van Mieris (1635-1681) of Leyde was the 'heir apparent' of that reignin prince of artists, Gerard Dou, who was s highly regarded in his day, and eventuall in fact succeeded to Dou's small but ele gant domain of *genre* production. Mieri both began and ended in the style of hi master, executing, in his best period, sma works noted for their minute and enamel like finish, of 'cabinet' size.

His son **Willem** (1662-1747), also activ at Leyden, an able but uninspired painte continued the *genre* tradition establishe by Dou. Both father and son are repre sented in the National Gallery, Londo and the Wallace Collection.

MIGNARD

The best-known of two brothers of thi name, Pierre was born at Troyes in 161 and died in Paris in 1675. He was one o those showy pseudo-geniuses whose glit tering reputations were fostered by th forcing-house of Versailles under the Sun King. His great talent was smothere under the gold heaped upon it by th innumerable would-be Midases of the ag

At fifteen, already a Master, he painte

rescoes in the chapel of the Maréchal de Bitry. The latter thereupon took him to Paris and placed him in the studio of Vouet for further training and supervision. Subsequently Mignard stayed for twenty years in Rome, becoming known, accordingly, as 'the Roman'. There he assimilated what he could from the works of Correggio and the Bolognese and Roman schools. In 1657 he returned to Paris with a great reputation, was appointed 'First Painter to the King', Director of the Gobelins Factory, Director of the Picture Collections and Director of the Royal Academy and received a title of nobility. He was a born portrait painter in the Titian tradition, though his favourite subjects, curiously enough, were Madonnas. Neither these, however, nor his frescoes, are his best work. One of his most successful portraits is that of Maria Mancini in Berlin.

MOLENAER

Jan Miense Molenaer, who was born in Haarlem c. 1610 and died there in 1668, followed several different fashions of his time during the first thirty years of his career. He began with half-length figures of drinkers or lute-players such as Frans Hals might have painted, in the style of his *Hille Bobbe* or *Singing Boys*, on one of his 'off' days. Molenaer's defective drawing is conspicuous in these works. He then turned to the representation of girls at the spinet and pseudo-smart gatherings. Finally, he fell under the influence of Adriaen Ostade, who had meanwhile achieved a high reputation, and composed scenes of peasant life. These pictures make a dark impression, the colours being only feebly brought out against a brown background. His many small figures are tightly packed into groups. The result is highly professional, but on the monotonous side. Both Molenaer and his wife, Judith Leyster, earned a great deal of money by their paintings.

Claes Molenaer (c. 1630-1676), also active at Haarlem, seems to have been related to Jan. He painted mainly landscapes, as a rule with a disarmingly simple technique, his snow-covered roofs, for example, being lightly touched in with pure white. His style in general recalls that of prints hung in 'respectable' drawing-rooms about the year 1900.

Cornelis Molenaer, active in Antwerp c. 1540-1589, and nicknamed 'Squinting Neel', was an excellent Early Flemish landscape painter, contemporary with and developing in the same way as Coninxloo. Of his unfortunately very rare works Berlin possesses his *Good Samaritan in a Forest Landscape* and Montpellier a *Winter Landscape*. His pictures are most interesting, but still little known, less than his life, which was miserable enough. He painted for a very low daily wage, earning sometimes as little as seven *sous* for landscape backgrounds.

MOLIJN

Born in 1595 in London, where his Dutch parents were staying at the time, and dying in Haarlem in 1661, Pieter de Molijn is represented in many galleries, usually by rather small landscapes, notable for the characteristic use he made of straight lines. They take the form of diagonals sloping slightly upwards throughout the picture-area. The foreground has a shadowed section, above which runs a sunlit road with precisely drawn figures of foot-passengers and horses and above the road again a darkly coloured strip of country, against which trees or single houses are silhouetted. The background also often includes the lines of hedgerows, heavily stressed by the brush. Much of the charm of his productions is due to this typical handling. His work has sometimes been mistaken for that of Goyen. He occasionally painted on a grander scale and depicted rural festivities. But these pictures have a more stilted effect.

MOMPER

The father, grandfather and great-grandfather of Joos de Momper (1564-1635) were all painters of Antwerp. In addition, they collected pictures, bought and sold them and issued engravings of works produced in many countries. In these circumstances it would have been perfectly natural for Joos to have turned out sophisticated, eclectic pictures. But in his case the long tale of family history was illumined by a sudden spark of ingenuous creative ability, as if he had been, not the last of an ancient, worn-out line of painters, but a Thurn and Taxis postilion unable to refrain from landscape painting.

His early works are dashed off with a splendidly uninhibited freedom. One is involuntarily reminded, by their astonishing simplifications, of Gobelins tapestries. And as it happens a record of payment, dated 1595, for Gobelins designs has been discovered. At this period the old convention of a brown foreground, a green middle distance and a yellow horizon area in landscape painting was already being ridiculed. But Momper, in his inspired innocence, elevated this expedient into a masterly style capable of expressing his gift for monumentality. His success arises from the impossibility of introducing Mannerism into work of this kind, leaving the field entirely free, once more, for a simple and natural delight in representation. He loved to depict mountains and deep valleys, always frequented by vehicles and travellers on horseback and afoot and by birds circling among the tree-tops.

At a later date his art grew more subtle. Such pictures as the two similar *Hilly Landscapes* at Pommersfelden and Warsaw, both masterpieces, have lost their resemblance to Gobelins tapestries. They are characterised, on the contrary, by a softness of line which lends them an inimitable atmospheric quality of positively impressionist type. The colour is laid on thick with bold strokes. The fading distance recall the artist from whom Momper learnt most, 'Peasant' Brueghel, i.e. Pieter the Elder.

Now that Momper's reputation is steadily increasing and the many work wrongly ascribed to him no longer bear his name he is regarded as approaching, at his best, the level of Jan 'Velvet' Brueghel.

The Antwerp painter **Frans** de Momper (1603-1660) was only distantly related to Joos. His landscapes are not important, the best of them being in the manner of Jan van Goyen.

MONACO

Piero di Giovanni Monaco, who was born at Siena c. 1370 and died in Florence in 1425, called himself Lorenzo Monaco— the Monk—after entering a monastery. His many extant altarpieces, *predelle* and panels prove him to have been a highly important predecessor of Fra Angelico. The older he grew, the more successfully he approached his ideal, the addition of further refinements, in the way of more subtle and delicate colouring and close execution of detail based on the practice of miniature painting, to the old style originated by Gaddi and the Sienese which he intended to preserve. His *Coronation of the*

J. DE MOMPER · LANDSCAPE WITH A DISTANT VIEW
28¾″ × 41¾″. Munich, Alte Pinakothek

Virgin, a magnificent altarpiece, is in the National Gallery, London.

MONNOYER

Jean-Baptist Monnoyer, an admirable French flower-painter, was born at Lille in 1636 and died in London in 1699. He deserves recognition for his introduction of unassuming *genre* works of this kind into the bombastic age of Louis XIV. He performed this feat surreptitiously, so to speak, by decorating bedrooms and the lintels of doorways with his flower pieces. He played a part in the great ornamental schemes of Le Brun at Vaux, Versailles and Marly. His style was the still-life equivalent of the rhetorical, monumental work of Le Brun.

MONTAGNA

Probably born c. 1440 at Orzinovi near Brescia and dying in 1523 at Vicenza, where his name is recorded as that of a citizen in 1480, though nothing is known of his previous life, Bartolomeo Montagna must, on the evidence of his pictures, have been trained in Venice. His colour is Venetian, though he does not employ the peculiarly bright vermilion of that school. His composition is based on that of Giovanni Bellini. He even occasionally permits himself solemn imitations of the exuberant anecdotal flourishes of the chronicler' Carpaccio. His sharply defined, uncompromising contours recall Mantegna. He may have observed such effects in the early works of Bellini or in those of Alvise Vivarini. For his painting shows, like that of Vivarini, a crystal-clear sense of construction and volume. His finest and most characteristic picture outside Italy, a *Risen Christ with St Mary Magdalene and John the Baptist*, is in Berlin. He is also represented in the National Gallery, London.

MOR

Born at Utrecht in 1519 and dying in Antwerp in 1575, Antonio Moro, as he called himself while in Spain, was trained by Scorel and visited Italy in 1550/1. Except for a single religious picture his extant works are all portraits.

In this field he was one of the most important artists of his time. In 1552 he accompanied one of his patrons, a cardinal, to the Court of the Emperor Charles V, where he soon achieved international celebrity. One after another of the grandees of the Empire employed him. From Spain he travelled to Portugal, Italy and England, painting portraits of Charles, Philip II, the Duke of Alba, William of Orange, Mary Tudor, Elizabeth of Valois, Alexander Farnese, Anne of Austria, Margaret of Parma and many men of learning. The list of his sitters rivals Titian's.

His portraits are very carefully painted and mostly life-size. The figures convey an effect of solidity and high relief. Their sternly set faces often express a disdain amounting to arrogance, always in a superlative degree, and are presented, technically, with masterly ease. But they differ noticeably from portraits of the first rank, such as those by Velasquez, Titian and Holbein, in suggesting a kind of artificially contrived rather than genuine sense of superiority in the sitter, as though the painter were trying to induce a shuddering feeling of awe in the spectator, even when portraying far from formidable personalities.

A remarkable and invariable characteristic of Mor's portraits is that one of the eyes of the model which contemplate the observer occupies the exact centre of the area assigned to the face as a whole.

MORALES

Luis de Morales (1509-1586), one of the most striking figures in the history of Spanish painting, lived at Badajoz, near the Portuguese frontier, at a time when Italian predominance in art was at its height. Philip II's ideal painter was Titian. The young artists of Spain, like those of Germany and Holland, set off at an early age to study in the 'Promised Land'. Any third-rate Italian was considered far superior to El Greco. At this date, moreover, the schools of Barcelona and Valencia

L. DE MORALES · MADONNA AND CHILD
19¼" × 13¼". Berlin, Staatl. Museen

were in decline and the new centres of Spanish painting, soon to be concentrated at Madrid, had not yet come into existence.

Such was the situation when Morales, of whose origins nothing is known, began to acquire reputation in a remote province on the whole hostile to Italian influence—though that of Leonardo must be admitted —and to the Renaissance in general. The pictorial imagination of Morales and the human types he portrayed were wholly his own. Stylistically he seems to have owed nothing to anyone. Nor can his mentality be compared with that of any other artist. His Berlin painting of the *Virgin and Child* is typical. A new variety of Madonna in a new attitude, one of positive timidity, is displayed. She appears as reluctant to touch the Child as any devout Christian would be to touch the Host.

Morales was called the 'Divine' even in his lifetime. The epithet is supposed to refer to his preference for representations of Christ. But his 'divine' style may well have shared responsibility for it. The tale is therefore probably untrue that he died in poverty. Not very many of his works have survived. Most of them are in Madrid. On the other hand, copies are legion. He was barely able to prevent their execution in his own day. A *Virgin and Child* by this artist is in the National Gallery, London.

MORANDO

(*see* CAVAZZOLA)

MOREAU

The Parisian painter Louis Gabriel Moreau (1739-1806)—not to be confused with the artist of the same name who taught Matisse nearly a century later—has never been accorded, from his own day to quite recent times, the recognition he deserves. He only obtained it after a great memorial exhibition of his works held after the First World War. He painted wonderfully attractive small views of the neighbourhood of Paris. Some of the best are in the Louvre. They include a Bellevue riverside scene bathed in the soft, faint light of an English day. Several anticipate the early work of Corot.

MOREELSE

Paul Moreelse (1571-1638) lived and worked all his life in Utrecht except for a visit to Italy in about 1600. He was a pupil of Mierevelt and the pictures he painted before his Italian journey, such as the *Portrait of a Woman* in the Berlin Gallery are in the style of his master. In Italy Moreelse saw the work of Titian and of the Baroque painters, and in his later work he reflects their influence in an intensified feeling for structure and form, a broader technique and the rejection of Mierevelt's preoccupation with detail. Pictures like *The Shepherdess* at The Hague, a similar subject at Amsterdam and *The Garden of Love* in the Hermitage, anticipate the art

Boucher. Moreelse was a popular portait painter, and he was also an architect of considerable merit. He designed the St atherine's Gate, Utrecht, demolished in 345.

MORETTO

citizen of Brescia, Alessandro Moretto (. 1498-1554) was the most important ainter of that city after Savoldo and omanino. Brescia was at that time subct to Venice, so that the influences of ellini and Titian on Moretto are intelli-ble, though he may never have visited enice. There are also some Raphaelesque atures in his work which he can only ave absorbed from engravings. Moretto terefore appears to have been a keen and ever student and probably also a man of ilture, well-informed in spite of his rovincial isolation. His palette of grey, reyish-green, faint blue and light red is lso proof of his fastidious taste.

In his biblical compositions, most of hich are at Brescia, though the important 't Justina is in Vienna, Moretto makes a reat effort to be inventive. His *Elijah lwakened by the Angels* has some sug-estion of Pan. The contrast between the gure of Elijah, given the rigidity of a tone giant, and the slim, active angel is nely imaginative. Unfortunately, the indscape is less appealing. It is a pity that iis artist's achievement is so uneven. Iis portraits are excellent. They show iuch psychological insight in their quiet, efined way. The London *Portrait of a Ian* is the first life-size, full-length ortrait, apart from frescoes, in the history f Italian painting.

MORLAND

Jeorge Morland, who was born in London n 1763 and died there in 1804, had an dventurous life. Extravagant habits led im to take refuge from his creditors on ne Isle of Wight, where he was obliged ɔ live with smugglers, whom he often ainted. On his return to London he was ventually arrested and died in prison. Iis scenes of rustic life, with tone-values in the Dutch style, are highly professional and ahead of his time. He was also probably the first artist to depict urban labourers. His manner is based partly on the tradition of Gainsborough, partly on that of the sporting painters. His *Shoeing the Bay Mare* is in the Tate Gallery, London, and *A Hunting Mishap* in the Victoria and Albert Museum.

MORONE

Of the two painters of this name of Verona, **Domenico** (1442-c. 1518), father of the famous **Francesco** (1471-1529) was by no means so negligible a painter as he is often represented. The chief work of the worthy, painstaking Domenico is a large canvas at Mantua, *The Rout of the Buonaccolsi*. If this spirited production, in which there is no bloodshed, had been of a size suitable for a small room, it would immediately have been universally appreciated.

Francesco was trained by his father, but remained wholly under the spell of the Venetians. A highly intelligent painter of a deeply romantic cast of mind, he had a special talent for clear and impressive construction. His landscape backgrounds are lit in the manner of Poussin. The foreground figures enacting his mostly biblical scenes look as if they, too, formed an integral part of the soothing serenity of the setting. The Samson and Delilah of his picture at Milan, tall and robust as they appear, seem inwardly lethargic, languid as the folds of their velvet mantles. They have no idea, one feels, any more than their creator had, what they are supposed to illustrate. They do nothing more, in the end, but envelop the spectator in their own melting mood. Such is the reason why Morone is not a more important artist. His *Madonnas with Saints*, of which there is a typical example at Berlin, are little more than conventional imitations of the work of Bellini and Cima.

MORONI

A Bergamo artist, Giovanni Battista Moroni (c. 1525-1578), was trained by

Moretto, but surpassed his teacher in the technique of portraiture, achieving likenesses of positively photographic precision. In the case of his women sitters this accuracy was obtained at the cost of warmth and the delineation of character. His male portraits are more sensitive and sympathetic, often with a suggestion of melancholy. His best and most appealing picture, the London *Portrait of a Tailor*, has acquired great popularity.

MOSER

The little church of Tiefenbronn, between Stuttgart and Pforzheim, contains a retable depicting episodes from the life of St Mary Magdalen. No other picture by Lukas Moser has so far been discovered. His very name would not be known if he had not concealed it in the flourishes of a decorative border of Persian type. The phrase reads: 'Lukas Moser, painter from Weil, created this work. Pray for him.' The opposite border contains the words: 'Wail, O art, wail, lament in misery! For none now craves thee more, O woe is me!' The date 1431 is added.

Moser was a great painter. In the simplicity of his composition he remains entirely faithful to the High Gothic style. But his vision had already outrun it. The newly awakened interest in the natural world clearly enraptured him. His ruffled seas and distant coasts are wonderfully fine, his shadowed waters under the lee of a vessel amazingly transparent. Nor does he depict figures of legend, but human beings of flesh and blood in various moods, even those of joviality, aboard ship, on a stairway or at table in the scene of the foot-washing of Christ. The guests whisper to one another or point to someone with their bread-knives, while Christ raises the table-cloth slightly to enable Mary Magdalen to reach His feet more easily. And this work is actually prior in date to the Van Eycks' Ghent altarpiece.

MOSTAERT

Information about Jan Mostaert is included in the biographical sketches of Van

J. MOSTAERT · PORTRAIT OF A YOUNG MAN
38" × 30". Liverpool, Walker Art Gallery

Mander, who had interviewed a pupil and a grandson of the master. None of his works, however, had been discovered before 1896, when Mostaert was found to be identical with the painter until then known as the 'Master with the Imperial Herald' and also with the 'Dutch Master of 1510/20'. Born at Haarlem c. 1475 and dying at Hoorn in 1555/6, he is stated by Mander to have been for eighteen years in attendance on the Imperial Regent of the Netherlands, Margaret of Austria. He belonged to an eminent family and was the kind of man who, on doffing his painter's smock, at once resumed the aspect of a nobleman. No doubt he was also wealthy.

He seems to have been trained by a pupil of Geertgen. His early pictures—for example, the delightful little panel at Cologne entitled *The Holy Family at Table*—are quite archaic in style, simple, naïve and with little trace of modelling, like Geertgen's. But Mostaert soon evolved his own manner, especially in his excellent portraits. His refined faces, with reserved

t courteously patient expressions, are
ng-headed, a cap often being drawn over
e low brows. Both ladies and gentlemen
e generally gloved and wear velvet and
rs. The backgrounds indicate Mostaert's
ve of anecdotal incident. That of the
verpool portrait refers to the legend of
Hubert. The paintings are technically
illiant, though neither outwardly nor in
irit do they really illustrate the subject.
ostaert was a distinguished landscape
tist, as his Munich *Miracle of St Hubert*
oves.

His later religious pictures, when they
e small, have much charm, though too
uch urbanity to be moving. But when-
er, as in a large work like the *Deposition*
arpiece at Brussels, he was obliged to
splay colour, his vision soared. In the
ece mentioned he actually returns to the
yle of Rogier van der Weyden, though at
is date both Lucas van Leyden and
abuse were active in the neighbourhood.

IULTSCHER

odern historians of the art of the past
gard the name of Multscher rather as
at of a firm than of an individual creator
all the paintings formerly or even now
rrent under this designation. Hans
ultscher, both sculptor and painter, was
rn c. 1400 near Leutkirch in the
avarian district of Allgäu. In 1427 he
oved to Ulm, where he eventually died
1467. He must have had a great reputa-
n in South Germany and the Tyrol
d no doubt maintained a large studio for
th sculpture and painting.
Probably he himself was primarily a
ulptor. Many of his works are unfortun-
ely lost. But eight wings of an altarpiece
Berlin are inscribed with a statement
at he painted them. Their technique by
means reaches the level of that of the
rly Dutch artists, whose works, how-
er, he must have seen. Nor does imagin-
on play much part in these pieces by
ultscher. Their surprising feature is
eir realism, wholly novel in the German
inting of the time. His humble, gaping
lookers at Christ and the Virgin are

such as might be seen in any fifteenth-
century street. His Joseph is an actor on
the scent of a successful career, his Mary
an embittered wife, who hates all the fuss.
Landscape and architecture are stylised.
The total impression is that of a monument in low relief painted in gold, red,
dark blue and yellowish green.

In the search for further works by
Multscher an unexpected difficulty arose.
Several pictures identical in style with the
Berlin panels and in some cases more
skilfully painted could only have been
produced by other persons employed in
Multscher's studio. It is therefore still a
matter of dispute whether not only the
sculptures but also the paintings of the
famous Sterzing altarpiece, now restored
to its original location, are by Multscher.
The altarpiece is commonly referred to as
his, though with a mention of an unknown
'Master of the Sterzing Panels'. The name
of Multscher is also used in connection
with two screens at Neuhausen near
Pforzheim and some other fragments of a
similar kind.

MURILLO

Bartolome Esteban Murillo was born in
Seville in 1618 and died there in 1682.
He was the most famous and popular
painter of the High Baroque period or,
more explicitly, the Counter-Reformation,
in Spain. No one could depict so well as
he the allurements, the fascination and the
intoxicating effects of Catholic belief or
the delicate and dreamlike beauty of the
visions and miracles which had all been
abjured on intellectual grounds by the
Reformation. Murillo's countrymen, especially in the south of Spain, hailed him
with rapture.

His expert understanding of popular
mentality, which he himself had every
opportunity to develop, his father being a
hairdresser with fourteen children, is
proved by the unvarying similarity of his
themes. His religious paintings illustrate
popular ideals and his scenes of common
life ideal domesticity. His famous picture
of *St Anthony and the Infant Christ*, at

Berlin, is imbued in the last analysis with the same spirit as that of his representations of melon-eating or dicing beggar-boys, of which there are examples at Munich. His general outlook varies as little as his style. He seems to imply that life is like a dream and that people should therefore be devout, meek and mild in their behaviour, even when begging or dicing.

This somewhat ironic view of Murillo's talent, generally held today, expresses a reaction against the extraordinary veneration with which his work was regarded up to the outbreak of war in 1914. Yet in spite of this artist's excessive indulgence in the picturesque, very clearly traceable to the methods of Correggio and Van Dyck, his achievement stands very high, though of course below that of his only slightly older rival Velasquez.

Murillo himself tells us that he never left Seville. Churches, monasteries and private citizens commissioned his work. He maintained a large studio and became a rich man. He was the first President of the Seville Academy, founded in 1660. Several hundreds of his pictures are extant. Among the most celebrated are the Munich representations of beggar children, the two paintings of *St Anthony*, at Berlin and Seville respectively, the Budapest *Madonna Distributing Bread*, the *Rosary Madonnas* of the Louvre, the Pitti Palace at Florence and the Dulwich Gallery, and the *Immaculate Conceptions* of the Prado and the Hermitage.

MYTENS

Daniel Mytens (1590?-1642) was a Dutch-

MURILLO · BEGGAR BOYS THROWING DIC
58¾" × 43¼". *Munich, Alte Pinakothek*

man from The Hague, possibly a pupil o Rubens. He came early to England an was appointed Court Painter to Charles in 1621. He painted the King in 1623 (th picture now hangs in the National Portrai Gallery) and was given a house and garde in St Martin's Lane. Mytens' Englis portraits, such as *James, Second Marques of Hamilton* (Hampton Court), anticipat Van Dyck in both spirit and style. Myten remained in England until 1634, then unable to compete with his great successo Van Dyck, he returned to Holland.

NADO DI CIONE

(see ORCAGNA)

NATIONAL GALLERY, LONDON

The National Gallery, probably the most representative collection of European painting in the world, was founded on April 2nd, 1824, when Parliament voted ₤57,000 for the purchase of thirty-eight pictures from the collection of John Julius Angerstein, including Claude's *Marriage of Isaac and Rebecca* and *The Embarkation of the Queen of Sheba* and Titian's *Venus and Adonis*. The pictures were first exhibited in the later owner's house, 100 Pall Mall; they were moved to 105 Pall Mall in 1834 and finally established in the present building, designed by William Wilkins in 1838. Among the many masterpieces in the National Gallery are Masaccio's *Madonna and Child*, Uccello's *Rout of San Romano*, Piero della Francesca's *Nativity* and *Baptism*, Botticelli's *Mars and Venus*, Michelangelo's *Entombment* and *Holy Family*, Leonardo's *Virgin of the Rocks*, *The Ansidei Madonna* by Raphael, Bellini's *Agony in the Garden* and *Doge Leonardo Loredano*, *The Agony in the Garden* by Mantegna, Titian's *Noli me Tangere* and *Bacchus and Ariadne*, Tintoretto's *St George and the Dragon*, Veronese's *Family of Darius before Alexander*, Holbein's *Ambassadors* and *Christina of Denmark*, Rembrandt's *Woman Bathing*, *Saskia as Flora*, *Margaretha Trip* and *Self-Portrait*, Vermeer's *Lady at the Virginals*, Van Dyck's *Charles I on Horseback*, Rubens' *Château de Steen*, *Silenus*, *Chapeau de Paille*, *Judgment of Paris* and *Rape of the Sabines*, *The Agony in the Garden* by El Greco, Velazquez's *Philip IV* and *The Rokeby Venus*, and Poussin's *Bacchanalian Revel*, *Worship of the Golden Calf* and *Landscape with Snake*.

NATIONAL GALLERY OF ART, WASHINGTON

This gallery was established by Act of Congress in 1937 as a division of the Smithsonian institute and was opened in 1941. The most outstanding pictures consist of about 150 works from the collection of Andrew W. Mellon, who also financed the building, a classical structure designed by John Russell Pope. The pictures include some of the finest examples of the work of Botticelli, Perugino, Raphael, Titian, El Greco, Goya, Chardin, Lancret, Van Eyck, Memling, Gerard David, Van der Weyden, Van Dyck, Rubens, de Hooch, Hals, Hobbema, Cuyp, Rembrandt, Holbein and Dürer. Fifteen of these pictures were purchased by Mr Mellon from the Soviet Government, having formerly been in the Hermitage, Leningrad. The Gallery also houses the Kress Collection, which includes examples of all the more important

J.-M. NATTIER · PORTRAIT OF AN UNKNOWN LADY · 22″ × 18⅞″. *Munich, Private Collection*

European painters from the thirteenth to the eighteenth centuries, e.g. Bellini's great picture *The Feast of the Gods*, El Greco's *St Martin and the Beggar*, *The Cowper Madonna* by Raphael, Mantegna's *Judith and Holofernes*, the *St Anne Altarpiece* by Gerard David, *The Woman weighing Gold* by Vermeer and *The Windmill* by Rembrandt.

A. VAN DER NEER · WINTER LANDSCAPE
$9\frac{1}{4}'' \times 13\frac{3}{8}''$. *Munich, Alte Pinakothek*

NATOIRE

Charles Joseph Natoire (1700-1777) was born at Nîmes and died at Castel Gandolfo after a most successful career as Director of the French Academy in Rome. His elegant mythological and historical paintings exactly suited the taste of the period. Natoire was a pupil of Le Moine, but derived his style from that of the far greater Nattier. He was considered as the rival of Boucher and in his splendid tapestry designs he indeed came close to the more celebrated master. Some of his portraits are also interesting. He is represented in the Louvre.

NATTIER

Jean-Marc Nattier (1685-1766) spent all his life in Paris. When he was twenty his father was imprisoned on a false accusation of murder and committed suicide. Nattier's chief aim was therefore understandably to lead a peaceful, undisturbed life. His career resembled that of Teniers, except that it ended less happily, for he died poor and neglected. He seemed at first destined for a better fate. Both his parents were painters and he was taught first by them and then studied at the Academy under Jouvenet, who befriended him. Nattier became a member of the Academy and travelled in 1717 to Amsterdam, where he painted the portraits of Peter and Catherine of Russia, who happened to be staying in Holland. The Czar invited the painter to Moscow, but Nattier refused and attached himself instead to the Court of Louis XV. He painted both the King and Madame de Pompadour. Then Boucher was taken into favour and Nattier was discarded and ridiculed for the allegorical compositions he had been compelled to paint against his own inclinations, for the mythological fancy dress in which he had been forced to deck out his pictures was not at all to his own taste. His real talent was for portraiture. In the medium of pastel, his fine colour sense and delicacy of execution are superior even to those of Rosalba Carriera and Quentin de La Tour. Some of his portraits of Madame de Pompadour and of the Princesses are among the most exquisite productions of the Rococo period. The two portraits in the London National Gallery, show Nattier at his best, but he is most extensively represented at Versailles. (Ill. p. 221.)

NEEFS

Pieter Neefs (1579-1656?) was born at Antwerp and was perhaps the pupil of H. van Steenwyck. In 1609 he entered the Guild in Antwerp, apparently in poor circumstances. He painted interesting church interiors often with candle lighting.

Sometimes the figures in his pictures were put in by J. Brueghel, Coques or Vrancx. His work can be seen at the National Gallery and the Wallace Collection, and in Amsterdam and Antwerp. Neefs had a son also called **Pieter** (1620-1675) who painted similar subjects, but without his father's spirit.

NEER

Aart van der Neer (1603-1677) was born in Gorkum, Holland. In his youth he was a steward in the Von Arkels family and only painted in his spare time. Later he moved to Amsterdam where he modelled himself on Raphael Camphuysen. His earliest dated picture was painted in 1639. In style Van der Neer's first pictures resemble those of E. van de Velde and are rather coarsely painted. His masterpieces fall between the year 1650 and 1660; they are usually winter landscapes with remarkably sincere and delicate interpretations of the effects of late evening or dawn. Van der Neer's name is usually associated with his late moonlight scenes, which are, however, not his best work and tend to mannerism. He was unable to live by his art, was forced to keep an inn and was in perpetual straits. There are fine examples of his work in the National Gallery, London; he is also represented at Amsterdam and Brussels. **Eglon** van der Neer (1634-1703) was Aart's son and a painter of conversation pieces and interiors in the manner of Ochtervelt.

NEROCCIO

Neroccio de Landi (1447-1500) was a Sienese painter and a pupil of Sassetta. It is not therefore surprising to learn that he was not a revolutionary artist. The Renaissance movement was in full swing, but Neroccio paid no heed to it. His sensitive pictures are in the same lyrical tradition as those of Domenico Veneziano. His *Madonna* and *Child* in Siena resembles a photographic plate reversing dark and light in the delicate and alabaster transparency of its quality. His *Madonna and Six Saints* and a frieze, also in Siena, are characterised

C. NETSCHER · THE LACEMAKER
13⅛" × 10¾". London, Wallace Collection

by striking pallor and a gentle lyrical feeling. There is an archaic half-length portrait by Neroccio in the National Gallery of Art, Washington, a lady with a pale, pearly skin and foaming hair.

NETSCHER

Caspar Netscher (1639-1684), Terborch's most important pupil, was born at Heidelberg of a Polish father. His widowed mother, a war refugee, took him to Holland in infancy and eventually, at the age of fifteen, he entered Terborch's studio at Deventer. By 1659 his apprenticeship was over, and to celebrate his independence he went by sea to Italy (1659-52) where he married. Later he visited England and worked at Bordeaux. He finally settled at The Hague, where he died.

By the time Netscher came to live at The Hague he had already done his best work. Deeply impressed by the charm and serenity of Terborch's pictures, but without grasping their inimitable nobility of spirit, he steeped himself in his master's vision. His finest picture during this period was *The Lacemaker* (Wallace Collection, London). Netscher never again succeeded in painting a composition of such harmony and such human warmth of feeling. Nevertheless, while he was under Terborch's influence he produced one good *genre* picture after another (*The Singing Lesson*, The Hague; *A Lady at her Toilet*, Dresden; *The Music Party*, Munich; *Kitchen Interior*, Berlin). In about 1670 Netscher's style suddenly changed. From then on he painted society portraits and banal allegorical scenes in French style. (Ill. p. 223.)

Constantin Netscher (1668-1723), Caspar's son, lived at The Hague and painted in the style of his father's later work.

NEUFCHATEL

Nicolas Neufchatel (working 1561-1567), also known as Lucidel, was born in the south of the Netherlands, probably at Mons, and worked and died at Nuremberg. He was trained in the workshop of Coecke van Aelst, the master of Pieter Brueghel the Elder. But Brueghel and Neufchatel are worlds apart. Neufchatel became an eminently bourgeois portrait painter. His pictures are imbued with an air of tranquillity and are in striking contrast to the turbulence of the painter's life. He was an ardent Calvinist and was forced to flee from Flanders and take refuge in Nuremberg. His pictures are unsigned and there is difficulty in identifying them. The principal work known to be by his hand is *The Mathematician Neudörfer and His Son* at Munich, painted in soft, subtle tones of brown and grey, a slightly weak, effeminate work, like all Neufchatel's portraits. *A Portrait of a Young Lady* is in the National Gallery, London.

NICCOLO DI LIBERATORE

Niccolo di Liberatore (working c. 1456-1502) worked at Foligno and elsewhere in Umbria and in the Marches. The many pictures known today to be by his hand all bear the mark of his tortuous piety and his almost physical preoccupation with the sufferings of Christ. His mature style is reminiscent of that of the Vivarini, but there is something in his pictures which is alien to beauty, a certain meagreness of spirit and lack of sensibility. It is as though his only aim was to bear witness to his faith, harshly and without a spark of imagination. The sackcloth and ashes are a little too much in evidence. As linear designs, however, his compositions certainly strengthened the tradition of the Umbrian School. A triptych by Niccolo is in the National Gallery, London.

NORTHCOTE

James Northcote was born in 1746, the son of a Plymouth watchmaker. He became the friend and biographer of Reynolds and between 1771 and 1776 he frequented Reynolds' house and studio. Northcote studied first at the Academy and afterwards, from 1777-1780, in Italy. It was his ambition to become a 'history' painter, but his failure is amply illustrated by the work in the Guildhall entitled *Sir William Walworth, Lord Mayor of London A.D. 1381, in the presence of Richard II, kills Wat Tyler at the head of the Insurgents, who are appeased by the Heroic Speech of the King.* Northcote succeeded better with portraits and is known for his *Memoirs of Sir Joshua Reynolds*. He died in London in 1831.

NOTKE

Bernt Notke (c. 1440-1509) was born in Schleswig-Holstein in the village of Lassahn and died in Lübeck. He was the most important wood-engraver and painter of the whole of eastern Germany of the period and also of Scandinavia. But very little of his work has been preserved. Among his documented paintings are an altarpiece and a frieze showing the Dance of Death at Reval and the high altar at Aarhus. The altarpiece at Lübeck with the famous *Mass of St Gregory*, which was ascribed to Notke, was destroyed during the last war. This work was remarkable for its terrifying psychological insight and its devastatingly cold objectivity. A splendid but macabre crowd of old men, eager to be saved, pressed about the tiny Gothic figure of Christ, who had come down from the Cross. This was no acclamation of beauty, but the angry monologue of an embittered spirit. And the painter of such sepulchral loom was the contemporary of Francesca, Botticelli, Giovanni Bellini and the young Dürer. It would be interesting to know more of him.

NOUTS

Little is known of Michael Nouts except that he was born c. 1628 in Delft and probably remained in his native place, where he in known to have been working in 1656. His principal portraits have all the

qualitites we associate with Delft: charm and tenderness, even when the model is plain. There is a remarkable *Portrait of a Young Woman* at Munich which was formerly ascribed to Hals, no mean tribute. Occasionally Nouts' style is reminiscent of that of Verspronck, who was indeed a pupil of Hals. His splendid *Portrait of an Old Lady* is in the Rijksmuseum, Amsterdam. A *Family Group* in the National Gallery, London, has recently been attributed to Nouts.

O

OCHTERVELT

Jacob Ochtervelt (working 1652, died before 1710) worked in Rotterdam and Amsterdam. He was an excellent minor master who painted in the style of Terborch and Metsu. Before he adopted this manner he painted hunting scenes and mythological pictures which are reminiscent of his master, Berchen, and of Jan Baptist Weenix. From about 1660 he began to be attracted by the interiors and *genre* subjects which were coming from the studios of Terborch, Metsu, Mieris, Vermeer and de Hooch. Ochtervelt aimed at greater elegance, an even lighter touch and more obvious charm, for he was of the mistaken opinion that Terborch relied for his effects on his brilliant rendering of materials and the attractiveness of his subject-matter. He produced pretty, delicately painted drawing-room pieces, glowing with warm red light; but the figures in his music parties, convivial groups and flirtatious couples, all painted with a faintly erotic overtone, are never properly related to each other and are without the inner tension of Terborch's figures.

OGGIONE

Marco d'Oggione (apprenticed c. 1490, died after 1524) was born and worked in Milan. D'Oggione was one of the first of Leonardo's pupils, and his dependence on his master was so great that it is impossible to imagine how he would have developed

without Leonardo's influence. He only showed some faint signs of individuality (greater interest in movement and a more pronounced twist in the pose of his heads) after the master vanished from his circle in 1515. The fine altarpiece at Mezzana is one of the independent works he painted at this period. D'Oggione made a copy of Leo-

J. OCHTERVELT · THE OYSTER EATERS
18¾″ × 13″. Castagnola, Thyssen Collection

nardo's *Last Supper* which hangs in the Royal Academy Diploma Gallery.

OIL PAINTING

The use of drying oils, such as linseed, poppy, walnut and hempseed, as mediums for painting superseded the tempera technique in Europe during the fifteenth century, though these oils were known long before that date. During the fifteenth century certain conditions created a demand for a new type of painting for which the oil medium was eminently suitable. Among these conditions may be mentioned the development of the easel-picture to satisfy the requirements of private patrons and collectors, the increased demand for portraiture and the beginnings of a realistic art of landscape. The direction which all these developments took was largely decided by the desire to imitate nature. For this purpose the oil technique proved to have great flexibility and could produce a wider range of effects than any other medium. The possibilities of oil were not at first fully developed. The fifteenth-century paintings by Flemish and Venetian artists generally referred to as oil pictures were produced by employing alternate coats of tempera and transparent oil glazes, and the gesso grounds of tempera were often still used. The direct process for easel-pictures which is what we now mean by oil painting did not come into universal use until the seventeenth century, although one or two masters of the previous century, such as Veronese and Tintoretto, had completely adopted the procedure. During the seventeenth century, however, the practice of painting pictures throughout with oils and varnishes became common. After 1700 oil grounds and oil colours were almost universally used and canvas, because of its light weight, became the most popular support, even though some artists preferred to paint on panels.

OLIVER

Isaac Oliver (1556-1617) was a Frenchman who came to England as a Huguenot refugee in 1562. He continued the Hilliard tradition in miniature painting, though he used shadows to suggest relief, wherea Hilliard had avoided them at the speci request of Queen Elizabeth. Some o Oliver's miniatures are full-length and th size of small easel-pictures. Such is th famous *Sir Anthony Mildmay* in the Cleve land Museum, Ohio.

OPIE

John Opie was born at St Agnes in Corn wall in 1761. He was a precocious boy, an came to London in 1780. He foolishl essayed the grand manner, as in th *Murder of Rizzio* (Guildhall), but his bes works are portraits which show a kee sense of pattern and a power of suggestin significant expression. *Self-portrait* an *Portrait of a Boy* (Tate Gallery), *Ann Charlotte and John Gillett* (Private Col lection, New York). Opie died in 1807.

ORCAGNA

Three brothers of the Florentine famil of Cione were painters—Andrea, Nard and Jacopa. The greatest of them, know to his contemporaries as Orcagna (Arch angel) was Andrea. The name is curiousl appropriate, for there was a new solidity, new plastic quality and yet somethin austere and archaic in his pictures. It i no surprise to learn that he was also sculptor.

Andrea Orcagna was born in Florence i about 1315 and died there between 136 and 1377. He was recognised as a grea painter even in his own day. His statur becomes apparent when one compares hi own completed works with those finishe by his brother **Jacopo** (after 1308-afte 1394) after his death. Jacopo has adapte his style to that of Andrea, but of the tru spirit of Orcagna there is no trace.

The tremendous power of Andrea' figures is strikingly apparent in his princi pal work, the altarpiece of the Strozz Chapel (S. Maria Novella, Florence), in th remains of a *Triumph of Death* (S. Croc and in the great altarpiece for S. Pietr Maggiore, Florence, now in the Nationa Gallery, London. These works also shov the painter's delight in rich stuffs an glittering accoutrements. His courtly Arch angel Michael with his green armour and his St Catherine flaunting her gold brocade like a princess herald the figures of Gentile da Fabriano. Orcagna's work indeed foreshadows the Renaissance.

Andrea's brother, **Nardo di Cione,** who died in Florence in 1366, was perhaps as great a painter, but unfortunately not a single work by him is fully authenticated and we are compelled to rely for information on Ghiberti, who attributed to him the frescoes of *The Last Judgement, Paradise* and *Hell* in the Strozzi Chapel. These important paintings owe more to Giotto and to the Sienese than to Andrea. They are quieter in feeling, the colour is clearer and more delicate and even in the representation of *Hell* the elongated figures of his women strike a charming lyrical note. The recently cleaned fresco of the *Crucifixion* in the refectory of S. Spirito, Florence, is the joint work of Andrea and Nardo.

ORLEY

Barend (or Bernart) van Orley was born in about 1492 in Brussels and died there in 1542. Early Flemish religious painting was above all the expression of a spiritual experience, of an unquestioning faith; and early Flemish portraits were factual records of the sitters' features. But in the period to which Orley belongs the aims of the fifteenth-century masters had been lost sight of. Painters were searching for new forms of expression. It was not the Italian Renaissance which destroyed Gothic painting, for the Late Gothic spirit was already degenerate and outworn. Orley's pictures show that the new restless spirit was not only incorporated in forms deriving from the Renaissance, but in the styles of previous periods. There is no proof that Orley ever went to Italy, though he is often stated to have done so. And Italian elements are by no means present in all his pictures. Many of them, especially the numerous straight-forward, matter-of-fact portraits which Orley executed as Court Painter to Margarete of Austria and Maria of Hungary, reflect the style of the Flemish School, in particular of Quinten Massys. During his last years Orley gave up painting and, apart from making designs for stained glass and tapestry, he left all his commissions to his many pupils and assistants.

OSTADE

Adriaen van Ostade is one of the most popular of Dutch painters. He owes his rather exaggerated reputation to the Victorians who prided themselves on being able to

A. VAN OSTADE
TAVERN SCENE
*11¼″ × 14¾″. Munich,
Alte Pinakothek*

unbend sufficiently to take an intelligent pleasure in Ostade's fresh, gay little peasant scenes.

Adriaen van Ostade (1610-1684) owed his style to the dramatic, deeply ironical Brouwer, to his master, Hals, and to Rembrandt, under whose spell he, like so many others, fell for better or worse. Ostade's early pictures closely resemble Brouwer's schoolroom scenes with boys being caned, but they were soon followed by a long period of peasant scenes and pictures of pedlars, organ-grinders and schoolroom interiors in which the drawing is very precise and the palette light in tone. The figures are dressed in blue trousers and pink jackets and the picture surface has a faintly chalky appearance. In about 1640 the influence of Rembrandt's chiaroscuro makes itself felt. The figures become larger, more dramatic and finally almost caricatures. Now and then Ostade would paint an interior with a Rembrandt-like atmosphere (*The Slaughtered Pig*, Frankfort). There have been innumerable copies and forgeries of Ostade's pictures.

Isaac van Ostade (1621-1649) was Adriaen's brother and pupil. Strangely enough, he is not nearly so well known, although if he had not died so young he might have become the better painter of the two. His first subjects were interiors with strong light and shade in the manner of Adriaen. Later he developed an individual style of landscape, especially in his winter scenes with frozen canals. His clear, silvery tone is unmistakable. He is well represented in the London National Gallery and Wallace Collection.

Both brothers spent the whole of their uneventful lives in Haarlem.

OUDRY

Jean-Baptiste Oudry was born in Paris in 1686 and died in 1755 at Beauvais. He was a pupil of Largillières and the painter of many outstanding animal pictures which not only adorned Versailles, but travelled to Schwerin, Stockholm and Copenhagen. But Oudry has another claim to fame—he established the reputation of Beauvais. He became Director of the Tapestry Works in 1734 and created an entirely new Gobelins style. One of his first acts as Director wa to employ Boucher. He made the mos impossible demands on his workers, bu under him the Beavais Factory flourishec as never before or since. Yet Oudry's worl at Beauvais must not blind us to the merit of his splendid pictures with their clea accents and cool colours. They can be seen in the Wallace collection, London.

OUWATER

Aelbert Ouwater is one of the great masters of early Netherlandish painting but very little is known about him. He probably came from Ouwater near Haarlem, where he is mentioned between 1440 and 1467. I has been thought that he was a pupil of Jan van Eyck, who was living at The Hague from 1424 till 1428, but the dates are too early.

Only one picture mentioned by Manders can be ascribed with certainty to Ouwater but no one who has seen it would hesitate for a moment to affirm the painter's high reputation. This picture is *The Raising of Lazarus* (Berlin). The scene takes place in a solemn circular church interior, where dark columns support a sunlit vault. The principal figure, towering above Lazarus who is fearfully rising from the tomb, is not Christ, but Peter, the mediator between a group of sumptuously dressed Jews and a group of believers. Jesus is performing the miracle almost anonymously. He stands inconspicuously among the others, one hand gently raised. But the expression on His face, a look of melting goodness and love, attracts attention as if by magic. The women by His side seem to glow with an inner light and they smile like people in a dream.

Because of the scarcity of his work, Ouwater means little to anyone who is not a connoisseur. Naturally, attempts have been made to ascribe other works to him on stylistic grounds. Among these are the *Scenes from the Life of the Virgin* in the Prado and *Christ taken Prisoner* at Munich. It is interesting that both these works were formerly attributed to Dirk Bouts. Ouwater has indeed great affinities with Bouts and there are reasons to believe that they were together in Haarlem for a time. Ouwater's pupil was Geertgen.

P

PACHECO

Francisco Pacheco, the master and father-in-law of Velazquez, was born in either 1564 or 1571 (both dates are mentioned) at Cadiz and died in 1654 in Seville. There is nothing especially exciting about either his life or his work. He became Court Painter, an Inquisitor, wrote a *History of Painting*, which is an important source book, and was a better teacher than painter. Only one of Pacheco's many portraits has survived. His religious pictures and altarpieces (nearly all of which are in Spain) are pedantic in manner and Roman in inspiration.

PACHER

The art of the German Gothic altarpiece reached its highest perfection in the work of a painter who did not come from a large, flourishing city, but lived in a small place in the Alps, in Bruneck. Michael Pacher was born at Neustift in about 1435, but settled in Bruneck in 1467 and founded a workshop famous for the production of altarpieces. His brother was also connected with it at a later date. Pacher died in 1498, it is not known where, though it may have been at Salzburg. Only a few of his masterpieces have been preserved. Among his chief authenticated works are the remains of the winged altarpiece of Gries, the high altar of St Wolfgang, the remains of the St Francis altarpiece at Salzburg (now divided between Salzburg and Vienna) and the altarpiece of the Fathers of the Church (Munich). The marvellous carving of the St Wolfgang altarpiece is also the work of Pacher and shows him to have been one of the greatest of the late Gothic wood carvers in Germany.

The fact that he was a sculptor helps to explain many of the characteristics of Pacher's painting: the sharply defined planes of his monumental figures, which do not so much give the illusion of volume as actually fill the space they occupy; the filigree-like ornament, the painted bald-achino by means of which he continues on

MICHAEL PACHER · ST GREGORY
(*From the Altarpiece, 'The Fathers of the Church'*)
86⅜" × 39¼". Munich, Alte Pinakothek

the picture surface the actual carving of the altarpiece; the tremendous strength and serenity, aloof rather than saintly, of his figures; the apparent simplicity of his composition, which is in reality carefully calculated to give the figures a three-dimensional quality as they loom up out of the twilight of the church nave; and his rows of box-like houses which draw the eye irresistably along the yawning streets. Mantegna, whom Pacher must have seen in Padua during his youthful travels in Italy, was influential in the formation of his style.

Pacher is one of the most important of the old German masters. The greatness of his work, with which he certainly broke new ground, lies in the grandeur of its spiritual content, in its quiet, undramatic monumentality, in its warmth of feeling and in its originality of colour and splendid draughtsmanship.

PADOVANINO

Padovanino's real name was Alessandro Varotari. He was born in Padua in 1588 and died in Venice in 1648. Berenson places him among those followers of Titian and Veronese who in his opinion 'shamelessly manufactured pictures which, in the distant markets for which they were intended, passed for the works of Titian, Veronese and Giorgione'. Padovanino

trained himself by making copies after Titian. He was antagonistic to the contemporary Mannerist style, clung to the Venetians, who had already become classics, and thus swam against the current. His religious pictures, the chief of which is *The Marriage at Cana* in Venice, are anaemic but painstaking. His small mythological compositions have more charm. They are painted with genuine feeling and in the case of one or two of them it remains uncertain whether they are actually by Padovanino or Titian.

PAINTERLY

This term, frequently employed today, was given its present meaning by Heinrich Wölfflin, who used in as a contrast to 'linear' in his *Kunstgeschichtliche Grundbegriffe* (Munich, 1915; English translation, *Principles of Art History*, 1925). By the 'painterly' as opposed to the 'linear' method, which expresses form by means of contour, Wölfflin means expression through mass, tone and colour in which the painter's brushwork and handling are of the greatest importance. Examples of 'painterly' handling may be found among the late works of Titian and in the pictures of Tintoretto, Hals, Rembrandt, Velaquez and Rubens. The painterly manner naturally lends itself far more than the linear to realism.

A. PALAMEDESZ
AFTER-DINNER MUSIC
18¾″ × 29¼″. *The Hague, Mauritshus*

PALAMEDESZ

Anthonie Palamedesz was born in 1601 in Delft and died in 1637 in Amsterdam. His best works were *genre* pieces painted under the influence of Dirk Hals and his circle. He may possibly have worked with Hals after he had finished studying with Mierevelt. He carried to its ultimate conclusion the hackneyed theme, so popular in his day, of guard-rooms and merry-making officers. Some of Palamedesz's pictures have great painterly qualities. His portraits are in the style of Mierevelt, but less harsh in contour and with more of the soft Delft manner.

Palamedes Palamedesz, Anthonie's brother, was born in 1606, supposedly in London, and died in 1638 in Delft at an unfortunately early age. He specialised in battle pieces.

PALMA GIOVANE

Jacopo Palma the Younger (Giovane) was a great nephew of Palma Vecchio and lived at Venice from 1544 to 1628. His pictures are to be found in every large museum where there happens to be room for the not very important followers of the great masters. Palma Giovane's work is an illustration of the way in which the vision of Titian, Tintoretto and Bassano degenerated into a stale mannerism. But Palma Giovane could paint all the same; it was

he who completed Titian's last work, *The Entombment* (Accademia, Venice), which the master had intended for his own monument.

PALMA VECCHIO

Jacopo Negretti Palma, known to posterity as 'Vecchio', was born at Serinalta, near Bergamo, in 1480, came early to Venice and died there in 1528. In the history of art Palma usually figures as a pure Venetian, but in reality he was always a native of Bergamo in alien territory.

The academic dispute as to whether he was a pupil of Giovanni Bellini, whether he was a friend of Titian and Giorgione or whether he lived apart in the colony of aliens is beside the point, for the pictures Palma painted after 1500, when Giorgione appeared on the scene, faithfully reflect all the subsequent developments in Venetian art. The half-length figures and the rather empty religious pictures of his early period give way to bucolic, lyrical compositions, nudes glowing with the warmth of high summer and saints gathered like shepherds of antiquity about Madonnas who grow ever more golden (*Jacob and Rachel* and *The Recumbent Venus*, Dresden, *Adam and Eve*, Brunswick, *The Holy Family*, Philadelphia).

At first sight Palma's portraits often resemble those of Giorgione so closely as to cause confusion, but a closer examination

PALMA VECCHIO
THE ADORATION
OF THE SHEPHERDS
56" × 84". Paris, Louvre

reveals subtle distinctions. Palma builds up his portrait busts on a pyramidal design accentuating the composition by patches of colour, such as white linen or spotted fur, and is at pains to give his personages a particular expression; Giorgione's characters, on the other hand, reveal nothing of themselves but merely look down from a calm, remote distance.

In about 1520, when Titian was painting pictures that were to make him world-famous, Palma approximated his style to that of the master, which for him meant greater vigour and more solidity. This resulted in those blonde, ample women who were like bourgeois sisters of Titian's Virgin of the *Assumption*. These pictures made Palma famous in his lifetime (*The Three Sisters*, Dresden, *Bust of a Young Woman* and *Young Woman in Front of a Hedge*, both Berlin). Even his religious pictures were from now on a glorification of classical, statuesque female beauty.

Palma had no pupils worth mentioning, but exercised great influence on succeeding generations of painters in Venice and Bergamo.

PANEL PICTURES

A panel picture is a painting on wood or metal, as opposed to canvas, pasteboard or paper. Painting on wood is older than on canvas, which was first used towards the end of the fifteenth century. Painters of the late Gothic period liked to purchase framed panels from the carpenter, and in Italy these were often cut in one piece. Apprentices then covered them with a firm layer of chalk, and the master drew his picture on this foundation and applied the colour in several transparent layers as thin as skin. The transparency of the layers of pure colour produced the final effect and explains the incredibly luminous effect of the old method. There was keen competition over the types and selection of wooden panels, and at first canvas was regarded as not likely to be durable enough. Time proved otherwise. The old panels were very susceptible to atmospheric conditions and, by the eighteenth century, a technique had been developed by which the wood

PARMIGIANINO · THE MADONNA WITH THE LONG NECK · *86⅜″ × 52¾″. Florence, Uffizi*

was rubbed away to within a millimetre of the paint and the oil-painted layer itself was then transferred to canvas.

PANNINI

Giovanni Paolo Pannini (born in 1691 at Piacenza, died in Rome in 1765) was trained as an architect before he became a painter. As an architect he has no claim to fame, but as a painter he created a new type of landscape. It was Pannini who first made the ruin motif the principle subject of an independent branch of painting. He had countless followers and imitators. His pupil, Hubert Robert, carried the theme to France and divested it in the process of all trace of the sentimentality and theatricality which cling to some of Pannini's historical and mythoogical ruins. Some of Pannini's religious pictures and splendid church interiors, such as *The Interior of St Peter's* in the London National Gallery, had no success in his own day.

PARMIGIANINO

Francesco Mazzola takes the name by which he is known to art historians from his birthplace, Parma. He was born there in 1503 and died at the age of thirty-seven in Casalmaggiore. Life was not exactly cruel to him, but never allowed him the peace which was essential to the realisation of his plans as a painter and an engraver (Parmigianino was the first important etcher known to history). It is clear from his pictures that he was an intellectual painter with a carefully thought-out theory of aesthetics.

He was trained by insignificant relatives and educated himself further by following the example of Correggio, who came to Parma in 1518. It has never been proved that he was actually Correggio's pupil, though they were both employed in about 1520 on the decoration of S. Giovanni Evangelista. He had been away from Parma for more than a year before that on account of war. In 1523 Parmigianino left his native place yet again and went to

Rome. There he painted his masterly picture of the courtesan Antea (Naples) in which there is surprisingly no trace of Correggio's influence. He has succumbed entirely to the formal discipline of Roman painting. But the head of Antea shows the first indications of a personal style. This is still more marked in the National Gallery *Vision of St Jerome*, upon which the artist was working during the sack of Rome in 1527. Repeated outbreaks of violence, which on one occasion led to his imprisonment, drove him from Rome, and he took refuge in Bologna. His most popular work, *The Madonna with the Rose* (Dresden), dates from this period. Here Parmigianino's style, a purely intellectual creation, is seen in its full maturity. The limbs of the figures are full and rounded, but overlong in proportion, the Madonnas have the refined air of society ladies who from a feeling of obligation submit themselves with a patient and indulgent smile to the gaze of the populace, while their attendants return the look with eagerness and without the slightest embarrassment (*Madonna with the Long Neck*, Uffizi). The classical serenity of Parmigianino's picture is anti-Mannerist; what makes him a Mannerist are his complex, restless diagonal patterns combined with the markedly erotic character of his figures.

PATENIER · LANDSCAPE
WITH THE ASSUMPTION
OF THE VIRGIN
$10\frac{1}{4}'' \times 14\frac{1}{4}''$. *Zurich, Kunsthaus*

From 1531 onwards Parmigianino was again living in Parma. He had become famous and his influence spread through Primaticcio to Fontainebleau. He died at Casalmaggiore in Cremona where he painted *The Madonna with SS. Stephen and John.*

PASTEL

A pastel is a stick of dried paste composed of pigment, chalk, zinc oxide and lime. A pastel picture therefore combines the qualities of both drawing and painting. The velvety, powdery surface of the pastel picture, which is its special quality, made it a peculiarly attractive medium to artists of the late Baroque and Rococo periods, though it was known and used as early as the sixteenth century. Among the most distinguished pastellists were Vivien (1657-1736), Rosalba Carriera (1675-1757), Nattier (1685-1766), Liotard (1702-1789) and Quentin de la Tour (1704-1788).

PATENIER

Joachim de Patenier was born in about 1480 at Bouvignes, near Dinant. We know very little about his life. He was a master in the Antwerp Guild in 1515, was a friend of Quinten Massys and Joos van Cleve and knew Dürer, who mentioned him as a landscape painter. He died not later than 1524 in Antwerp.

Patenier was born at a time when explorers were sailing round the world for the first time. This may have intensified his innate feeling for landscape and have inspired him to paint the first pure landscapes in the history of European art, for the tiny figures which give them their titles are only pretexts. It was a bold step at the time, and though the art of landscape has enormously developed since then, Patenier's work has lost none of its greatness.

For the first time a sense of distance was depicted in landscape. Patenier's landscapes are conceived in quite a different spirit from those of his contemporary, Altdorfer, who sees trees, bushes and hills

in minute detail, but without Patenier's overwhelming apprehension of the vastness of the world. Patenier is an epic rather than a lyric painter. His meadows, cornfields, rivers, rocks, bridges and villages are descriptive rather than poetic. His landscapes are indeed often imaginary, but the details are derived from the most careful observation of fact. Patenier's fantasy only gains the upper hand when he is painting rocky heights.

He was the first painter to grapple with the problem of aerial perspective. He solved it by dividing his picture into three a brown foreground, a green middle distance and a blue background.

In some of his works the subject plays a real part: *The Baptism* (Vienna), *The Rest on the Flight* (Prado), *St Christopher* (Escorial), *The Temptation of St Anthony* with figures by Quinten Massys (Prado). But already in *The Journey to Hell* (Prado) the subject is only a pretext and in *The Assumption of the Virgin* (Kunsthaus Zürich) the minute figure of the Virgin in glory above the little town perched on a rock is hardly noticed. (Ill. p. 233.)

PATER

Jean-Baptiste Pater was born in 1695 in Valenciennes and died in 1736 in Paris. He was a pupil and follower of Watteau, not an imitator like Lancret, for his pictures have their own individual character. The qualities which make Watteau's work so convincing, his brilliant handling of stuffs, the clarity of his outline, the expression of his faces and his fine sense of recession, scarcely exist in Pater's painting, which remains two-dimensional and schematic. In his work we see the final results of that sensitive, lyrical style which is based neither on nature nor on intellect. Yet pictures such as *The Bathers* (Grenoble) and *The Hunting Party* (Munich) are daydreams which never fail to enchant us.

PEALE

Charles Willson Peale, an American painter and naturalist, was born in 1741 in Annapolis. He was apprenticed at first to a addler, then in 1765 he went to Boston and watched Copley at work, and during 1766-69 he was in England, studying with Benjamin West. Returning to Annapolis he set up as a portrait painter. At the outbreak of hostilities he moved to Philadelphia. He became an officer under Washington in the Revolutionary Army and made a great many sketches of military figures. At his best Peale combined the tradition of Copley with a touching sincerity. His *Staircase Group* (Philadelphia), a portrait of his two sons, is one of the best portraits painted by an American. His portrait of Charles Waterton, the naturalist in the National Portrait Gallery, also gives a good idea of Peale's powers. He was not only a painter, but also coachmaker, silversmith, dentist and taxidermist.

PENTIMENTI

The Italian word 'pentimenti' means 'that which is to be regretted'. A curious use has been made of the term in the history of painting. It signifies the traces of older painting or earlier states of a painting that gradually become visible through the picture surface. Posterity is often not particularly pleased to see something emerge which the painter had wished to cover up. But pentimenti are often extremely helpful in solving problems of style and attribution. In some rare cases (and then only from the seventeenth century onwards) painters have been known to make conscious use of pentimenti. Thus an old painting of a nude might provide the basis for the flesh tones of a portrait painted over it.

PERIODICALS

The following are some of the leading periodicals dealing with old master painting; date of foundation and interval of issue are given (M = monthly: Q = quarterly):

Académie royale de Belgique Bulletin (text in Flemish and French), 1915, irreg.
Alte und neue Kunst; Wiener kunstwissenschaftliche Blätter, 1952, Q.
Bolletino d'arte, 1907, Q.
Burlington Magazine, 1903. M.

Gazette des Beaux Arts (text in English and French), 1859, M.
Metropolitan Museum of Art Bulletin, 1942, M.
L'Œil, 1955, M.
Revue des Arts (*Conseil des musées nationaux*), 1951, Q.

PERRONNEAU

Jean-Baptiste Perronneau, who was born in 1715 in Paris and died in 1783 in Amsterdam, was unaccountably neglected in his own life time and quite forgotten in the nineteenth century. This is inexplicable,

J. PERRONNEAU · MADAME DE SORQUAINVILLE
40⅞″ × 32⅜″. Paris, Louvre

for his portraits, both in oil and pastel, have unusual charm and sweetness of colour. The fact that Perronneau was less penetrating than Latour in his delineation of character should have recommended him to the French Rococo. The Court ignored him, he was overlooked by society and only among the bourgeois and fellow artists did he find patrons. His commissions took him to London, Amsterdam, Rome and St Petersburg. Two fine examples of his work are in the London National Gallery.

PERUGINO · THE VISION OF ST BERNARD
(*Detail*) 69¼"×68". *Munich, Alte Pinakothek*

PERSPECTIVE

Perspective is the means by which in a picture the effect of three dimensions is created upon a two dimensional surface. By means of perspective, objects in a painting are made to diminish in size as they recede. In nature we observe that with distance parallel lines appear to converge and horizontal lines assume various angles. By the application of a geometric perspective, it is possible to approximate these relationships so that a drawing appears more or less correct, according to the impression on the eye.

Perpsective in all its complexity plays a most important rôle in the representational art of Europe. The Renaissance painters, above all, devoted themselves to the study of perspective as a science. Alberti, in his

della Pittura, deals at length with the science of vision, and states that a painter must have a thorough knowledge of geometry to set down what he sees. He insists on a given distance and a given position and mentions many times a transparent plane, or screen (*velo*), which, placed between the artist's eye and the conical rays converging upon it from the objects viewed, would make it possible to give those objects their precise position in space. Such a screen was not in Renaissance times always imaginary; an actual transparent, squared screen was often used, especially in dealing with problems of foreshortening. Representations of it occur in the works of Dürer and Holbein, and it must have been responsible for the astonishing precision of Holbein's perspective. Alberti's views influenced the work of Uccello and Francesca, two of the most outstanding of the many Italian painters who devoted themselves with enthusiasm to the creation of the illusion of depth. This enthusiasm is shown in their predilection for architectural vistas. Perspective, as practised by the old masters, has far less significance in contemporary painting, which is no longer concerned with the accurate recording of what the eye sees.

PERUGINO

Pietro di Cristoforo Vannucci, who was known in his lifetime as Perugino and signed himself thus, was born in 1450 at Città delle Pieve, not far from Perugia and died in 1523 at Fontignano. This great Umbrian master was the teacher of Raphael, the decisive influence on generations of artists, the painter of serene, reserved Madonnas and saints, the creator of a world where the legends of Christianity are enshrined in an atmosphere of eternal noonday calm, and yet Vassari (in this case exceptionally reliable) describes him thus: 'Pietro was not a religious man and would never believe in the immortality of the soul, obstinately refusing to listen to all good reasons. He relied entirely upon the good gifts of Fortune and would have gone to any lengths for money.' Berenson calls him a great painter, but a villain. If he were, both his contemporaries and posterity have ignored it; only his fame as a painter has survived.

Perugino was first trained in Perugia, then went to Florence, where he completed his education in the studio of Verrocchio. He may also have worked with Piero della Francesca. By 1475 he was independent and by 1479 he had already been summoned to Rome. Together with Ghirlandaio, Verrocchio and Signorelli, he executed frescoes in the Sistine Chapel. Three of them were later removed to make way for Michelangelo's work. *Christ giving the Keys to Peter* is still well preserved. Its design and its tremendous effects of space inspired Raphael's *Marriage of the Virgin*; the figures in Raphael's picture might be by Perugino, so strong was his influence on the young Raphael.

After he had completed this important commission, Perugino was considered one of the foremost painters in central Italy. He was summoned to Venice, Cremona, Florence, Prato, Panicale and Siena, but he always returned to his native place. His characteristic style is indeed a product of the old Umbrian School. Perugino died of the plague while he was working on a fresco at Fontignano.

'How refreshingly quiet are his Crucifixions and Entombments! The air is soundless, and the people wail no more; a sigh inaudible, a look of yearning, and that is all. How soothing must such paintings have been after the din and turmoil and slaughter of Perugia, the bloodiest town in Italy! Can it be wondered at that men, women and children ran to see them?' (Berenson). The Louvre possesses two of Perugino's most beautiful panel pictures, *Apollo and Marsyas* and *The Conflict of Love and Chastity*, pagan, mythological works reminiscent of Piero di Cosimo. Perugino's best portrait, *Francesco delle Opere*, hangs in the Uffizi, while his altar-piece, *The Virgin and Child with SS. Raphael and Michael*, commissioned in 1496 for the Certosa of Pavia, is in the National Gallery, London.

PESELLINO

Francesco di Stefano Pesellino was born c. 1422 in Florence and died there in 1457. He was one of the most delicate draughtsmen and colourists of the early fifteenth century. If their faces were less aristocratic, his Madonnas might be confused with those of Fra Filippo Lippi, under whom he probably studied. Fra Filippo is full of humanity and Pesellino follows his example in his delineation of the Holy Child, St John and the angels; he even includes Fra Filippo's red noses, but when it comes to the face of the Madonna, he, like Domenico Veneziano, is overcome with longing for the spiritual. In his small compositions, such as the three *predelle* in the Accademia, Florence, he is almost indistinguishable from Veneziano. Pesellino's pictures are rare. The National Gallery, London, owns one example, an altarpiece with *predella* panels by Lippi, painted for the church of the Compagnia della SS. Trinita, Pistoia. There are further a *Pietà* in the Poldi Pezzoli, Milan and the *Miracle of SS. Cosimo and Damiano* and *St Francis* in the Louvre.

PESNE

Antoine Pesne was born in 1683 in Paris and died in 1757 after having been Court Painter to three successive Kings of Prussia. As a young man, Pesne was awarded the Prix de Rome, but Mansard, Curator of the Académie Royale, took a dislike to Pesne's picture and revoked the prize. The artist left France in a dudgeon. He chanced to meet a Herr von Knyphausen, who commissioned a portrait from him. Frederick I saw this picture and summoned Pesne to Berlin. Under Frederick the Great, who often sat to him, Pesne became famous. But he was not only a portrait painter; he was also the author of countless mythological, *genre*, history and religious pictures. There were

PIAZZETTA · A SEASHORE IDYLL
68″ × 58¾″. Cologne, Wallraf Richartz Museum

synthesis of Caravaggio's powerful, earthy naturalism and a strain of pastoral poetry. This quality, together with a straight-forward, often noble, sense of composition and rich colour, was new, and replaced the worn-out conventions of the time with a truly painterly conception. It was to Piazzetta and not to Amigoni that Tiepolo was indebted.

Among important works by Piazzetta may be mentioned *The Ecstasy of St Francis* (Vicenza) and the ceiling painting in the Chapel of S. Domenico in SS. Giovanni e Paolo, Venice. Piazzetta worked slowly and with difficulty, and this was probably the reason he died poor.

so few painters of any significance at that time in Germany that it was not difficult for an artist who had grown up with the work of Largillières, Desportes and Rigaud to make his mark. Pesne was a source of inspiration to the whole succeeding generation of German painters. His painting is pure Rococo. If it has a slightly Prussian flavour, that is due to his sitters rather than to him.

PIAZZETTA

Giambattista Piazzetta (1682-1754), who lived and died in Venice, is one of the principal masters of eighteenth-century Venetian painting. He was not a painter of townscapes in the manner of Canaletto or Guardi, but encouraged painting in the direction of Tiepolo. The two paintings which show Piazzetta's style at its best are *The Soothsayer* (Venice) and the *Seashore Idyll* (Cologne). This style is a pleasing

PICKENOY

Nicolas Eliasz Pickenoy of Amsterdam (1591-1655) has only been esteemed at his true value since the turn of the century. For many years his pictures were attributed to others, in particular to Thomas de Keyser, which perhaps did him too much honour. He was a solid, technically able painter whose aim was to free the portrait and the group portrait (in which he specialised) from the feeble colour and stiff drawing which had characterised Dutch portraiture since it had succumbed to the influence of pseudo-classical Mannerism. Pickenoy surpasses Ravesteyn and Cornelis van der Voort, who was probably his teacher. The art of Van Helst, the rival of Rembrandt, represents a further development of the style of Voort and Pickenoy.

PILO

Carl Gustaf Pilo (1711-1793) was a Swedish painter born at Nykoling. He studied at the Stockholm Academy and lived in Denmark from 1740-1772, where he was Court Painter and Director of the Danish Academy. From 1772 onwards Pilo was in Sweden and became Director of the Stockholm Academy in 1777. Pilo was important among eighteenth-century Swedish painters in that unlike them he never travelled to France. He thus evolved a personal style free from French influence.

hough not exclusively a portrait painter, is best work was done in this field; he avoured theatrical but soft effects of light nd greenish flesh tones. Pilo's masterpiece s a great unfinished canvas in the National Museum of Stockholm, *The Coronation of Gustavus II.*

PINTURICCHIO

Bernardino Pinturicchio was born in 1454, probably in Perugia, and died in 1513 in Siena; he was therefore a native of the same town as his contemporary Perugino, a somewhat surprising fact in face of his pictures. They appear to have been painted at least fifty years earlier, the drawing is sometimes laboured and Pinturicchio does not scorn the use of gold ornament. His pictures are not contemplative like those of Perugino; they are diffusive narrative pieces; his famous Piccolomini frescoes in the Library at Siena with their hard, spiky outlines and bright colours are magnified book illustrations; and his faces have nothing in common with the thoughtful countenances of Perugino. His slender, aloof young girls, men and boys cast careless sidelong glances or look unreflectingly straight into our eyes. Pinturicchio's works, both his frescoes and panel pictures are refined and polished, more elegant and more lively than Perugino's gentle, subdued pictures. Yet they do not rank with them, as even Pinturicchio's contemporaries realised when they referred to him as 'the next after Pietro'.

Pinturicchio lived chiefly in Perugia, but executed a large number of commissions in Rome (Sistine Chapel, Aracoeli, apartments in the Pope's palace, for which he was rewarded with two farms), Orvieto and Siena. He maintained a large workshop. Towards the end of his life he suffered from very poor health; he was probably never of a robust constitution, for he was almost a dwarf.

PIOMBO

Sebastiano del Piombo was born in Venice in 1485 and died in 1547 in Rome. He came of the family of de' Luciani and only took the name Piombo (seal) in 1531 when the Pope appointed him Frate del Piombo.

Piombo once signed himself as a pupil of Bellini, but it is now established that Cima and not the greater Bellini was his master. Piombo's false description of himself is in keeping with the character revealed in many of the letters he wrote and which have been preserved. He seems to have been vain, calculating, malicious, revengeful, suspicious and utterly egocentric. The only friend whom he never exploited or deceived was Giorgione. After Giorgione's death in 1510 Piombo completed his unfinished picture, *The*

SEBASTIANO DEL PIOMBO · DETAIL FROM ST JOHN CHRYSOSTOM ENTHRONED AND OTHER SAINTS · *80″ × 66″. Venice, S. Giovanni Crisostomo*

Three Philosophers (Venice). He not only did the work extremely well, but he never once bragged about it. He was already by this time a brilliant painter in the Giorgionesque manner, foreshadowing the later Titian in his colouring, as in his noble *Portrait of a Roman Lady* in Berlin. This was clearly one of the first works he painted in Rome, where he settled in 1511 at the invitation of the banker, Agostino Chigi. Piombo met Raphael in Rome, and the impact of this meeting is reflected in Piombo's adaptations of the colour range of such of Raphael's compositions as *The Mass at Bolsena*. He painted a number of pictures in Raphael's manner, including *Cardinal Carondelet*, *The Violin Player* (private collection, Paris), *Portrait of a Lady* (Barcelona) and the *Fornarina* (Uffizi), which for many years was actually ascribed to Raphael. But Piombo's admiration for Raphael changed to hatred and contempt when he met Michelangelo.

PISANELLO · A PRINCESS OF THE HOUSE OF ESTE · 16⅞" × 11¾". *Paris, Louvre*

From that moment Michelangelo was the dominant influence in his work, though Piombo never slavishly imitated him. He even used to criticise sketches and drawings which he begged from Michelangelo, often sending them back to Florence after having corrected the composition. Piombo's drawings are sometimes almost indistinguishable from those of Michelangelo; his great work in the London National Gallery, *The Raising of Lazarus*, combines Michelangelo's nobility and sense of design with the romantic quality of Venetian painting. During his last years Piombo produced a number of austere masterpieces, which include the *Pietà* in Viterbo, the *Portrait of Andrea Doria* (Rome), the *Head of Clement VI.* (Naples) and *Christ in Limbo* (Madrid).

In 1534 Piombo's friendship with Michelangelo came to an end and the great master became, like Raphael, Cellini and Giovanni da Udine before him, the object of the painter's hatred. But Piombo did not go unpunished. He became ever more solitary, the commissions from the Vatican which he so greatly prized, fell off, and his creative powers rapidly declined.

PISANELLO

Antonio di Puccio, called Pisanello, was born in 1395 at Pisa and died in 1455 in Rome or Naples. His mother came from Verona, and returned there when her son was still a small child, so Pisanello was educated in Verona and was taught to paint in the manner of Altichiero, who had died in the year of his birth. While still a student, Pisanello visited Venice. It was at the time when Gentile da Fabriano was creating a stir there, and the young student must have come into contact with him. As a painter, Pisanello's fame is exceeded by that of Gentile da Fabriano, yet it is clear that he had the makings of a very great artist. He chose, however, to become a medallist instead of a painter, and left only two portraits (Louvre and Bergamo) two religious panels (London) and two frescoes (Verona). The outstanding characteristics of these works are nobility of feeling, exquisite delicacy of drawing and olour and, above all, an unusual elicity in the rendering of natural detail. 'He painted birds as only he Japanese have painted them', writes Berenson.

PITTONI

Giovanni Battista Pittoni (1687-767) was one of the most charming of the Venetian eighteenth-century painters. The influences which went to the creation of his fluent style are obvious at a glance: Ricci, Piazzetta and, above all, Tiepolo. Pittori is less robust than these masters and his slap-dash technique is probably not so much an expression of tempera-ment as a fashionable mannerism. But his religious and mythological pictures are extremely elegant and, especially the smaller works, very tasteful. Carlo Carlone (1686-775) worked in a similar style in Como.

PLEYDENWURFF

Hans Pleydenwurff, who was probably a native of Bamberg, settled in Nuremberg during the mid-fifteenth century. He was given the freedom of the city in 457 and died there in 1472. Until the advent of Dürer, Pleydenwurff was the most important painter in Nuremberg, and a powerful source of fresh inspiration. A great gulf separates a stiff, devotional picture like the 'Tuch altarpiece' (by an unknown master) and a work such as Pleydenwurff's *Portrait of Count Löwenstein*, painted at exactly the same time. This sensitive interpretation of the over-refined features of a highly-strung old man ranks as one of the most astonishing achievements of the period (Nuremberg, Germanisches Museum).

Pleydenwurff's great altarpieces, the last and most beautiful of which is the Munich *Crucifixion*, show that he must

H. PLEYDENWURFF · THE CRUCIFIXION
(Detail) 11¾″ × 17″. Munich, Alte Pinakothek

have been subjected during his formative years to the influence of Rogier van der Weyden. His distant landscape backgrounds, his love of sumptuous materials and his unfaltering sense of composition all derive from Flemish example, and his figures and faces resemble those of Van der Weyden. It was Pleydenwurff who took the Flemish style to Nuremberg.

POELENBURG

Cornelis van Poelenburg of Utrecht (c. 1586-1667) was by no means considered a genius by his contemporaries, but he was very popular. People were fond of his gentle, indeterminate little landscapes, such as *The Cascades at Tivoli* (Munich) and of his mythological scenes, which showed groups of charming, porcelain-like nudes (usually sitting at the bottom of the picture, almost perching on the frame) gathered about the figure of Diana or Amaryllis in a dreamy landscape. Even his

biblical scenes, such as *The Rest on the Flight* (Dresden) are composed in the same manner. His portraits are just as agreeable but quite empty. Poelenburg was very successful. He was employed for a time as Court Painter in Florence and also in London. When Rubens paid a visit to Utrecht in 1627, he called on Poelenburg as a matter of course. Poelenburg's pupils, Vertangen, Cuylenburg, Haensbergen and Lisse, followed him closely enough to give trouble to modern collectors of his work.

POLACK

Polack went to Germany from Poland, hence his name. He is mentioned for the first time in the Munich records of 1482.

A. POLLAIUOLO · DAVID
18¾″ × 13⅝″. Berlin, Staatl. Museen

He was a very industrious painter, never refused a commission, even if it was only to whitewash a wall, produced a great deal of work, and when he died in Munich in 1519 his reputation was high, especially for his frescoes. He was probably sixty to sixty-five years of age at the time of his death.

A number of panel pictures are known to be by Polack's hand. Among the most beautiful are the fully documented *Holy Altarpiece of St Stephen*, the parts of which are divided between Nuremberg, Freising and Munich, the *Blutenburg Altarpiece*, the *St Peter Altarpiece* (National Museum, Munich) and *The Madonna* (Schliersee). In spirit Polack is entirely Gothic; he favours strange faces, often distorted with passion and expressive of a naïve acquiescence in the joys and terrors of Christian legend.

POLIDORO DA CARAVAGGIO

Polidoro (c. 1495-1543) entered Raphael's studio in 1512 and worked on the Vatican frescoes. He left Rome after the city was sacked by the Germans in 1527 and moved first to Naples and later to Messina where he met his death by murder.

Polidoro's principal works were the monochrome façade frescoes representing scenes from the works of Livy with which he decorated the exteriors of many Roman houses. It was largely on account of Polidoro's influence that this kind of work became popular in Austria and Germany in the latter half of the sixteenth century. To-day most of Polidoro's exterior paintings have disappeared, and we can only form a vague idea of their style from decorative interior frescoes. In this he shows himself to have been one of the originators of the classical landscape. Both Claude and Poussin admired his work. A fine example of it is the *Landscape with the Legend of the Magdalen* at S. Silvestro, Rome.

POLLAIUOLO

The brothers Antonio and Piero Pollaiuolo were both painters, sculptors, engravers and goldsmiths They were two of the most fascinating personages of the Renaissance, and Antonio in particular was a most important painter, for his work links that of his great teacher, Castagno, directly with that of Verrocchio and Botticelli. Without Antonio the whole edifice of Florentine painting would collapse.

PONTORMO · THE SUPPER AT EMMAUS
92″ × 70″. Florence, Uffizi

Antonio, the son of a goldsmith, was born in 1433 in Florence, and died in Rome in 1498. He was therefore living just at the time when the first wave of burning interest in the newly discovered sciences of perspective, volume and anatomy was beginning to subside, when the intense zest for life of the early Renaissance was beginning to yield to a gentle scepticism and there was a general tendency to dwell on the past and to humanise classical mythology and reconcile it with the every-day reality of the present. Antonio's *Apollo and Daphne* (National Gallery, London), painted c. 1475, was in perfect tune with the spirit of the times and was an immediate success. The drawing in this little picture is powerful but sensitive, the expression on the faces is slightly ironical, and the miracle by which Daphne is turning into a laurel is made to look like an optical illusion. The rhythm and swiftness of Apollo's pursuit are conveyed with irresistable verve and the two branches of the tree look like the wings of some dark angel in the embrace of an impetuous Florentine youth. Antonio's contemporaries were impressed by his handling of the theme and by its symbolism. Antonio's drawing and predilection for violent movement (*David*, Berlin; *The Rape of Deianeira*, New Haven, U.S.A.) were inspired by Castagno's example. Pollaiuolo tackled one of the most difficult of painter's problems, the representation of the naked male in action, and

243

succeeded so well that he enlarged the field of painting for all his successors (the two Hercules panels in the Uffizi and *The Martyrdom of St Sebastian*, National Gallery, London). His landscape backgrounds are among the first realistic interpretations of nature in the history of European painting.

The part Antonio's brother **Piero** took in his paintings, designs for tapestries, frescoes and sculptures cannot always be clearly defined. Piero Pollaiuolo was born in Florence c. 1441 and died in Rome in 1496. His chief work is *The Coronation of the Virgin* in the Duomo of San Gimignano. His pictures are less spirited than those of his brother. He was probably a gentler and more sensitive person. Some of the portraits of girls which are ascribed to him (New York and Berlin) are as graceful as those of Domenico Veneziano.

PONTORMO

Jacopo Carrucci, who like so many Italian painters of the Renaissance took the name of his birthplace and made it famous, was the son of a painter whose works are unknown, or rather unrecognised, for they are among the pictures produced in Ghirlandaio's workshop, where he was employed. Pontormo thus grew up surrounded by good painting. He was born in 1494 and died in 1557 in Florence. He was apprenticed at a very tender age, not to his father, who was already dead, but to Leonardo, then to Albertinelli, afterwards to Piero di Cosimo and finally to Andrea del Sarto. Vasari is the source for this list of distinguished names and, as he did not greatly care for Pontormo, the information is probably correct. But Pontormo only studied seriously and for any length of time under Del Sarto, who at first completely dominated him, though by 1514 he was already aware that Pontormo had something quite new to offer. Soon after that date he painted the *Santa Conversazione* (Or San Michele, Florence) of which Venturi says: 'With this picture a young painter, only twenty-four years of age, ill at ease in the moral and intellectual climate of his age, changed the whole aspect of the Renaissance.'

If art historians had not already given a name to the movement inaugurated by Pontormo we might be tempted to call it 'expressionism'. His style derived from Michelangelo's frescoes in the Sistine Chapel, but he entirely eschews naturalism and uses colour to further aims which can only be called expressionist. The writhing tortuous figures in one of his principal works, *The Entombment* (Cappella Capponi, Florence), look like ghosts whose frozen gestures are illumined by magnesium flares. It is a pity that Pontormo is officially labelled a Mannerist, for he was far from being just another of the later spiritless imitators of Michelangelo.

Voss calls Pontormo the last important representative of the Florentine Renaissance, while Berenson describes him as 'an academic constructor of monstrous nudes' referring to a composition which is indeed rather feeble, the *Martyrdom of Forty Saints* (Pitti, Florence). Pontormo was an admirable portraitist, and in this field his influence is reflected in the work of his pupil, Bronzino. Through Rosso Fiorentino, Pontormo's Mannerism spread to Fontainebleau. Pontormo's character was not very aimable: he was eccentric and a misanthrope. (Ill. p. 243.)

PORDENONE

Giovanni Antonio de Sachis was named Pordenone after the little town in the north-eastern corner of Italy where he was born. At one point it seemed as if Pordenone might rank higher than the young Titian in popular esteem. When he went to Rome in 1515 his provincial training was still apparent in such works as *The Madonna Enthroned* (Venice), but Raphael and Michelangelo (whose frescoes in the dome of the Cathedral at Treviso he later copied) opened his eyes to recent developments in painting. Pordenone was quick to absorb these new trends, and when he returned to Venice his pictures were characterised by the movement and the sweeping gestures of the Baroque. This was the moment when Pordenone was held to be a serious rival of Titian. But he soon succumbed to the influence of the greater master. This influence does not appear

so much in Pordenone's frescoes as in the deep colour and crowded compositions of his other pictures.

Pordenone was born in 1484 and died in 1539, shortly after he had left Venice for the court of Ferrara. His death was attended by mysterious circumstances which have never been satisfactorily explained. Four years previously Pordenone had been knighted by the King of Hungary. His works include frescoes in the Duomo, Cremona and at Pordenone, *Portrait of a Lady*, *Madonna of Carmel*, *St Lorenzo Giustiniani and Three Other Saints* (Academy, Venice) and *The Annunciation* (S. Maria degli Angeli, Murano).

POST

In his choice of subject, Frans Post was one of the most eccentric of the Dutch painters. He was born in 1612 at Leyden and died at Haarlem in 1680. The great experience of his life was a seven-year journey through South America in the train of the Prince of Nassau. When he returned to Holland in 1644 Post found that besides describing the sights he had seen he could also make paintings of them, and that these paintings found a ready market. With few exceptions, he went on painting Brazilian landscapes for the rest of his life. They are not specially informative as topographical works, but these pictures of half-naked, strange little figures running about between exotic trees have a naïve charm. They make rather the same impression as the pictures on the lids of cigar boxes. Post is represented in the Mauritzhus.

POT

Hendrick Gerrit Pot (1585-1657) was born in Haarlem and worked there and at Amsterdam. He is said to have worked with Frans Hals in the studio of Van Mander, and some of his pictures, such as the Civic Group at Haarlem, show affinities with Hals. But Pot's most characteristic canvases, scenes of merrymaking, resemble Rubens rather than Hals in style and colouring. Pot's picture of *The Apotheosis of William the Silent* at Haarlem certainly shows the influence of Rubens. Pot came to England and painted the portrait group of Charles I, Henrietta Maria and the Prince of Wales now at Buckingham Palace, a curious composition in which the centre of the picture is occupied by a large table.

POTTER

Paulus Potter, the important Dutch

animal painter, came of a family of painters and received his first lessons from his father. **Pieter** Potter, who was born c. 1597 at Enkhuizen and died in 1652, in Amsterdam, was a humble painter of *genre* pictures and landscape and could not teach his gifted son more than the rudiments of his art. Paulus Potter, who was the first to raise animal painting to the level of great art, probably owed more to himself than to any teacher. He must have made endless studies of animals. Yet it was not this alone that made him a great animal painter. The powerful effect of his pictures is due to the fact that he did not see and paint animals in isolation, but conveyed their special atmosphere and environment more faithfully than any other painter before Stubbs. There is a picture in Berlin in which a bull is walking up a slope, almost silhouetted against the sky. It is a small canvas, not more than $8\frac{1}{4}$ by $11\frac{5}{8}$ inches, but the impact it makes can only be described as gigantic. Potter never faltered in either drawing or colouring. At one period he painted in tones of brown and gold and at other times he reproduced local colour. He had great influence on Adriaen van de Velde, a more poetic painter. Paulus Potter was born in 1625 at Enkhuizen and died in 1654 in Amsterdam at the early age of twenty-nine.

POURBUS

Three generations of painters of this name made a reputation as portraitists. Pieter Pourbus (born in 1510 at Gouda, died in 1584 in Bruges), his son, Frans Pourbus the Elder (born in 1545 in Bruges, died in 1581 in Amsterdam), and his son, Frans Pourbus the Younger (born in 1569 in Antwerp, died in 1622 in Paris). **Pieter's** unostentatious portraits of citizens of Bruges, painted in restrained tones of black, grey and dull green, are straightforward, austerely conceived faithful likenesses in the best Flemish tradition. In his historical and religious compositions he shows himself to be a sober Mannerist.

Frans the Elder was a pupil of Floris, which was not altogether to his advantage. His many religious pictures are rather coarsely painted. But his portraits, infinitely more up-to-date than those of his father, are reminiscent of Adriaen Key in their charm and serenity.

Frans tho Younger was a more cosmopolitan painter. He went to Italy, was Court Painter in Mantua from 1600 until 1609, and afterwards became Court Painter in Paris to the Queen Mother Maria de' Medici, who was also the patroness of Rubens. Pourbus' portraits show many influences, particularly Spanish, and vary considerably in quality.

N. POUSSIN
APOLLO AND DAPHNE
$38\frac{3}{4}'' \times 52\frac{3}{4}''$. *Munich,*
Alte Pinakothek

He had a predilection for life-size figures, which during his Italian period had great individuality, but later degenerated into stiff, polite family portraits.

POUSSIN

Nicolas Poussin was born of peasant parents in Normandy in 1594. His interest in painting was first aroused by Varin in 1611. The following year he went to Paris and there he worked with Ferdinand Elle, Philippe de Champaigne and perhaps Lallemant and studied the royal collection of antique sculpture and engravings after Raphael and Giulio Romano. These engravings had great influence on the young painter, and when he left Paris for Rome in 1624 his style was full of Mannerist tricks and motifs taken from these authorities. In order to obtain the means of getting to Rome, Poussin had assisted Duchesne with decorations in the Luxembourg and had painted a group of pictures for the Jesuits.

When he reached Rome, Poussin immersed himself in the study of classical antiquities, studied anatomy and perspective and worked in the studio of Domenichino, whom he considered the first master in Rome. At the end of the twenties he began to concentrate on relatively small pictures for private patrons, taking his subjects from Roman mythology and basing his style on that of Titian. In 1630 he was commissioned through the help of Cardinal Barberini to paint the *Death of Germanicus* and *The Capture of Jerusalem* and he began to use colder colour and clearer modelling, emulating Roman sculpture and the late Raphael. At this time he painted a number of biblical subjects. From 1640 to 1642 Poussin was again in Paris at the request of Louis XIII, who wished him to decorate the Long Gallery of the Louvre. This was an unhappy period, owing to the antagonism of established artists in Paris. Poussin never again returned to France, though by now he had a group of devoted French patrons, to whom he sent works which were even then regarded as his most perfect, the embodiment of French classicism, characterised by monumental calm and mathematical clarity. Poussin died in Rome in 1665 and was buried in the church of San Lorenzo in Lucina.

The intellectual content of Poussin's pictures has often been stressed, and indeed it cannot be exaggerated. Every detail of his great compositions was the result of profound thought. He gave logical form even to the disorder of natural scenery, thus imposing upon landscape an air of order and permanence. He achieved this by means of an harmonious balance between the horizontal and vertical elements of the design. There are forty paintings by Poussin in the Louvre, and there are several magnificent examples in the National Gallery, including the *Bacchanalian Revel, The Adoration of the Golden Calf* and *Landscape with a Snake*. One of his finest works, *The Gathering of the Ashes of Phocion* is in the collection of Lord Derby at Knowsley Hall.

PRADO

The Spanish National Gallery in Madrid, the Museo del Prado, completed in 1785,

PREDIS · GIRL WITH CHERRIES
15⅞″ × 16¼″. *New York, Metropolitan Museum*

was built over a period of thirty years on the site of a little park which had always been known as the 'Prado'. The new and imposing building housed all the treasures which the Spanish and Habsburg rulers of Spain had amassed in the course of many centuries. The paintings from these royal collections form the most important part of the contents of the Prado. The gallery is particularly rich in the works of Titian, the Flemish masters and, of course, the Spanish painters, Velazquez, Goya, Murillo and El Greco.

PREDELLE

Predelle or *predella* panels are the small pictures which often decorate the base of a winged altarpiece (for illustrations, see *Angelico*). When the simple altarpiece was embellished with wings, it became necessary to raise it up on a base so that the wings could be freely opened and closed. Painters made use of this base to introduce small compositions bearing on the main theme of the altarpiece. Thus the *predelle* of a Crucifixion often show an Entombment. When systematic collecting became common during the Renaissance many altarpieces were dismembered and the small predella panels were disposed of as individual pictures.

PREDIS

Ambrogio de Predis was born in Milan in 1455, where he probably died. The year of his death is not known, but he was still alive in 1509 when he received part payment for some tapestry designs he had delivered to the Emperor Maximilian in 1500.

Predis began his career together with his elder brother **Cristoforo** (died in 1486) as a medallist and miniaturist, and in 1482 he became Court Painter to the Sforza. While Leonardo was in Milan, Predis shared his studio. He assisted Leonardo with his commissions and when copies of pictures were ordered Predis did most of the work on them. The National Gallery version of *The Virgin of the Rocks* is partly by his hand.

Predis also produced some excellent works of his own which, despite their stylistic dependence on Leonardo, have a personal charm. His *Girl with Cherries* (New York) could not have been painted without knowledge of Leonardo, yet it could not possibly be taken for a Leonardo. The girl's expression is vigilant and rather affected, and the picture has a slight undertone of mockery and eroticism; there is little interest in chiaroscuro. Other good pictures by Predis include *Bianca Maria Sforza* (Philadelphia), *Anna Sforza* (Milan), perhaps painted in conjunction with Leonardo, and *Francesco Brivio* (Milan). (Ill. p. 247.)

PREVITALI

Andrea Cordelliaghi Previtali, who was born in Bergamo in 1480 and died there in 1528, was a Venetian in spirit. He was a pupil of Giovanni Bellini, but was more strongly influenced by Cima. His pictures have much in common with those of the latter, though his colour scheme is brighter, with passages of pink, violet and wine-red, the feeling less memorable and the composition less well organised. His landscapes never equal those of Cima. Previtali belongs to the group of Bellini's followers which included Basaiti, Bissolo, Iganatis and Girolamo da Santa Croce.

PRIMATICCIO

Francesco Primaticcio was born in Bologna in 1504 and died in Paris in 1570. He worked for many years with Giulio Romano in Mantua and his style is a synthesis of Giulio's conception of the linear beauty of antique sculpture and the softness of Correggio. If he had remained in Italy, Primaticcio would never have been so highly esteemed as he was in France after Francois I summoned him to Paris in 1532. After the death of Rosso Fiorentino, the Italians who were working at Fontainebleau fell completely under the influence of Primaticcio. He originated the style of a whole school. He painted chiefly murals at Fontainebleau. Easel pictures by him are to be seen in the museums of Bologna, to which city he several times returned, and Florence. Primaticcio also executed a few sculptures.

PROVENENCE

The provenence of a picture, which is one of the aids to establishing its authenticity, consists of bills or receipts given by the artist, published descriptions in documents or journals of the period, engravings of works made during or shortly after the painter's lifetime, the succession of collections to which the picture has belonged and the important exhibitions in which it has appeared.

PROVOST

Jan Provost or Prevost was born c. 1465 at Mons and died in 1529 at Bruges. Provost came to Bruges in 1494, the year of Memling's death. Artistically the town was already stagnating; Gerard David, who was about the same age as Provost, was still painting, but his work was so conservative that the newcomer's appearance had the effect of a tornado on the town, though he was far from revolutionary. Provost's religious paintings express the spirit of a transitional period, though his composition is less laboured than that of other masters of the time; there is even a strain of light-heartedness to be discerned in the brightness of his colour, in the slight eroticism of the nudes in his various *Last Judgments* (of which the only authenticated example is at Bruges) and in the good-humoured irony of his caricatures of patriarchs and matrons. Provost was a very able painter, but, like so many others of that period, he lacked drive. His pictures are rare. When Dürer visited Antwerp in 1521, Provost happened to be there, and much to his satisfaction he persuaded the celebrated German painter to accompany him to Bruges. Dürer painted the portrait of the fashionable Provost and that of his third wife.

PRUD'HON

Pierre Prud'hon (1758-1823) was born at

J. PROVOST · THE NATIVITY
24¾″ × 21″. Geneva, Private Collection

Cluny and was educated by the monks of the Abbey of Cluny. In 1774 he was sent to the Academy at Dijon; he went to Paris in 1780, and two years later won a prize which took him to Rome. There he studied Raphael, Correggio and Leonardo and formed a friendship with Canova. He returned to Paris in 1789 and earned his living as a portrait painter. At the turn of the century he was given apartments in the Louvre, commissioned to decorate public buildings and elected a member of the Institute. He is widely known for his pale, sensuous nudes. Typical pictures are *The Rape of Psyche* and *Crime pursued by Justice and Divine Wrath* in the Louvre and *Venus and Adonis* in the Wallace Collection, London.

PYNACKER

Adam Pynacker, who was born in Delft in 1622 and died in Amsterdam in 1673, appears to have been a pupil of Both. It is clear that he himself also visited Italy. His landscapes consist of romantic ruins reflected with a cloudless sky in limpid water or distant views of classical temples seen through the sharply defined trunks of trees. Though, like all painters of the picturesque, Pynacker borrowed motifs from other artists, he had genuine feeling for architecture. Two of his best works are in the Wallace Collection, London.

Q

QUAST

Pieter Quast, who was born in 1606 in Amsterdam and died there in 1647, painted numbers of pictures of brawling, tippling peasants in the style of Adriaen Brouwer, yet without ever capturing Brouwer's spirit. But he was also the author of one or two extremely beautiful and tranquil *genre* pictures which might be mistaken for the work of Ostade, lightly brushed-in peasant interiors, brown in tone, with subtle effects of chiaroscuro. His pictures of guardrooms, in which he aped the style of the painters who followed Dirk Hals, are rarely successful.

QUELLINUS

Erasmus Quellinus, who was born in Antwerp in 1607 and died there in 1678, was a pupil of Rubens, popular in his own day for his decorations for festivals and state receptions. His pictures at once reveal the source of the painter's inspiration, but they lack Rubens' powerful vitality and look like the work of a pupil. Yet Quellinus has a striking gift for large-scale composition. His pictures derive their stability and compactness from his abundant use of deep shadows. After Rubens' death Quellinus was made official painter of the city of Antwerp.

The cartouches in the flower garlands of D. Seghers were often painted by Quellinus.

QUERFURT

August Querfurt was born in 1696 at Wolfenbüttel and died in 1761 in Vienna. In addition to a few portraits and *genre* pictures, he painted mostly battlepieces, in the art of which he had been instructed by his father, **Tobias,** who, according to his signature, was Court Painter at Brunswick. Querfurt's second teacher, Georg Rugendas of Augsburg (1666-1742), also painted battlepieces, for such pictures were certain of a good reception among the German petty princes of the day. All these painters stemmed from Wouwerman. Some of Querfurt's small pictures of battles and horses are very painterly.

RAEBURN

Sir Henry Raeburn (1756-1823), Scotland's foremost portrait painter, was the son of a prosperous Border millowner. He was apprenticed at the age of fifteen to a goldsmith. Raeburn soon afterwards tried his hand at miniatures and finally at oil painting, receiving encouragement from David Martin (1736-1798), a fashion-

RAEBURN · THE REV. WALKER SKATING
29¼″ × 14¼″. *Edinburgh, National Gallery*

able Scottish portrait painter. In 1778 he married the Scottish-born widow of a wealthy Frenchman, Count Leslie. In 1785 Raeburn visited London, where he met Reynolds, who advised him to go to Italy and gave him introductions to painters in Rome. Raeburn worked in Rome from 1785 to 1787, but his work shows no trace of Italian influence. On his return he built himself a house in Edinburgh which is still known as 'Raeburn's House' and settled down to record the features of all who were distinguished in the Scottish society of the day. Raeburn occasionally exhibited at the Royal Academy, of which he was elected to full membership. He was knighted in 1822 when George IV visited Edinburgh. All Raeburn's finest portraits are in the National Gallery of Scotland. They come as a revelation to those who only know the few examples in the south. They are conspicuous for their vigorous modelling, robust colour and understanding of character. Raeburn made no preliminary sketches, but painted straight on to the canvas.

RAMSAY

Allan Ramsay (1713-1784) was the son of Allan Ramsay, the author of *The Gentle Shepherd*. In 1724 he went for two years to Rome, where he worked at the French School. His style was influenced by that of Quentin de la Tour. Ramsay returned to his native city, but in 1756 he settled in London, where he was very successful, excelling as a painter of women. Ramsay's best work is in private collections, and it is only recently that his fine qualities have been appreciated. He is outstanding for his unusual palette, in which pink, vermilion and indigo are prominent, and for his sense of pattern. Dr Johnson praised Ramsay's charm and intelligence.

RAPHAEL

Raphael Santi (born in 1483 in Urbino, died in Rome in 1520) was the son of **Giovanni** Santi, a painter of repute at the Court of the Montefeltri. Although Raphael died young, it is a misrepresentation to describe him as a 'youth of infinite 'promise': he had developed to full maturity. The blind adoration of the nineteenth century did him a disservice by idolising him to the extent of investing him with a halo. He was not a radiant young god, but a man completely and unobtrusively average with a grace and felicity not typical of the Renaissance. 'Raphael's brush', so often quoted as a 'mystery' in story and poem, was not a magic wand, but the tool in his hand that often drove him to overwork and exhaustion. He certainly was not 'the greatest', but, equally certainly, he was one of the truly great.

He received his main training under Perugino in Perugia. Characteristics of this important Umbrian painter can be seen even in Raphael's later work: in his early paintings they are very conspicuous. In these, similar female figures appear with the full, rather formalised faces, narrow mouths and pronounced lower lips. They are placed, just as Perugino placed them, almost floating in the pellucid landscape: or, again, St Georges charge cast-iron dragons on steeds of large dimensions that derive something from the Gothic Multscher, and lances are broken in red-and-white striped lists (*St George*, Louvre). The characteristics which are peculiar to Raphael are less easily detectable, but lie mainly in the absence of Perugino's warm, brownish tints. Raphael had begun his quest for his own personal colour, clear as early morning light, and simplified planes.

At the end of 1504 he moved to Florence. There he came in contact with Leonardo and immediately surrendered to his preoccupation with chiaroscuro. This influence is startlingly apparent in the *Madonna del Granduca* (Florence), one of Raphael's early masterpieces. After he had controlled the first tumult of confused feeling, both drawing and colour were clarified again, with a heightened loveliness and grace. Masterpieces appeared, such as the *Madonna as Beautiful Gardener* (Louvre), the *Tempi Madonna* (Munich), the *Madonna with the Goldfinch* (Uffizi), and, for a second time, a *St George* (National Gallery of Art, Washington), which shows that Raphael still remained a boy at heart. A mood of boyish exaltation is in the picture, and the landscape is exquisitely 'free from dust'. The impression of festivity, the luminous atmosphere, the purity of his phantasy will appeal to every heart and eye. Correctly perceived and understood, the intense simplification of form reveals his deliberate, uneasy striving after the monumental.

In 1509 Raphael, already eminent in his profession, went to Rome. There he created his world-famous frescoes in the Vatican, among others *Parnassus*, *The Dispute*, *The School of Athens* and the *Heliodorus* series. It goes without saying that he had minutely studied Michel-

RAPHAEL · POPE LEO X WITH TWO CARDINALS
61¼" × 47⅜". *Florence, Uffizi*

RAPHAEL · THE MADONNA DEL GRANDUCA
33⅞″ × 22⅞″. Florence, Pitti

angelo's frescoes in the Sistine Chapel, but they no longer overwhelm him. This too was the period of his friendship with Sebastiano Piombo, and it is noticeable to what a large extent he adopted the Venetian colouring: in the night setting of *The Liberation of St Peter* he is more romantic than the dreamiest Venetian.

In the Vatican rooms painted with his frescoes, Raphael created the marvel of illusion, though not in the sense of 'deception' as in Baroque art. His interpretation of the antique ranks as a final verdict from which there is no appeal. Also for the first time his religious themes show a splendour purged of all fear and satanic evil.

Besides other frescoes and pictures, such as the lovely *Madonna with the Fish* (Madrid) and the majestic *Sistine Madonna* (Dresden), his portraits are notably out-

standing. These glorious, masterly portraits of individuals and of groups show Raphael at his best, and amazingly they reveal the 'eternal youth' as a keen, penetrating observer.

At the end of March, 1520, Raphael fell ill: he died of fever in a few days. He was buried with every honour and pomp in the Pantheon at Rome.

RAVESTEYN

Jan Antonisz Ravesteyn (1572-1657 at The Hague) is the best-known of that essentially Dutch name. Jan painted portraits, but nothing else is known about his life as an artist. His pictures show some similarity to those of the more important Mierevelt, a contemporary who lived in Delft, though they are more reminiscent of Cornelius van der Voort (1576-1624), who worked first in Antwerp, then in Amsterdam. Ravestenyn's portraits of which there are a great many at The Hague, are smooth and sober. In 1618 he painted groups of The Hague Civic Guards.

REDOUTÉ

The Redouté family produced a number of painters in the seventeenth century. Originally they came from Dinant in Flanders, but migrated to Paris. *Redouté* has become a synonym—chiefly among art-dealers and private collectors—for small, bewitching flower pictures exquisitely painted. Their delicacy is the acme of decorative art.

RELINING

When injuries or decay in a canvas have occurred to such an extent that minor operations will not check the process of disintegration, the picture must be relined. This means that the entire picture, including the old canvas, must be remounted upon a new support, usually a new linen canvas. The traditional procedure is to stretch the new canvas on a temporary stretcher eight or ten inches longer each way than the original and to

253

size it. The picture, the front of which has been protected by paper applied with glue, is then placed face downwards on a board. Hot glue is next applied to the front of the new canvas and to the back of the old painting. The two canvases are then pressed together. When the picture is almost dry, it is ironed on the back with an extremely heavy tailor's iron. When the relining process has been completed the canvas is at once removed from the temporary stretcher and placed upon the original one.

REMBRANDT VAN RIJN

Rembrandt's father was the miller Harmen, his mother was the daughter of Neeltgen, who owned two Rijn mills. He was born at Leyden in 1606 and died at Amsterdam in 1669. Much has been written about his tragic life—factual and fanciful biography and even a film. The underlying reason for this continued probing lies in the consoling magic of his pictures, in his tireless quest for human dignity whatever the depth of humiliation or suffering.

After a year at Leyden University, Rembrandt gave up studying and started serious work: indeed, he became obsessed by work in his desire for mastery. In 1632 he moved to Amsterdam and conquered the city. Into his studio flocked a stream of burghers, rich, inquisitive, vain, eager to be immortalised by him. He painted innumerable portraits and his fame grew. But in the days of wealth he remembered and visited his less fortunate friends, notably Hercules Seghers, whom he helped by buying his engravings.

He painted pictures at this period such as his contemporaries had never before envisaged. Peter Lastman had brought chiaroscuro from Italy and taught it to his great pupil. Rembrandt used it with infinite delicacy and achieved a remarkable golden luminosity. He painted splendid Old Testament pictures, and also domestic scenes overflowing with vitality, using his wife, Saskia, as model. He bought a large house in the Breestraat and filled it with treasures of every description, including pictures by Hercules Seghers, Brouwer, Lastman, Raphael, Bassano, Carracci and Rubens. Many pupils passed through his workshop—Backer, Bol, Eeckhout, Koninck, Flinck, Victors and, later, Carel and Barent Fabritius, Maes and Hoogstraten.

But the good days passed. Saskia died in 1642, preceded by three of their children. In this fateful year Rembrandt painted *The Nightwatch*. It was intended to be a huge portrait group of Captain Banning Cocq's Militia Company, for which he was to be paid 100 gulders per head. Something quite different emerged—a ghostly scene, an allegory of the muddle and aimlessness of all human activity, the magic power of delusion. For Rembrandt the theme was wonderful, but the result was of no more value as

REMBRANDT · THE SMALL SELF-PORTRAIT
19⅞" × 16½". Vienna, Kunsthistorisches Museum

REMBRANDT
STORMY LANDSCAPE
20¾″ × 29¼″.
Brunswick, Museum

portraiture than the animated head of any old man. His sixteen clients were furious and returned the picture.

This was the turning-point. The world suddenly became aware that this marvellous artist had gone mad or, at any rate, that his feet were not on the ground. They regarded him as half sinister, half ridiculous, and shunned him. Rembrandt himself saw clearly that he had chosen the road to despair: from then on he wandered in the slums and the Ghetto, fascinated by the inhabitants. He studied the faces of the wretched and the diseased: he painted incessantly, but always and only on the one theme—the human spirit rising superior to its experience of suffering. And his colour became ever more wonderful and his expression more profound.

His material circumstances deteriorated rapidly. No orders came in and he went bankrupt. His young son, Titus, who was already fatally ill, and Hendrikje Stoffels, the maid, did their best for him. Because of a clause in a will, he could not marry Hendrikje, though he loved her and often painted her, notably as Bathsheba. She bore him a daughter, Cornelia, and in consequence was excluded from the Sacrament and denied burial in consecrated ground. Titus died in 1668.

Impoverished, ridiculed and despised,

Rembrandt still wandered about the streets like a King Lear. His self-portraits are truly devastating. The last was painted in 1669 and is now in Amsterdam.

Important dates in Rembrandt's life are: *1621*, he studied under Swannbach at Leyden and then under Pieter Lastman (q.v.) in Amsterdam. He returned to Leyden to work with Lievens (q.v.). Gerard Dou became one of his pupils. *1632*, he migrated to Amsterdam (possibly as a result of his first important commission, *The Anatomy Lesson of Dr Tulp*). *1634*, marriage to Saskia von Uylenburgh. *1642*, Saskia's death and *The Nightwatch*. *1654*, Hendrikje Stoffels gave birth to Cornelia. *1656*, bankruptcy. *1657* and *1658*, forced sale and ejection from home. In *1661/2* appeared *The Syndic of the Drapers*. The *Conspiracy of Claudius Civilis* and the *Triumph of Quintus Fabius Maximus* were rejected by the Corporation. Aert de Gelder, his last pupil of importance. *1662*, death of Hendrikje. *1668*, death of Titus.

Rembrandt was a master in all branches of painting—landscape, still-life, portrait, mythological, biblical, *genre*. His technique, at first precise and detailed, gradually developed into a broad impressionist style with a thick impasto. He restricted his palette to yellow ochre, red, brown, black and white but the lustre of the

255

colours grew ever more intense. Finally there was nothing left for him to achieve in composition, drawing or colouring. After drastic sorting by experts many hundreds of pictures are recognised as genuine, though not the two thousand claimed in the nineteenth century: also over a thousand marvellous drawings and three hundred and fifty etchings are known.

Rembrandt's masterpieces include, apart from his numerous self-portraits: *The Anatomy Lesson of Dr Tulp* (The Hague); *Landscape with Baptism of the Eunuch* (Hanover); *Stormy Landscape* and *Family Group* (Brunswick); *Holy Family*, *David and Absalom*, *The Disgrace of Haman* and *The Prodigal Son* (Leningrad); the *Marriage of Samson* and *Manoah's Sacrifice* (Dresden); *The Nightwatch*, *Jan Six*, *The Denial of St Peter* and *The Jewish Bride* (Amsterdam), *Jacob's Blessing* (Cassel); *Woman Bathing*, *Saskia as Flora*, *Margaretha Trip* and *Self-portrait* (London); *Man with Golden Helmet*, *Jacob Wrestling with the Angel* and

Hendrikje Stoffels (Berlin); *David Playing Before Saul* (The Hague and Frankfurt); *Hendrikje*, *Bathsheba*, *Christ at Emmaus* and *The Angel Leaving Tobias* (Louvre).

RENI

Guido Reni, the son of a musician, was born in 1575 at Calvenzano and died in 1642 at Bologna. His reputation has fluctuated. In his own day he was lauded to the skies, but soon after he was despised. Then the nineteenth century applauded him and the twentieth held him in contempt. Today the verdict on him seems to be 'acquittal by default', and interest in him remains. There are two clearly marked periods in his work. In the first he used chiaroscuro—not the chiaroscuro of Caravaggio, but more that of Ribera, with elements obviously taken from Raphael. In the second period he adopted a plainer, lighter, more delicate sculptural style. He shows more command in the first period,

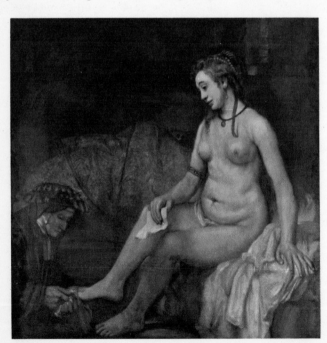

REMBRANDT
BATHSHEBA
56⅝" × 56⅝". *Paris, Louvre*

but the second is more individual and therefore of greater interest. His later pictures, in spite of excessive sweetness, lack of atmosphere and insincerity, show an extraordinary feeling for form.

Reni was a pupil of the Calvaert and Carraci School. He worked for several years in Rome, painting frescoes in the Vatican, St John Lateran and San Gregorio Magno. Finally, he returned to Bologna, where his passion for gambling reduced him to dire poverty.

REPLICA

Replica, a Latin word, really means a 'reply'. As used in art the word has come to mean a copy in the artist's own hand. It would be more accurate to call it a duplicate. A duplicate by the same hand as the original, and however similar, tends to be esteemed less highly. The first picture is usually more readily authenticated than the replica.

RETABLE

The Latin *retabulum* means a rear wall or reredos. In the history of art the word designates a small painted or carved altar-back. Retables were common in medieval churches before winged altar-pieces became general, but after 1400 they were only found in smaller churches, except in Spain, where they remained popular for considerably longer.

REYMERSWAELE

Marinus von Reymerswaele takes his name from the village in Zealand where he was born in 1493, and which probably disappeared in a flood. He died in 1567. Latterly he lived in Middelburg, where he was once sentenced as an iconoclast for plundering churches. He was a very good painter, but not a great one. He is important because the birth of *genre* painting owes a great deal to him. In style he follows Quinten Massys, though his pretensions are far smaller, and he is rather crude and coarse in his sarcastic mimicry. Specialisation began in his day. His territory might be termed 'Finance-*Genre*'. Variants of the subject *A Money-changer and His Wife* (a theme originally treated by Massys) hang in many places, such as Copenhagen, Dresden, Madrid, Florence and Nantes, and there are at least twenty copies of his *Tax-collector*. In some of his truly beautiful religious pictures he goes back unashamedly to Dürer's engravings.

REYNOLDS

Sir Joshua Reynolds (1723-1792) was born at Plymton Earl, near Plymouth, the son of a parson. He showed great promise in drawing at a very early age, and at seventeen he was placed under the portrait painter, Hudson. In 1746 he came under the influence of William Gandy, an Exeter painter, whose father had been a pupil of Van Dyck. In 1749 Reynolds accompanied Captain, afterward Lord, Keppel on a Mediterranean cruise. He stayed for three years in Italy making careful studies of Raphael, Michelangelo and the old masters. Very few painters have been such astonishingly accurate copyists as Reynolds; it is thought that one of the pictures attributed to Rembrandt in the National Gallery is actually a copy by Reynolds. On his return to England, Reynolds settled in London with his youngest sister, being determined from the outset to remain a bachelor. He enjoyed success for the rest of his career. Between 1760 and 1769 he often painted as many as four portraits a week. In 1769 Reynolds was knighted and elected first President of the newly constituted Royal Academy. In 1773 the degree of Doctor of Civil Law was conferred on the painter by Oxford University, and about this time he executed the designs for the 'Virtues' of the windows of New College. In 1784 Reynolds succeeded Allan Ramsay as Painter to the King. In 1789 he lost the sight of one eye. 'All things have an end,' he said. 'I have come to mine.' He was buried in St Paul's Cathedral by the side of Sir Christopher Wren, and left a fortune of over £100,000 to his niece, Mary Palmer, together with a collection of old masters which realised £30,000.

Reynolds' character was not attractive. Blake called him a 'sly dog' and said, 'I consider Reynolds' *Discourses* as the Simulations of the Hypocrite who smiles particularly where he means to betray.' He had all the distasteful qualities of a strong-willed man determined to succeed at all costs: he was a social climber, pompous, condescending, astute, urbane, calculating and irritatingly discreet. By continually recommending the study of the old masters in his *Discourses* and by urging that a composite style of excellence could be extracted from them, Reynolds exercised a harmful influence on English painting. But though he himself was so close a student of the old masters, his work, despite himself and his theories, shows the absurdity of the eclectic doctrine. As an artist, Reynolds was unnecessarily modest and lacking in confidence, and felt the need to rely on the old masters. In reality, he was gifted with marvellous creative power. 'Damn him,' cried Gainsborough, 'How various he is.' And Reynolds' pictorial invention is superb. His colour has deteriorated owing to his use of bitumen, but his forms and rhythms are indeed impressively varied. Among a great number of outstanding works may be mentioned *Dr Johnson* (National Portrait Gallery, London), *Kitty Fisher* and *The Brummel Children* (Kenwood), *Lord Heathfield*, *Lady Cockburn and Her Three Children* and *Captain Robert Orme* (National Gallery, London) and *Battle Scene* (Dulwich).

RIBALTA

Francisco Ribalta, about whose life very little is known, came from Catalonia, but worked chiefly in Madrid and Valencia. He died in 1628. He probably visited Italy some time before 1600, for the influence of Raphael and the Carracci is clear in his early work, and later he was the first Spanish painter to succumb to the spell of Caravaggio. But Ribalta remained essentially Spanish in his feeling for the spectacular and his gloomy naturalism.

RIBERA

Jusepe de Ribera was born c. 1590 in Jativa, near Valencia. He died in Naples at that time the capital city of the Realm of the Two Sicilies, which belonged to the Spanish crown. Life was much freer in Naples than in Madrid, so Spanish artists all longed to reside there. However, it is a mistaken idea to suppose that Ribera was called there: in fact, he drifted there after his schooling under Ribalta by way of Padua and Rome. In Naples he found patrons, notably the Carthusian monks and later the Viceroy. His fame reached Spain, and even Velazquez paid him a visit, and the Pope presented him with the Order of Christ. His last years were clouded by illness and embittered by the seduction of one of his daughters by Prince Juan of Austria. His mood at the end of his life is demonstrated by his last picture—the malicious, disdainful *Boy with a Clubfoot*

Ribera is not only one of the greatest

REYNOLDS · SELF-PORTRAIT
$29\frac{1}{4}" \times 24\frac{3}{8}"$. *London, Royal Academy*

Spanish painters, but one of the greatest painters of the seventeenth century in Italy. It is plain that he was influenced by Caravaggio and his chiaroscuro, but there is far more passion and intensity in Ribera's colours. In course of time his palette changed from browns to lighter ones, but he remained Spanish in his love of stirring, agitated scenes, such as accusations and persecutions. As the majority of his works have religious themes, he tended to overstep the borderline of cruelty and bloodthirstiness. He is represented in the National Gallery, London, by *The Lamentation over the Dead Christ.*

RICCI

Sebastiano Ricci, or Rizzi, was born in 1659 in Belluno and died in 1734 in Venice. He was a great traveller and several times visited London, Vienna, Paris and the Low Countries. His gay, easy style moved in the direction that Venetian painting, led by Tiepolo, had taken. Ricci no longer paints religious subjects, as it were, on bended knee, but confronts them all with a cavalier smile and bow. Saints no longer stand enthroned; they float around everywhere. To landscape he gives closer attention, thereby opening Venetian eyes a little wider to the beginnings of 'Veduta' painting, a movement that was carried on by his nephew.

Marco Ricci (born in 1676 in Belluno, died in 1729 in Venice) painted landscapes and landscape backgrounds in a novel, sketchy style. His acquaintance with Magnasco and his revolutionary handling of paint affected him strongly. For the rest, Marco himself was a good-for-nothing brawler and killer.

RICHARDSON

Jonathan Richardson (1665-1745) wrote about painting and owned a famous collection of old master drawings. He was a pupil of John Riley and the painter of the National Portrait Gallery likenesses of Steele, Pope, Matthew Prior and George Vertue. He was a sound, solid painter with the reputation of being able to obtain a good likeness.

RIGAUD

Hyacinthe Rigaud was born in 1659 at Perpignan. In 1681 he joined Le Brun in Paris and was wisely persuaded to take up portrait painting. He made a very meagre living until he received his first commission from the Court and at one leap became the fashionable painter of the day. He died in Paris in 1743. Rigaud painted the kings of France, Spain, Sweden and Poland, evolving a style based on Van Dyck. Later he developed a more intimate manner, which he used for portraits that were not official. Some of these show the influence of Rembrandt, seven of whose works were in Rigaud's possession. Rigaud is important as a bridge between the formal

J. DE RIBERA · BOY WITH A CLUB FOOT
$65\frac{5}{8}'' \times 36\frac{1}{4}''$. *Paris, Louvre*

Baroque Court portraiture of the seventeenth century and the more intimate naturalism of the eighteenth century. Represented in the National Gallery and the Wallace Collection, London, and the Louvre.

RIJKSMUSEUM, AMSTERDAM

The State Museum of Holland was founded in 1808 by Louis Napoleon and was housed at first in the Royal Palace. The present building was opened in 1885. It houses one of the most important collections of old masters in the world. All the important Dutch masters are represented, as well as Fra Angelico, Bassano, Brueghel, Cranach, Goya, El Greco, Murillo, Rubens, Teniers, Tintoretto, Van Dyck and Veronese. The most celebrated picture in the collection is Rembrandt's *Nightwatch*.

RILEY

John Riley (1646-1691) was one of the most interesting of all the many Stuart portrait painters. He was a pupil of Isaac Fuller and later worked with Soest. His work is characterised by a romantic spirit and by rare insight into character. There are fifteen portraits by him in the National Portrait Gallery, including the revealing study of *Lord William Russell*.

ROBERT

Hubert Robert (1733-1808 in Paris) painted charming landscapes, romanticising antiquity at a time when painting was turning to novel forms and ideas. He was a man of varied talent. He painted pictures that were often only suggestions for new gardens or his own conceptions for the new gallery at the Louvre. Some of his gardens materialised at Versailles, and he accepted the post of first Curator of the Louvre Gallery. He is responsible for top-lighting so general nowadays. Twice he even painted the gallery as a ruin, having imbibed a partiality for 'landscape with ruins' from Pannini after a ten-year spell of imitating him in Rome. Robert was

highly esteemed in Paris both before and after the Revolution, in spite of being imprisoned for a time during which he painted indefatigably.

Robert's pictures are to be found in many museums. The majority are Italianised landscapes with *genre* figures either in softly-lit colours or muted grey-greens, showing some affinity to Fragonard and very vaguely to the Dutch painters in Asselyn's circle. But Robert was also the chronicler of events in Paris, such as the demolition of houses at Neuilly, the burning of the Opera House and the storming of the Bastille.

ROBERTI

Ercole de Roberti (1456-1496) was the son of a Majordomo of the Dukes of Este. He grew up at Ferrara in the aura of the renowned Cosimo Tura, whom he certainly saw passing in and out of the castle, and may even perhaps have been his pupil. In any case Roberti is saturated with Tura, Mantegna and Squarcione, and completely insensitive to the dawning of the High Renaissance. His colours are harmonies of autumn tints and he nearly reaches Tura's level, but, like all preachers, he emphasised too much and cannot altogether escape the charge of spiritual exhibitionism.

Roberti appears to have finished some of Cossa's altarpieces, and there is often a similarity to Cossa in his own work. *John the Baptist* (Berlin) is perhaps his best picture. The Ferrarese dukes esteemed him highly, and he accompanied them on their journeys, even as far as Hungary.

ROMANINO

Girolamo Romanino seems to have been uncertain of the date of his own birth. He varies the date between 1484 and 1487 in Brescia. He could not have died before 1562, as there is a portrait of his at Innsbruck dated that year.

He was a contemporary of Titian and had met Bellini and Giorgione. The influence of these distant Venetians remained clear in Romanino's work to the end of his days. He adored vitality and strong movement and his palette varied from rather bright colours to the almost sketchy grey-on-grey of his self portrait in the Uffizi. His efforts to be different from Titian, Lotto or Pordenone are obvious. His *Beheading of St John the Baptist* (Berlin) reverts back to one of Dürer's woodcuts. Romanino also painted a series of frescoes. An important work, *The Nativity*, is in the National Gallery, London.

ROMANO

(*see* GIULIO)

ROMBOUTS

Theodor Rombouts (Antwerp 1597-1637), probably a pupil of Abraham Janssens, later went to Rome as had Rubens and so many others before him. His pictures fall into two categories: the Valentin-style (that is, Caravaggio-style) *genre* paintings (card-players, smokers) and the religious themes, which are more reminiscent of Rubens. Unconsciously he clung to this strict division even in colouring.

Gillis Rombouts, probably of Flemish origin though he was born and died in Haarlem (1630-1678). Although he was no more than an average painter, he was not a mere imitator of Salomon Ruysdael and Hobbema as is often thought. His crowd scenes on the beach and his village squares show that he must be regarded as a painter in his own right.

Salomon Rombouts, his son and pupil (lived from 1650 to about 1702 in Haarlem) painted in the same style as his father for a while, then turned to the themes which were to be characteristic of him— tall, dark masses of trees, bordered by a few patches of bright foliage, thrown into relief, with a brightly lighted foreground— reminiscent of a coarser Ruysdael. The details often show Italian influence. His broad pictures of ponds may be compared with Roelof Vries.

ROMNEY

George Romney was born in 1734 at Dalton-in-Furness in Lancashire and he died in 1802 at Kendal. His father was a

cabinet-maker. For ten years he followed his father's trade; then he was apprenticed to an itinerant portrait painter. He soon realised the value of his style and in 1762 he went to London. From 1763 onwards his portraits were always a centre of attraction at big exhibitions, although he never showed at the Academy, owing to his hostility to Reynolds. In 1764 Romney visited Paris, where he made the acquaintance of Vernet and studied Rubens. On his return he settled in London in a house near that of Reynolds, and soon gained as many commissions as his rival. In 1773 he went for two years to Italy. Unlike Reynolds, Romney was indifferent to money. He often turned away wealthy

ROBERTI · ST JOHN THE BAPTIST
21⅞″ × 12⅞″. Berlin, Staatl. Museen

sitters to devote more time to Lady Hamilton, with whom he was obsessed from 1783 onwards. He survived Reynolds by ten years, but by then he was already ill. Though he returned to his somewhat neglected family at Kendal before he died, he was paralysed and quite senile.

Romney was exclusively a portrait painter. He left behind him at least 1,800 portraits, perhaps as many as 2,000. Today most of them are in the private possession of English owners. All of them are extraordinarily ingratiating, with their deep, soft tints and the painter's wonderfully effective use of chiaroscuro so like the old masters. The colour is refined and rich, always established with one or two pleasing effects—a small blue handkerchief or a piece of brocaded waistcoat. Romney had no interest in psychology: none of his subjects give away more than a visiting-card would. The result is that his portraits are beautiful aristocratic still-life studies.

ROSA

Salvator Rosa, who was born near Naples in 1615 and died at Rome in 1673, was most lavishly gifted. He was painter, poet, musician, actor, orator and theatrical director, yet he does not ultimately rank as a great master. Nature really endowed him too profusely, though today justice is not done him: he was a very good painter. Some of his themes were undoubtedly beyond him, but his landscapes are always good. His devotion to nature was wildly romantic, but he expressed it in vivid lines and colours. His harbours in sunlight are Vernet dramatised, and the subject on which, he mistakenly, most prided himself, horsemen in battle became realistic, grim massacres among Abruzzi bandits, while the well-worn theme of the temptation of St Anthony becomes in his hands a misconceived scene of slaughter that is undeniably comic. Nevertheless his pure landscapes are under-rated, and among them should be included the powerful *Adoration of the Shepherds* in Vienna.

Rosa's life was crammed with adventure. It is easy to believe that at one period he roamed the mountains with bandits. His work was mainly done in Rome and Florence. A landscape and his most interesting self-portrait are in the National Gallery, London.

ROSLIN

Alexander Roslin (1718-1793) was born at Malmoe and studied in Stockholm. He visited Italy in 1750 and in 1752 settled in Paris, where he established himself as a portrait painter and became in 1753 a member of the French Academy. Roslin was a portrait painter in a purely French style much resembling that of Nattier. Swedes, including the Royal Family, commissioned him with portraits when visiting Paris, and in this way Roslin was influential in encouraging the French manner in Sweden. He is represented at Stockholm and in the Louvre.

ROSSELLI

Cosimo Roselli (1439-1507 in Florence) was trained in the studio of Neri di Bicci, a painter of charm and delicacy. He had as little temperament as his teacher; he peopled traditional scenes with large drily painted, dimly coloured figures and it is plain that his highest aspiration was to become a second Ghirlandaio. But, however lacking in ability to put over his own feelings, he must have been the most perceptive and sensitive of teachers. Both Piero di Cosimo and Fra Bartolomeo blossomed and ripened to maturity under him.

Matteo Rosselli (1578-1650/1) was born in Florence of a family of painters known as Rosselli da S. Giorgio, though their real name appears to have been Buontalenti. Matteo was a painter, a pupil of Gregorio Pagani, and worked all his life in his native city. His principal paintings include frescoes in Santa Annunziata and a fresco of the *Death of S. Antonio* in S. Marco, the *Martyrdom of S. Andrea* at the Ognissanti, *S. Carlo in Glory* in Or San Michele, and further examples in the Uffizi and Pitti Palaces.

ROSSO

Rosso Fiorentino, whose real name was Giovanni Battista di Jacopo, was born in Florence in 1494 and died in Paris in 1540. He is a very interesting figure in the history of painting—one of those people who, though not in the highest rank themselves, yet open new spiritual vistas for final discovery and illumination by others.

Rosso who had steeped himself in Del Sarto, Raphael and Michelangelo, was one of the founders of Mannerism (q.v.). He raised the connection between movement and emotion as shown in Michelangelo's frescoes, from a revelation to an accepted principle. In all probability it was Michelangelo who procured for him the post of Court Painter in 1530 in Paris to assist in the decoration of the newly-built Palace of Fontainebleau. Once there Rosso soon became the leading painter. The frescoes he painted at Fontainebleau have been well preserved.

Rosso's followers, particularly Primaticcio and Niccolo dell'Abbate, developed his mannerism into the style of the School of Fontainebleau (q.v.). (Ill. p. 264.)

ROTTENHAMMER

Hans Rottenhammer (1564-1623), a German painter, was born at Munich. He studied there and in Rome where he painted a number of altarpieces. He then spent ten years in Venice and his *Marriage at Cana* (Munich) shows how strongly he was influenced by Veronese. His mythological subjects with their enamel finish and groups of nudes in classical postures are typical Mannerist pictures. Rottenhammer was employed by the Duke of Mantua and the Emperor Rudolf II. He returned to Bavaria in 1606 and lived in Augsburg for the remainder of his life.

ROWLANDSON

Thomas Rowlandson (1756-1827) was born in London and was trained at the Academy Schools. At the age of sixteen he was sent to Paris to stay with a French aunt and he remained with her for three years, working at the École de l'Académie Royale. He became familiar with the art of Fragonard and St Aubin and he knew Janinet. On his return to London Rowlandson settled down after a year or two of extravagant living as a humorous commentator on social life. He painted in watercolour and was one of the greatest virtuosi of this medium as well as the greatest English caricaturist. He produced a complete, rich and boisterous comedy of the public and private manners of his day. His colours are of a rare delicacy and he also had an individual feeling for landscape. There are examples of his best work in the Victoria and Albert and British Museums.

RUBENS

Peter Paul Rubens (1577-1640) is one of the most brilliant figures in the history of painting. To call him a second Titian is not to rank one above the other, but to compare two giants alike in the complete fulfilment of their lives, their virtuosity, and the compass and splendour of their work. And they have another likeness in common. Their appeal is not to the young: a certain ripeness of age in both mind and eye is needed fully to understand and appreciate their work.

Puyvelde wrote: 'Rubens is the greatest improviser the world has ever known. He "thinks" with his brush, he imagines with his brush, and, at the same time, he organises brush in hand. . . . He magnifies life and glorifies it. He turns his people into giants.'

Rubens painted his great mythological and biblical scenes in a mood of titanic emotion, outwardly a respectable citizen, busily occupied with his canvas and not in the least bohemian, but inwardly erupting like a volcano. In the *Triumph of Silenus* and the *Fall of the Damned* he gazed, absorbed and fascinated, into a steaming cauldron of a world and revealed it to those who had eyes to see. He could evoke tremendous drama on a grand scale as in the *Battle of the Amazons*, or quite simply as in *Andromeda*. His feeling for life can be compared to Homer's; he has the same robust zest, as shown for example

ROSSO FIORENTINO
MOSES DEFENDING JETHRO'S
DAUGHTERS · *64" × 46¾"*.
Florence, · Uffizi

in *The Rape of the Daughters of Leucippos*, where the ladies do not appear to object to their fate. And like Homer, too, he is an observant psychologist, as witness his superb portraits.

When Rubens, at the age of thirty-one, returned from Italy, he had brought his style and technique to their highest pitch. As time passed he had lost the last remnants of heaviness, darkness and mannerism, which he imbibed from his teachers, Adam van Noort and Otto van Veen (1556-1629). Pictures of all sizes, from vast canvases down to tiny drawings, came equally easily to him: it was merely a question of which dimensions were most suited to his vision. Munich possesses a large number of sketches that show him at the peak of his powers.

Peter Paul Rubens was born at Siegen in Westphalia, Germany. When Peter Paul arrived, his father, a well-known magistrate from Antwerp, was serving a five-year sentence of exile in Siegen, but on his death the family returned to Antwerp. Peter Paul received a sound education and then was accepted as a page in a nobleman's household. The boy decided firmly that he wanted to be an artist. When, in 1600, his apprenticeship was over, Rubens made the conventional journey to Italy, but he was held up in Mantua. Influential people, having seen his pictures, recommended him to Duke Gonzaga, in whose service he remained for eight years. The Duke soon entrusted him with small diplomatic commissions and sent him first to Florence and then to Rome, where he made friends with Elsheimer. Later he was sent to Genoa and, in 1603, to Spain. When the death of his mother obliged him to return home to Antwerp he was no longer an unknown painter.

Rubens became Court Painter to the Regent and his wife, drew a large salary, married the charming young Isabella Brant and built himself a patrician house, in which he worked from dawn to dusk. Commissions streamed in from all sides, engravers copied his pictures, manufacturers wove carpets to his designs, yet he found time to spend the evenings with his family and his friends.

Rubens' contacts bore fruit. In 1622 Maria de' Medici, the Queen-Mother of France, commissioned twenty-one pictures from him for the palace at Luxembourg. The theme was homage to the Queen-Mother, the fee 20,000 ducats.

Rubens' astounding diplomatic career began about this time. The reason why the Infanta Isabella selected him must lie in the factors that influenced her: first the fact that he was on the spot, then that he was educated, astute and popular, that he had travelled and made contacts far and wide in Church, Court and Government circles, and, finally, that his embassies never caused trouble or complications.

From then on Rubens was, on many occasions, either secret ambassador or official representative during the long years of the peace negotiations between England and Spain. He visited London and Madrid frequently and met Velazquez. Both Charles I of England and Philip IV of Spain knighted him, and he was responsible for the signing of the peace treaty between the two countries. An idea of the style of life he led can be gleaned from a memorandum, dated 1627, reporting the sale of his collection of antiques to the Duke of Buckingham for 100,000 Dutch guilders.

RUBENS · RUBENS AND ISABELLA BRANT IN
THE HONEYSUCKLE ARBOUR · *70″ × 53½″*.
Munich, Alte Pinakothek

RUBENS · THE RAPE
OF THE DAUGHTERS OF
LEUCIPPOS · 87⅜″×82¼″.
Munich, Alte Pinakothek

Rubens' first wife died in 1626. In 1630 he married Hélène Fourment, the sixteen-year-old girl he has immortalised in so many pictures. He began to weary of diplomatic missions and to long for peace and quiet to paint; finally, the death of the Infanta Isabella released him from all burdensome duties. He bought the little Château de Steen near Malines and passed the summer months there. But during the last five years of his life Rubens was afflicted by gout and fever, and in the spring of 1640 he died at his town house in Antwerp.

His major works include: *Adoration of the Magi* (1609, Prado), *The Ascent of Calvary* and *The Descent from the Cross* (1610-1612, Antwerp), *Rubens and Isabella Brant in the Honeysuckle Arbour* (1610, Munich), *The Conversion of St Paul* (1617, Berlin), *The Fall of the Damned*, *The Last Judgment*, *The Rape of the Daughters of Leucippos*, *The Battle of the Amazons* and *The Triumph of Silenus* (c. 1618, Munich),

Adoration of the Kings (1619, Malines), *Holy Family* (c. 1620, Florence), *Christ between Thieves* (Antwerp), hunting pictures in New York and Dresden, *Homage to the Medici* (Louvre, sketches in Munich and Leningrad), *Adoration of the Magi* (1624, Antwerp), *Madonna with the Parrot* (Antwerp), *War and Peace*, *The Judgment of Paris*, *The Triumph of Silenus*, *The Rape of the Sabines* (London), *Andromeda* (c. 1637, Berlin), *The Judgment of Paris* and *The Garden of Love* (Prado), landscapes in Munich, Florence, Vienna, London and Paris, portraits and life studies of Hélène Fourment in Munich, Vienna and Paris.

RUBLEV

Andrei Rublev was a Russian icon painter and the greatest influence in Russian art throughout the fifteenth century. Possibly a pupil of Theophanes of the School of

Novgorod, Rublev collaborated with him in the church of the Virgin Annunciate in Moscow and thus became one of the founders of the School of Moscow. Rublev's most famous single work is *The Old Testament Trinity*, painted about 1410 for the Troitse Sergieva Monastery, Moscow, where the painter was a monk. It is a symbolic representation of the Trinity in the form of the three angels who appeared to Abraham. The subtle linear rhythms, the visionary power, the trans-lucency of the colour surpass anything achieved by the earlier icon painters. Rublev is also known to have restored the twelfth-century frescoes on the great central piers of the Uspenski Sobor, Moscow.

RUISCH

Rachel Ruisch (1664-1750 in Amsterdam) was the daughter of Frederick Ruisch, professor of anatomy and an amateur painter, wife of the engraver, Poop, mother of ten children, niece of the famous Brazilian painter, Frans Post, pupil of Willem van Aelst, and she surpassed them all. She is considered among the best flower-painters that Holland has ever pro-duced. She liked to paint her flowers in tight nosegays as well as direct from nature, often using flowers, leaves, fruits, birds' nests, beetles and caterpillars all heaped on to one dinner-plate. Her microscopic drawings were as precise as those of Abraham Mignon (born in Frankfurt in 1640, died in Wetzlar in 1679). She pre-ferred an old-fashioned 'black' background, though she was essentially a lady of the Rococo. As Court Painter to the Elector Palatine, she was greatly sought after. There are examples of her pictures in the National Gallery, London, and Amster-dam, Brussels, Munich and Rotterdam.

RUISDAEL

Jacob van Ruisdael, the loftiest exponent of landscape painting in the romantic style of the Netherlands of his time, is still considered among the most important painters of the seventeenth century. His fame has remained constant, and for long it completely eclipsed that of another great Ruisdael, his uncle Salomon.

Dr Jacob van Ruisdael, son of an art-dealer and landscape painter, was born in 1628 or 1629 at Haarlem and probably died there in 1682. His father and his uncle taught him to paint, but he also studied medicine at the same time, took his degree and practised. In fact it seems that he never gave up doctoring, which perhaps explains his opulence.

Dutch landscape-painting after Vroom (q.v.) had forked in two directions. One branch which might be called visionary landscape, painted purely for light effects, led through Cuyp and Seghers to culmin-ate in Rembrandt; the other branch, naturalistic, documentary landscape, tar-ried until Ruisdael came along and brought it to its culminating pitch. By the time he was in his middle fifties he had mastered nature in all her moods and conveyed them straight to the mind and heart of the spectator without any artificial effects of light. Towards the end of his life a romantic note crept into his pictures.

His chief works include: *Mill at Wyk*, *Watermill* (Amsterdam), *A View near Haarlem* (National Gallery), *Jewish Cem-etery* (Detroit and Dresden), *Oak Forest*, *Landscape with Farmhouse* (Berlin), *Corn-fields* (New York), *Waterfall* (Amsterdam and London) and *The Great Forest* (Vienna).

Hobbema was Ruisdael's pupil.

Salomon van Ruisdael was born c. 1600/02 in Haarlem and died there in 1670. A generation divides him from his nephew, and this is apparent in his works. They depend to a great extent on drawing and often on shading, and they incline towards atmosphere, scintillating light on trees, reflections in gleaming water. His sponsors were Esias van der Velde and the young Goyen, who, in 1634, lived in his brother's house. Pictures typical of Salomon are *Water with Oaks* (Sarasota, U.S.A.), *A River Landscape* (Munich). Towards the end of his life new themes appear with larger buildings, giant trees,

J. RUISDAEL · WATER-
FALL NEAR A FOREST OF
OAKS · 56¾″ × 78″.
Amsterdam, Rijksmuseum

more dramatic harmonies (*The May-tree*, Vienna; *The Watchtower*, Munich).

RYCKAERT

David Ryckaert (1612-1661), third of his name, lived in Antwerp. Not much is known of his father and grandfather, but David made his reputation by his pictures of peasants and his domestic *genre*. His early works are reminiscent of Brouwer. Later his painting lightened and his themes were more akin to those of Teniers, though he never achieved the height of either master.

His uncle, **Martin Ryckaert** (1587-1631), was a landscape painter of less importance.

SACCHI

Andrea Sacchi, who was born in 1599 at Nettuno and died in 1661 in Rome, was a pupil of Albani, and therefore influenced by the Carracci. Although he lived in the middle of the Baroque period he inclined even more than the Bolognese painters towards impressive formal gesture and elements of classicism. His reputation soared to almost exaggerated heights with the revival of classicism after the Rococo period. Sacchi's best frescoes and altar-pieces, among them *The Vision of St Romuald*, are in Rome. Maratta was his pupil.

SAENREDAM

Pieter Jansz Saenredam, who was born in 1597 in Assendelft and died in 1665 in Haarlem, is today considered one of the most important of the Dutch painters, though he is one of the most unpopular. His pictures are austere and restrained, and yet they are easier to like than the character of the man himself. Fate, in jest, breathed genius into the soul of a dull, dry official. Saenredam, as if to emphasise his lack of temperament, elected to paint church interiors. Jan van Eyck's superb picture in Berlin of the nave of a church had shown what a grand subject naves could make, but no one before Saenredam had made an architectural feature the sole theme of a picture. Hendrik van Steenwyck (1550-1603) and his younger namesake (1580-1649) were merely forerunners who scarcely distinguished between a church nave and a Renaissance palace. Saenredam's daring lay in the fact that he only wanted to paint bare walls, one of the most

difficult and exciting of tasks. But if Saenredam was excited, he did not show it. He has left practical notes on his work in which he is so pedantic that he mentions every detail in his pictures in which he has deviated in the slightest degree from actual fact. His work became ever more limpid and more simplified as the years passed. Some of his masterpieces convey the sensation that behind his walls lie dream-cloisters of serenity and truth, for Saenredam's sobriety has a compelling quality.

Two of his best works are in the London National Gallery. None of his followers attained his stature, least of all Isaac Nickele (active c. 1660-1703 in Haarlem)

P. SAENREDAM · THE INTERIOR OF THE CHURCH OF ST LAWRENCE · *21⅝″ × 17¼″. Rotterdam, Boymans Museum*

who may have been Saenredam's pupil and who thought of himself as a most faithful follower. Houckgeest and Vliet were more successful.

SAFTLEVEN

Cornelis Saftleven, who was born in 1607 in Gorkum and died in 1681 in Rotterdam, still enjoys a certain reputation as a painter of ingenuous peasant scenes after the manner of Ostade and Brouwer, but his landscapes and his dimly-lit barn interiors are finer works.

Herman Saftleven, his brother, who was born in 1609 in Rotterdam and died in 1683 in Utrecht, was a much better painter. His earlier pictures are striking woody landscapes in which all the interest is concentrated in the dark foregrounds. His later pictures are quite different. Here the foreground is only a frame for distant river and valley landscapes, as with Verhaecht, only Saftleven paints more thinly and directly. Herman travelled up the Rhine and lived for a time at Elberfeld. He is well represented in the London National Gallery and at Dulwich.

Jan Griffier painted very like Saftleven. He was born in Amsterdam in 1645 and died in London, where he was known as 'the gentleman from Utrecht'. He spent most of his life in England, where, like Monet later, he painted the Thames in summer from his houseboat, and in winter devoted himself to recalling little scenes of the Rhineland and painting them from memory.

SALVIATI

Francesco de' Rossi, called Salviati, was born in Florence in 1510 and died in Rome in 1563. He was greatly influenced by Parmigianino and also by Pontormo, who, like him, was trained in the studio of Andrea del Sarto. The best of his works, which embrace almost every branch of painting, are his accomplished seated portraits, though they are not very profound. His *Portrait of a Boy* is in the National Gallery, London.

SANDBY

Paul Sandby (1725-1809) was born at Nottingham and at the age of sixteen he was employed for two years as a draughtsman at the Tower; he was then sent to survey the Highlands. He lived from then onwards as a topographical painter, travelling about in England and Wales sketching mansions, parks and landscapes and selling his pictures to the owners of the scenes he depicted. He reproduced some of his drawings in aquatint, a process he was the first to use in England. Sandby was a foundation member of the Royal Academy and Deputy Librarian there 1790-1809. He was the first English landscape painter of any importance to use watercolour; he was also a pioneer in the appreciation of the beauty of English landscape. Represented in the Tate Gallery and the Victoria and Albert Museum.

SANDRART

Joachim von Sandrart was born at Frankfurt in 1606. He was the son of a Flemish emigrant. After a lifetime of wandering round Europe, he died at Nuremberg in 1688, honoured and respected as Director of the Academy. He painted chiefly portraits—baroque, skilful, often slightly humorous portraits. He is better remembered as author of the first history of German art. He was a member of the Claude-Poussin circle in Rome and is the source of invaluable information about his artist friends.

SANTA CROCE

Girolano da Santa Croce was working in Venice from 1516 until c. 1556, but little is known of his early life and training. He studied under Basaiti in Venice and may possibly have also been a pupil of Giovanni Bellini. In his later work he modelled himself on Giorgione and Titian. His *St John the Evangelist* and *St George* are in the National Gallery, London.

ANDREA DEL SARTO · A SCULPTOR
28″ × 22″. London, National Gallery

SANTVOORT

Dirk van Santvoort (1610?-1680), a Dutch painter who worked in Amsterdam, may have been a pupil of Rembrandt. He painted a few religious compositions but was chiefly known for his 'society' portraits which were extremely popular in his own day. He became President of the Guild at Amsterdam in 1658. His works include a fine portrait group in the Amsterdam workhouse, a religious composition in the Louvre and a *Girl with a Finch* in the National Gallery, London.

SARTO

Andrea d'Agnolo, son of a tailor, is one of the most famous names in the history of art. The nineteenth century particularly idolised him, and poets sang his praises.

He was born at Florence in 1486 and probably only left his native city once, when in 1518 he spent a year in Paris executing a commission from the Court. He died in 1530 at the early age of forty-four. There was nothing in the least dramatic about his life, and in character he was gentle and irresolute. From his teacher, Piero de Cosimo, he absorbed nothing, but set up a studio with a fellow-student, Franciabigio, whose taste and talents were more congenial to him. These two friends were both inspired by the colour of the Venetians and by the super-sensitivity of Correggio.

Buschek describes Andrea del Sarto as the 'only Florentine who painted in the sense that the Venetians understood painting'. In the last ten years of his life he changed from quiet symmetry to more animated scenes, foreshadowing the Mannerism of his pupils, particularly of Pontormo and Rosso Fiorentino.

Andrea del Sarto's work is unequal. His major works include: *Betrothal of St Catherine* (Dresden), *The Entombment* (Vienna), *Charity* (Louvre), *Portrait of a Sculptor* (London), *The Entombment, Legend of Joseph* and *The Disputation* (Pitti Palace), and *Madonnas* in Berlin, Budapest and Florence (Uffizi): also frescoes in Florence.

SASSETTA

Stefano di Giovanni, called Sassetta (1392-1450), was a Sienese painter, perhaps the pupil of Paolo di Giovanni and Bartolo di Fredi; he was also influenced by the Lorenzetti. He designed a font for the Duomo, Siena, in 1427 and his earliest dated picture was painted in 1436. Siena, incurably old-fashioned, knew nothing of the fierce intellectual life of Florence, and, long after it was dead elsewhere, it preserved the gentle, courtly Gothic spirit of chivalry of the fourteenth century. Sassetta

SASSETTA
THE PROCESSION OF THE
MAGI · 8¾″ × 11¾″. New York,
Metropolitan Museum

was the last and the most delicate and imaginative interpreter of this spirit. A comparison of Sassetta with Francesca, who in the 1440s was working in the same little town as Sassetta, Borgo San Sepolcro, clearly shows Sassetta's essential Gothicism. Among his principal works are the frescoes of the Porta Romana, Siena, finished by his pupil, Sano di Pietro, and the scenes from the life of St Francis in the National Gallery.

Sano di Pietro, who was born in 1406 in Siena and died there in 1481, was Sassetta's pupil. In his early pictures he followed his master closely, but never equalled him in sincerity, for he was trying too consciously to achieve naïve and lyrical effects. Finally, his pictures became quite mechanical.

SASSOFERRATO

Giovanni Battista Salvi (1609-1685) adopted the name of his birthplace, Sassoferrato, though he worked principally in Urbino and died in Rome. He may have spent some time in Domenichino's studio. The output of this eclectic painter was small, and previous centuries have tended to overestimate him. Theoretically he derived much from Raphael, and his repetitive Madonnas are based entirely on Raphael's drawings and the etchings of Guido Reni. His pictures tend to be sentimental and over-colourful.

SAVERY

Roelant Savery, who was born in Courtrai in 1587 and died in 1639 in Utrecht, painted small panel pictures of dark forests inspired by Jan Brueghel and Coninxloo, while the wooden-looking wild animals that stand or lie about among the trees were obviously taken from engravings. It is only when the animals are reduced to insignificant background features that Savery's landscapes make harmonious compositions. These pure landscapes are of great interest, and so are some of the flowerpieces which Savery produced while he was Court Painter in Prague and Vienna. Like Jan Brueghel, he was a pioneer in his choice of subject matter, but in handling he never advanced beyond the sixteenth century.

SAVOLDO

Giovanni Girolamo Savoldo, who was born c. 1480 in Brescia and died c. 1550 in Venice, is among the Italian painters rescued by Duveen from oblivion and accorded a tardy recognition. Savoldo was a modest man; he lived quietly in retirement, was an invalid in his old age and was forgotten before he died. He was trained in Florence, but when he moved to Venice he fell under the spell of Giorgione, Titian and Palma Vecchio. In Florence he had acquired Leonardo's love of twilight effects; he combined this with the qualities of Venetian painting in the romantic image of a woman seen by night, half hidden by her enveloping shawl (*The Venetian Woman*, sometimes known as *Mary Magdalen Approaching the Sepulchre* or *Courtesan in a Shawl*, Berlin and London). In Savoldo's picture *An Angel Dictating to St Matthew* (New York) the setting is definitely night.

SCHAFFNER

Martin Schaffner was born c. 1472, and he died during the plague at Ulm in 1547. He was one of the Swabian painters in the Augsburg or Ulm tradition, in whose pictures the first glimmerings of the Renaissance make an appealing appearance. Yet there is nothing Italian about Schaffner's submissive Madonnas and saints, which, if they are not altogether German, are more Dutch than Renaissance in conception. The influence of Cranach is obvious in Schaffner's excellent portraits, but they are reserved in colour, matt rather than luminous. These portraits and the *Wettenhausen Altarpiece* (Munich) are his chief works.

SCHALCKEN

Godfried Schalcken, who was born in 1643 in Made and died in 1706 at The Hague, was the son of a minister who must have been very apprehensive when his thirteen-year-old son started to swagger about as an art student. However, the boy's most important teacher was Gerard Dou, though he studied also under Van Hoogstraaten at Dordrecht (1656-1662). In fact, for years he imitated Gerard Dou so closely that he might be accused of plagiarism (*An Old Woman Scouring a*

SAVOLDO · A VENETIAN WOMAN
36¾" × 29¼". Berlin, Staatl. Museen

Pot, National Gallery, London). He likewise adopted Dou's candlelit themes in *genre*, but to these he added the Rococo charm which made his little panels so famous in the eighteenth century. In between he painted pictures like *A Boy Fishing* (Berlin), which he himself probably regarded as unsuccessful, but which combined vigorously drawn tree stumps and water-lilies with the figure of a boy that might have been painted in the nineteenth century. His father's fears were groundless. Godfried Schalcken prospered, travelled a great deal and spent some time in London.

His nephew, **Jacob**, and his pupil, **Arnold Boonen**, imitated him without capturing any of his charm.

SCHÄUFELEIN

Hans Leonhard Schäufelein was born in Nuremberg c. 1480 and died c. 1540 at Nördlingen, where he owned a house in which he lived from 1515 onwards after a period of travelling about in the Tyrol. Schäufelein painted a number of portraits and religious subjects, very varied in style and colouring, some of great beauty, others ineffective. They exhibit a frank delight in narrative and are usually linear in character, the forms often actually outlined. Schäufelein was also an excellent wood-carver, but he is a curious product of his age. He obtained his greatest satisfaction in imitating other painters, and he openly boasted of having copied Dürer, Cranach and others to perfection.

SCHIAVONE

Giorgio di Tomaso Chiulinovoc, called Schiavone, was born in Dalmatia in 1436 and died in Sebenico in 1504. He was one of Squarcione's pupils and proud of the fact, for he always signed himself as such. His Madonnas in Berlin and Turin, and his altar piece in London are worth attentive study being syntheses of Squarcione and Tura.

Andrea Meldolla was also called Schiavone: he too came from Dalmatia (born c. 1522, died in Venice in 1563). He may have been a pupil of Titian. His large forest scenes, full of Greek gods and goddesses, are noteworthy and his massy foliage is quite Flemish in character.

SCHMIDT

Martin Johann Schmidt was born at Grafenwöhr, near Krems in 1718. He is known as 'Krems Schmidt', which makes it easier to remember his pictures with their gentle supple Venetian figures glancing from a Correggio-like dusk. Schmidt painted many altarpieces in Austria. He and Maulbertsch were the most important painters of their day. He died in 1801 at Stein on the Danube.

SCHONGAUER

Martin Schongauer, of old Augsburg ancestry, was the son of a goldsmith and magistrate. He was born at Colmar in 1430 and died at Brescia in 1491.

Munich possesses a portrait of him by his pupil, Burgkmair: apart from the inscription, there is a note written 450 years ago with the words, 'Mayster Martin Schongawer, painter, called "Handsome Martin" on account of his looks'. Martin's face is indeed anything but handsome. He looks a ruthless dare-devil, but his heart must have been in the right place, for he painted tender, sincere pictures with simple, serene Madonnas.

Undoubtedly Schongauer is one of the most important German painters, and is still more important as an engraver. He is the only artist before Dürer whose influence extended to Italy and Spain through the fame of his engravings. His earliest authenticated picture is dated 1473, and it places him at once as an outstanding master of his art. The picture is *The Virgin in the Rose Bower* (Colmar, Collegiate Church), and has been called 'the German Sistine Madonna'. The comparison is inept, because Schongauer's Virgin is not majestic and relaxed like Raphael's. God has not revealed to her that one day she will be called holy too.

Schongauer always painted people going about their daily life, but illumined by the most tender poetry: at first the faces are Dutch but later more German in type. With the technique of his engravings he blended the formality of Roger van der Weyden and the naïveté of German folksongs. The majority of his pictures are less than 18 inches in height: *The Birth of Christ* (Munich), *The Holy Family* (Vienna), *The Adoration of the Shepherds* (Berlin), *The Virgin in Front of a Rosehedge* (Leipzig). The sixteen panels of the *Passion of our Lord* (Colmar) were certainly painted with the assistance of friends. Unfortunately, much of Schongauer's work was destroyed during the religious risings, and much has been falsely attributed to him.

SCHOOL

This word is used in relation to old master painting in a double sense. When a picture is labelled 'School of Botticelli', the painter is thus classified as one who was either trained under Botticelli in his workshop at Florence, or was so strongly influenced by Botticelli's example as to be easily remembered by his resemblance to his model. In its second application the word 'School' takes on a more complex meaning. The term covers any group of artists united by some common civic or racial tendency. When associated with the name of a city or country, like the Schools of Florence, Venice, Siena or Antwerp, it carries with it a distinct territorial significance, the suggestion of a local achievement. Sometimes when the precise origin of a picture is uncertain, it is more loosely described as Flemish or Dutch School, while such a term as 'North Italian School' may be used for work which cannot be ascribed to any single town or district in Northern Italy, but which is clearly sub-Alpine in character.

M. SCHONGAUER · THE NATIVITY
10⅞" × 6¾". *Munich, Alte Pinakothek*

SCHOUBROECK

Pieter Schoubroeck was born about 1570 at Hessenheim, near Frankenthal, during the 'emigration'. His parents were Flemish Protestants who had fled from religious persecution to Frankenthal near Mannheim. There the *émigré* painters founded a colony. Coninxloo and Valkenborch lived in it for many years. The influence and dependence of the painters on each other was great, and gradually the 'Frankenthal Style' emerged. In the next generation it was represented by Schoubroeck and Mirou (c. 1585-1661 in Frankenthal). Later Schoubroeck moved to Nuremberg, but he returned to the colony before his death in 1607. He was a landscape painter, chiefly of attractive wooden gorges and mountain valleys abounding with tiny, sprightly figures. Sometimes his subject was religious (*John the Baptist Preaching*, Brunswick) and sometimes a peasant scene or a cavalcade of horsemen.

SCHÜCHLIN

Hans Schüchlin was one of the early Swabian masters. He died in Ulm in 1505. It is difficult to say from whom he inherited his style as only one authenticated work of his exists, the *Tiefbronn Altarpiece*. In it there are traces of Dutch influence and of Dirk Bouts. The unusually soft tones he uses were lost by his successors, one of whom Zeitblom, was his son-in-law.

SCHUT

Cornelis Schut (1597-1655 in Antwerp) was one of the best known of Rubens' disciples. His contemporaries admired his huge allegoric and religious canvases on account of their vitality, pleasing colouring and the beauty of the figures. Schut is like Rubens but never succeeds in catching either his polish or his strength.

SCOREL

Jan van Scorel was the son of a Catholic priest. He was born at Schoorl (Scorel) in 1495 and died as a priest himself at Utrecht in 1562. He was a well-educated man, a fluent linguist, and he had travelled in Italy, Rhodes and Palestine. At the age of twenty-seven he was selected by Pope Hadrian to be Raphael's successor as director of the papal collection of antiques. He was offered, and accepted, the gift of a canonry, but, although he was ordained a priest, he died a wealthy and honoured man of the world.

Scorel's influence on the next generation was great, as he was the first Dutch painter of his century to have seen Italy, and he brought Raphael and Romanism back to the north with him. Maerten van Heemskerk and Anton Mor were his pupils.

The influence of the study of the antique and of Raphael is very clear in Scorel's pictures: even his contemporary, Mander, speaks of his 'Raphaelite faces'. But in his landscapes he could not throw off his Dutch inheritance, even when he sprinkled ruins and castles over his plains.

Scorel's chief works are: the Falkenstein Triptych which was painted before his Italian sojourn, *The Presentation in the Temple* (Vienna), already in the spirit of Raphael's frescoes; *The Virgin and Child* (Berlin). In his portraits which are strong and full of character, his Dutch side is very apparent, probably because his sitter was so often his sweetheart, Agathe Schoonhoven. The fine portrait in the Doria Gallery, Rome, is of her.

SCOTT

Samuel Scott (1710-1772) was a painter of topographical landscapes and naval subjects, executed with a precision and delicacy reminiscent of Canaletto (who was in England from 1746 to 1750 and again in 1751). Scott's works were greatly admired, and collected by Walpole. He is seen at his best in *Old London Bridge* (Kenwood) and *The Thames* (Victoria and Albert Museum).

SEGHERS

Two painters bore this name. **Daniel** Seghers (1590-1661) lived and worked in Antwerp and was a pupil of Jan Brueghel, from whom he learnt to paint flowers. Daniel was the most important of the early Flemish flower painters. He was highly esteemed by the Princes of Holland, who once presented him with a palette made of gold. His flower pictures are of two types: they consist either of garlands hung about Italianate reliefs or cartouches (which are generally by another painter) or of short-stalked flowers arranged in vases. (Verendael, 1640-1695, imitated both types.) Daniel Seghers and Jan Brueghel remained the prototypes for Flemish flower painters until Rembrandt's chiaroscuro, as practised by Jan Davidsz de Heem, introduced another element. The final stage was represented by Huysum's Rococo flowerpieces.

J. VAN SCOREL · MADONNA AND CHILD
17⅞" × 14¾". Berlin, Staatl. Museen

Hercules Seghers was one of Holland's most important painters. He was probably born at Haarlem c. 1589 and he died in 1638, presumably at The Hague. The important dates in Seghers' tragic, troubled life are unknown: even Hoogstraten, who grew up while Seghers was still alive, can tell us nothing with certainty, and Houbraken speaks of him as a doomed figure. It was neither poverty nor lack of success that caused Seghers to despair, but the melancholia which so often haunts his engravings. He was never so utterly abandoned as he imagined. Rembrandt admired him and bought pictures and engravings from him, and doubtless dealers visited him. But in 1630 Seghers left Amsterdam, and went first to Utrecht and then to The Hague, completely vanishing from the circle of friends who had done their best for him.

Hercules Seghers was a pupil of Coninxloo, but he had more in common with Brueghel and Scorel. It might be thought that he was influenced by Rembrandt, but on the contrary it was he who influenced Rembrandt. He taught him a great deal about the light effects of weather. In fact, one of Seger's best pictures, a *Mountain Landscape* in the Uffizi, was attributed to Rembrandt until 1925, when Bode discovered the mistake.

Seger's most important work is the *Maas Landscape* (Vierhouten), but very few of his pictures survive. Berlin possesses two *Views of the Rhine*, Amsterdam a *River Valley*, London a *Mountain Landscape*, Philadelphia a *Landscape with Ruins* and Rotterdam a small, signed *Landscape*.

SEGNA

Segna di Buonaventura, mentioned for the first time in Siena in 1298, probably died in 1326/31. He must therefore have been the same age as Ugolino and, like him, one of Duccio's pupils. Segna did not achieve his master's strength, but their pictures are comparable in delicacy, Segna gaining his effects by narrowing the heads and elongating the fragile limbs of his figures.

SELLAIO

Vasari states that Jacopo del Sellaio (1441-1493 in Florence) was a pupil of Fra Filippo Lippi, so Botticelli may have been a fellow-student, as they were the same age. This may well have been so, because Sellaio adopted Botticelli's style completely and also worked for him. Sellaio was not a great painter, but a good one and not merely an imitator. His cassone panels show individuality. These panels are spread far and wide, for Sellaio was a zealous painter of cupboards and chests. There are examples in the Uffizi, the Louvre and the National Gallery, London.

SERRA

The brothers **Jaime** (active 1361-1395) and **Pedro** Serra (active 1363-1400) worked in Gerona, where they were born, Saragossa, Manresa and Barcelona, and maintained a large and famous workshop, where Luis Borrassà was trained. The Serra brothers are important for their projection of the Italo-Gothic style in their own work and for the wide influence they exerted through their many followers. Pedro Serra's retable of the Pentecost (c. 1394) in Manresa Cathedral shows a lack of facility in figure organization but incorporates new landscape elements against the gold ground and is characterised by a new psychological awareness in the faces of the personages. Jaime's work includes the Holy Sepulchre Retable, Saragossa, and the panel, *The Adoration of the Shepherds* (c. 1360) in the Montillor Collection, New York. Borrassà (1380-1424) was the principal upholder of the International Style inaugurated by the Serra brothers. He worked in Catalonia and though, like his masters, he was influenced by the Sienese painters, he dispensed with the gold background and set his figures in more realistic surroundings. An outstanding example of his work is the Retable of the Guardiola (c. 1410-1420) in the Soler y March Collection, Barcelona.

H. SEGHERS
MEUSE LANDSCAPE
*28″ × 34¾″. Vierbouten,
D. G. Beuningen Collection*

SIBERECHTS

Jan Siberechts was born in Antwerp in 1627. He went to England in 1672 and died in London about 1700. He was a very important painter who, in his best period, produced pictures of an unforgettable quality. They are, as it were, fragments of nature, a meadow, or one or two cows or dogs, a farm cart crossing a ford, a girl asleep in the grass, all in a matt silvery green picked out by a reddish tinge in a bodice or a coat. There are beautiful pictures from this period in Brussels, Munich, Budapest and Lille. Before this good period he painted Italianate pictures rather similar to those of Both and Dujardin, and in later years in England he changed his style once again. He painted several views of Chatsworth which show the influence of Rubens.

SIGNATURES

The custom of signing pictures with the painter's name or initials began rather late. The reason for this is very simple, though not the one usually believed—namely, that people of the Gothic age had no consciousness of individuality and preferred their work to remain anonymous. The painters of those days most certainly valued popularity and advertisement, but—and this is the point—they thought only in terms of the present and not of posterity. Not until the Renaissance was immortality a consideration in their minds.

Very early dated signatures are occasionally found, and always on particularly important works. In 1307 Giotto signed his greatest fresco in Padua, and Jan van Eyck his double portrait of the Arnolfini in 1434. By about 1500, signatures, initials or ciphers had become general, and some of them are very curious. Lack of a signature only lessens the value of a picture when it is known that it was the painter's habit to sign his works. (Ill. pp. 280-1.)

SIGNORELLI

Luca Signorelli (1441-1523), one of the greatest Italian masters of the late fifteenth century, was born at Cortona and was a pupil of Piero della Francesca, with whom he worked at Arezzo. He may also have studied for a time under Fioranzo di Lorenzo, and he was greatly influenced by Antonio Pollaiuolo. Signorelli's earliest recorded work was the decoration of the organ in the Church of the Laudi at Cortona in 1470. In 1471 he was at Arezzo, where he decorated the chapel of St Barbara in S. Lorenzo with frescoes and painted a panel of St Niccolo da Tolentino for S. Agostino and a panel, *Virgin and Saints*, for S. Francesco, but these have since disappeared. Signorelli's movements between 1475 and 1479 are uncertain. During that time he may have painted the *School of Pan*, formerly in the Berlin Gallery, but destroyed during the Second World War, and two panels of the Madonna, one the tondo reproduced here, now in the Uffizi. Important frescoes at Loreto were probably executed c. 1478-9. Signorelli visited Rome in about 1482 and painted the fresco of *The Journey of Moses* in the Sistine Chapel. In 1485 he contracted to paint a chapel in S. Agata, Spoleto, but this was never carried out. In 1488 he was made a citizen of Città di Castello in recognition of his services in painting a standard of the Virgin. Possibly he visited Volterra soon after this time and painted *The Annunciation* in the Duomo and *The Virgin Enthroned with Saints* in S. Francesco. To this period may also belong the magnificent *Circumcision* in the National Gallery, London. In 1496 Signorelli painted the *Martyrdom of St Sebastian* (Munich) for S. Domenico, Città di Castello. In 1497 Signorelli was engaged on the well-known series of frescoes illustrating the life of St Benedict in the cloister of the Monastery of Monte Oliveto Maggiore di Chiusuri, near Buonconvento, Girolamo Genga acting as his assistant. In April 1499 he was commissioned to complete the frescoes on the vault of the Chapel of S. Brizio in the Cathedral of Orvieto, commenced by Fra Angelico; and in April 1500 the commission was extended to the side walls of the chapel, the subject of these frescoes being *The Last Judgment*. In addition to the sum of 575 ducats, Signorelli received for this work a measure of wheat and new wine each year and a convenient habitation with two beds. In 1506 the painter was summoned to Siena to execute frescoes in the palace of Pandolfo Petrucci; and the following year he painted the altarpiece

The Virgin Enthroned with Saints for the church of S. Medaro in Arceria. In 1508 he was called to Rome by the Pope Julius II together with Pinturicchio, Perugino and Sodoma to decorate the Camere of the Vatican; but Raphael was preferred, part of the work Signorelli and his colleagues had executed was taken down and Signorelli returned with Pinturicchio to Siena. He then finished the frescoes he had begun in the Petrucci Palace. One of these, *The Triumph of Chastity*, is now in the National Gallery. The painter's latest works include a *Virgin in Glory* (Arezzo) and an unfinished fresco of the *Baptism* in the chapel of Passerini Palace, near Cortona.

Signorelli took an active interest in the affairs of his native city and in 1488 held the post of chief magistrate. He was elected to the office of Prior twelve times between 1479 and 1522. Twice he was despatched to Florence on public business. Signorelli was twice married, first to a sister of Lazzaro Vasari, father of the author. and secondly to Galizia di Pier Antonio

J. SIBERECHTS · WOMAN ASLEEP
IN A MEADOW
42¾" × 33¼". Munich, Alte Pinakothek

A. ALTDORFER

J. ASSELYN

H. BALDUNG GRIEN

J. DE' BARBARI

IOANNES BELLINVS·

GIOV. BELLINI

A. BERRUGUETE

A. BLOEMAERT

H. BOSCH

P. BRIL

CLAUDE LORRAINE

L. CRANACH

A. DÜRER

A. VAN DYCK

F. FLORIS

F. GOYA

URS GRAF

EL GRECO (DOMENICO THEOTOCOPULI)

FRANS HALS

M. HOBBEMA

H. HOLBEIN
THE ELDER

H. HOLBEIN
THE YOUNGER

P. DE HOOCH

J. LEYSTER

N. MAAS

FRANS CRABBE

MASTER I. B.

A. VAN DER NEER

AERT PIETERSZ

RAPHAEL VRBINASA F,

RAPHAEL

Rembrandt · f

REMBRANDT

J. VAN RUISDAEL

S. VAN RUISDAEL

H. L. SCHAUFELEIN

M. SCHONGAUER

A/ · STALBEMT Fe
A° 1619

Double
signature

P. Brveghel. Fe,
1618

A. V. STALBEMT - P. BREUGHEL
THE YOUNGER

G. TERBORCH

Titianus
P.

TITIAN

Diego Velazquez

D. VELAZQUEZ

Meer

JAN VERMEER VAN DELFT

P.£.W.

PH. WOUWERMAN

Ianu: Zick Iunior

J. ZICK

281

Carnesecca. He had two daughters and three sons, one of whom, **Antonio,** followed his father's profession. Signorelli was one of the greatest fresco painters, distinguished by the dignity and gravity of his style, his power of expressing deep emotion, by his dark, glowing colour, fine sense of scale and mastery in depicting the human form in action.

SISTINE CHAPEL

The official private chapel of the popes in the Vatican was built for Sixtus IV by Giovanni de' Dolci (1473-81) and owes its fame to the frescoes which decorate its walls and ceiling. The frescoes on the two long walls were all executed between 1481 and 1483 and depict parallel events in the lives of Moses and Christ. *Moses and his wife Zipporah in Egypt, The Circumcision of the Son of Moses and Zipporah* and *Christ Giving the Keys to Peter* were the work of Perugino assisted by Pinturicchio. Botticelli was responsible for *The Burning Bush with Moses killing the Egyptian and driving the Midianites from the Well, The Punishment of Dathan, Korah and Abiram, The Healing of the Leper* and *The Temptation of Christ*; Domenico Ghirlandaio is seen at his best in *The Calling of Peter and Andrew* and his pupils painted the *Crossing of the Red Sea.* Signorelli executed *Moses giving his rod to Joshua* and the *Lamentation for the Death of Moses,* assisted by Bartolomeo delle Gatta, and Cosimo Rosselli painted *The Last Supper, The Worship of the Golden Calf* and worked with Piero di Cosimo on *The Sermon on the Mount.* Two frescoes by Ghirlandaio and Salviati on the east wall were repainted by Arrigo Fiammingo and Matteo da Lecce at the end of the sixteenth century. On this wall and between the windows are 24 portraits of popes by Domenico Ghirlandaio, Fra Diamante and Cosimo Rosselli.

The ceiling is entirely covered with the famous frescoes begun by Michelangelo at

SIGNORELLI · MADONNA AND CHILD
(Detail) 68" × 46". Florence, Uffizi

the request of Pope Julius II on May 10th, 1508 and completed by him on October 31st, 1520. Contemporary records describe Michelangelo's reluctance to undertake the work, for he regarded himself as almost exclusively a sculptor. He conceived of the ceiling decoration as an architectural whole with Prophets and Sibyls projecting between massive pillars; the *Ancestors of Christ* wait for redemption in pointed arches and lunettes and the *Brazen Serpent, Ahasuerus, Esther and Haman, David and Goliath* and *Judith and Holofernes* are represented in the pendentives at the four corners above the altar. The centre of the ceiling is divided into wide rectangles, alternately large and small which are bordered with painted architraves supported by pillars on which imposing nudes are seated. The subjects in the rectangles are *The Creation* and *The Fall, The Sacrifice of Noah, The Flood* and *The Drunkenness of Noah.*

More than twenty years afterwards (1534-1541) Michelangelo walled up two windows in the west wall, eliminated three frescoes by Perugino and painted his great *Last Judgment*.

SNAYERS

Peter Snayers, who was born in 1592 at Antwerp and died in 1667 at Brussels, was a pupil of Vranx and carried on with the same themes—fights, travellers in woods, realistic raids on villages. Some of his quiet landscapes with travellers have a foretaste of Momper. After Snayers was given the appointment of Court Painter to the Governor of Brussels, he regularly executed commissions for panoramic scenes of historical battles. Unfortunately, owing to the fancifulness of an 'armchair warrior', these cannot be considered his best work.

SNYDERS

Frans Snyders (1579-1657 in Antwerp) does not seem to have come into his own as a still-life painter until 1610. In the intervening years he returned to Antwerp from a journey to Italy and met Rubens, who was already world-famous. Rubens gave Snyders several commissions and they worked together for several years.

Snyders is known today as the great painter of animals and fruit. He owes his success to the friendship and teaching of Rubens. The fact that his pictures hang well beside Rubens' is significant. His most famous work is incorporated into one of Rubens' pictures, the popular *Garland of Fruit* (Munich). One of his most beautiful animal paintings is in Rubens' *Diana* (Berlin). Rubens, in return, painted a figure in Snyders' superb *Kitchen-piece* (Munich). The Prado has a fine collection of Snyders' work.

SNYERS

Pieter Snyers (1681-1752) was born at Antwerp and studied under A. van Braedael in 1694. In 1741 he was made Director of the Royal Academy in Antwerp. He painted fruit and flower pieces, landscapes, portraits and figure subjects of low life. At one time he went for a few months to London, where he painted a number of successful portraits.

SODOMA

Giovanni Antonio Bazzi, ironically nicknamed 'il Sodoma', was born in 1477 at Vercelli, Piedmont, and died in 1549 at Siena, the town he loved most. He was the son of a cobbler. Sodoma is usually designated as a disciple of Leonardo, but this is only partially correct. His particular use of light and shade came from Perugino, and Raphael quite as much as from

F. SNYDERS
THE KITCHEN TABLE
*54″ × 80⅞″.
Munich, Alte Pinakothek*

Leonardo, and his *St George and the Dragon* at Washington shows how inferior was his use of it. His best and characteristic work is in his Madonnas, which definitely do show Leonardo's influence. Sodoma was a happy-go-lucky fellow: if he had taken his work more seriously he would have risen higher.

SOEST

Gerard Soest (c. 1605-1681) was a painter of German birth who worked in England. He was probably born at Soest, near Utrecht. He settled in England in 1656, painting portraits in the style of Lely. Several examples of his work are in the National Portrait Gallery, London, and the fine portrait of Aubrey de Vere, Earl of Oxford, at Dulwich is probably his.

SOLARIO

Andrea Solario was an important artist because, though belonging to Leonardo's circle, he was the only one who successfully resisted the master's hypnotic effect. He was born in 1465 at Milan and died there in 1522. He struggled for years not to be dragged down into slavish imitation, and he broke away by hardening and 'enamelling' Leonardo's twilight effects. Without Leonardo, his lovely *Madonna with the Green Cushion* (Louvre) would be unthinkable, but, unlike any work by Leonardo, she is fresh and animated.

Solario diverged still further from Leonardo in his portrait painting. He insisted on strong colouring and sharp definition (*The Lute-player*, Rome). In fact, his most notable portrait, painted only a year before his death, of *Chancellor Morone* (Private Collection, Milan) is strikingly close to Holbein.

SOLIMENA

Francesco Soliman (1657-1717)

was a Baroque decorative painter who worked principally in Naples. He claimed to be able to paint in a dozen different styles and was a master of astonishing skill, covering walls and ceilings with a riot of hovering, fore-shortened figures, flying draperies and illusionist architecture. Solimena had a famous school, and characteristic works by him and his pupils can be seen in the churches of Gesu Nuovo and S. Paolo in Naples.

SORGH

Hendrik Sorgh (c. 1611-1670 in Rotterdam) was a pupil of Teniers. He also studied Brouwer and imitated his peasant and market scenes. Marine pictures and biblical scenes painted by him also exist. In his *Adoration of the Shepherds* (Hamburg) he practically copied Rembrandt, but his still-life details are often fascinating.

A. SOLARIO · THE MADONNA WITH THE GREEN CUSHION · *24″ × 20″. Paris, Louvre*

SPAGNA, LO

Giovanni di Pietro, a Spaniard known as Lo Spagna, was working in Italy from 1504 until 1528. He may have been a pupil of Perugino and his work also shows the influence of Pinturicchio and Raphael. Few of the circumstances of his life are known; he was an established painter in Umbria by 1504. In 1516 he was made a citizen of Spoleto and in 1517 he was elected head of the Society of Painters there. His best works are those painted in the manner of Perugino such as the *Madonna Enthroned* (1516) in the chapel of San Stefano in the lower church of San Francesco at Assisi. In his latest works Lo Spagna imitated Raphael's Roman style. He is represented in the National Gallery, London, at Assisi, Perugia, Rome, Spoleto and Trevi.

SPINELLO

Spinello di Luca Spinelli, called Aretino, lived from 1333 to 1410 in Arezzo. In his quest for simplicity and austerity in drawing, Spinello was forced to revert back to Orcagna, Nardo and to Giotto himself. His best frescoes include *The Legend of St Benedict* in San Miniato, Florence, and *The Legend of St Catherine* at Antella, near Florence, parts of the paintings in S. Francesco at Arezzo, and the *Ephesus* and *Potitus* scenes in the Campo Santo at Pisa. His panel paintings, chiefly remains of altarpieces, are to be found in many museums, and the Academy at Florence possesses a Madonna triptych.

SPRANGER

Bartholomäus Spranger, who was born in 1546 in Amsterdam and died in 1611 in Prague, had from his youth up something donnish about him. He studied under three painters for seven years, and, according to Mander, frittered away the time in reading. After that he travelled in Italy, the classic land of his dreams, and was fortunate in securing powerful patrons, becoming in

1575 Court Painter to the Emperor Maximilian II in Prague and later to Rudolph II. His friend, Mander, lived in Prague, and soon many other court painters came to the city. Spranger was their lode-star to good posts, advancement and comfort.

Spranger painted numerous allegorical and mythological pictures and, after his return from Italy, his distinctive style had an enormous influence on his contemporaries through his engravings. It was a mixture of Correggio, Parmigianino, empty rhetoric and polite pornography.

SQUARCIONE

Francesco Squarcione (1399-1468 in Padua) is a very controversial figure in the history of art. Recently, however, evidence has been forthcoming to prove that he really was a painter of note. For example, he was called on as an authority when a contract was made between Donatello and the city officials of Padua in 1443. The 'Paduan style', which was, and still is, a particular conception, could only have emanated from him. It was based on the closest study of the antique. Mantegna derives his style from Squarcione, Crivelli and Tura studied in Padua, and the development of this whole circle of painters was due to Squarcione's example.

There are only two authenticated pictures by Squarcione: one, *St Jerome with the Baptist and Saints* (Padua) and the other a *Madonna and Child* (Berlin).

STARNINA

Gherardo di Jacopo Starnina lived in Florence in the second half of the fourteenth century and died in about 1409. A fog of uncertainty still hangs over his work. All his documented works have been destroyed, except his frescoes of *St Jerome* (only discovered in 1932) in the Carmine Church in Florence. But his hand has been detected in the *St Anthony* frescoes in S. Croce, Florence, and in a large Agnolo Gaddi painting. This is reported by Vasari, so from these two works it should be possible to point to panel pictures by Starnina. But the *Thebias* (Uffizi), the landscape with hermits, is almost the sole example. It might have been painted by a younger, more austere Fra Angelico. It is amazing to observe how Starnina makes a gesture or an attitude convey a whole act, and how his diminutive toy-like landscapes seem entirely normal. Starnina gives the idea that all techniques and styles were at his disposal but that he himself preferred this archaic form.

STEEN

Jan Steen was born in 1626 and died in 1679. His home was at Leÿden and he died there, but in between he lived at The Hague, Warmond, Haarlem and Delft. Nothing is known about his youth or his training. Houbraken (q.v.) is responsible for the gossip and stories about Jan Steen. Many of them are demonstrably improbable, but it is certain that Steen was a light-hearted, boon companion who paid his way with quick, casual pictures, that he enjoyed life and public-house debates. But Steen was a most gifted artist and a witty chronicler of everyday life. His portraits and landscapes are scarce, but he painted gardens and interiors superbly.

It is surprising that Steen's fame reached its highest pitch in the nineteenth century, and that today it is still high enough for him to be considered as 'one of the greatest Dutch painters'. He never painted an entirely serious, solemn picture in his life; there is nearly always a touch of humour about them, and they are singularly free from weak or shoddy passages. His technique is sometimes polished (*à la* Metsu), sometimes bold (*à la* Brouwer) with scribble effects in thin brown pigment. All subjects were grist to his mill, but, as he was a vagrant, he never stuck to anything for long. Line, colour, vitality and humour make up a typical Jan Steen. His pictures number many hundreds.

JAN STEEN · THE FEAST OF ST NICHOLAS
32¾" × 27¾". Amsterdam, Rijksmuseum

STEENWYCK
(*see* SAENREDAM)

STEFANO DA ZEVIO

Stefano di Giovanni da Verona, known better as 'da Zevio', was born c. 1375 and died c. 1438/43 in Verona. The great Altichiero must have been a contemporary, but Stefano's pictures do not show his influence at all, only the German influence of the so-called 'soft style' of the Cologne School. However, Stefano was immersed in North Italian pictorial ideas, and his *Madonna of the Rose-bush* (Worcester) is, if authentic, the most extreme expression of German characteristics. Elsewhere he inclines towards Pisanello, who may have been his pupil. The majority of his frescoes and panel pictures are in Verona.

STOSKOPFF

Sebastian Stoskopff (1596-1657) was born

in Strasbourg and was a pupil of Daniel Soreau in Hanau. From him he learnt to paint still-life in the manner of the Netherlanders. He then spent more than twenty years in Paris and during the 'thirties became one of the most subtle of the French still-life painters. The Musée de Strasbourg contains some of Stoskopff's best works from the Paris period. They combine large foreground figures with still-life groups in a manner not seen again for more than two hundred years. In 1641 Stoskopff returned to Strasbourg, where his style became less exciting; he painted smaller, less bold, more conventional pictures.

STREATER

Robert Streater, who was born in Covent Garden in 1624 and died in 1680, was the first Englishman of marked ability to practise mural painting, a form of art stimulated during the seventeenth century by the erection of great houses and encouraged by the example of Rubens who had decorated the ceiling at Whitehall during his stay in London from June 1629 till March 1630. Evelyn thought highly of Streater and Pepys records a visit to Streater's studio in 1669 where he found Sir Christopher Wren and other virtuosos admiring his work. The decorations on the ceiling of the Sheldonian Theatre, vigorous, though florid, show Streater at his best. He also executed decorations in the Chapel of All Souls College, Oxford, in St Michael's, Cornhill, and at Whitehall.

STRIGEL

Bernhard Strigel (1460/61-1528) had a great reputation as a portrait painter in his own day. He was Court Painter to the Emperor Maximilian, who ennobled him. Strigel's home town was actually Memmingen, but it was to the nearby city of Augsburg that he owed his fame and his wealth. His painting is reminiscent of Zeitblom whose pupil he may have been.

During the Rococo period Gothic and Renaissance painting lost favour, and Strigel's name sank, with many others, into oblivion. Even in the last century it was not known who had painted the greater number of Strigel's pictures. But since he was recently rediscovered his reputation has risen from year to year.

There are works by him in the galleries of Munich, Nuremberg, Vienna and Berlin, which show that he approaches the great masters.

STROZZI

Bernardo Strozzi was born in Genoa in 1581 and died at Venice in 1644. He

B. STRIGEL · PORTRAIT OF SIBYLLA VON FREYBERG · 20″ × 13¾″. *Munich, Alte Pinakothek*

originally intended to study philosophy, but when his stern father was dead, he hesitated, and eventually joined the Carthusian monks as a means of devoting his life to painting without realising how much he desired worldly success. One day he escaped from the monastery, fled to Venice and hid himself there (1631). The astounding sequel is that the Church not only pardoned him immediately, but, at the height of his fame, made him a Cardinal.

To begin with, Strozzi favoured Caravaggio's naturalism giving it an almost Spanish twist. Then in Genoa Rubens broke on him like a divine revelation: finally, in Venice, the transformation of his work was completed by his discovery of Veronese. Strozzi succeeded in putting an end to the Venetian Mannerism from which Johann Liss had already tried to break away. The best of Strozzi's works are his portraits of which there is a fine example in the National Gallery, London.

STUART

Gilbert Stuart (1755-1828) was a distinguished American painter. He studied under Benjamin West in London, travelled in Europe and returned to New York in 1793. He stands out on account of his superb handling of paint and for his pearly flesh tones. Among his better-known works are his portrait of Washington (whom he painted many times) in the National Gallery, Washington, and his portraits of his countrymen, Benjamin West and John Singleton Copley, in the National Portrait Gallery, London.

STUBBS

George Stubbs (1724-1806) ranks as one of the great animal painters of the world, and as a painter of horses he has never been excelled. It is only comparatively recently that his qualities have been fully recognised; the grandeur of his composition, his feeling for landscape, the subtlety of his tones, his insight into character, his

most un-English objectivity and his powe of rendering the weight and movement o animals. Stubbs was born at Liverpool and began to study anatomy at an early ag under a surgeon in York. He lectured on the subject to students in the hospita there. He went to Rome in 1745 with th declared intention of finding out whethe art was superior to nature. He decided tha it was not. In 1766 Stubbs published hi great work, *The Anatomy of the Horse* which is still an authority on the subject. His most famous picture is the *Hamble tonian* (private collection). *The Phaeton an Pair* is in the National Gallery, Londor and *A Gentleman Holding His Horse* is i the Tate Gallery, London. In his old ag Stubbs began an illustrated work calle 'A Comparative Anatomical Exposition the Structure of the Human Body wit that of a Tiger and Common Fowls', bu he died before this was completed. A one time he was interested in the techniqu of painting in enamel on earthenware, an produced a number of large panels in th medium, which were fired by Wedgwoo It was in this medium that he executed th equestrian portrait of Wedgwood himsel

SUBLEYRAS

Pierre Hubert Subleyras was born Toulouse in 1699 and died in Rome 1749. He studied in his native town and Paris, then settled in Rome, where h married Maria Tibaldi. He painted larg decorative religious compositions. He well represented in the Louvre and *Th Bark of Charon* in the National Galler London, is attributed to him. In 1745 h painted a *Mass of St Basil* which wa reproduced in mosaic in St Peter's. Th painting itself is in Sta Maria degli Angel

SUSTERMAN

Justus Susterman (Suttermans) was bo in 1597 in Antwerp and died in Florence 1681. While still quite young, he went Paris and joined Franz Pourbus, who that time was at the height of his reputatio and had good contacts. In 1620 a group of tapestry designers were invited to Florence by the Duke of Tuscany, and by some means Susterman attached himself to the party. He was an adept in the art of pleasing, and eventually the whole of Italy, including the Vatican, took him up. He was in great demand as a portrait painter, and when Van Dyck visited Florence he stayed with Susterman.

Susterman was purely a portrait-painter with a very distinctive style. He made his models look like vigorous people with penetrating expressions and all at the prime of life, and he used dark shadows even when tinting flesh. The Uffizi possesses one of his best paintings—the portrait of *Galileo*. Other fine works hang in the Galleria d'Arte Antica, Rome.

SUSTRIS

Lambert Sustris, who was born c. 1520 in Amsterdam and died after 1568, probably in Padua, is a painter who has still not been sufficiently studied. He went to Italy when he was quite young and found his feet in Venice, where for a long time he worked for Titian and Tintoretto, principally painting in backgrounds. When Titian visited Augsburg as the guest of the Emperor Charles V, Sustris accompanied him, and the prominent citizens of Augs-burg regarded his arrival as chance of having their portraits painted (Waldburg, Fugger, Vöhlin). Munich possesses two typical portraits which hang, not unintentionally, beside a large *Diana* from the School of Fontainebleau. In both the style derives from Primaticcio. Mander praises Sustris' 'dolcissima maniera', the suppleness of his lines and the dignity of his colouring. The way in which he developed can be clearly traced from his early *Women Bathing* (Vienna) which is Dutch in feeling.

SWEERTS

Michiel Sweerts was born about 1614 in Brussels and died in 1656 in Goa. He had gone to India with a missionary society, which was a tremendous undertaking in those days, with little hope of return, so Sweerts' religious enthusiasm must have been extreme. Nothing is known about his artistic development. An exquisite picture, painted in delicate shades of grey, like his *Inn Parlour* (Munich), is reminiscent of Terborch and his circle, while *Taste* and *Hearing* (Stuttgart) recall the circle round Vermeer van Delft. Still, he may only have been an intelligent follower of Duck and Duyster. Wilhelm Leibl was devoted to his grey picture in Munich, which is readily understood.

T

TACCONI

Francesco Tacconi was born in Cremona and worked there and in Venice from 1458 until 1500. In a document dated 1464 he and his brother Filippo are praised for their paintings in the loggia of the Palazzo Pubblico, Cremona. A *Virgin and Child* by Francesco in the National Gallery, London, shows a tendency to imitate the Vivarini. In 1490 Tacconi was commissioned to paint the shutters of the organ of St Mark's, Venice; these works are feebly executed in the style of Squarcione.

TASSEL

Jean Tassel (c. 1608-1667) was the son and pupil of **Richard** Tassel, and he also studied under Jean Leclerc. When he went to Rome in 1634 he moved in the circle of Van Laer (Bamboccio). On his return to France he worked in Dijon and Langres. His style betrays many influences, those of Guido Reni, Veronese, Vouet and La Hire, while his contrasts of light and shade suggest Caravaggio. Tassel's work is unequal in quality, but at his monumental best, as in *The Coronation of the Virgin by the Infant Christ* he is a considerable painter with an unusual strain of fantasy. His masterpiece is thought to be a portrait of Catherine de Montholon, also at Dijon, painted while Tassel was working for the Ursuline Convent at Dijon, of which she was the foundress.

TEMPERA

The word 'tempera' has the same derivation as 'temper', and was used in early Italian writings to denote any liquid medium with which pigments could be combined to make a paint, the result being distinguished from fresco, which contained no added medium. Later the word was applied specifically to work executed with egg yolk. The process of tempera painting as it was practised in Italy before the oil medium began to come into use, c. 1450, is described in detail by Cennini. The yolk is first separated from the white of the egg. The pigments are well ground in distilled water with the muller, and when the painter is about to begin work an equal volume of colour and egg yolk are mixed. Some painters added a little water to the egg and some preferred to grind the colours directly into the egg. The egg colour of the yolk has very little effect on the paint, though Cennini recommended town eggs as being paler than those from the country. The painting is best executed on a rigid panel covered with gesso. Cennini refers on several occasions to the use of fig-tree sap introduced by beating the egg with cuttings of the young shoot. No satisfactory explanation of this procedure has ever been offered.

The traditional tempera techniques are all based on a deliberate methodical procedure, and are not suitable to spontaneous, direct painting. Usually a complete drawing is made and traced upon the gesso panel, which has been brought to a smooth ivory-like finish. An early surviving example of a drawing which was traced on to a panel for a tempera painting is that of Raphael's *Vision of a Knight* in the National Gallery, London, where it can be seen together with the finished picture. The painting is thinly executed, usually with sable brushes. Italian tempera painters generally painted the design in a monochrome undercoat, usually green. Michelangelo's *Madonna and Child* (National Gallery, London) is an interesting example of an unfinished work in tempera, showing the monochrome underpainting.

Tempera paintings are characterised by a brilliance and luminosity unequalled by the use of other mediums. Furthermore, the dried paint film does not become yellow or darken with age, as oil paintings may do, because the medium itself is non-yellowing. Tempera pictures are also less

DAVID TENIERS THE
YOUNGER · THE
GALLERY OF THE ARCH-
DUKE IN BRUSSELS
38⅜″ × 51¼″.
Bavarian State Gallery

likely to crack than oil paintings. The medium is suitable for the painting of minute and careful detail but does not lend itself to any breadth of handling or to bold effects of chiaroscuro and wide range of tone. The medium lacks the flexibility of oil because it dries so rapidly. It was for this reason that, when the oil painting process came into use in the fifteenth century, it gradually supplanted tempera.

TEMPESTA

Antonio Tempesta's real name was Pieter Mulier. He was born in Haarlem in about 1637 and died in Milan in 1701. He went early to Italy where he is reputed to have spent a wild life. He painted a large number of sea pieces which are without much significance, but his decorative landscapes, most of which are in Milan, are vigorously executed and highly original in colour.

TENEBROSI

The name given to the school of Caravaggio, which concentrated on heavy contrasts of light and shade. They met with much success in Naples and Venice.

Pietro Ricchi, Carlo Saraceni, Francesco Rusca, Matteo da Pittocchi and Bastiano Manzoni were the most prominent of the Tenebrosi.

TENIERS

In his day, David Teniers the Younger was one of the most famous painters of the Netherlands, and he is still regarded as among the most important Flemish painters of the seventeenth century. He was born in 1610 at Antwerp and died at Brussels in 1690. His father was **David Teniers the Elder** (1583-1649 in Antwerp), known to art history as a painter of a few religious pictures, landscapes and portraits. But Teniers the Elder speculated so foolishly that he landed himself in prison and his family in misery. The effect on his son was to make him concentrate on becoming rich and famous in his desire to wash out the past. By the time Teniers the Younger had reached the age of thirty-five he had accomplished his ambition and recorded his achievement in *The Artist with His Family* (Berlin). In this picture the painter is seen playing the 'cello, surrounded by his wife and children, all sumptuously dressed, with every sign

TERBORCH
BOY PICKING FLEAS
FROM A DOG
$13\frac{3}{4}'' \times 10\frac{3}{8}''$.
Munich, Alte Pinakothek

of prosperity, even to the costly curiosity of a monkey sitting on his garden wall. His wife was a daughter of Jan Brueghel.

In 1651 the Archduke Leopold lured him to Brussels by appointing him Court Painter and Director of his Art Collections. Teniers hoped to be knighted, but this dream was never realised.

Teniers had been taught to paint by his father, but in style he inclined more to Brouwer, though lacking his robustness. By 1640 he had found his own personal style, which, as the years passed, was characterised by an ever more subtle handling and texture. He also widened the field of his subject-matter. He painted scenes in the squares and streets of Brussels (*The Shooting Match*, Vienna), and delighted in broad village panoramic scenes (*The Bleaching-ground*, Dresden and *Consecration of a Church*, Brussels, Vienna, Amsterdam). He painted his family once again in *Teniers at His Castle Near Perck* (London), and finally even pure landscape (*Flemish Landscape*, Brussels, and *A Winter Scene*, Vienna).

A subject which he painted several times, and which has become very famous, was *The Temptation of St Anthony*. The scene is laid in a rocky cave full of ghostly figures, but it is all utterly different from Hieronymus Bosch. Obviously, he painted the supernatural with a twinkle in his eye. Some of the colouring in the figures is exquisitely delicate.

The most remarkable subject Teniers ever painted—apart from his monkeys—is *The Picture Gallery of Archduke Leopold*

(Brussels). In this painting he left to posterity a rich source of information: through it the fate of many pictures by Titian, Giorgione and Veronese can be established.

TERBORCH

Gerard Terborch was born in 1617 at Zwolle and died in 1681 at Deventer. His father was a tax-collector and an amateur painter, so Gerard grew up in an educated home. When he was fifteen he met Rembrandt in Amsterdam and resolved to be a painter. He studied under Pieter Molijn, a talented landscape painter. Then his father suggested travel, so Gerard visited Italy, France, Germany and England, where he met Van Dyck. He had made his name by the time he revisited Germany in 1546 to paint the signing of the Peace of Münster. Two years later Philip IV invited him to Madrid and raised him to the rank of a nobleman. In 1650 Terborch returned to Zwolle, but in 1654 he moved to Deventer, when his reputation was at its height. He took very few pupils: Caspar Netscher was his best.

Today Terborch's work is held in high esteem, but sometimes a patronising note creeps in which is unjustified in so far as it detracts from his unique skill in depicting the simplest happenings of everyday life with convincing humanity. The *Woman Peeling Apples* (Vienna) might be any young mother quietly intent on her work, while the child at her side looks up at her with an inimitable half-comprehending glance, so moving that it is almost holy. To the power of expression Terborch added wonderful colouring, from the softest shades of grey to brilliant red. The atmosphere of his pictures is somewhere between that of Rembrandt and Vermeer. His portraits are unusual, and are

clearly the work of a most distinguished painter. They are small in size and show the whole figure easily and yet formally posed against an austere neutral background.

Terborch's principal works include *The Despatch* (The Hague), *Conseil Paternel* (Berlin and Amsterdam), *The Concert* (Berlin), *The Letter* and *Boy Picking Fleas from a Dog* (Munich), *Woman Peeling Apples* (Vienna) and *A Young Woman playing a Theorbo to Two Men*, *Portrait of a Young Man* and *An Officer Dictating a Letter* (London). The pictures Terborch brought back from Münster are interesting, but not outstanding (London and Münster).

TERBRUGGHEN

Hendrik Terbrugghen was born in 1588 at Deventer. His father was a barrister at Utrecht. Terbrugghen studied under Abraham Bloemart, who was considered the apostle of Italian naturalism. At the end of his training Terbrugghen went to Italy himself and stayed there several

TERBRUGGHEN · THE CONCERT
36″ × 50″. Rome, Borghese Gallery

years. He was home again by 1614 and died at Utrecht in 1629.

Although he uses Caravaggio's dramatic, artificial lighting, the influence of the Italian master on him is much less pronounced than his likeness to Vermeer van Delft. Both his beautiful pictures of *The Flautist* (Cassel and Gotha) are fantasies in colour, and in that respect no more 'subject pictures' than the works of Vermeer. (An exception, however, is the *Woman Singing* in Basle.)

Beyond doubt, Terbrugghen would have been a greater painter if he had followed Vermeer more consistently: as it is, his work is patchy. Marvellous passages are there for the seeking as, for instance, the turbaned head of a boy in the crowded *Call of St Matthew* (Utrecht), or one of the *Tricktrack Players* (Utrecht), or the flautist in the *Concert* (private collection, Ledbury), and in his most important picture, *The Laughing Girl* in Utrecht.

TESTELIN

Louis Testelin (1615-1657) was the pupil of his father Gilles and of Vouet. He enjoyed a successful academic career as a painter of large decorative compositions and religious pictures, but he also made interesting drawings satirising contemporary life. Some of these are in the museum at Dijon. Testelin's paintings include *The Resurrection of Tabitha* (Rouen Museum), *The Flagellation of St Paul and St Silas* (Notre Dame, Paris), *The Marriage of Louis XIV* (Versailles) and *The Magdalen* (Grenoble Museum).

THORNHILL

Sir James Thornhill (1675-1734) was a decorative painter in the Italian Baroque tradition—the only English exponent of it, indeed—who painted the cupola of St Paul's Cathedral, the Painted Hall at Greenwich Hospital, altarpieces for several Oxford colleges and ceilings at Blenheim. Thornhill's manner resembles that of his contemporary, Tiepolo. Thornhill was the

G. B. TIEPOLO · THE ADORATION OF THE KINGS · *162¾″ × 84¾″. Munich, Alte Pinakothek*

father-in-law of Hogarth, and he was the founder of an academy of painting later conducted by Hogarth in St Martin's Lane, London.

TIBALDI

Pelligrino Tibaldi, a late Renaissance painter, sculptor and architect, was born in 1527 at Puria and died in 1596 at Milan. Mannerism was at its height when he started painting, and he absorbed it directly he joined the circle of Michelangelo's followers in Rome about 1550. In his early work, under the influence of Parmigianino and dell' Abate, his attraction to the monumental is clearly visible. His best work was done in Bologna—his Odysseus frescoes. They are accounted among the most outstanding examples of Mannerism anywhere. Their success created a demand for his work in various towns, including Ancona, where he decorated the Loggia dei Mercanti with similar interesting paintings. In 1587 he was invited to Madrid, and his progress there was a triumph for him. The Spaniards even preferred him to El Greco, and when he left in 1596 the King made him a marquis!

TIEPOLO

Giovanni Battista Tiepolo, who was born in 1696 in Venice and died in 1770 in Madrid, is, with Guardi, the last of the great Venetian painters and one of the most inspired artists of the late Baroque and Rococo periods. Every age has loved his grace, his delight in the pleasures of the senses and his light touch. He lacks one gift—motive power—so, in spite of all his talents, he remains among the great but not the greatest painters.

Tiepolo came of a good family, and Gregorio Lazzarini (1655-1730), under whom he studied, taught him not only to draw, but to express the purely visual delight which had so long been frowned upon by 'intellectual' painters. Veronese was another good influence: it almost seems as if he actually had a hand in early works, such as *The Last Supper* (Louvre) and *Cleopatra's Feast* (Melbourne). Tiepolo devoted himself to his work, made a careful study of Piazzetta, and soon mastered his early uncertainty in the depiction of light and the drawing of the nude.

His rise to international fame began when he was called to Würzburg in 1751. He stayed there for two years and painted the wonderful frescoes in the episcopal Residence. His fame reached its peak in 1762 after an invitation from the King of Spain. He decorated rooms in the Palace in Madrid and the King pressed him for more work, but Tiepolo had by this time grown weary of incessant labour. He and his two sons, who accompanied him everywhere as his assistants, wanted time off to enjoy life. He was getting old and Court intrigues wearied him, but it was too late, and death overtook him in a strange land.

Tiepolo's frescoes are his best-known work, but he also executed a number of fine oil paintings, many of them works of importance, such as *The Martyrdom of St Agatha* and *Christ Carrying the Cross* (Berlin, Venice), the *Adoration of the*

TINTORETTO
MARS AND VENUS
SURPRISED BY VULCAN
*55½″ × 77⅜″. Munich,
Alte Pinakothek*

TINTORETTO
CHRIST WALKING ON
THE SEA OF GALILEE
46¾″ × 67⅞″. *Washington,
National Gallery*

Magi (Munich, New York), and *Telemachus* (Amsterdam).

Tiepolo's wife was a sister of Guardi, so their sons had a double inheritance of artistic blood, but only **Domenico's** name (1727-1804) has survived. He helped his father with many of his frescoes.

TILLEMANS

Peter Tillemans (1684-1734) was a Flemish painter who worked in England. He came to London from Antwerp with his brother-in-law, Peter Casteels, and was first employed as a draughtsman. Later he made a name for himself with his landscapes with horses and dogs. He made about five hundred drawings for Bridge's *History of Northamptonshire*, and was a pioneer in the development of both landscape and sporting pictures in England.

TINTORETTO

Jacopo Robusti was the son of a dyer (*tintore*) in S. Cassiano, a slum-quarter of Venice; hence the boy was known as Tintoretto (the little dyer) and made that name immortal.

Jacopo Tintoretto was born in 1518 in Venice and he died there in 1594. A mist of uncertainty hangs over his artistic education: it is reported that he worked for Titian 'for a few days'. The style of his early work seems most like Paris Bordone —the same technique, the same method of creating depth by means of *coulisses*, the same threatening atmosphere and stormy skies, the same feeble illusion of space are common to both, though Tintoretto shows a particular love of firmly modelled female forms (*Venus and Vulcan*, Munich; *Leda*, Florence). He may have been a pupil of Bonifazio. He exhibits no more of the influence of Titian than any other painter of that time, except perhaps in his choice of colour. And the legend above the door of his workshop is said to have read: 'Michelangelo's drawing and Titian's colour.'

As far as is known, Tintoretto never left Venice. He led a quiet, uneventful life and was fond of the society of monks, who commissioned many paintings from him. His marriage was happy and, out of his seven children, **Domenico** (1560-1635) and **Marietta** (c. 1555-c. 1590) have often been called his collaborators. (Domenico made his mark as a portrait painter.)

Michelangelo, Salviati and Parmigianino all strongly influenced Tintoretto. Indeed, it was under the impression made by Michelangelo's work in the Sistine Chapel that Tintoretto painted *The Brazen Serpent* (Venice), and *The Miracle of St Mark*

(Venice), which laid the foundation of his reputation in 1548. The huge *Crucifixion* in San Rocco, Venice, is perhaps his finest work and is so broadly painted that it has the effect almost of a sketch.

Tintoretto's work cannot be reduced to any brief formula. His secular pictures (*Susanna and the Elders*, Vienna; *Venus and Vulcan*, Munich) make an impression of great clarity and solidity; his religious pictures are ecstatic and agitated. *The Last Supper* (San Giorgio, Venice) is an eerie scene taking place in the ghostly light of the catacombs. Tintoretto expresses his religious fervour in his predilection for melodramatic, supernatural effects of light. It was he who was responsible for the direction taken by El Greco. The dun light, the flame-like figures and the volcanic-looking blue-green colour of *Christ Walking on the Sea of Galilee* (Washington) might almost be the work of El Greco.

There is a third side to Tintoretto's output—his remarkable portraits. His thoughtful paintings of old men, *Cornaro* (Pitti, Florence), *Sansovino* (Uffizi), *Morosini* (London) and *Old Man* (Berlin) are outstanding.

TISCHBEIN

There were four painters of this name.

Johann Heinrich or **Cassel** Tischbein, who was born in Haina in 1722 and died 1789 in Cassel, was the eldest. He studied in Paris and in Piazzetta's studio in Venice and became Court Painter and Director of the Academy at Cassel. He was a brilliant technician, and his early portraits are cabinet pieces in their delicacy of painting (*Portrait of His Wife*, Hamburg). He was just the right man to help the Landgrave realise his dream of assembling a fine collection in Schloss Wilhelmstal near Cassel. Some of his biblical and mythological etchings are also very attractive.

Johann Jacob or **Dutch** Tischbein (born in 1725 in Haina, died 1791 at Lübeck) was Johann's brother. His nickname comes from his early landscapes in the Dutch style which are small and painted on wood.

Johann Friedrich or **Leipzig** Tischbein, who was born in 1750 at Maastricht and died in 1812 at Heidelberg, spent his last twelve years as Director of the Academy in Leipzig. His only importance is in the field of portraiture. He was greatly influenced by Gainsborough and by the contemporary slightly effeminate French school.

Wilhelm Johann Heinrich or **Goethe-**Tischbein, who was born in Haina in 1751 and died in 1829 at Eutin, is the best-known of a large family, of whom over twenty members painted. He was the friend and travelling companion of Goethe in Southern Italy. The talented, enthusiastic young painter of *Goethe in the Campagna* (Frankfurt) gradually developed into one of the earliest of the nineteenth-century naturalists. His still-lifes of apples and pears are reminiscent of Courbet.

TISI

Benvenuto Tisi, called Garofalo, was born at Ferrara in 1481 and died there in 1559. He was a pupil of Domenico Panetti by the time he was ten years of age and studied later in Cremona and then in Rome (1499-1501). He returned to Ferrara and worked there with Dosso Dossi. In 1509 he was again in Rome and met Raphael. He went blind in 1550 and his last work bears that date. His style was based on that of the Ferrarese painters Roberti and Costa and was later influenced by that of Raphael and of the Venetians. But he never became a Mannerist and his work looks old-fashioned beside that of his contemporary Parmigianino. He worked chiefly for the d'Este family. Eight of his works are in the National Gallery, London, and include both religious and mythological subjects.

TITIAN

Tiziano Vecellio was born in Pieve di Cadore, a village in the Dolomites, where his father was a clerk to a magistrate. The date of his birth has always been queried, and even Vasari, who met Titian

TITIAN · VENUS
47⅞" × 66".
Florence, Uffizi

at the Vatican, reports it alternatively as 1480 or 1490. His contemporary, Dolci, mentions the year 1489. Titian himself in a letter to the King of Spain, gives it as 1477. He, if anyone, ought to know, but there are practical and psychological reasons for doubting his information. Titian's earliest pictures date from 1505/10. The spirited *Assumption*, painted in 1516, is clearly a youthful work rather than the creation of a man approaching forty. Three years before that Titian had applied for the first time for a public appointment. There was nothing unusual in such an application from an ambitious young man of twenty-three, but it would have been a curious action on the part of an established painter of thirty-six. Furthermore, Titian always liked to think of himself as unique. He therefore described himself in his old age to the King of Spain as ninety-five instead of eighty-two years of age, not only so that he should appear even more remarkable than he was, but to disguise the true nature of his connection with Giorgione. He made out that, instead of being twelve years younger than Giorgione, he was his senior by a year, and it was thus doubtful whether he or Giorgione had been responsible for the new developments in Venetian painting. The question of Titian's age has never been satisfactorily settled, but the official dates generally given today

are: Titian was born in 1477 in Venice and died there in 1576.

He was a pupil of Giovanni Bellini and it was in his studio that he made the acquaintance of Giorgione. Like all young painters, Titian was completely enthralled by the novelty of Giorgione's work and followed him like a satellite. Their friendship grew, and when Giorgione died suddenly Titian completed one of his unfinished pictures, the *Venus* (Dresden).

Titian's Giorgionesque period lasted a long time. To it belong many famous pictures: *The Gipsy Madonna* and *The Madonna with the Cherries* (Vienna), *Sacred and Profane Love* (Borghese Gallery, Rome), *The Concert* (Pitti, Florence) and *Noli me tangere* (National Gallery, London). A restrained, yet growing vitality underlies the pastoral tranquillity of these pictures.

At length, in 1516, Titian broke free from the spell of Giorgione. He painted *The Assumption of the Virgin*, which ushered in the Baroque as if with a trumpet blast. The dedication of this picture was the occasion for a public holiday, and Titian himself was made State Painter. The Virgin of *The Assumption*, as Titian portrays her, is not being wafted or even carried up to Heaven; she is a heavy, excited, gesticulating figure forcing her way upwards. The *Bacchanal* in the Prado and the *Bacchus and Ariadne* in the National Gallery belong to the same period.

In his thirties Titian underwent a transformation. He realised that his gift did not lie so much in the painting of obviously dramatic events as in seeing and revealing the beauty of colour. He concentrated more and more on deep, intense, darkly-glowing colour. Outward circumstances contributed to this change. In 1530 Titian's wife died, and in the same year he met the Emperor Charles V in Bologna. He was much affected when the Emperor made a friend of him and when, three years later, in 1533, he appointed him Court Painter, made him a Count and gave him the right to use the title of 'Imperial Counsellor'. This recognition of his talents gave him fresh impetus and the desire to extol in paint the virtues of maturity and dignity, elegance and patriarchal gravity.

Titian also received commissions from the Dukes of Ferrara, Mantua and Urbino. In 1545-46 the Pope invited him to Rome and presented him with the Belvedere. Michelangelo visited him, and he was given the freedom of the city. In 1548 and again in 1550-51 he was among the Emperor's guests at Augsburg. Lucas Cranach painted his portrait (now lost) and everyone of note who came to Venice visited him. He lived in Venice in the style of a nobleman and looked and behaved like an aristocrat. But he was neither grateful nor content. Always tense and overworked, always gnawed by suspicion, despite his great popularity, Titian at last could not prevent his underlying arrogance from becoming evident in his pictures. They are pictures for the eyes of age, for those who, perhaps like the painter, see too much. Gradually Titian's technique loosened till his last pictures (e.g. *Christ Crowned with Thorns*, Munich) are painted directly on to

the canvas with wild brush strokes and little or no drawing, composed in colour alone and animated by flecks of light and dark. No painter before Titian had ever attempted to convey the lack of precision which characterises the vision of the aged.

Other important works from Titian's middle and late periods include *La Bella* (Pitti, Florence), *Venus* (Uffizi), the *Venus del Prado* (Louvre), *Danaë* (Madrid), *The Madonna* (Munich), *The Vendramin Family* (National Gallery, London), *Lavinia* (Berlin), *The Entombment* and *Religion Succoured by Spain* (Madrid), *Pietà* (Venice) and *Ecce Homo* (Leningrad). It is impossible to enumerate

TITIAN · CHRIST CROWNED WITH THORNS
72" × 72¾". Munich, Alte Pinakothek

Titian's many portraits, which include some of his most striking works.

Orazio Vecellio (c. 1520-1576) was Titian's son. He worked with his father, and also succeeded him in various official posts. His authenticated pictures are rare, but he is not considered an important painter.

TOCQUÉ

Louis Tocqué (1696-1772 in Paris) was the son-in-law of Nattier and a pupil of Rigaud. He was a popular painter, often invited to the Courts of St Petersburg and Copenhagen; he was also a man of the world who recognised his own limitations. He enjoyed the last ten years of his life on a retirement pension. His pictures are as cool and smooth as porcelain but without Nattier's charm or La Tour's keen and penetrating observation. The current view that he was better at portraits should not be accepted without qualification, though his Rococo courtiers are perfect in their way.

TOMASO

Tomaso da Modena (c. 1325-1379 in Modena) was trained in the manner of Vitale de Bologna and the illuminators of manuscripts, and was one of the painters whose works are believed to have been discovered in Prague. In actual fact he did have contacts with the Emperor Charles IV, and two signed paintings of the Madonna hang in the Castle of Karlstein, near Prague. Even if Tomaso never went to Prague in person, he is certainly the bridge by which Italian influences were transported to the Bohemian School. And, reversing the process, he came in touch with the Gothic spirit of the north, a spirit not yet extinct in German painting.

Tomaso's fresco of the *Dominican at His Writing-desk* (San Niccolo, Treviso) anticipates Lucas Moser, with the spirit of whose work it has so much in common, by about two generations. The Dominican is proudly wearing spectacles, which had only just been invented! Tomaso is distinguished by his studies from nature: he uses all his powers of observation and

imagination, which combine to make him the most important of the painters of his century who emanated from Modena and Treviso.

TORBIDO

Francesco di Marco Torbido was born c. 1482 in Venice and died in 1562 at Verona. The paintings in the Fontanelli Chapel in Venice are considered his principal works, and, judged by size, they certainly are. But more truly beautiful are a couple of portraits about which Berenson writes: 'Torbido, who before he was swept away by the deluge brought down by Giulio Romano, tasted of the springs of Giorgione's art and, refreshed by them, painted two or three haunting portraits, such as the wistful young man in the Doria Gallery, or the ivy-crowned youth at Padua.' It is possible that the so-called *Broccardo* was painted by him, though the Budapest Museum persists in attributing it to Giorgione.

TOURNIER

Nicolas Tournier (1590-after 1657) worked in Rome from 1619 to 1626, and seems to have been more influenced there by Valentin than by any other painters. His pictures were until recently often confused with those of Valentin. He has the same tendency towards stylisation and classicism and the same mood of melancholy intensified. In 1632 Tournier settled for the rest of his life in Toulouse, working also for patrons in Carcassonne and Narbonne. His best work was done in Toulouse and can be seen in the Musée des Augustins there. The masterpiece of the period is the *Pietà*. This has a monumental severity and profound religious feeling and is painted in the Caravaggesque style.

TOURNIERES

Robert Levrac Tournières was born at Ifs, near Caen, in 1667 and died at Caen in 1772. A *genre* and portrait painter, he was a pupil of Lucas de la Haye and of Bon Boullogne. He was admitted to the Academy as a portrait painter in 1702 and as a history painter in 1716. He became

assistant professor in 1725. A picture of
La Barre, the flautist and composer, and
other musicians in the National Gallery,
London, is ascribed to Tournières. Other
pictures by him include *The Daughter of
Dibutades drawing the Portrait of her Lover*
(Louvre) and a *Portrait of Racine* (Caen).

TOWNE

Francis Towne (1740-1816) was born in
Devon and worked in Wales, Italy and
Switzerland. He particularly liked mountain subjects. He worked in watercolour
only and his pictures are rare. (Examples
are in the Victoria and Albert Museum.)
He was astonishingly in advance of his age,
deliberately eschewing the picturesque
traditions of landscape painting of his
period and concentrating on geological and
architectural structure, and simplifying in a
manner that foreshadows the style of Paul
Nash.

TRAINI

Franceso Traini, first mentioned in Pisa
between 1321 and 1363, was the leader and
the most outstanding personality of the
Pisan School. Quite recently the extremely
interesting frescoes in the Campo Santo
were recognised as his work. In 1340
Ambrogio Lorenzetti had painted his
Good and Bad Government in Siena and,
in the same spirit Traini covered the walls
in Pisa with a series of imaginative frescoes,
like giant book illustrations of the *Triumph
of Death*. The *St Dominic Altarpiece* in
Pisa is his only absolutely authenticated
work.

TROGER

Paul Troger was born in 1698 at Welsberg
and died in 1762 at Vienna. He studied in
Northern Italy and was much influenced
by Piazzetta and Solimena. He settled in
Vienna c. 1728, and from 1754 to 1757 was
Rector of the Academy. Frescoes and altarpieces by Troger can be seen in Vienna,
Brixen and Salzburg, and in many Austrian
monasteries. He was a most skilful illusionist painter, and among the most
impressive of his works is the ceiling fresco
of the *Triumph of Religion* in the Cathedral

at Brixen, for which there is a sketch in the
Vienna Academy.

TROY

François de Troy (1645-1730) spent
several years as a student in Toulouse,
where he was born, then moved to Paris
and joined the workshop of Claude Lefebre, taking over his clientèle at his death
in about 1675. He also took over the pattern of Lefebre's portraits, but added
elements from Van Dyck and made them
more decorative and warmer in colour.
He specialised in portraits of the Parisian
bourgeoisie and of the Court as did
Rigaud and Largillière, and was responsible for the training of a large number of
pupils. There are good examples of his
work in the Louvre, the Musée de Rouen
and the Musée de Toulon.

Jean Francois de Troy, his son (1678-
1752), also studied in Rome and in 1738
became Director of the French Academy
in Rome. He executed huge classical and
historical pictures and designed tapestries
for Louis XIV and painted much more
attractive small scenes of gallantry, and
genre and biblical pictures for his own
pleasure. Represented in the National
Gallery, London, and the Wallace Collection, London.

TRUMBALL

John Trumball (1756-1843) was an American painter who served as aide to General
Washington during the Revolutionary
War. He came to London in 1780 to study
under Benjamin West, but was imprisoned
because of his execution in America of
Major André as a spy. Trumball's works
include portraits of Washington and
many distinguished soldiers of the Revolution as well as scenes from the war,
including *The Battle of Bunker Hill*, *The
Death of Montgomery*, *The Surrender of
Lord Cornwallis* and *The Signing of the
Declaration of Independence*. In 1831
Trumball's pictures of the Revolution
were purchased by Yale University and in
1832 the Trumball Gallery was erected on
the campus to house them.

COSIMO TURA · MADONNA AND CHILD EN-
THRONED · (*Detail*) 94″ × 40″. *London, National Gallery*

TURA

Cosimo Tura lived from about 1430 to
1495 in Ferrara. Together with Cossa, he
was the most important of the brilliant
Ferrarese painters of the fifteenth century,
but as Court Painter to the Dukes of Este
Tura asserted his claims to leadership
more strongly and insistently than Cossa
and his work imposed itself on the whole
succeeding generation of painters.

Tura must have spent about fifty years
in Padua. Many artists travelled to Padua,

but none of them were so profoundly impressed as Tura by what they saw in the
studio of Squarcione and Mantegna. Later
Tura also saw and admired the work of
Piero della Francesa in Ferrara, but it
could not divert him from his own remarkable imaginative conceptions. Berenson
has described his style as follows: 'Tura's
figures are of flint, as haughty and im-
mobile as Pharaohs, or as convulsed as the
gnarled knots in the olive tree. Their faces
are seldom lit up with tenderness, and
their smiles are apt to turn into archaic
grimaces. . . . His landscapes are of a
world which has these many ages seen no
flower or green leaf.'

The same carving of feature and groov-
ing of muscle were used also by Castagno
to express asceticism and inflexibility.
Castagno lived far away from Tura in
Florence, so it would seem that the style
must have been in some way a product of
that period.

Tura, then as now, was considered an
important painter. His pictures are almost
all religious, and many of his panels have
lately been taken to America, among them
The Flight into Egypt (New York). Berlin
possesses a *Madonna with Saints* (appar-
ently finished by Roberti), London a
Madonna with Angels and *An Allegorical
Figure*. There are *Lamentation* pictures in
Venice (Correr), Paris and Vienna, and a
fine *Madonna* in Venice (Academy). In
Ferrara there is a *Fight with a Dragon*, and
Modena possesses his last work *St
Anthony*.

TURCHI

Alessandro Turchi, l'Orbetto, who was
born in 1578 in Verona and died 1649 in
Rome, is easy to remember because of his
tiny religious scenes, painted on panels of
slate or black marble, which can be seen
in many museums. They show no influence from Venice or from his birthplace
but incline more towards Carracci and
Reni. His uninspired eclecticism is very
pronounced in his large canvases, where
his flesh tints are lobster red and the
picture surface seems to be powdered with
chalk.

UCCELLO

Paolo di Dono, who signed his pictures Paolo Uccello, was born in 1397 in Florence. At the age of ten he was apprenticed to Ghiberti and by the time he was eighteen he was a master-painter. He spent six years, from 1424 until 1430, in Venice; he was living in Padua with his friend, Donatello, in 1445 and was in Urbino in 1457. By then commissions were few and far between. Poverty, loneliness and sickness were the lot of this great painter towards the end of his life and he died in hospital in 1475.

Vasari has no compassion for him. He describes Uccello as a neurotic recluse, a brooder, who would have been 'the most pleasing painter of all the followers of Giotto if he had not wasted his time and worn out his imagination in futile speculation over problems of mathematics and perspective'. The Renaissance revered science, but Vasari felt that Uccello foolishly indulged his passion for perspective at the expense of a full life.

If it is ever possible to speak with absolute certainty of the personal style of any painter of that period it is so in the case of Uccello. His three enormous panels of the *Battle of San Romano* (London, Paris, Florence) are stupendous; they consist of cubic planes with never a shadow, and rigid areas of colour without depth, like a map, and yet these compositions of mathematically converging lines and frozen figures are monumental in their effect. Uccello's characteristic style is already established in his early work and can be seen in the monochrome *Portrait of Sir John Hawkwood* in the Duomo, Florence, which is the first equestrian portrait of the Renaissance period. As the painter grew older his style slightly softened. *The Midnight Hunt* (Ashmolean Museum, Oxford) and *St George and the Dragon* (Musée Jacquemart, Paris) show a growing inclination for naïve effects which in Uccello's last years triumphed over everything else. In the little panels of *The Legend of the Jew and the Host*, painted for the Duke of Urbino, the monumentality of the battle pictures has been sacrificed to this toy-like quality.

PAOLO UCCELLO · THE ROUT OF SAN ROMANO, 1432
72″ × 125″. London, National Gallery

UDEN

Lucas van Uden was born in Antwerp in 1595 and died there in 1672. Between 1620 and 1630 he painted various landscape backgrounds for Rubens, and the resemblance of his own landscapes with their wooded valleys and gentle hills to those seen in Rubens' pictures confirms this fact. But Uden's little landscapes (*Hilly Landscape with Rainbow* and *Landscape with Woodcutters*, Berlin) are unheroic and lack the bold touch of Rubens. When Uden wanted figures for his landscapes he had recourse to another painter, no less an artist than Teniers, who scattered glittering little figures like beads over Uden's pictures.

UDINE

Giovanni da Udine (Giovanni Nanni or dei Ricamatori) as born at Udine in 1487 and died in Rome in 1564. He worked principally in Rome and was one of the most interesting decorative painters of the period. While working with Raphael he invented a style of ornament based on the newly discovered decorations of the Baths of Titus and created a new art form combining painting and stucco which became the basis of sixteenth-century decoration. His work is naturalistic and richly coloured and represents a synthesis of the fifteenth-century Umbrian tradition with Roman classical forms. He studied first with Giovanni Martini da Udine and later in Venice under Giorgione. When he came to Rome in 1511 he entered Raphael's workshop and began his long career as a decorative artist in Rome, Florence, Cividale, Venice and Udine. His numerous works include decorations in the loggia of the Vatican (1517-19) and the Hall of Pontiffs and in the Medici Palace (1520) in Florence.

Giovanni Martini da Udine (c. 1453-1535) was perhaps a pupil of Cima in Venice but was back in Udine by 1497 and remained there until his death. An altarpiece in the National Gallery, London, is ascribed to him and other works include a *Madonna* (Museo Civico, Venice) and *St Mark Enthroned* (Cathedral, Udine).

His style is based on that of the Vivarini and Cima.

UFFIZI

Uffizi is the same word as office in English, and it originally signified the administrative office of state, town or court. Vasari was the architect of the Uffizi in Florence, which was built between 1560 and 1574. The Dukes of Tuscany filled more and more rooms with their collections of pictures, till finally the Uffizi Palace became the Uffizi State Gallery, the name that now stands for one of the most important picture-galleries in the world. No other museum has so large a collection of early Italian painting, including works by Botticelli, Fra Filippo and Filippino Lippi, Pollaiuolo, Castagna, Uccello, Ghirlandaio, Veneziano, Piero di Cosimo and Leonardo.

UGOLINO

Ugolino da Siena (died c. 1348 in Siena) is known to have been a pupil of the great Duccio and his chief work demonstrates this fact. It is a signed altarpiece that he painted for the church of Santa Croce in Florence, and which in drawing, composition and colour follows Duccio completely. Today parts of this altarpiece are in Berlin, London and private collections. The National Gallery possesses no fewer than seven of his works. They are close to Duccio in style, but they have less grace and charm than Duccio's work and greater dramatic intensity. This is specially noticeable in the remarkable *Betrayal*.

UTRECHT

Adriaen van Utrecht (1599-1653 in Antwerp) was essentially a pure still-life painter of fruit and game, even when he set them in a kitchen interior or on a breakfast table, in a *genre* piece. Any objects that did not interest him he let others paint in for him. Artists such as Jordaens, Teniers, Thulden and Rombouts usually painted the groups of people gossiping that are dragged into some of his pictures. His pure still-lifes are reminiscent of Fyt, but his colour tends to be rather dark, just as if he had never seen the work of either Rubens or Snyders.

V

VAGA

Pierino del Vaga (Pietro Buonaccorsi) was born in Florence in 1501 and died there in 1546. He was a pupil of Ridolfo del Ghirlandaio and later assisted Raphael in Rome. He painted decorations in the Loggia of the Vatican from cartoons by Raphael, *The Crossing of the Jordan*, *The Taking of Jericho* and *Joshua Stopping the Sun*. He also worked in the manner of Giovanni da Udine with whom he collaborated in decorations in the Vatican. In 1523 he left Rome for Florence, Siena and Genoa, where he worked in the Palazzo Doria. On his return to Rome he was employed by Paul III and executed decorations in the Castel Sant' Angelo and the Palazzo Massimi. He was essentially a decorator inclining towards Mannerism.

VAILLANT

Wallerant Vaillant (1623-1677) was born in Lille, but passed the greater part of his life in Holland and Germany, working in Middelburg, Amsterdam and Frankfurt. For a short period, from 1659 until 1665 he was in Paris and came under the influ-ence of the austere style of Champaigne. Vaillant's work is a most interesting combination of the Dutch and French traditions. Both are apparent in the *Boy Seated Drawing* in the National Gallery, London.

VALCKENBORCH

Three painters of this name became famous: **Lucas,** who was born in Louvain in 1530 and died in 1597 in Frankfort, **Martin,** his brother, who was born in 1535 in Louvain and died in 1597 in Frankfort, and **Frederik,** Martin's son, who was born in 1571 in Antwerp and died in 1627 in Nuremberg. All three painted the same subjects in the same style, landscapes with the tiny figures of huntsmen, people promenading, woodcutters or quarrymen and an occasional unpretentious *Adoration* or *Building of the Tower of Babel*, a theme which Pieter Brueghel had made popular.

Lucas van Valckenborch, who represents the so-called Frankenthal School, was the most important of the three painters. His landscapes, usually distant views seen from a height, are meticulously painted (*The Vintage*, Vienna; *Landscape with*

L. V. VALCKENBORCH
MOUNTAIN LANDSCAPE
WITH A MINE AND
FOUNDRY
30⅛" × 42⅜". Vienna,
Kunsthistorisches Museum

Huntsmen and Smelting-house, Frankfort). Though they are so early in date, these landscapes, without being works of genius, are characterised by unity of atmosphere and show skill and power in handling.

VALDÈS

Juan de Valdès Leal, who was born in 1622 in Cordoba and died 1690 in Seville, was, like Velazquez, half Spanish and half Portuguese. He was a temperamental painter whose pictures have something of Murillo's ecstatic faith in spite of their stark realism. It was Valdès' misfortune to be Murillo's contemporary and fellow-countryman, and inevitably, he was over-shadowed by him. Valdès best work can only be seen in Seville and Madrid, but there is a typical *Immaculate Conception* in the National Gallery, London.

VALENCIENNES

Pierre Henri Valenciennes (1750-1819) was born at Toulouse and studied there and under Doyen in Paris. He spent some time in Italy where he was influenced by Claudo and Poussin. He painted classical landscapes in the manner of those two masters and was the author of a work entitled *Elements of Perspective*. He is well represented in the Louvre.

VALENTIN

Valentin (or Valentino) de Boulogne was born in 1594 at Coulommiers, not far from Paris, but his ancestors were Italian, probably from Bologna. He went back to Italy in 1614 and lived in Rome until his death in 1632. Fortunately, the circle in which he moved in Rome had no effect on him artistically. He was serious-minded and without worldly ambitions, so he sat quietly at his easel turning out impressive and fantastically naturalistic pictures like *The Prophetess* (Louvre), *Martyrdom of Saints* (Vatican), *The Cardsharper* (Dresden). For a long time his Dresden picture was attributed to Caravaggio, his great prototype. He received many commissions from Italian collectors and was admired by Louis XIV.

VANLOO

Jean Baptiste Vanloo (1684-1745) was born at Nice and studied under his father. He worked in Turin for a time, then in 1737 went to London, where he became the leading portraitist of the day. He became a member of the French Academy in 1740. A number of his portraits are in the National Portrait Gallery, London.

VANNI

Andrea Vanni (c. 1332-after 1396) was a Sienese painter whose linear style stemmed from that of Simone Martini and Lippo Memmi. He may have been a pupil of the latter. He shared a workshop in 1353 with Bartolo di Fredi. Vanni was a close friend of St Catherine of Siena and painted her portrait. Important works by him include a polyptych of *The Madonna and Saints* in S. Stefano alla Lizza, Siena, an *Annunciation* in the Fogg Art Museum, Harvard, and the fresco of St Catherine in the Church of San Domenico, Siena. His style is more rigid and angular than that of Simone Martini and his mood and colour are sober and without the humour that enlivens Bartolo di Fredi's work.

VASARI

Giorgio Vasari, who was born in 1511 in Arezzo, and died in 1574 in Florence, was a painter, an architect and a biographer. Fate was kinder to him than to his Dutch counterpart, Karel van Mander (q.v.). Vasari was a pupil of Michelangelo and Andrea del Sarto, and, although his portraits and his frescoes in Florence have not given him a claim to immortality, he is still honoured in that city as the architect of the Uffizi Palace. His biographies of painters, sculptors and architects, the *Vite*, have provided posterity with some invaluable documents. They start with Cimabue and end with Titian, and today they are still interesting to study, with the proviso that due allowance is made for Vasari's imaginative flights.

VECCHIETTA

Vecchietta, whose real name was Lorenzo di Pietro, was a notable painter, sculptor, bronze-founder, builder and engineer. He was born at Castiglione di Val d'Orcia in 1412 and died at Siena in 1480. Sassetta was probably his teacher and Neroccio his pupil, while he himself filled the breathing-space between the two great names. In his taste for naturalistic scenes (*The Flagellation* and *Christ Bearing His Cross*, Siena), Vecchietta diverges from Sassetta and, though he vacillated later, the distinction was maintained.

The triptych, *The Assumption of the Blessed Virgin Mary*, in the Cathedral of Pienza (Corsignano) is accounted his best work. There is a large panel of the *Madonna and Child with Saints* in the Uffizi.

VELAZQUEZ

Diego Rodriguez de Silva y Velazquez is Spain's most important painter and one of the world's great masters. The admiration accorded him in his lifetime has increased with the centuries until it has almost become veneration. Michelangelo is the only other artist of this calibre whose work was not in the least affected by his popularity. As Velazquez progressed from the bold, heavy manner of Caravaggio to his final subdued and economical style his pictures grew ever more aloof and distinguished until no trace of intimacy remained. Intimacy is still present in his celebrated early works such as *The Kitchenmaid* and *The Water-carrier* (private collection, London) and in *Christ in the House of Martha* (National Gallery, London), and though he no doubt chose these subjects for their painterly possibilities, it is delightful to be reminded in them of the everyday experiences they enshrine. Later Velazquez utterly renounced such subject-matter; and his

VELAZQUEZ · THE INFANTA MARGARITA
84¾″ × 58¾″. *Madrid, Prado*

development as a man is said to have been very similar; he became more and more distant, reserved and aristocratic.

Velazquez was born in Seville in 1599; his parents belonged to the lower ranks of the nobility. He was given an exclusive education at school and then was apprenticed to the eccentric Herrera, with whom, however, he remained only a few weeks before changing to Pacheco, who did not teach him much about painting, but helped him a great deal in other ways. Velazquez eventually married Pacheco's daughter, Juana. It was during this period that he painted his *bodegones* (kitchen-pieces), completely under the spell of

Caravaggio. But they nevertheless contain the germs of Velazquez's subsequent development, for even in them he rejects Caravaggio's colouring and his plebeian gestures.

Velazquez made two attempts to move to Madrid before he succeeded in getting there. The Duke of Olivares, whose name would have long since been forgotten if Velazquez had not immortalised him, became interested in the young painter and recommended him to the notice of the King. In 1623 Velazquez was appointed Court Painter. Then in 1628 Rubens arrived in Madrid and persuaded the King to give Velazquez two years' leave to visit Italy. In 1631 he returned to Spain after having studied and copied Titian, Veronese and Tintoretto and

VELAZQUEZ · THE INFANTE DON CARLOS
83⅜" × 50". Madrid, Prado

after having met Ribera in Rome. This was the beginning of his great period. By 1643 he held a variety of appointments at the Court, and was made Officer of Works in charge of the building of a Royal Gallery, to buy pictures for which he again visited Italy from 1649 until 1650. In 1652 he was appointed Court Marshal and was made a member of the Most Noble Order of St James. In the spring of 1660 Velazquez accompanied the King on a journey to the Pyrenees to meet Louis XIV. On the way back to Madrid he caught cold and by the autumn of the same year he was dead.

Velazquez's genius increased with age. He had overcome every problem of drawing and composition, so in his great picture *Las Meninas* (Madrid) he hazarded an experiment. He depicted the Infanta with her maids of honour in his studio while the King and Queen were only visible in a mirror. He also ventured to paint the radiant garden of the Villa Medici in monochrome. And he openly attempted something at which he had only hinted in his early work: in *The Spinners* (Prado) he combined two distinct subjects on two different levels in the picture. Again, in *The Surrender of Breda* he boldly cut the landscape into sections by painting twenty-nine lances piercing the sky; he also succeeded in giving the victorious Spanish general a most humane and benevolent expression as he lays his hand on the shoulder of his defeated enemy. There is an abundance of painterly detail in this picture—the huge horse beside the victor, the touching figure of the young standard-bearer in his bloodstained tunic, the pastel figures in the background and the extraordinary light in the smoke-filled sky.

Every stroke of Velazquez's brush counts; his colours are subdued, and as he grew older he softened his light and shade until the silvery-grey tone predominated that Monet later so greatly admired. In the field of portraiture Velazquez is the equal of Rembrandt. His most admired portraits include *Portrait of a Young Girl* (New York, Hisp. Soc.), *Lady with a Fan* (London, Wallace Collection), *Philip IV: Bust Portrait* and *Philip IV in Brown and*

W. VAN DE VELDE THE YOUNGER
VESSELS SALUTING
$31\frac{1}{2}'' \times 26\frac{3}{4}''$. *Amsterdam, Rijksmuseum*

Silver (London, National Gallery), *Cano* (private collection, London), *Pareja* (private collection, Salisbury), *Pope Innocent X* (Rome and Washington), *The Infanta Margarita with a Vase of Flowers* (Vienna), and *Equestrian Portrait of Duke Olivares, The Infante Don Carlos, Pablo, Don Fernando as Huntsman, The Dwarf Sebastian, Philip IV in Old Age* and *The Infanta Margarita with a Shawl in Her Hand*, all in the Prado.

VELDE

Dutch marine painting reached its brilliant peak with Willem van de Velde the Younger at a time when it was particularly appreciated in Holland after the Dutch naval victory over England made her, temporarily, the greatest sea-power in Europe. Dutch painting had come a long way from the early efforts by Hendrik Vroom to the authentic and technically correct pictures of ships and naval battles of Willem van de Velde. He did not romanticise or dramatise, he quite simply

painted seascapes instead of landscapes. He is the Heyden of the sea.

Willem, born at Leyden in 1633, was the son of the unimportant seascape painter, **Willem van de Velde the Elder,** and was a pupil of Simon de Vliegers. It is thought that during the seventies he was captured at sea and taken prisoner to England. He did not return to Holland, but settled in Greenwich where he died in 1707. He is buried in St James's, Piccadilly. His best works are not oil paintings, excellent though these are, but reed pen drawings on a painted white background. There are a number of these in the National Maritime Museum at Greenwich.

Adriaen van de Velde (1636-1672 in Antwerp) was Willem's brother and a prominent landscape painter. He succeeded in combining all that Wouverman, Potter and Berchem were striving for in his wonderfully luminous river or seashore scenes, meadow landscapes or winter pieces. In some of his small landscapes, such as the *Forest Scene* (National Gallery) he anticipates the Barbizon School as a *plein-airist*.

Esias van de Velde, who was born c. 1591 in Amsterdam and died in 1630 at The Hague, was apprenticed to Goyen and later became the teacher of Aert van der Neer. His scenes of skaters or of pleasure parties on the banks of rivers are firmly and skilfully drawn. His style is like that of folk art, unfashionable but lasting. His group portraits and his battlepieces are unequal.

Jan Jansz van de Velde (active in 1620 in Haarlem, died in 1662 at Enkhuizen) painted small still-life pictures of breakfast tables, which, in the economy of their construction are reminiscent of Heda, but are painted on a dark ground in yellow, blue and white and create a harmony that is almost as exquisite as that of Vermeer. Jan was also an engineer.

VENETO

Bartolomeo Veneto (or Veneziano or da Venezia) signed himself as a joke on his first picture 'half-Venetian, half-Cremonese', but on later pictures as 'Venetus'.

BARTOLOMEO VENETO · PORTRAIT OF A LADY
17¼″ × 13⅝″. Frankfurt, Staedelsches Kunstinstitut

Little is known of his life, but he was active soon after 1500 in Venice, Ferrara and Milan. The female bust-portraits of his best period are decisive in outline and rather acid in colour. Costa is partly responsible for this which is not surprising, as Veneto worked for Lucrezia Borgia for two years in Ferrara, which was Costa's native place. Veneto's most famous picture is the truly enchanting *Portrait of a Young Courtesan* in Frankfort.

VENEZIANO

Domenico Veneziano, the painter of the tender Lucia altarpiece in the Uffizi, the majestic *Madonna and Child Enthroned* (National Gallery), and the lovely tondo of *The Adoration* (Berlin), must, as his name implies, have come from Venice, but his spirit, his eye and his hand are Florentine through and through. Venice at the time of his birth (1400/10) was still steeped in Byzantine influence, while Masolino and Fra Angelico were already painting in Florence and Domenic's painting stems

from them. Very little is known about his life. He died in Florence in 1461.

The Madonna of the Lucia altarpiece is seated between the tall, upright figures of saints and the slender marble columns of an arcade, the composition forming a subtle harmony of pink and grey which has its equal only in the work of Piero della Francesca. And light which in Fra Angelico's picture is merely the attribute of a divine subject, is introduced for purely aesthetic reasons in Veneziano's compositions. The *predelle* are in Berlin, Washington, Cambridge and Florence. The little panel in Washington, *John the Baptist in the Wilderness*, clearly shows Veneziano's conception of human beauty. The Baptist is a naked Florentine boy standing on the sandy shore of the Adriatic, just about to plunge into the water.

Unfortunately, the frescoes of S. Egidio in Florence are lost. Piero della Francesca and Piero del Pollaiuolo assisted Veneziano with them.

VENNE

Adriaen van de Venne, born 1589 in Delft, died 1662 at The Hague, painted fine landscapes with a pointed brush, scenes with wagons and peasants and horsemen, exactly like those that **Theobold Michau** (1676-1765) painted a century later. Pictures by both these painters lie around like cuckoos' eggs and are attributed by the dozen to Jan Brueghel, which is not to his advantage. In later life Van de Venne changed his style and painted crude peasant scenes in dull monochrome, making a name for himself with them at the time.

VERELST

Simon Verelst was born c. 1644 at The Hague and died in London in 1721. He was the son of **Pieter** Verelst, whose small pictures with figures, reminiscent of Gerard Dou's work, can occasionally be found in museums.

Simon inherited his father's rather limited talent, but lucky circumstances took him young to England where, under the Duke of Buckingham's patronage, he became a flower-painter of repute. Today his flower pieces and his portraits with floral accessories are considered second-rate. Pepys describes a visit to Verelst on 11th April, 1669, when he offered him £20 for 'a little flower-pot of his doing, the finest thing that ever, I think, I saw in my life'.

Simon's brother **Herman** (1643?-1700?) also settled in London and painted similar pictures.

VERHAECHT

Tobias Verhaecht (1561-1631 in Antwerp) was Rubens' teacher, but he himself had not a trace of his pupil's style or spirit. He was purely a landscape-painter, and in style he was midway between his two intimate friends, Jan Brueghel and Momper. His landscapes, usually of distant lakes, cities and strange rocks seen from a height, depend entirely on his fascinating topographical drawing; his colour is indifferent.

VERKOLJE

Jan Verkolje was born at Amsterdam in 1650, but when he married he moved to Delft, and died there in 1693. His pictures show that it was still possible to paint the same threadbare subjects as Metsu and Terborch, the fireplaces, and the silk-clad ladies and cavaliers. But Verkolje's pictures have no depth and his figures incline to be flat, except in his best picture, *The Temptation* in Dresden.

His pupil, **Thomas van der Wilt** (born 1659 in Piershil, died 1733 in Delft) painted in his master's style for another century and their pictures are almost interchangeable.

Nicolaes Verkolje was Jan's son, and perhaps a better painter. Unfortunately, it was the taste of the period to treat most subjects frivolously. His pictures are small and colourful and quite charming. The less said the better about his mythological and biblical efforts on a larger scale. Nicolaes was born in 1673 at Delft and died in 1746 at Amsterdam.

VERMEER

Jan Vermeer is recognised by the twentieth century as one of the greatest painters ever produced in Holland, but for two hundred years he was forgotten and his name almost passed into oblivion.

He is the painter of *The Woman Weighing Pearls* (Philadelphia), *The Girl in a Blue Jacket* and *The Little Street* (Amsterdam), *View of Delft* and *Head of a Girl* (The Hague), *Girl Reading a Letter* (Dresden), *Soldier and Laughing Girl* (Washington), *The Milkmaid* (Amsterdam), *Woman at a Window* (New York), *Lady and Gentleman Drinking Wine* (Berlin), *The Pearl Necklace* (Berlin), *The Lace-maker* (Paris), *The Artist in His Studio* (Vienna) and *The Love Letter* (Amsterdam). Astronomical prices are now given for his pictures, though shortly after his death some of them were auctioned for almost nothing.

Vermeer van Delft is a magician in the creation of pure colour, form and effects of light. He loved plain surfaces, whether of bare walls or of smooth materials, he favours pastel-coloured jackets and black

J. VERMEER VAN DELFT · A WOMAN OPENING A WINDOW · 17⅞″ × 15⅞″. *New York, Metropolitan Museum*

J. VERMEER VAN DELFT · A STREET IN DELFT
21¾" × 17¾". *Amsterdam, Rijksmuseum*

hats. Strictly speaking, he is neither a *genre* nor a portrait painter. His faces are formally pleasing, but as similar to each other as those of Leonardo. They express no feeling, and when they smile they seem as remote as the Mona Lisa. Vermeer is a stranger to passion, drama and impulsiveness, so that his pictures are almost without human sympathy. But he reaches the height of perfection in his colour harmonies. Discussions about abstract art often lead to the same observations as Vermeer's pictures, and it is perhaps owing to its mysterious affinity with modern abstraction that Vermeer's art is so highly prized today.

As for his life, Jan Vermeer was born at Delft in 1632 and died there in 1675, when he was only forty-three years old. His father was a silk-weaver who later became a publican and, as a side-line, an art-dealer. It is safe to assume that Jan was apprenticed to Carel Fabritius, the myster-

ious pupil of Rembrandt who lost his life in an explosion at Delft in 1654. By that date Vermeer was already married and independent. In view of Vermeer's early, much debated Italianate pictures such as the *Christ in the House of Mary and Martha* (Edinburgh), it is important to know whether he ever visited Italy. It seems unlikely that he left Holland, as he is mentioned nearly every year as being in Delft: there are six signatures of his on promissory notes alone. Things were not going well for him, for though he was esteemed and later became head of the Guild of St Luke, he had eleven children to provide for. Commissions came in slowly and were as slowly executed, for Vermeer worked with great difficulty. Only about forty pictures by him exist and it is unlikely that many have been lost. He tried to improve his situation by dealing in pictures, but times were bad and ill luck dogged him. When he died some of his pictures had to be put up to auction to cover his debts. A generation later Vermeer was forgotten; Houbraken did not know of his existence.

VERMEER VAN HAARLEM

The Vermeers, or Van der Meers, of Haarlem, were not related to the family in Delft, but they produced an important landscape painter, Jan Vermeer the Elder, who was born in 1628 and died in 1691. His early powerful woody scenes are like those of Ruisdael, or rather, he, like Ruisdael, was influenced by Cornelis Vroom, who also lived in Haarlem. Around 1660 he changed his style, and the little panels of his second period depict landscapes of dunes, broad, undulating country with distant towns, in cooler colours and flooded with broken light. The pictures are highly valued, often counterfeited and wrongly attributed. Verburgh and Kessel painted in a similar manner.

Jan's son, **Jan Vermeer the Younger**

(1656-1705), was a pupil of Berchem, and a visit to Rome italianised him still more, but his sunny southern landscapes of shepherds with their flocks always retained an element of Dutch heaviness. Among many pot-boilers, a good picture, like the *River Landscape* (Hamburg), occasionally makes its appearance.

Jan's second son, **Barent** (1659-c. 1700), painted still-life with fruit and vegetables piled up in the foreground. He had a taste for black-and-white effects and often introduced a Negro head.

VERMEYEN

Jan Vermeyen, who was born c. 1500 in Beverwyk, and died in 1559 at Brussels, travelled in Spain and Tunis and was considered a great portrait painter in his day. His portraits show the influence of his teacher, Mabuse, and still more of his friend, Scorel, whose firm drawing and sharply-defined planes he copied in his later years. Apart from portraits, he occasionally painted religious subjects and, in a few instances, factual historical themes that he had brought back from Spain.

VERNET

Claude Joseph Vernet was born in 1714 at Avignon and died in 1789 at Paris. His pictures immediately recall those of Claude Lorraine: they exhibit the same enthusiasm for hilly, classical landscape bathed in sunlight, the same delight in the sparkling sea. Claude Vernet was in his element when he was commissioned to paint the ports of France, and he produced his best work then (Louvre). He idealised, of course, but he took great care to study his subjects and paint from experience. An authentic record describes how he had himself lashed to the mast of a ship in a storm so that he could watch the sea undisturbed.

Carle Vernet (1758-1836), the son and pupil of Joseph, was born at Bordeaux. He also studied under Lepicié and won the Prix de Rome. On his return to Paris he began to paint classical landscapes with animals. His passionate interest in horses gave him a close first-hand knowledge of these creatures and qualified him to paint them in a realistic manner rare in France before the nineteenth century. Carle Vernet is represented in the Louvre and at Versailles.

VERONESE

Paolo Caliari (1528-1588) was born at Verona and died in Venice, but was known to his contemporaries as 'Veronese'. After his apprenticeship to Badile and when he had painted a few independent works, Veronese moved to Venice at the age of twenty-five. Under the aegis of both Titian and Tintoretto, the son of the humble stonemason rose to the position of a Venetian nobleman in whom society recognised a kindred spirit. Sometimes it is said that beneath the mask of the luxury and sumptuousness of his pictures there lies a note of regret at the decline of Venice. This seems unlikely, as Veronese genuinely admired beautiful women, masterful men and all the advantages of wealth and ostentation. He was utterly worldly and was even brought before the Inquisition to defend his picture, *The Feast of Levi* (Venice). He was acquitted, but if he had only called the work *Cleopatra's Feast* he would have been spared the tedium of lengthy explanations.

Although Veronese's style is founded on the Venetian School, he developed it to suit himself, and some of his pictures are nearer Bassano than Titian (*The Holy Family*, London). His colours, fabulous as they are, especially his golden orange, pale blue and glowing red, lack depth and look as though they were all jostling together in the foreground of the picture. One of his masterpieces, *The Marriage at Cana* (Louvre), which was commissioned by the monks of S. Giorgio for 325 ducats, anticipates Tiepolo in colouring. There is nothing restless about the composition, but the dazzling colour gives it an air of turbulence. Among the wedding guests are the Emperor Charles V, his sister, François I, Henry VIII's sister, Suleiman the Magnificent and Vittoria Colonna; among

VERONESE · UNFAITHFULNESS
75" × 75". London, National Gallery

greater part as a painter than a sculptor. Many artists have had great influence as teachers and have imposed their style on their pupils, notably Leonardo, but in Verrocchio's studio a great number of painters very different from himself were trained and encouraged to follow their own bent. Leonardo, Perugino, Credi, Ghirlandaio, Botticini and probably Botticelli all passed through his studio. It is not known for certain who were Verrocchio's own teachers: his painting is reminiscent of that of Castagno and Pollaiuolo.

Verrocchio was born in 1436 in Florence. In his lifetime he was equally famous as a painter and a sculptor. He died in Venice while working on the Colleoni statue.

Some experts evaluate Verrocchio's own work as low as possible in order to enhance Leonardo's prestige. But their opinion is flatly contradicted by the unquestioned authenticity of *The Baptism of Christ* in the Uffizi. It is known exactly what portions of this picture were painted by Verrocchio's pupil, Leonardo, the left angel and part of the landscape. All the rest is by Verrocchio and proves him to be a most important painter. Three *Madonnas* by him are in Berlin, London and Budapest. He also had a hand in the following works from his studio: *The Madonna with Standing Child* (Berlin), *Tobias and the Angel* (London) and *The Madonna with SS. John and Donatus* (Pistoia).

the musicians in the centre Titian can be seen playing the contra-bass, while Tintoretto and Veronese himself are performing on the violin. So brilliant an explosion of colour and wit console the spectator for any lack of spiritual depth.

Apart from his frescoes in S. Sebastiano, Venice, and in the Villa Barbaro, Maser, and the ceiling painting in the Doge's Palace in Venice, Veronese's chief works are *The Feast in the House of Levi* (Venice), *The Marriage at Cana* and *Christ at Emmaus* (Paris), *The Finding of Moses* (Madrid), *The Rape of Europa* (Ante Collegio, Venice), *The Battle of Lepanto* (Academy, Venice), *The Family of Darius before Alexander* and *S. Helen: Vision of the Cross* (National Gallery, London).

VERROCCHIO

Andrea del Verrocchio is one of the most debated yet fascinating figures in Italian art. To most people his name only recalls the imposing equestrian statue of Colleoni in Venice, but in reality he played a far

VERSCHURING

Hendrik Verschuring, who was born in 1627 at Gorinchen and died in 1690 at Dordrecht, is represented in most large museums, though he is only one among many of Wouverman's and Berchem's followers. Holland produced such painters by the dozen, and all had some talent. Verschuring was a pupil of Jan Both.

After ten year's residence in Italy, he, not surprisingly, painted Italianate peasant scenes, huntsmen with horses camping, not altogether convincingly, in an idealised landscape. They look much more as if they were standing in front of a thinly painted backcloth.

VERSPRONCK

Jan Cornelisz Verspronck (1597-1662 in Haarlem) began with portraits which were far removed from Frans Hals, although he was his pupil. They are rather harshly drawn and in their chalky texture resemble work done with coloured crayons. Perhaps his later portraits, after he had suddenly become aware of Frans Hals and the young Rembrandt, are more skilfully executed and composed, but Verspronck is more original and true to himself in his early pictures, such as the *Girl in a Blue Dress* in Amsterdam.

VICTORS

Very little is known about the two step-

VERROCCHIO · THE ANGEL RAPHAEL AND TOBIAS · *33″ × 25½″. London, National Gallery*

brothers, Jan and Jacob Victors. **Jan** was born in 1620 at Amsterdam and was a pupil of Rembrandt. He tried to imitate his master in his religious pictures, but his sense of drama and of light and shade has more than a whiff of the Meiningen Court Theatre. His peasant scenes and his *genre* streets are less artificial, but he only rises above mediocrity in his portraits, some of which can almost vie with Rembrandt's. Jan emigrated to the East Indies, where he died in 1705.

Jacob Victors (1640-1720 in Amsterdam) lived for a long time in Italy and liked to sign himself 'Jacomo'. Like Hondecoeter, he painted animals and, particularly poultry. He sets his cackling fowls in Italianate scenery (*The Poultry Yard*, Dresden), or goes to the opposite extreme and places a pair of pigeons like a still-life in front of bare plaster walls (*Pigeons*, Hamburg). In later life he gave up painting and devoted himself, appropriately, to the feather business.

VIEN

Joseph Maria Vien was the teacher of Jacques Louis David and prepared the way for Neo-classicism. He was born in 1716 at Montpellier and died in 1809 in Paris.

He began by being a purely Rococo artist: then he rediscovered the antique in Italy. He and the poet, Diderot, the pope of art, encouraged each other in enthusiasm for this new ideal which, being anti-Rococo, was in the air. It spread immediately to England, where it was taken up by Benjamin West.

VIGÉE-LEBRUN

Marie Louise Elizabeth Vigée (1755-1842) was born in Paris, the daughter of **Louis** Vigée (1727-1767) a portrait painter and pastellist. She had little training apart from what he was able to teach her in girlhood before his early death, but by the age of fifteen she was earning her living as a portraitist. In 1776 she married **J. B. P. Lebrun**, painter, dealer and critic. From him and from his friend, Joseph

Vernet, Marie received the greatest encouragement and assistance. She became a member of the French Academy in 1783. Meanwhile she had become a society favourite and the friend of Marie Antoinette, of whom she painted more than twenty portraits. At the beginning of the Revolution she went to Italy, then to Austria, Russia, Switzerland and England, in all of which countries she was given numbers of commissions. In her old age she settled again in Paris and once more became a society leader. Though her pictures have too much self-conscious charm and sweetness, Vigée-Lebrun was a better artist than her enormous output might suggest. She is represented in the Louvre, in the National Gallery, London, and the Wallace Collection, London.

VIGNON

Claude Vignon (1593-1670) was born in Tours and spent the years from about 1616 until 1624 in Rome, where he fell particularly under the influence of Domenico Fetti; he was also influenced by the work of Caravaggio and Elsheimer and by the work of their northern followers such as Lastman. Vignon's paint in his early work has a rich impasto similar to that of Lastman and of Rembrandt. In his later pictures, painted some time after his return to Paris, Vignon's touch is lighter. He is represented in the Louvre, at Angoulême and in the Musée de Tours. Vignon was a founder member of the French Academy; he was also a dealer in pictures and is known to have sold Rembrandts.

VINCKEBOONS

David Vinckeboons, who was born in 1576 at Malines and died in 1629 in Amsterdam, was a charming painter of small woody landscapes with distant views of enchanted castles on the shores of lakes or vistas sweeping away to a church or a village. Genuine Vinckeboons are rare, but forgeries are very common; the cipher which is supposed to authenticate them, a

VIGÉE-LEBRUN · THE BARONESS DE CRUSSOL
46″ × 34″. Toulouse, Musée des Augustins

finch on a tree, is a pure invention, delightful though it is.

Vinckeboons' landscapes have something in common with those of Coninxloo, Valckenborch and Jan Brueghel. His little figures of travellers are lively enough, but he preferred to paint peasant scenes. In pictures such as *The Fair* (Hamburg) he is as unrestrained as Jan Steen, and his pictures in Frankfort of village streets, organ-grinders and pedlars are in the spirit of Ludwig Richter.

VITALE DA BOLOGNA

Vitale da Bologna was born c. 1300 in Bologna and died there in 1365. He is considered to be the founder of the Bolognese School. His chief work, a signed *Madonna* which shows his style very clearly, is in Bologna, as are three fine panels and the Mezzarata frescoes. In those days it was next to impossible not to be influenced by Giotto and the Sienese painters: besides, Vitale lived near Rimini and its School, and this helped to make him into a lively expressive painter, very uninhibited for his times. He was also a miniaturist. This narrative element in his art has strengthened the conviction of some historians that the Traini frescoes in Pisa may in reality be by him, but this is purely hypothetical.

VITERBO

Lorenzo da Viterbo (c. 1437-1476 in Viterbo) has left frescoes behind him that make it worth while to stop off at Viterbo on a journey from Siena to Rome. It is like coming across a well in the desert to find such frescoes, reminiscent of Gozzoli and Melozzo, in this isolated provincial town.

Lorenzo died too soon: he might have become the successor of Piero della Francesca.

VIVARINI

Of the three painters of this name, two brothers, Antonio and Bartolomeo, hold a noteworthy place in Venetian painting.

Antonio Vivarini was born between 1415 and 1420 on the Venetian island of Murano, and he died in Venice 1476/84.

Doubt has lately arisen of the authenticity of the famous *Adoration of the Magi* in Berlin, which is attributed to him and with its early Renaissance fairy-tale qualities it has been regarded as the forerunner of Gentile da Fabriano. However, the fact remains that Antonio Vivarini was one of the liberators of Venetian painting from Byzantine influences. Venice had such strong economic and political links with Constantinople that she did not break away from Byzantinium until long after the rest of Italy had severed all ties.

Antonio's friend, **Giovanni d' Alemagna** (probably from Cologne), seems to have been equally remarkable. A *Madonna* altarpiece in the Accademia in Venice is their combined work.

Bartolomeo Vivarini, who was born c. 1432 in Murano and died in 1499 in Venice, represents a further development.

He had been at the Paduan School and had met Rogier van der Weyden when he visited Italy. Bartolomeo's early pictures have the sculpturesque qualities of the Paduan school, but some of his later works, such as the *Adoration* in New York, show, by contrast, a curious mixture of Flemish and Italian influences.

Alvise Vivarini (c. 1445-1504 in Venice) was Antonio's son. By the time he came to paint, the Venetian style was already established. Alvise, who was at first influenced by the rigid linear technique of his uncle Bartolomeo, based his style more and more closely on that of Giovanni Bellini and Cima. A fine portrait by him and a *Virgin and Child* are in the London National Gallery. (Ill. p. 318.)

VIVIEN

Joseph Vivien was born in 1657 at Lyons, went to Paris, but soon turned his back on France as a result of depression at his lack of success. He wandered restlessly from place to place in Germany and for a time was Court Painter in Munich. He died at Bonn in 1734.

His work consists of portraits in pastel and oil, a few religious pictures and a few designs for tapestry. His importance lies in his lively portraits. *Fénelon* (Munich) is one of his best and reveals a dry objectivity and a power of penetration that even Rigaud and Lagillière, his contemporaries, rarely equalled.

VLIEGER

Simon de Vlieger, who was born c. 1600 in Rotterdam and died in 1653 in Weesp, was the teacher of the great Willem van de Velde the Younger and Jan van der Capelle. He himself was an outstanding marine painter and an important link in the chain of artists—Vroom, Porcellis, Van de Velde—who led marine painting from its infancy to its brilliant peak. His pictures are extremely painterly and full of variety. He was the author not only of sea pieces, but of some *genre* scenes showing subjects such as a sailor on leave staggering along,

ALVISE VIVARINI · ST JOHN THE BAPTIST
$52\frac{5}{8}'' \times 20\frac{3}{4}''$. *Venice, Accademia*

bow-legged, through a landscape shrouded in a Rembrandt-like dusk.

VLIET

Hendrik van Vliet, who was born c. 1611 in

Delft and died there in 1675, was the pupil of two portrait painters, so at first he aspired to become one himself. But at the age of forty he began to paint church interiors in the manner of Houckgeest. The fact was that Houckgeest had left Delft and his clients were all flocking to Vliet. From an insignificant portrait painter, Vliet developed into nearly as successful an artist as Houckgeest.

VOS

Cornelis de Vos, who was born in 1584 in Hulst and died in 1651 in Antwerp, was, apart from Rubens and Van Dyck, the most important Flemish portrait painter of his day. Though his religious and allegorical pictures are generally relegated to museum basements, his portraits are among the most talented of any painted at that date. Vos was a brilliant technician and a penetrating observer. He never flattered his sitters, yet saw and brought out every attractive quality they possessed. Above all, he loved the alert expression of young faces, and an attentive observant look is a common characteristic of his portraits. His groups are excellently composed. He was not only a painter; he was a connoisseur and an art-dealer.

Marten de Vos was born in Antwerp c. 1532 and died there in 1603. He left the Romanist painter, Floris, under whom he was studying, and went to Venice where he became the pupil and assistant of Tintoretto. He was later employed by the Medici. He then returned to Antwerp where he met with great success especially in the fields of religious painting and portraiture. Vos is one of the most characteristic Flemish Mannerist painters. His works include *The Tribute Money* (Antwerp) and *St Paul at Ephesus* (Brussels).

Paul de Vos (c. 1596-1678 in Amsterdam), Cornelis' brother, was well known for his paintings of animals and hunting scenes. His pictures are reminiscent of Snyders', who was his brother-in-law, but are usually more dramatic. His brush strokes have a restless, nervous quality which emphasises the emotional tension of his pictures.

VOUET

Simon Vouet (1590-1649) was the pupil of his father, Laurent, and is reputed to have come to England at the age of fourteen to paint portraits. By 1614 he had settled in Rome, having already been in Constantinople and Paris. He stayed in Rome until 1627, except for visits to Naples, Genoa and Venice, and was elected President of the Academy of St Luke. He spent the last twenty years of his life in Paris. He was at first strongly influenced by the followers of Caravaggio, then began to evolve a more monumental style, gradually freeing himself from the violent and emotional elements of the Caravaggiesque idiom. Vouet was very successful in Paris, and his importance in French painting was considerable: in decorative painting he established a tradition that remained dominant throughout the seventeenth century; Mignarf, Le Sueur and Le Brun were all his pupils and all were powerfully influenced by him. Represented in the Louvre and many French provincial galleries.

VRANCX

Sebastian Vrancx, who was born in 1573 in Antwerp and died there in 1647, was a man of energy; he was president of the Guild of St Luke, wrote plays for a dramatic society, was a captain in the Civic Guard and travelled a great deal in Italy. He painted with equal zest any subject for which he was asked— peasant scenes, brawls, church interiors, battle pieces with cavalry or bandits. But his pictures, which are often weak in drawing, prove that versatility is not all. It would seem that Vrancx often permitted friends to work on his canvases, and he did the same for them. When the authenticity of a picture attributed to Vrancx is in doubt his hand can usually be detected by his trick of adding red and black flecks of pigment to the clothes of his personages to create an effect of sparkle and liveliness.

VREL

Jacob Vrel signed a couple of pictures: otherwise there is no evidence of his existence. He must have been a contemporary of Vermeer, and he was working in Delft sometime during the mid-seventeenth century. He painted small pictures of streets, some of which were until a few decades ago attributed to Vermeer. One of the most confusing—it even deceived Bode—is in Hamburg, but all doubts vanished when Vrel's signature was discovered. His mediocrity is revealed in the bad drawing of his interiors.

VRIES

Roelof van Vries was born c. 1631 in Haarlem and died in 1682 in Amsterdam. It is sometimes said of him that he painted like a ham-fisted Ruisdael, but in reality there is no comparison. Ruisdael's pictures are big and daring in conception,

C. DE VOS · THE PAINTER'S DAUGHTERS
31¼" × 36¾". Berlin, Staatl. Museen

while those of Vries are timid and non-committal. Yet, measured by less exacting standards, Vries is by no means negligible, particularly in his early work.

VROOM

Hendrik Vroom (1566-1640 in Haarlem), today an almost forgotten pioneer in art, was the painter of enormous precisely drawn seascapes with swarms of people on shore or on board sailing ships. Vroom was a porcelain painter who took to marine painting after a sea voyage that ended in shipwreck. He was breaking entirely new ground. As there were no models on which to base himself, he allowed his fancy full play and this is the source of attraction in his pictures despite the fact that they are too large. They caused a sensation at the time and Vroom sold them for huge sums.

Adam Willaerts, who was born in 1577 in Antwerp and died in 1664 in Utrecht, was Vroom's first follower of consequence.

Cornelis Vroom (c. 1591-1661 in Haarlem) was Hendrik's son and pupil. All the Vrooms seem to be *avant-gardistes*, body and soul. Cornelis blazed a new trail in the field of landscape painting. His first pictures still showed Elsheimer's influence, but around 1630 he began to paint pure wooded landscapes. What Lastman was to Rembrandt, Vroom was to Jacob Ruisdael, and both worthy forerunners stemmed from Elsheimer. However, in his last years Vroom began to imitate Ruisdael, and their pictures are almost indistinguishable.

VUIBERT

Remy Vuibert was born c. 1600 and died c. 1561, but little is known of the life of this French painter, who is at present the subject of research. He appears to have stayed a considerable time in Rome before 1635 and was influenced not only by Caravaggism but by Domenichino and Poussin. The last years of his life were spent in France, possibly in Paris. A large painting of the Death of St Cecilia in the Musée Fabre at Montpellier, for many years thought to be by Poussin, has now been attributed to Vuibert by M. Thuillier, who considers the picture to be one of the artist's Roman works.

WALLACE COLLECTION

This collection, housed in Hertford House, Manchester Square, London, began to take shape when the 3rd Marquess of Hertford, an intimate friend of George IV purchased numbers of Dutch and French pictures from French collectors at the time of the Revolution. It is however to the 4th Marquess that the Collection chiefly owes its present form. It was he who assembled the works of French eighteenth-century art for which the Wallace Collection is especially famous. The collection of Boucher's work is unequalled elsewhere; the gallery also possesses eight pictures by Watteau, twenty-two by Greuze and seven by Fragonard, including the celebrated *Swing*. The Dutch paintings at Hertford House include a portrait of his son by Rembrandt and Hals' *Laughing Cavalier*. There are also fine examples in the Collection of the work of Velazquez, Rubens, Van Dyck, Gainsborough, and Reynolds.

WALSCAPELLE

Jacob Cruydenier van Walscapelle, who was born in 1644 in Dordrecht and died in 1727 in Amsterdam, stands midway in time and style between Jan Davidsz de Heem and Huysum. He painted fruit and flowers in the manner of De Heem, putting them against a dark background and giving his foregrounds a luminosity reminiscent of Huysum, even if it is less brilliant. His pictures are characterised by meticulously painted insects with transparent wings, snail-shells and dew drops. He is represented in the National Gallery, London.

WARD

James Ward (1769-1859) was the brother-in-law of George Morland, and was at first influenced by him, painting rural and anecdotal pictures. He soon, however, developed into a most original painter, one who has seldom been justly estimated. Ward's mature style was inspired by Rubens. It is rich, vigorous and grandiose, imbued with a sense of magnitude and drama. Characteristic works by him include *Landscape with Cattle*, painted as a deliberate challenge to Paul Potter's *The Bull* (The Hague), *Cattle Piece, Harlech Castle* and *Gordale Scar*, all in the Tate Gallery, London. Ward's dynamic power moved Delacroix to admiration, and his work was also seen and praised by Gericault on his London visit.

WATTEAU · L'ENSEIGNE DE GERSAINT
(Left side) 72¾" × 123". *Berlin, Charlottenburg*

WATTEAU

Antoine Watteau, though often mentioned in the same breath as the Rococo boudoir painters, is in reality in quite another category. It is just as inept to describe him as a painter of *fêtes galantes* as it would be to label Michelangelo as a painter of nudes. Watteau was never popular and his pictures never graced the boudoirs of Versailles. But he was as essentially a child of his time as Mozart, and they have much in common—powdered wigs, Italian comedies, secret grief and an early death. Watteau's pictures, apparently sparkling with joy, are coloured by the melancholy of a man who knew he was an outcast and must die young. In his despair he painted fashionable pictures, as he thought, but they were lacking in the light-hearted frivolity which would have pleased the Court circle. *The Embarkment for Cytherea* (Louvre), his entry picture for the Academy painted in 1717, is entirely without eroticism.

Watteau's palette changed by degrees from the glowing range of bright colours of the *Cytherea* to the shimmering, low tones—giving the effect of shot-silk brocade—of his last famous picture, *L'Enseigne de Gersaint* (Berlin). The splendid *Fête Champêtre* (Berlin) has the same soft iridescence casting a veil over its underlying vitality. This picture, the subject of which Watteau painted many times, stands about halfway in his development towards his final style, represented by the *Enseigne de Gersaint*, the signboard which the art dealer Gersaint commissioned from him for his new shop. Watteau's circumstances at the time were wretched. He had just come back from a visit to England desperately ill with consumption. He felt that the end was near, but he finished the signboard, one of the most beautiful and poetic pictures of the whole eighteenth century.

Antoine Watteau was born in 1684 at Valenciennes, the son of a tiler. He began to study in Valenciennes at the age of fourteen, but at eighteen he went to Paris, poor as a church mouse. He worked at first in the studio of Gillot, to whom he always remained grateful, and then with Audran, who held the post of Custodian at the Luxembourg Palace. There Watteau saw the pictures of Rubens and the Venetians. It was not long, however, before he left Audran and the Academy, where he had been accepted as a pupil, and went his own restless, solitary way, continually changing his lodgings, always melancholy. He very rarely received a commission, and though he had a little money, he lost it all in a bank crash. In 1719 he travelled to London to consult a famous physician. But his case was hopeless, and he returned to France in 1720. He accepted a few social invitations, met Rosalba Carriera, painted *The Halt during the Chase* (Wallace Collection, London) and, presumably in three days, *L'Enseigne de Gersaint*. Then he retired to a small house at Joyent-sur-Marne lent him by a patron. There he died, alone and forgotten, in 1721 at the age of thirty-seven.

Watteau's pictures, apart from those already mentioned, include *La Polonnaise* (Warsaw), *L'Accordée de Village* (Berlin), *French Actors* and *Italian Actors* (Berlin), *Mezzetino* and *The French Players* (New York), *Dance in a Park* (Edinburgh), *The Judgment of Paris* and *Gilles* (Louvre), *Fête in a Park* (Madrid) and *Harlequin and Columbine* and *The Music Lesson* (Wallace Collection, London). (Ill. p. 321.)

WEENIX

Jan Baptist Weenix the Elder, who was born in 1621 in Amsterdam and died in 1663 at Deutecum, was a pupil of Bloemaert. He went to Italy for four years (1643-1647) but even when he was surrounded by classical ruins his heart was half in Holland. The figure in his *Sleeping Girl* (Munich) lying beneath a crumbling Italian arch is a wench from Utrecht and no Italian maid. This picture is enchanting in colour and much more successful than the painter's larger, crowded canvases.

Jan Weenix the Younger (1640-1719) was his son and pupil, and though he never visited Italy he inherited his father's divided interest. He too painted a *Sleeping Girl* (Munich); and she might well be the sister of the Utrecht baggage. This picture is smaller and less colourful than the father's painting. Jan painted a series of cabinet pictures in the same *genre* (*Huntsman*, Munich; *Landscape with Sleeping Shepherds*, Dulwich College, London).

His second master, Gisbert Hondecoeter, provided him with the second of his principal themes, the large still-life with dead game, usually hares propped up against antique stone urns.

WERFF

Adriaen van der Werff, who was born in 1659 in Rotterdam and died there in 1772, was overwhelmed during his lifetime with honours, wealth and titles, courted by the King of Poland, the Dukes of Marlborough and of Brunswick and by the Elector Palatine, and flattered by the open-mouthed admiration of the populace. He is no longer regarded as a great painter, though it is easy to realise why he was such a success. Over and over again he painted seductive groups against a dusky, park-like background, including only one or two figures, for whom he chose the most alluring, silken-skinned of models (*The Dancing Class*, Amsterdam; *Arcadian Scene*, Berlin; *Susanna Bathing*, Budapest).

Werff's influence was considerable. It is harder to enjoy the pictures in which he aped the French manner (*Self Portrait*, Amsterdam) and his religious pictures, which are as smooth and hard in texture as porcelain.

WEST

Benjamin West was born in 1738 at Springfield, Pennsylvania, of Quaker parentage. He was a precocious child and painted a watercolour at the age of nine which he said in later life was equal in some ways to anything he had ever done. By the time he was sixteen he was earning his living as an itinerant portrait painter, and a few years later he was established in Philadelphia, then in New York. In 1760, helped by friends, West went to Italy to study seriously. On his way back to America three years later he visited England and was persuaded to settle in

London. One of his pictures attracted the attention of George III, who became his lifelong patron. West succeeded Reynolds as President of the Royal Academy. A large group of American painters studied under him in London. He died in 1820 and was buried in St Paul's Cathedral. West's talent was mediocre, but he painted one picture which is good in itself and of great interest in the history of painting, *The Death of General Wolfe* in the National Gallery of Canada. West decided, against the practice of the day, to paint the figures in contemporary costume. When this became known, Reynolds was so agitated that he called on West, accompanied by the Archbishop of York, to persuade the artist to clothe his figures as Greeks or Romans. But when he saw West's finished composition he at once withdrew his objections. From that time classical dress was replaced by the correct period costume in historical pictures.

WESTALL

Richard Westall (1765-1836) was born at Hertford and was apprenticed to a heraldic engraver. In 1785 he became a student at the Royal Academy where he met Lawrence. He was made A.R.A. in 1792 and R.A. in 1794. He painted portraits, among which were four of Nelson, history pieces and mythological subjects. His *Cassandra Prophesying the Fall of Troy* is in the Victoria and Albert Museum, while the Wallace Collection possesses his *Venus Sporting with Cupids*. Westall also produced watercolours which were exceptionally rich in tone and far in advance of the tinted drawings of the late eighteenth century.

WET

Jacob Willemsz de Wet (1610-after 1671) was born probably in Haarlem and appears to have been a pupil of Rembrandt in about 1632, though the resemblances between his work and that of the master are only superficial. His *Expulsion of Hagar* (Munich) is a typical painting, like Rembrandt in atmosphere, but timid in organisation and colour. Occasionally, however, Wet painted an outstanding picture. Such is The *Adoration of the Shepherds* (Hamburg). A Rembrandtesque landscape by him is in the National Gallery, London.

WEYDEN

Rogier van der Weyden was born in 1399 at Tournai and died in 1464 at Brussels. The work of this great painter has always been admired, but little was known about the man himself before the nineteenth century, and many facts remain to be discovered and corroborated. Rogier was the son of a cutler, Henri de la Pasture, and was probably apprenticed to Robert Campin (q.v.), the Maître de Flémalle, though the relation of Rogier van der Weyden to Campin has been the subject of lengthy dispute. He is mentioned several times in the records of Tournai. In 1421

R. VAN DER WEYDEN · PORTRAIT OF A YOUNG WOMAN · 18¾″×12¾″. *Berlin, Staatl. Museen*

'Rogelet de la Pasture' was given a present of wine by the town of Tournai and in 1432 he was received into the Guild there. In 1435 Rogier's name, in its Flemish form of Van der Weyden, occurs for the first time in the records of Brussels. Rogier is mentioned as 'Painter to the Municipality', a high honour not again accorded to anyone after Van der Weyden's death. In 1450 he was in Rome and possibly visited Ferrara. It was while he was in Italy that he painted the *Entombment* in the Uffizi, in which the rocky background so much resembles that in the picture of the same subject painted a little earlier by Fra Angelico.

Van der Weyden's reputation had preceded him to Italy and his visit gave the Italians much food for thought. But when he himself returned to Brussels he rid himself of all recollection of his Italian journey and carried on with his work exactly where he had left off before setting out from home. The result was that by 1460 Italian painters were making pilgrimages to him. The Duchess of Milan herself requested permission to send the young painter Bugato to him for further instruction. At this time Rogier's fame as a great painter of the north was second only to that of Jan van Eyck. He died revered, prosperous and already almost a legendary figure.

One of Rogier's three sons, **Pieter**, was a painter and the talented **Goosen** van der Weyden (c. 1465-c. 1539) was his grandson.

Two painters were responsible for the remarkable flowering of Flemish painting at the beginning of the fifteenth century. One of these two men was Rogier van der Weyden. Van Eyck preceded him by about half a generation. The two painters were not at all alike. Rogier's genius was for drama, while Van Eyck was epic in feeling. Van der Weyden was intellectual in his approach; his first concern was not to express his own feelings, but those he had observed in others. His characters therefore have a greater range of expression than those of Van Eyck, and they are always absolutely clearly depicted, with none of the ambiguity of Van Eyck. Van der

R. VAN DER WEYDEN · THE COLUMBA ALTARPIECE *(Centre panel)*
55¼″ × 61¼″. *Munich, Alte Pinakothek*

Weyden constructs his pictures dramatically, placing his figures in the scene like actors on a stage. He always makes great play with gesture and the movement of hands. But his hands are not differentiated: they are all fine and slender. This shows that he was no realist, despite his meticulous technique.

In style, Van der Weyden's early pictures, with their sharp definition and use of black, are close to the work of Campin. But his palette soon grew lighter and clearer in tone, while his line became increasingly elegant. The colours in a picture like the Columba Altarpiece are like a firework display, which cannot be said of any of Van Eyck's pictures.

Rogier's immediate influence was far greater than that of Van Eyck. His ideas, his types, his palette and his elegance nourished generations of painters. He left about 100 pictures which today are among the great treasures of museums and a few private collections. They include *The Deposition* and *Golgotha* (Prado), *The Last Judgment* (Beaune), *The Adoration of the Kings* (Columba Altarpiece, Munich), the St John Altarpiece, the Altarpiece of the Blessed Virgin and the Bladelin Altarpiece (Berlin), the Altarpiece of the Blessed Sacrament (Antwerp), *The Entombment* (Uffizi), *The Madonna with Four Saints* (Frankfort), the *Braque Triptych* (Louvre) and *Portrait of a Lady* and *The Magdalen Reading* (National Gallery, London).

WILDENS

Jan Wildens, who was born in 1584 in Antwerp and died there in 1653, spent five years in Italy, but the experience had little effect on his work owing to his contact

RICHARD WILSON · THE RIVER DEE NEAR EATON HALL
21¼″ × 35″. Birmingham, Barber Institute

Leubus). For a time Willmann was Court Painter to the Great Elector, but he suddenly left Berlin without warning to join the Monastery of Leubus, whose Abbot had for long admired his painting. He remained there until his death.

WILSON

Richard Wilson (1714-1782) was born at Penegoes, Montgomeryshire, the son of a clergyman. With the help of his relative, Sir George Wynne,

with Rubens. On his return to Antwerp he was overwhelmed with commissions from Rubens and for three or four years he was busy painting foliage and landscape backgrounds for the great master. His work can be seen in the *Diana* (Berlin) in the *Cimon* (Vienna) and in the *Pan* in the Royal Collection, Buckingham Palace. Wildens' own works, such as the *Winter Landscape with a Huntsman* (Dresden) lack zest, but his landscape backgrounds are extraordinarily atmospheric and poetic.

WILLMANN

Michael Lukas Willmann was born at Königsberg in East Prussia in 1630 and died in 1706 at the Monastery of Leubus in Silesia. He was one of the most important German painters of the late Baroque.

Willmann studied in the Netherlands, and when he returned to Germany at the age of twenty-three his painting was an undigested mixture of early Rembrandt and Rubens. In *Susanna Bathing* (Nuremberg) the influence of Rubens is paramount. The violent movement and chiaroscuro of the late Baroque were increasingly dominant in Willmann's work, and his inharmonious and disturbing use of light and shade turned his pictures into wild dramas, like some of the canvases of Tintoretto (*The Crucifixion of St Andrew*,

he was sent to London in 1729 to study under an obscure portrait painter, Thomas Wright, and also under Hudson, the master of Reynolds. In 1749 Wilson went to Italy, where he remained for six years. His inclination was for landscape painting, and though he painted portraits both before and after his visit to Italy, he was not fitted by temperament to flatter his sitters or to tolerate their whims. In Rome Wilson established himself as a landscape painter and was admired by Zuccarelli, Mengs and Vernet. On his return to England Wilson was made a foundation member of the Royal Academy, but he found there was little demand for pictures of the English countryside, and it became increasingly difficult for him to earn a livelihood. A notebook of Wilson's in the Victoria and Albert Museum records how he sent out his landscapes on approval and with what depressing frequency they were returned. He managed to paint an occasional portrait, such as *Peg Woffington* (Garrick Club), and these and £50 a year he received after his appointment in 1776 as Librarian of the Royal Academy saved him from utter destitution. Wilson returned to Wales in 1781 and died at a relative's house at Colomondie. Like Claude, from whom he derives his sense of light and atmosphere, Wilson is essentially classical in that he is grandly detached, serene and preoccupied with the typical rather than the particular.

These virtues are most striking, not in most of his Italian landscapes, but when he applied them to the English scene, in such pictures as *The Thames at Twickenham* and *Cader Idris*, both in the National Gallery, London.

WITTE

Emanuel de Witte was born c. 1617 in Alkmaar. He committed suicide in Amsterdam in 1692 after a life of unrelieved misery caused by quarrels, law-suits, humiliations and anxieties, including the death of two wives.

Witte was the son of a schoolmaster and completed his training at the age of nineteen. In 1640 or 1641 he moved to Amsterdam and soon afterwards to Delft. Until then Witte had only painted mythological scenes in the manner of Elsheimer, but in Delft he found himself subjected to quite a different influence. The little town had for long been important in the world of art and, though apparently less was going on there at that time, Houckgeest and Vliet had excited attention by painting a novel subject—church interiors. Witte immediately followed the new fashion, at first perhaps in the hope of improving his wretched circumstances. When he moved to Amsterdam in 1651 he painted an occasional portrait or market scene, but he invariably returned to the subjects which were by now nearer to his heart—church interiors and other scenes which conjured up thoughts of man's mortality.

Chiaroscuro is of prime importance in Witte's church fantasies. The emphasis with him is not on bare walls, as with Saenredam, but on the vast space of the vaulted church interior. He very often groups his figures, dressed in black or bright red, about an open tomb, thus creating a Hamlet-like atmosphere. Nevertheless, one of his finest pictures is a domestic piece, *Bedroom with a*

Woman Playing on a Spinet (Rotterdam).

WITZ

Conrad Witz was born c. 1400 at Rottweil in Württemberg and died c. 1445, probably in Geneva, but perhaps in Basle, where he had lived since 1434. His name and some of the details of his life have only been known since the turn of the century. Now he is recognised as a great painter, although the sources of his splendid work, the Basle Altarpiece, with its two monumental figures of Sabothai and Benaja, are shrouded in mystery. It would be fascinating to know how a contemporary of Francke, Moser and Lochner, a man living in an isolated town like Basle, had learnt to paint in a style which embraced elements of Masaccio,

K. WITZ · THE ANNUNCIATION
62⅜″ × 48″. Nuremberg, Germanisches Museum

327

Dürer and Campin (cf. Basle Altarpiece, *St Bartholomew*, Basle, *The Annunciation*, Nuremberg). It is not impossible that Witz started a revolution in art of the same nature as Campin, Van Eyck and Masaccio without knowing any of them or having visited either the Netherlands or Italy. But his affinity with Masaccio may be a pure coincidence, and perhaps we underrate the rapidity with which the innovations of Campin and Van Eyck spread to Germany.

Only a few of Witz's pictures have survived, fragments of altarpieces. All his frescoes have perished. His most popular picture at the present time is *The Miraculous Draught of Fishes*, the wing of an altarpiece in Geneva. Not everything is admirable in this picture, for large groups of figures are not Witz's strong point, but the atmospheric landscape is of extraordinary beauty. It is a faithful interpretation of the Lake of Geneva, the earliest German true landscape, in fact.

Witz died rich and esteemed by his contemporaries.

WOLGEMUT

Michael Wolgemut, teacher of the great Albrecht Dürer, lived from 1434 to 1519 in Nuremberg. His reputation has fluctuated over the centuries: he has been regarded as a worthy craftsman, as the principal German master before Dürer, and, finally, as an ambitious tyrant who kept down other painters and represented their work as his own. It is true that he had a high opinion of himself (and that is not unjustified), but his character must have been above suspicion, for Dürer all his life held him in high regard and painted him when he was an old man of eighty-two.

Wolgemut has many merits. He did not co-operate with Pleydenwurff, who introduced the Flemish style to Nuremberg. He went back to the direct observation of nature and found enough new aspects and ideas to content him. As he was treading new ground, he painted very precisely. Later his outlines became very hard and his figures looked as if they had been frozen in full action. But his colour always remained fresh and lively.

WOOTTON

John Wootton (1678?-1765) was a painter of hunting and racing scenes and portraits of Newmarket favourites, and he also executed a number of ambitious landscapes in the style of Claude and of Gaspar Poussin. He was so enthusiastic about classical painting that he often placed his horses among Roman columns. There is an imposing series of large pictures of horses by him at Althorp; and there are two fine examples of his work at Welbeck, *Bonny Black* and the *The Bloody-shouldered Arabian*. Wootton was highly esteemed in his day and was commissioned to paint a state portrait of George II on horseback.

WOUTERS

Frans Wouters was born in Lierre, Brabant, in 1612 and died in Antwerp in 1659. He was a pupil of Pieter van Avont and of Rubens and devoted himself to history and landscape painting. He entered the Antwerp Guild in 1634, but soon after went to Germany where, in 1637, he became Court Painter to Ferdinand II. Later he accompanied Ferdinand's ambassador to England and became Court Painter to Charles I. He returned to Antwerp and was made Dean of the Guild in 1649. Wouters' works include a *Dance of Amoretti* (Hampton Court), *Venus and Adonis* (Copenhagen), *A Conflagration in a Dutch City* (Staedl. Museum, Frankfort), *Diana Hunting* (Vienna) and *Nymphs and Satyrs* (National Gallery, London).

WOUVERMAN

Philips Wouverman is one of the most lovable painters that the seventeenth century produced in the Netherlands. About 1,000 of his pictures can be authenticated. The general public is readily inclined to under-estimate him. His hunting scenes, horses, riders by streams or outside smithies, dallying with girls, camping, or drawing up at an inn, his red jackets and white horses, all seem too facile and almost too obvious. But this is a superficial judgement. Wouverman had no secrets in his art, yet he is one of the most ingenious, many-sided and imaginative of painters, and a master of drawing and atmosphere. Towards the end of his life his powers declined.

Philips Wouverman lived from 1619 to 1668 in Haarlem, and came of a family of painters. Three of the few facts known about him are illuminating: he was a pupil of Frans Hals; as a Protestant, he showed great courage in eloping with a Roman Catholic girl and marrying her in Hamburg; and he became rich enough to give one of his daughters 20,000 guilders as a dowry.

Pieter Wouverman, who was born in 1623 in Haarlem and died in 1682 in Amsterdam, was Philips' brother and probably his pupil, as their style is very similar. Pieter failed: he was without Philips' light touch for crowded scenes of action. His pictures are too charming to be convincing.

Jan Wouverman, (1629-1666 in Haarlem) was the youngest brother. He would have been an interesting landscape-painter if he had not been beguiled by horses. His heavy-boned old nags in sandy, hilly landscapes, nearly always include a white horse, such as Philips had made famous.

WRIGHT OF DERBY

Joseph Wright of Derby (1734-1797) was an eccentric in the history of painting. In his impressive pictures he coarsened and modernised Honthorst's style to suit England's march of progress in an age when everyone was applauding scientific, technical and mechanical developments. Wright painted people doing experiments by candle-light (*à la* Honthorst) with machines and apparatus (*Experiment with an Air-pump*, Tate Gallery, London; *Scholar in the Planetarium*, Derby). These

PH. WOUWERMAN · BOY WITH A WHITE HORSE
17¾″ × 15¼″. Amsterdam, Rijksmuseum

pictures were revolutionary in their day, but to eyes accustomed to photography there is nothing very unusual about them. Wright even liked to introduce his favourite effects into pure landscape (*The Burning of the Stock Exchange, Vesuvius in Eruption*).

WTEWAAL

Joachim Wtewaal lived from 1566 until 1638 in Utrecht. He was a highly-paid and much sought-after painter in his day. He was occupied in the linen trade, but as relief from this prosaic occupation he painted religious and learned subjects like *David and Abigail* (Amsterdam), *Diana and Actaeon* (Vienna), *Marriage of Poleus and Thetis* (Brunswick), which depict swarms of small wide figures in Mannerist postures in leafy landscapes. Wtewaal carried on the style of Beuckelaer in some of his large kitchen pieces.

WURMSER

Niklaus Wurmser came from Strassburg, and was one of Emperor Charles IV's highly esteemed Court Painters in Prague and Burg Karlstein. He is mentioned as being in Prague about 1360, so he was probably born between 1320 and 1330. Unfortunately, it is not possible to establish which of the paintings at Karlstein are by his hand. If, as is assumed, the fresco *Charles IV with the Reliquary of the Holy Cross* is his, then he takes his place with the great masters of the Bohemian School. The picture, moreover, is strikingly French in conception.

WYNANTS

Jan Wynants was born c. 1625 in Haarlem and died in 1684 in Amsterdam. The work he has left behind him is very varied in quality. Some of his more pleasing landscapes are very simple, consisting of but a hill, a track across a field, a tower and one or two figures. The golden brown tone of these pictures is enlivened by the colourful accents of the little figures, mostly painted by Ph. Wouwerman or by Wynants' pupil, Adriaen van de Velde. Wynants' later compositions are unnecessarily large;

Lingelbach painted the elegant groups of riders in these pictures and the rest of the canvas is filled up with picturesque trivialities, fences, sandy hollows, bushes and fallen tree trunks. This is Wynants' characteristic style. His early pictures, which were far more sensitive, influenced Gainsborough and even Constable. He is represented by pictures from his best period in the London National Gallery and the Wallace Collection.

WYNTRACK

Dirk Wyntrack, who was born c. 1625 in Drenthe and died in 1678 at The Hague, was exclusively an animal painter. Occasionally, like Melchior Hondecoeter, he painted them big against a wide landscape arranged like a stage scene with *coulisses*. But mostly he fills his barns and farmyards with a multitude of small animals—goats, lambs, ducks and hens. His barns are reminiscent of those of Jan Steen, while he took his farmyards from Hobbema, with whom he was acquainted and for whom he sometimes painted animals.

YÀÑEZ

The name of Fernando Yàñez de la Almedina, whose paintings belong to the years 1500 to 1540, is highly regarded in Valencia, the town of his birth. He brought Leonardo da Vinci's style to Spain, as can be seen in his picture, *St Catherine*, in the Prado. It has been conclusively verified that in 1504/5 Yàñez was one of Leonardo's assistants in Florence. Raphael's influence is also visible in his pictures. Yàñez' style flourished for a short time in Castille, but it was too alien to the spirit of Spain to last long.

YKENS

Frans Ykens was born in Antwerp in 1601 and died there in 1693. He was a still-life painter, a pupil of Osias Beert. He travelled in France c. 1629 and entered the Guild of Antwerp in 1630. From 1665 to 1667 he was living in Brussels. Rubens owned five of his paintings and his work is to be found in most museums. At his best he is reminiscent of Snyders.

Peter Ykens was born in Antwerp in 1648 and died there in 1695. He was the son and pupil of Jan Ykens (1613-1679) a painter and sculptor. Peter entered the Antwerp Guild in 1673 and became Dean of the Guild in 1689. He painted religious compositions including *St Catherine Disputing with the Philosophers* (Antwerp), *Christ Appearing to St Teresa* (Lille) and *Episodes in the Life of St Francis Xavier* (Mechlin). Two portraits by him are in the Antwerp Museum.

ZANOBI

Macchiavelli Zanobi, known as Macchiavelli, a little studied Italian painter, was born in Florence in 1418 and died there after 1476. A few signed works reveal him to have been a follower, perhaps even a pupil, of Pesellino and to have been influenced by Benozzo Gozzoli. Signed works by him are in Berlin and Dublin and an interesting triptych by him of the *Virgin and Child with Saints* is in the

B. ZEITBLOM · THE VIRGIN AND CHILD, WITH ST ANNE AND FOUR SAINTS
14¾" × 46¾". Munich, Alte Pinakothek

National Gallery, London, as well as the left and right wings of another altarpiece showing St John the Baptist and St John the Evangelist and St Mark and St Augustine.

ZAGANELLI

Francesco Zaganelli was born at Cotignola during the latter half of the fifteenth century and died in 1518. He was influenced by the Bolognese painters and by Palmezzano and may have been a pupil of Rondinelli. One of his best works is *The Baptism* in the London National Gallery. This has far more sense of design than pictures such as *The Madonna and Saints* (Brera) or *The Annunciation* (Berlin). His *Madonna with Portraits of the Pallavicini Family* is another of Zaganelli's more successful compositions.

ZEITBLOM

Bartholomäus Zeitblom was born c. 1455 in Nördlingen and died in 1522 at Ulm. His level as a painter was assessed correctly for four hundred years, and so it is today, but there was a short interim period in the middle of the nineteenth century when his reputation was exaggerated, even to calling him 'the German Leonardo'. Nothing, and no connection with Leonardo, supports this absurdity. Zeitblom was a favourite painter in the days when Ulm was a wealthy, progressive city. He painted portraits of the city worthies in a rather stereotyped fashion, always standing and all exactly alike. His altarpieces too—and there are quite a few of them in Bavaria—are mechanical and very definitely Gothic, without charm. However, his portraits are imposing in a statuesque way, and his religious pictures have a compelling austerity. Zeitblom's charm as a painter lies in his use of colour.

ZENALE

Bernardino Zenale (1436-1526) came from Treviglio and studied under Foppa in Milan. He was also influenced by Bramante, with whose style his own has

affinities. He is fond of architectural details and indeed for the last twenty years of his life he entirely abandoned painting for architecture. He wrote a treatise on perspective in 1524. Many of his pictures were painted with the assistance of Butinone, but the *Virgin and Saints with the Kneeling Duke and Duchess Sforza* in the Brera Gallery and *The Annunciation* in the Casa Borromeo, Milan, are by his own hand alone.

ZICK

Januarius Rasso Zick is virtually unknown, yet, once seen, his pictures are unforgettable. The experts who admired him as a painter of frescoes did not realise the profusion and originality of his oil paintings until a memorial exhibition of his work was held in Cologne in 1934. Since then Zick has been elevated to the rank of an important painter of the Rococo period.

Zick was born in 1730 at Munich, where his father held various appointments, including that of Court Painter, and he died in 1797 at Ehrenbreitstein near Coblenz. He was well taught by his father before he went to Paris. He loved Rembrandt and must have been a receptive youth, for in Paris he saw and absorbed Watteau's pictures, and when he went to Rome to study under Anton Raphael Mengs (then a painter of repute, but now almost forgotten), Zick absorbed his style and especially his use of white. In 1762 the Elector of Trier invited him to paint frescoes there, and after that his life was uneventful.

Two of Zick's oil paintings are absolutely typical. In them he managed to combine the influence of Rembrandt, Teniers, Pieter Aertsen, Watteau and Mengs without discordance and with an incomparable grace and serenity. The first is *Dance at the Inn* (Munich Pinakothek) and the second a religious picture in which Rembrandt's influence predominates, an *Entombment* in the Rheinhardt Collection at Munich. Zick painted many other less exciting pictures, including a sentimental composition in which Jean Jacques Rousseau is the principal figure.

Zick's excellent frescoes can be studied best in the monasteries of Wiblingen, near Ulm, and at Rot, near Leutkirch. His frescoes in Mainz and Coblenz were destroyed by bombs.

ZOFFANY

Johann Zoffany (1734/5-1810) was born in Frankfort, the son of a German architect. He went to Italy at the age of thirteen and spent twelve years there studying painting. At the age of twenty-five he came to England and, except for a further long visit to Italy and seven years' sojourn in India, Zoffany spent the rest of his life in London. He found favour with George III and was among the forty original members of the Royal Academy. Zoffany was the most original of those artists who were directly influenced by Hogarth; he developed the 'conversation piece' which Hogarth had originated. Zoffany's work is unequal in quality, but he painted with fluency, exuberance and freshness. Two fine examples of his work are in the National Gallery, London, *Mrs Oswald* and *The Bradshaw Family*.

ZOPPO

Marco Zoppo de Ruzieri, who was born in 1432 in Cento and died c. 1478 in Venice, is mentioned in documents as Squarcione's apprentice, but as the old man was a miser and failed to pay his apprentices, it seems more probable that Zoppo was his assistant. The records further add that Zoppo usually painted chests and benches. But his two chief works are an altarpiece in Bologna and a *Madonna Enthroned with Saints* in Berlin. Surprisingly, they both point to a different teacher—namely, Cosimo Tura. The *Madonna* in Berlin is a large powerful canvas and the figures are vigorously modelled, just like Tura's.

J. ZICK · A TAVERN BRAWL
19¾" × 31¼". *Stuttgart, Staatsgalerie*

Zoppo's colours are usually sober; he was fond of greys and browns, but here and there he interspersed them with vivid purple or red patches. A *Pietà* and *A Bishop Saint* are in the National Gallery, London.

ZUCCARELLI

Francesco Zuccarelli was born in 1702 in the little Tuscan town of Pitigliano and died in Florence in 1788. But he was a Venetian in spirit and spent most of his life in Venice, where he fared very much like Canaletto, though their work is not to be compared. Like Canaletto, Zuccarelli found patrons in the English colony in Venice and like him he spent a considerable time in London.

Zuccarelli was a landscape painter; his subjects, however, were not views of Venice, but biblical and mythological scenes in arcadian settings.

ZUCCHERO

Federigo Zucchero (1543-1609), or Zuccaro, was an Italian painter who came to England from Rome in 1574. He was the founder of the Academy of St Luke in Rome, which was the model for later institutions, including the English Royal Academy, and he was famous for two

333

portraits, *Mary Queen of Scots* at Chatsworth and *A Lady in Fancy Dress* at Hampton Court, a portrait of Queen Elizabeth.

ZURBARAN

Francisco de Zurbaran was born in 1599 at Fuente de Cantos, Estremadura, and died in Madrid in 1664. He is one of the most independent of the great Spanish painters; his pictures show no trace of Velazquez's influence, although they were close friends and admired each other's work, and they are equally removed in style from those of Cano, with whom Zurbaran was never friends, although they were neighbours in Seville. Zurbaran is a completely individual painter. He was a deeply but not a fanatically religious man, and considered it a waste of time to paint secular subjects, an attitude that must be regretted in face of his three outstanding still-life pictures in Florence, Tangier and Kiev, and the portraits in Strassbourg, Berlin, London, Paris, Montreal, Detroit and Boston.

Most of Zurbaran's religious pictures were painted for monasteries, and usually consist of cycles illustrating monastic legend and history. These pictures are sharply defined, austere, unsentimental and almost oppressive in their lack of joy or compassion, their sculptural qualities enhanced by strong lighting. Zurbaran modified these characteristics as he grew older and even made a timid approach to Murillo's sweetness of manner. He moved to Madrid in 1658 in the hope of obtaining more commissions and making a better livelihood, but he does not seem to have painted anything there at all.

He is represented in most important galleries and in many Spanish monasteries.

ZURBARAN · ST APOLLONIA
45¼″ × 26⅝″. Paris, Louvre

His most important work was the *Bonaventura Cycle*, of which three of the pictures, formerly in Berlin and Dresden, were burnt, while the remaining two are in Paris and Genoa. Only in one instance did Zurbaran paint a smiling face—in the astonishing picture of Christ as a small boy who has pricked himself while plaiting a crown of thorns (Seville).

BRIEF BIBLIOGRAPHY

Sources

MANDER, KAREL VAN *Het Schilder-Boeck*, 1st edition, 1604; 2nd edition, 1618; annotated translation into French by H. Hymans, 1884/5.

This book is the basis for the study of the history of painting in the Netherlands.

VASARI, GIORGIO *Lives of the Painters, Sculptors and Architects*. Everyman's Library, London, 1927 (4 vols.).

The most important source-book for the art of the Renaissance in Italy. The original text, *Vite de piu eccellenti pittori, scultori ed architetti*, was first published in 1550 and revised and enlarged in 1568. It is a book that can be read for pleasure as well as for information.

WALPOLE, HORACE *Anecdotes of Painting in England* (1762) ed. Ralph N. Wornum, 1876.

A valuable and entertaining source-book based on the notes and memoranda of George Vertue (1684-1756).

Modern Dictionaries

Bryan's Dictionary of Painters and Engravers. New edition, 1903.

A standard biographical dictionary, illustrated.

BÉNÉZIT, E. *Dictionnaire critique et documentaire des peintres, sculpteurs, dessinateurs et graveurs de tous les temps et de tous pays par un groupe d'écrivains specialistes français et étrangers*, 1st edition, 1911-13, 3 vols.

A very comprehensive list including many minor names. A list of chief works is usually given and of museums where they can be seen.

CHAMPLIN, JOHN DENISON AND PERKINS C. C. *Cyclopaedia of Painters and Paintings*, New York, 1885-87

Includes biographies and descriptive articles on famous paintings with line illustrations.

THIEME, ULRICH, AND BECKER, FELIX *Allgemeines Lexikon der bildenden Künstler*, Leipzig, 1911-47.

The most complete and authoritative dictionary of artists. There are good bibliographies and the longer articles are signed.

WURZBACH, A. *Niederländisches Künstler-Lexikon*, Leipzig and Vienna, 1904-11.

An important biographical dictionary with bibliographies, lists of works, locations of pictures and in many cases facsimiles of signatures.